Conversations with Directors

An Anthology of Interviews from *Literature/Film Quarterly*

Edited by
Elsie M. Walker
David T. Johnson

THE SCARECROW PRESS, INC.
Lanham, Maryland • Toronto • Plymouth, UK
2008

SCARECROW PRESS, INC.

Published in the United States of America
by Scarecrow Press, Inc.
A wholly owned subsidiary of
The Rowman & Littlefield Publishing Group, Inc.
4501 Forbes Boulevard, Suite 200, Lanham, Maryland 20706
www.scarecrowpress.com

Estover Road
Plymouth PL6 7PY
United Kingdom

British Library Cataloguing in Publication Information Available

Library of Congress Cataloging-in-Publication Data

Conversations with directors : an anthology of interviews from Literature/film quarterly /
    edited by Elsie M. Walker, David T. Johnson.
        p. cm.
    Includes index.
    ISBN-13: 978-0-8108-6122-0 (pbk. : alk. paper)
    ISBN-10: 0-8108-6122-4 (pbk. : alk. paper)
    1. Motion picture producers and directors—Interviews. 2. Motion pictures—Production
and direction. I. Walker, Elsie M., 1975– II. Johnson, David T., 1972–

PN1998.2.C615 2008
791.4302'330922—dc22   2007050206

⊗™ The paper used in this publication meets the minimum requirements of
American National Standard for Information Sciences—Permanence of Paper
for Printed Library Materials, ANSI/NISO Z39.48-1992.
Manufactured in the United States of America.

For my father, Marshall Walker, a big man
—Elsie M. Walker

For Rick and Page Ciordia, and in memory of Dave Johnson
—David T. Johnson

Contents

Acknowledgments

*W*e wish to thank Jim Welsh and Tom Erskine for their pioneering work in founding *Literature/Film Quarterly*, and we thank Brenda Grodzicki and Dean Cooledge for their meticulous assistance in maintaining the journal. We are indebted to the contributing editors of *Literature/Film Quarterly*, past and present, for their invaluable reports on the submissions we receive. The Department of English and the Fulton School of Liberal Arts at Salisbury University have been very supportive of our work on *Literature/Film Quarterly* and, for that, we are grateful. Finally, we wish to thank the interviewers who first conducted the fascinating interviews in this volume, our families, and our loved ones who have been as excited about this book as us.

Introduction

$\mathcal{F}$ounded in 1973 by James Welsh and Tom Erskine, *Literature/Film Quarterly* has made its name as the preeminent journal of the study of adaptation, a concept once defined as the processes by which films adapt preexisting texts but which has come to mean a broader, more permissive study of intertextuality. Over the years, one of the interests of the journal has been to provide high-caliber interviews with some of the major figures of literary and film studies (particularly the latter). Although *Literature/Film Quarterly* has conducted interviews with people who have worked in film in various ways—screenwriters, producers, actors, and other personnel—this book will focus on directors in particular. Part of the reason for that focus is the large volume of interviews with filmmakers since the journal's inception. In reviewing the archives, we were pleased to discover interviews with directors from 1973 to 2007; interviews representative of the classical Hollywood era through to contemporary independent filmmaking; interviews with directors from America, the United Kingdom, France, Poland, Mexico, and Australia; interviews with documentary, narrative, experimental, and mainstream directors; and interviews which are fascinating both individually and for the ways in which they illuminate each other. Some of the interviews come from issues of the journal which are either rare or no longer in print, and many of the earlier interviews were conducted when the total circulation of the journal was still relatively modest. In addition, several of these interviews are with directors who have since died but who continue to influence filmmaking today—directors like Robert Altman, Frank Capra, René Clair, Federico Fellini, and Billy Wilder. We have collected these interviews in one volume both for readers who are familiar with our journal and for those who are new to our publication.

Particularities of context for each of the directors and their work are provided in our brief introductions for each interview as well as through the interviews themselves. These interviews, arranged in the chronological order in which they were published, were all conducted and conceived separately; however, in the act of placing them together, we have found many intersecting threads of argument, connections in the concerns, preoccupations, and creative hopes that are discussed. This book, in itself, constitutes a new intertext that has been created through placing the interviews together. What follows is a brief summary of the points of connection and contrast among the interviews and of how they take on meaning in relation to each other. The purpose of this introduction is not to sidestep crucial industrial, national, cultural, ideological, social, and personal contexts for understanding the films discussed but, rather, to foreground some fascinating points of connection and difference.

Given *Literature/Film Quarterly*'s primary interest in adaptation, it is hardly surprising that so many of the interviews are concerned with that subject. These interviews are representative of the key shift in the focus of adaptation studies: from attempting to slavishly evaluate adaptations in terms of their relative fidelity to source-texts, to understanding adaptations as part of the intertextual matrices through which we understand all works of literature and film. We include several interviews focused on adaptations that are representative of directors' personal preoccupations: Wayne Wang's adaptation of Amy Tan's *The Joy Luck Club* (1993), partly inspired and informed by Wang's own experiences as a Chinese-American "pulled between" two cultures; John Schlesinger's adaptation of James Leo Herlihy's *Midnight Cowboy* (1969), which reflects the director's thematic focus on fantasy as it intersects with reality; and Richard Linklater's adaptation of Philip K. Dick's *A Scanner Darkly* (2006) which, in its combination of comedy and tragedy, reflects Linklater's personal and artistic "view of the world." Two of the other adaptations discussed in this book are especially concerned with broad-scale, social issues: Terence Davies' adaptation of Edith Wharton's *The House of Mirth* (2000) which, despite its beautiful and painterly mise-en-scène, emphasizes the ugliness of society in Wharton's text (in keeping with the socially focused narratives associated with Davies); and Patricia Rozema's adaptation of *Mansfield Park* (1999) which, influenced by Edward Said's essay "Jane Austen and Empire,"[1] foregrounds Rozema's reading of Austen's "subtle statement about [the] captivity" of women as well as slaves.

Several of our directors foreground the immediate problems of adaptation: Alain Robbe-Grillet (novelist as well as filmmaker), for instance, speaks of how the "raw materials" for literature and film are "completely different." Jonas Mekas professes himself against adaptations of great literature: he asks "what insights can you add to [*Moby Dick*]? . . . You can only simplify, banalize, distort." Andrzej Wajda (having directed both theater and film) speaks of how "when you read [*Hamlet*] it makes for the whole world. When you see it on the stage there is just a conception—of Orson Welles, or Laurence Olivier, etc. *Hamlet* itself remains untouched:" for Wajda, the adaptation is a conceptual frame in which ideas of the play are selected and reduced. Yet the interview with Franco Zeffirelli, about his adaptation of *Hamlet*, emphasizes how much he wanted to avoid reducing the impact of Shakespeare's language, in *all* its tonal complexity.

Other directors privilege the importance of adaptations as forms of interpretation *and* processes of selection: Clair, for instance, speaks of needing to put the play upon which *Un chapeau de paille d'Italie* (*An Italian Straw Hat*, 1927) is based aside, eschewing concern for fidelity given the necessary changes in adapting the text to film. For Rozema, "interpretation is impossible to avoid" and "must be openly declared by filmmakers." Furthermore, she felt "morally obliged" to create an adaptation of *Mansfield Park* that could help inspire a "collective re-awakening" to Austen's novel through its audacious development of the author's subtexts. Baz Luhrmann similarly emphasizes the importance of using "aggressive" devices to translate a text, that of Shakespeare's *Romeo and Juliet*, for a new audience. That said, Luhrmann also voices a Lévi-Straussian understanding of the fundamental, transcendent myth that is, for him, at the heart of *Romeo and Juliet*: "that myth has been with us forever—youth in conflict with society, the extreme danger of absolutism of idealistic love and youth. The great point of the piece is that if the incumbent generation propagates hate of any kind—racial hate, hate over religion, sexuality, whatever reason—it will come back on them. And the greatest loss is that you lose your children over your hate." Despite his great reverence for Shakespeare's language and its very particular tonal complexity (perhaps unconsciously echoing Zeffirelli), Luhrmann thus suggests that the text's essential thematic concerns belong to all time as well as a new medium.

Just as many of these interviews feature discussion of adaptation, they also, inevitably, invoke the idea of cinematic authorship, of *auteur*ism and the troubled history within film studies of that concept (or "policy," if one goes back to its original use in the *Cahiers du Cinéma*). And yet, while the ways in which directors discuss their work has undoubtedly been inflected by the history of *auteur*ism—and while such an influence is evident throughout this volume—those same directors often complicate or explicitly reject any single way of thinking about directing. Schlesinger puts it bluntly when he states, "I think there's a lot of rubbish talked about the *auteur* theory," and Wajda seems to be responding to this notion when he says, "what bothers me lately in film is just this tendency to promote the work of director into dangerously exaggerated proportions." Like Wajda, Robert Wise does not directly refer to the term *auteur*, but clearly his interest in final cut rights—and, perhaps, even, his animosity toward television—comes very much from an *auteur*ist approach to the medium. To be sure, there are other skeptics and supporters: William Friedkin talks disparagingly about "the auteur stuff," leveling a whole series of critiques against *auteur*ist critic Andrew Sarris, while, in contrast, Jean-Charles Tacchella states, "Of course, there is much to be said for Bazin's idea of the style of a director, of the identification of the director by the films he worked on." Wherever readers of this volume locate themselves in the spectrum of possible responses to *auteur*ism, the interviews here are likely to stimulate further considerations of this influential, contentious concept.

*Auteur*ism, of course, invokes preconceptions of artistic control, and these interviews represent directors' wildly contrasting experiences in terms of their relative control over production and reception. In Gregory Mason's retrospective interview surveying Clair's career, the director not only admits that he does not keep any of his own films, he gently refuses to establish himself as an expert on his own work. His unassuming position does not appear disingenuous but is, rather, part of his perhaps paradoxical detachment from as well as affection for his films: he was "the *auteur* of his films in their conception and making" yet did not maintain control of his films after their release. Mason discusses absurdities of English subtitling, the "mutilation" of Clair's film prints in others' hands, critical interpretations unreflective of the director's intentions as well as Clair's famous disinterest in a plagiarism suit against Charlie Chaplin for those obvious borrowings from Clair's *À Nous la Liberté* (1931) in *Modern Times* (1936). Clair's detachment from such issues of control, along with Clair's candidly critical assessment of several films he directed, could not be more different from Louis Malle's apparently total recall of the details in his films (though not without irony or humility) or Friedkin's manifest desire to control the reception of his films, notwithstanding his disavowals of interest in what critics think. Friedkin discusses his various roles in editing, promotion, distribution, script-writing, subtitling and dubbing: yet, despite this "*large measure* of control" Friedkin laments that "the best film stock in existence fades in two years. The colors that you strove for are gone!" His ultimate concern, then, that which is beyond his control, is the perishability of film itself.

Directors who worked within the classical Hollywood studio system also emphasize industrial measures of control upon them. Wise, for instance, speaks of the many supervisions and orders from "the front office" as to "the final cut of the picture, how it should look, what should be done," and Capra emphasizes his desire for artistic control beyond the studios, the concept of "One Man, One Film," which prompted him to co-create the short-lived independent production company Liberty Films. Other directors express anxiety about controlling spectators' reception of both them and their work. Wes Craven says he "doesn't even regard himself as a 'horror director,'" although his name is often connected with the spectacles of violence associated with that genre: "I still get the usual knee-jerk sort of reactions like 'Gee, it was really neat the way that guy fell off the cliff.'" Craven reacts against such superficial responses to the violence of his films, claiming (in agreement with his interviewer) they are instead "a form of reaction against bourgeois society"; they work as critiques of American myths in which the "violence itself is almost incidental." He thus challenges preconceptions of his ideological purposes. Edward Dmytryk's part in the Hollywood Ten will perhaps forever influence how audiences understand the ideological place of his films:

Dmytryk was an unfriendly witness for HUAC but, after being forced to testify, changed his position and retestified as a friendly witness. Lester Friedman's interview is much less focused on Dmytryk's films than on the director's understanding of these events, suggesting that the filmmaker's work was eclipsed by his concern for control over his good name.

But perhaps the most memorably devastating account of what happens when a filmmaker loses control over his or her work *and* its reception is in the interview with Marcel Ophüls. In Frank Manchel's interview, Ophüls explains the processes by which his documentary *The Memory of Justice* (1976), his exploration of the nature of war crimes and the Nuremberg Trials, was taken from him, re-edited, and presented in such a way as to undo his original intentions. The financial backers (from English and German production companies: the BBC and Polytel, respectively) had particular ideas for what the film should represent which Ophüls fully understood too late. According to Ophüls, the backers wanted a film about evil that is not confined to the Third Reich and, more specifically, which would make correlations between Nazi Germany and the Vietnam War (My Lai in particular)—a vision to help counter anti-German prejudice and to flatter "what they assumed to be radical chic conceptions on the American market." In the beginning, Ophüls grants that his approach was comparatively harmonious with such views but, through the process of filming, there was a shift in his approach: he was loath to make correlations implying his right to ultimate judgment. Ophüls notified his backers of this shift and, after the rough-cut screening, the film was confiscated from him and controversial scenes were excised. Cuts included an interview with former Wing Commander Rose explaining why the attack on Dresden was a war crime and footage showing economic bosses of the Third Reich who "got top jobs after the war and took over German industry." Perhaps the most damaging distortion of Ophüls's work was in the manipulation of an interview with the chief of the prosecutors of the Nuremberg Trials (author of *Nuremberg and Vietnam: An American Tragedy*), Telford Taylor. In the reedited film, Taylor was shown saying that the "American forces at Vietnam had been guilty of the same crimes and to the same degree as the Nazis that we had convicted in Nuremberg." Yet in his interview with Ophüls, Taylor had specifically stated that such a correlation would be against his understanding. It took six months for Ophüls and Taylor to have the falsified statement removed and, in the interim, the reedited version was seen by "millions of Germans": the impact was "not only ironic" but "traumatic" for Ophüls, especially since the film was subsequently attacked for "equating My Lai with Auschwitz." As Ophüls puts it, "Auschwitz was unique. I think that the Holocaust of World War II, in its proportions, in its premeditation, in its ideology, in the fantastic support that this ideology obtained with the majority of the German people is unique." Using such a "monument of evil" to vindicate views on other events—such as atrocities in Vietnam or Israel—is, for him, "indecent and obscene." This interview thus represents our most extreme example of what is at stake when a director loses control of both production and reception.

Ironically, some directors encounter a loss of control in more creatively generative ways. There is clearly an awareness among many of these filmmakers of the potential dangers—and, perhaps, even, opportunities—in contingencies and accidents of production. When discussing her adaptation of *Mansfield Park*, Rozema reflects on the unpredictable "conditions [that] affected production most": "Chance. Weather. Actors' moods and love lives. . . . Various amusing issues like that." Rozema's frustration with such issues, though offered here humorously, relates to Wise's dislike of "too many surprises." As a result, he favors copious research and preplanning prior to a shoot. And yet, despite anxieties over accidents here and in other interviews, many directors note how often ideas will arise in the course of shooting—ideas that they had not previously planned for. It was only when he was actually on the mausoleum set for *Romeo and Juliet* that Luhrmann realized he must shoot his final, climactic scene somewhere else, and the moment in Wilder's *Double Indemnity* (1944) when the car will not start came to the director on a lunch break, when his own car would not start (and he rushed back to say, "Don't touch a thing! I'm going to do it again—I'm going to do it differently!"). And beyond these examples, there are directors who actually seem to take pleasure in what they cannot control. It is as though the film becomes a means by which to catch life unawares, as when Altman notes his desire for films to be "occurrences" or Richard Leacock mentions a related investment in "discovery." Perhaps the most extreme example is Wajda, who notes succinctly, "I think that every piece of art is an accident" and "My work is of an accidental nature," though, on the latter statement, concedes, "although I know the direction in which I am going." These interviews thus represent a range of possible responses to the inevitability of contingency.

Although each one of our directors might be regarded as an *auteur*, one given primary credit for the distinguishing vision of his films, notwithstanding the unexpected, many of them stress the necessity of collaboration in filmmaking—whether it be collaboration with a producer (Davies on Olivia Stewart), cinematographer (Zeffirelli on David Watkin), editor (Robbe-Grillet on Bob Wade), composer (Fellini on Nino Rota) or cowriter (Malle on Polly Platt). Among the possible collaborations, many directors place working with actors at the heart of successful narrative filmmaking. Their comments represent different points on a continuum between allowing full improvisation and assuming paternalistic control of the actors' delivery of the script (both Altman and Fellini speak of their films as their "children"). Wise admiringly notes Altman's penchant for having actors improvise, though Wise himself relies on more preproduction planning: he storyboards entire films but without staying "married to the sketches." However, Wise notes that it is crucial to give actors "a free hand" so as not to inhibit what they can "generate and bring to the scene" (he mentions a key argument scene in *Au-*

drey Rose (1977) which became fully improvised). He insists, therefore, on a balance: "mine is a *prepared* approach with ample room for improvising as we go along." Altman himself mentions that he gets much credit for "having the actors improvise all the time," and he emphasizes the importance of improvisation through rehearsal. However, he also emphasizes that once scenes are filmed they are "very well rehearsed." Altman's discussion of his own collaborative process with actors underlines the intentionality behind the apparent ease with which his actors appear almost spontaneously engaged with their scenes. Clair speaks of combining improvisation with prepared scripting ("there was no rule"). Similarly, Linklater speaks of the script as "a really good place to start" for collaboration with actors even if "major architectural aspects of the structure of the story" remain fixed. In addition, several directors discuss many specific collaborations with actors: Schlesinger directing Jon Voight in *Midnight Cowboy* and casting Karen Black in *The Day of the Locust*; Davies directing Gillian Anderson in *The House of Mirth*, Capra directing Barbara Stanwyck in her first feature film (*Ladies of Leisure*, 1930); Clair directing as well as writing several parts for Paul Olivier; Wajda directing Zbyszek Cybulski (whom he calls a Polish equivalent to the "phenomenon of James Dean in America, "like a revelation in religion").

The directors conceive of their role in relation to the actors in different terms: Altman calls himself a "cheerleader," "trying to set up an atmosphere and a focus of energies" for the actors, and Friedkin calls himself "a kind of road guide, a tourist guide, making sure that [the actors] don't wander off onto byways that will lead them nowhere." Wajda speaks of himself as the "leader" chosen by the group involved (in theater or film) but insists that "the quintessence of the film is the actor." He argues: "even if the director is superb, it is not he who lends his face to the crowds of people. Someone else emits the light, exposes his body and soul . . . I am fully aware that everything I want to say on the screen has to be filtered through someone else's individuality." His words echo Capra's insistence that, not only are the actors the "principal tools" of storytelling, but directors who indulge in "ego-massaging" feats of technical display risk boring the audience for the "people-to-people medium" of cinema.

Several director-scriptwriters discuss script revisions as a necessary part of collaborating with actors. Eric Rohmer, who is famously focused on the importance of dialogue, speaks of aiming to put "familiar words in the mouths of actors, words familiar to them personally. The script is very often made as a function of the actor": such practice avoids "uniformity of tone," even when the scriptwriter/dialoguist and director are one (as in his case). Yet Rohmer insists that the original conception of a script is entirely determined by him: "I don't need collaboration. Not at all. I work alone. I speak to no one. Only when I have finished do I have someone read it." Friedkin works hard on scripts with actors who are then "free to throw away the script" and "just *become* the character[s]": in order to facilitate this, he tries to cast people based on their "inherent" qualities. Similarly, Tacchella writes a shooting script having met the actors, taking each of their personalities into account and inserting details of their actual lives into the script.

In addition to considerations of performance and script, the directors in this volume discuss a range of conceptual and practical approaches to the technical aspects of cinema, including cinematography. Some directors recount ingenious ways of manipulating the most intangible aspects of mise-en-scène—light and air—as they are recorded by the camera. Zeffirelli, for example, describes using white sheets in *Hamlet* to "bounce the light, to reflect it back into the scene," while Wilder recounts his cinematographer and his actually blowing aluminum powder into the air prior to shooting scenes in *Double Indemnity*, in order to make up for lost values in black-and-white film. Clair discusses employing the swish pan in *Les Grandes Manoeuvres* (*The Grand Maneuver*, 1955) to make up for the poor quality in color-film dissolves at the time of the film's making. Other directors feel strongly that style should never overtake narrative, especially with regard to cinematography. Capra calls attention to the issue of lens length and soft focus (as, for example, with the shots of Claudette Colbert in *It Happened One Night* [1934]), but he also reflects more generally on the connection between style and narrative: "if you see the machinery, the story's going to go out the window." Similarly, Tacchella recalls Carl Theodor Dreyer's advice on cinematography: "Dreyer said you should 'use the camera to eliminate the camera,'" and Leacock argues for a related suppression of overt style in the context of shooting documentaries, although here it is less about the audience and more about affecting the profilmic reality: "LIGHTS! People following with lights, lights! My God! If you want to change the situation, just start turning on lights!" And yet, for all of the pragmatic reflection and advice in this volume, directors are often apt to reflect in much more metaphorical, almost lyrical ways about their approaches to cinematography. Coolidge says of her film *Rambling Rose* (1991), "The whole concept of the film was light," and Robbe-Grillet says of his film *La Belle captive* (*The Beautiful Prisoner*, 1983), "sculpting light was one of the organizing plans for this film." Whether revealing the day-to-day, practical decisions about cinematography that films require, or engaging in poetic reverie about the possibilities inherent in the intersection of camera, celluloid, and light, directors in this volume reflect on their visions as manifested through cinematography.

Several of our directors also emphasize their involvement in, and understanding of, editing and montage, though at different stages of the filmmaking process. Robbe-Grillet describes how films are "born" to him, not only as images taking shape, but as "montage structures." Mekas speaks of editing his footage "in the camera," differentiating his practice from the "classical, the traditional idea of editing" because his approach to making non-narrative films "require[s] a much more personal, intuitive and automatic kind of editing [that] can be done only during the shooting." Capra, most of whose work was made in classical Hollywood studios, speaks of editing after scenes had been filmed with the editing possibilities already in mind. Capra's emphasis is on achieving a "smooth flow" with editing, on keeping the narrative "dynamic of film" not only intact but unobtrusively so. For Capra, the ideal editing happens without the audience's awareness because "they remain fascinated by what is going on." Where these directors emphasize editing as the realization of a preconceived film, others emphasize editing as its own process of creation. Leacock, for instance, speaks of how much he loves editing as it leads to discovery, as he works through footage in the order it was filmed: "you have to go through from the beginning to the end and it is like going through a maze. You take a wrong turn and oops, you are in trouble!" Friedkin similarly argues that editing is "more exciting, more interesting, more discovery-prone, more important, than any other facet of filmmaking" (and thus he insists on unusually strict editorial control on his films). Despite their different approaches to editing, many directors are here united in expressing great concern over holding rights to the final cuts of their work. Clair stands alone in being dismissive of such proprietorial concern. He also speaks of cutting those parts from *I Married a Witch* (1942) during which a sneak preview audience coughed because he read the coughs as an expression of boredom. Such editing decisions reflect Clair's professed anti-intellectual, primary focus on the democratically enjoyable potential of film: a concern which transcends the importance of any statement on personal vision, industrial circumstance, or *auteur*istic control in his interview.

It is an often uncontested cliché to refer to film as a "visual medium," one in which editing, cinematography, and mise-en-scène are paramount. Even Wise, who began his career as a sound editor, regards cinema as primarily "visual" to the extent that he fears developments in sound technology that might compromise the audience's "full concentration on the screen." Other directors, however, explicitly emphasize the crucial impact of the soundtrack, and music in particular. Malle speaks of using both sound and music in "counterpoint" to the main visual action: for instance, the soundtrack for *Pretty Baby* (1978) is designed to suggest "the world outside the house" because the characters are "like prisoners." He describes the ways in which diverse forms of music (Erik Satie, Miles Davis, Charlie Parker) have entered and influenced his films, sometimes by happenstance, and yet which now seem integral to their form. Robbe-Grillet speaks of how music sometimes has "a kind of initiating role" for his conception of film. For *Le Jeu avec le feu* (*Playing with Fire*, 1975) he imagined a "tryptych structure" of "three musical domains" that were chosen for their "dissonance": the third act of *Il Trovatore* (especially the "fire" aria); a Brazilian dance song performed by the popular singer Elisete de Cardoso; and a German military march from the Wehrmacht. Robbe-Grillet painstakingly explains the ways that his film's form (the script, visuals, psychological preoccupations, and dialogue) intersects with these diverse forms of musical composition, each of which, in turn, has its own implicit structures, narratives, themes, and intertextual associations. Similarly,

Davies speaks of using what Robbe-Grillet calls the "diegetic tie-ins" of music in *The House of Mirth*: "When I knew that there had to be a transition from America at the end of the season to Monte Carlo it had to be something that had all that yearning for hope that had been dashed. [Mozart's "Così fan tutti" aria] has it: two young women, wanting their lovers to come back." For Davies, the aria matches his film's "transition from a rain-soaked Hudson River to that wonderful light upon the Mediterranean water, just full with sensuality and implied sex." Luhrmann reflects on the usual method of adding music at the post-production stage, without originally conceiving of visuals and soundtrack together: "Traditionally what you do . . . is you shoot your film and then you sort of add music a bit like you add wallpaper. But we write our music *into* the film." Like Robbe-Grillet and Davies, he emphasizes the affective power of music and his practice of making music integral to the conception of a film (even the pop songs that were composed or adapted for *Romeo and Juliet*, in addition to Craig Armstrong's score, were written into the original script by Luhrmann and Craig Pearce).

Several directors conceive of filmmaking processes in musical metaphors: Altman, for instance, speaks of recording his actors' voices in ways akin to recording separate instruments (mixing the lines of music later); Leacock aligns the editing process to that of composing music. Luhrmann says, "all movies are a piece of music in that they have rhythm and structure and rise and fall and then you have other movements . . . which are the tracks within them." Perhaps the most elaborately ingenious metaphorical language belongs to Davies when he speaks of being influenced by Douglas Sirk's and other "women's films" of the 1950s: "Of course, I was influenced by them; they went into the psyche and came out refracted. . . . If I could use a musical analogy, it's like the "trill" in eighteenth-century music, particularly Mozart. It begins as decoration, but by the time you hear it in Mahler it has become very dark, full of angst, but it's still a trill. So are all the things in your own psyche." Other directors use different metaphors in the process of self-definition or of conceptualizing cinema: both Malle and Craven invoke the long-standing association between cinema and dreaming Mekas speaks of his films as diaries; Friedkin describes shooting the mise-en-scène of *The French Connection* (1971) to imitate cubist paintings. And Leacock also frequently uses nonmusical metaphors to describe his filmmaking processes in a way that foregrounds the pragmatic realism of his approach: in relation to a failed project of filming a flood that never happened, he says, "sometimes you catch a fish, sometimes you don't catch a fish."

Other directors raise the broader concept of realism and how it may be achieved in various ways through cinema. Tacchella asserts: "I refuse to have anything to do with anything that looks like cinema. I like to use dramatic devices as they appear in our own lives: Love, problems of everyday life, death." Other directors draw more specific correlations between their film narratives and actual people, events, or places: Coolidge connects a character from *Real Genius* (1985)

(Professor Hathaway) with real scientists developing nuclear power in the 1980s, and Wajda describes his film *Kanal* (1957) as an attempt to show a "real, if not understated, experience of the Polish underground during the Warsaw uprising." He notes that this film was critically reviled for its visceral horrors (at the Cannes Film Festival in 1957) only to be dismissed for its sentimentality decades later; he thus emphasizes how cinematic constructions and perceptions of reality shift because "we are all aiming at a greater truth, always more precise and exact than before." Robbe-Grillet speaks of how a project takes shape within his head usually because he is inspired by "some real setting": for instance, the huge forest of trees reaching to the sky in *L'Homme qui ment* (*The Man Who Lies,* 1968) is an actual place which separates Ukraine from Slovakia and Poland). For Robbe-Grillet, the concept of a novel "takes place within the structuring of sentences, independently of any idea of where the action takes place," but a film necessitates not only specificity of, but actuality of, setting. Other directors call attention to specific stylistic elements and casting requirements for achieving realism. Altman, a director whose work typically features ingeniously overlapping lines of dialogue, insists that audiences should work to select and interpret aural detail rather than having a soundtrack which establishes straightforward hierarchies of noise because, in his words, "you don't hear everything somebody says in real life, do you?" For Friedkin, the cinematic camera has the ability to communicate *heightened* reality because it "has a tendency to reflect further than the mirror does. The camera has the tendency to magnify facets of human behavior and to suggest many more things than are there. It's like putting a pebble into the water, and from it flow all of the many waves." Coolidge emphasizes the importance of the microcosmic details (of mise-en-scène, research, training the actors according to their particular environments) which, in the truth of their specificity, "automatically" expand into a believable "macrocosm." Capra is one who especially professes his "passion for credibility" and he argues that the realistic believability of a film begins with having good actors "for all the small parts" so the audience is "more liable to believe the derring-do of the stars."

Although these directors are concerned with realism in narrative filmmaking, the subject of documentary and the forms of realism it may represent is one that also arises quite often throughout this book. Most directly, both Leacock and Ophüls offer valuable insights into documentary production and distribution (though Ophüls's nightmarish scenario with his film *The Memory of Justice* is an extremely negative case). And many other filmmakers invoke the subject both directly and indirectly, at times in the ways they do not seem to accept the division between documentary and fiction in the first place. Mekas might, in light of his own statements about film, be added to our list of documentary filmmakers, when he notes, "The only distinction I accept is non-narrative and narrative"; yet he is tentative in his formulations, adding, "Even there, there are complications." So too is Malle, when he admits, after being asked about the relationship between documentary and fiction, "I don't mean to say that documentary and fiction are the same, but as I have found out more about both aspects of filmmaking I have realized you could, for instance, speak about the fictional aspects of documentary." Friedkin states, "I seem to want to begin my films with a documentary," and while he cites this tendency as one that has caused him more work in the editing room, he recognizes its origins in his own early experiences in documentary production ("I guess it goes back to my documentary days with Wolper, when I first came to Hollywood"). Like Friedkin, both Schlesinger and Marcela Fernández Violante have had early, formative experiences with making documentaries that inflected their narrative filmmaking. While the main focus of this volume, then, is decidedly on mainstream, narrative filmmaking, documentary has an important place here as a subject that directors, in considering the potentials of the medium, quite often return to.

The interaction of politics, history, and film is one that inevitably arises in these interviews, whether in relation to narrative or documentary productions. Various filmmakers discuss the politics they are attempting to represent, their own historical experiences, and the ways in which their films may or may not be catalysts for social change. In his interview, Dmytryk contemplates many of these questions as an often reviled member of the Hollywood Ten. Whether or not readers' opinions will be altered by Dmytryk's words collected here, it is clear that he has continued to think about politics, film, and history, both in the time leading up to the HUAC hearings and in the contemporary context of the interview (Reagan-era America). Craven, from a very different perspective, offers some thoughts on any overly optimistic approaches to the social role of popular cinema: "People who look at horror film politically forget that there's still an enormous gap between watching a film like *Hills* [*The Hills Have Eyes*, 1977] or *Videodrome* [1983] or something and getting involved in social action." The social role of film is one that Coolidge considers as well; when asked whether she believes that "part of the social role of film is to exert a leveling influence," she responds, "I believe that. It's not what everybody thinks, but that's what I'm trying to do." In discussing the important influence of Said's essay on her film, Rozema concedes that not every audience member is going to sense its political content: "I knew it could function for some merely on the domestic romantic comedy level and for others more like myself on a political level. I try to make it simple and strong and true for those who don't wish to know that there is really sugar on the pill." Linklater also adapts his text, *A Scanner Darkly,* in light of his desire to explore a contemporary climate that seems to count on people's lack of interest in politics: "Someone's counting on you not really having any analytical ability. . . . I won't say ability, because that implies people are stupid, which I don't think they are. I just think it's [lack of] interest. They don't want to know." In a very different context, Ophüls reflects on the politics of his grim experience with distributors: "Whenever people try to censor a filmmaker, they never admit that what they are talking about are political issues, because this would be extremely primitive and extremely unsophisticated. They always find other issues." And, in one of the most haunting anecdotes on the relationship among film, politics, and history, Wang describes the extras on *The Joy Luck Club* being particularly moved by a scene involving a reunion of family members split by the Second World War—and how one extra approached him later to relate her own experience of separation during the war: she "told me she had had to leave her baby during the war and never found it again." Although these and other filmmakers offer opinions and anecdotes from many different political moments, their opinions on the interaction of film, history, and politics will likely provoke further reflection for readers of this volume.

Given the various historical, political, national, industrial, and cultural contexts represented by the films discussed in this book, it is scarcely surprising that our directors conceptualize artistic creation and commercial imperatives in radically different ways. Several directors express revulsion toward the American blockbuster: Altman insists "I don't make 'mainstream,' 'shopping mall' kinds of films, like *Pretty Woman* [1990]. I'm not an 'in demand commodity'"; Violante describes the difficulty of getting her own films made in the context of many other Mexican films awaiting domestic distribution while films like *E.T.* (1982) dominate theaters; Malle says "I feel this religion of the blockbuster is very unhealthy," after he discusses the importance of not compromising even after success brings pressure to join the Establishment." Clearly these directors differentiate their work from the commercialism of blockbusters and yet, as Mekas argues, there can be "a great danger in dividing films in terms of avant-garde and non-avant-garde, of commercial and non-commercial. . . . So that, at the very end, we can speak only about the individual artists." Later in his interview, Mekas also discusses the importance of context, of intertextuality, of genre. He is perhaps ultimately less concerned with reinforcing a Romantic notion of unique *auteurs/* artists than with rejecting any Platonic ideal or definition of film. For Wise, both the art and commerce of filmmaking must be focused on involving the audience: "I don't think there's necessarily a contradiction between a good movie artistically and a good movie commercially." This does not mean, for Wise, pandering or catering to what a perceived audience wants but, rather, considering the potential thematic impact should the film appeal to a "great mass of people."

Wise was, of course, most often working within the classical Hollywood studio system and with comparatively high budgets. Conversely, Clair speaks of making films with "no budget" and he confirms having had to stop filming *Paris qui dort* (*Paris Asleep/The Crazy Ray*, 1925) on one day because he could not afford the entrance fee for the Eiffel Tower. For some directors, working with small budgets is a trade-off for artistic freedom: Violante speaks of having to make "very cheap" films because the wealthy producers of Mexico want to make films that are the antithesis of her work, "films about singing prostitutes having fun."

Leacock speaks of choosing to make smaller and smaller, cheap and personal films, of making films on budgets as small as $70 and resisting more expensive options (even projects of $2,000) which entail becoming answerable to financiers. Tacchella explains how he, with some difficulty, financed his films through advances from the Centre National de la Cinématographie and negotiated comparative freedom (including writing his own scripts): he has always made films with comparatively small budgets so that he could retain "a hundred percent free hand" as much "as money allows." Coolidge provides an equivocal statement on the pros and cons of *both* independent and mainstream filmmaking: "if you just do independent film, then you can be limited—pigeonholed—into a more restricted budgetary and marketing pattern. So the point is to do big budget pictures in Hollywood film because they reach many people and you have a chance to really do a broad spectrum appeal picture. And I want to do those. For my soul, though, I prefer independent filmmaking. The corporate structure of Hollywood filmmaking gives it an inflexibility." Of course, for Coolidge, such concerns are compounded in her being a woman filmmaker: at the time of her interview in 1999 she said, "discrimination against women is absolutely everywhere and absolutely constant."

A further source of much anxiety and speculation in these interviews is television. Violante states her critiques quite clearly: "The problem with television is that it reduces the cultural level and conforms to a dangerous uniformity for all tastes." For Violante, this issue is particularly corrosive to cultures other than those of the United States, such as her native Mexico because, as she says, "It [television] also promotes the 'American Way of Life,' thus reducing the sense of national pride. Thus the values and ideals portrayed in Mexican culture tend to disappear." Although he is critical for very different reasons, Wise also derides television, noting how he must "butcher" his films to make room for commercials and, in a more general complaint, suggesting that television is too driven by mass desires: "I am very much a believer in not catering to an audience, not to say, 'Hey, what do they want? Let's give it to them,' like television does so much." Clair offers a different perspective than these directors. Speaking in 1979, he complains not so much about the medium itself as his sense that television had yet to find its own ideal means of expression: "What I have seen on the television screen is something that could be theatre or could be motion pictures. I always expect, I hope I will see something one day that belongs to television." Like Clair, some directors are at least open to its possibilities. Coolidge, for instance, acknowledges some of the problems with working in television but also notes some advantages, such as "the freedom of dealing with more serious material," especially with larger cable companies like HBO or TNT. And Wilder notes in passing that, rather than dulling the senses, television may just be sharpening them: "The audience is so far ahead of you. Nowadays even farther because their eyes and their ears have been so sharpened by all the television they see."

In contrast to such wildly differing positions on the subject of television, directors often show a remarkable uniformity of opinion when it comes to the other directors they most admire. Luis Buñuel, for example, is cited by directors as different as Craven, Leacock, Malle, Robbe-Grillet, and Wajda. The directors of the French New Wave crop up frequently, too; Jean-Luc Godard in particular is mentioned several times. Michelangelo Antonioni is also singled out in more than one case, as is Fellini, who himself cites other directors in his own interview: Alfred Hitchcock ("There was an artist, such an artist!"), Roberto Rossellini ("It was mainly Rossellini, as you must know, because I began with him"), and Costa-Gavras ("But I'm no Costa-Gavras" [331]). Davies owes much to Sirk, though he only invokes the director through his examples of "women's pictures" such as *Magnificent Obsession* (1954) and *All That Heaven Allows* (1955). Linklater, in the most contemporary interview in this volume, talks about watching *Vertigo* (1958) and *3 Women* (1977) with his daughter ("things I think she's vaguely ready for") and discusses, in reference to other films, the idea of a filmmaker's (and, for that matter, anyone's) continuing cinematic education: "It's kind of an endless lifetime project of trying to see as many great films that are out there." Such a project is one that the filmmakers of this volume clearly took to heart, as they reminisce on the work of their peers and predecessors—and how that has influenced the work that they, in turn, have produced.

In counterpoint to the effusive praise reserved for groundbreaking filmmakers, directors frequently use the interviews to take their critics to task. Clair, for example, discusses the general problem of critical misinterpretation: "the author of a motion picture as well as a play or novel does something or writes something, but later an explanation comes from a critic which is completely different from what he intended to do." In his interview, Robbe-Grillet responds much more specifically to an actual excerpt of writing about his films; "It's remarkably stupid!" he states emphatically, adding, "This critic isn't someone who is particularly sensitive to modern cinema." Friedkin snubs almost all of his contemporaries in the field of criticism, saying, "Film criticism has declined to such an extent that I can't look at it." Although he admires James Agee, he disdains Pauline Kael and likes Andrew Sarris and "the *auteur* stuff" even less. Kael is mentioned again in Mekas's interview, when he discusses her as one of the mainstream critics "more interested in producing entertaining copy . . . than in providing the correct information on things they are writing about." As someone who has written extensively on cinema, Mekas also offers many of his own ideas about criticism, though he hastens to add, "I'm not a critic! The furthest I can go is to say I'm a midwife." Responding to critical prejudice to a genre, Craven characterizes the critical population's passionate dislike of horror films by reflecting, "I would say that ninety-five percent wanted to lynch me and the rest of us"—the "rest of us" being his peers in horror-film direction. Despite the often heated tone of these comments, however, at least one director is fairly indifferent: Schlesinger, who notes of his critics, "They've got their job to do, and I've got mine." And finally, Altman conflates critics with the general audience in a humorous response to a serious question. Asked "What do you think of critics?" he deadpans, "A lot of people see my films and say, 'I don't get it.' But I've created at least a cult following. That's not quite enough people to make a minority!" However directors characterize their critics, these interviews illustrate their often contentious and amusing relationships.

Most of the original interviews in this book are preceded by substantial introductions by the interviewers (some of whom themselves discuss critical responses). Our own brief notes for each interview provide further reflection on the place, meaning, and potential fascination of each interview for our readers today. What is perhaps most remarkable about this selection of interviews, beyond the intricate (though obviously unintentional) points of connection between them, is the comparative openness with which most directors respond to questions. For instance, Capra's description of mistakenly anticipating a Best Picture Academy Award for *Lady for a Day* (1933) is hilariously candid: "I rehearsed speeches, I wrote lots of acceptance speeches; and I practiced them before a mirror so my voice would break in just the right place. My wife was in her ninth month of pregnancy, and she just locked the door and thought I'd lost my mind. And I had!" With equally unflinching candor, Coolidge speaks of how the death of her father (when she was nine) left her family socially vulnerable, an experience which made her "identify with outsiders" as is reflected in the points of view that she privileges through her films. Similarly, Malle says that *Le Feu follet* (*The Fire Within*, 1963) is an attempt to cope with the question of suicide, without finding answers, because the story "more or less happened to a friend" of his. In reading each interview, we might learn more about particular films, but many interviews (whether directly or indirectly) also establish the virtual presence of the director: Hammond describes Tacchella as having "the aspect of the serious and the aloof school-boy until he starts to speak"; Linda Cahir describes Davies's nonverbal response to her praise of his film: "he just smiled at me, quietly looked up through his glasses, and then he laughed, roundly, a laugh filled with good-natured mirth." The interviewers have obviously created contexts for what read as comparatively unmediated, uncensored encounters. For instance, we can recognize the relaxed openness that John Tibbetts encouraged in Altman, especially if we note Altman's comparatively terse manner of responding to a series of questions in a forum which Tibbetts has transcribed as occurring after his one-to-one interview. Most of the other interviews are in the traditional format of one-to-one questions and answers with two notable exceptions beyond Altman. Cahir provides interview transcriptions for Davies and the producer Olivia Stewart that are interspersed with Cahir's own comments on the film and its primary source. And Rocco Fumento's interview is more like an essay about the overwhelming and brandy-infused experience of meeting Fellini. This essay nevertheless answers a fantasy of access to the "maestro": especially when Fumento emphasizes Fellini's jovial candor in the presence of his student (Gianfranco Angelucci) in front of, whom Fellini says, "I don't have to wear the mask."

While some directors remove the mask, others perhaps create new masks whenever they discuss their work. The interviews of this book reflect and respect the many differences among the directors, in terms of sensibility, persona, and vision. They are united, however, in providing us with new contexts for understanding a diverse range of cinema which reflects numerous forms of art, reality, history, politics, ideology, and personality. We hope this book will serve as tribute, not only to the bodies of works the directors have created (and, in many cases, are still creating) but also to the interviewers who have taken the time to sit down with filmmakers over the years and record, for our benefit, what they have to say.

NOTE

1. Edward W. Said, "Jane Austen and Empire," in *Culture and Imperialism* (New York: Vintage Books), 80–96.

CONVERSATIONS
WITH DIRECTORS

Jonas Mekas

Non-narrative forms require a much more personal, intuitive and automatic kind of editing, and this can be done only during the shooting.

*T*he practice of publishing interviews in *Literature/Film Quarterly* did not begin with a director of an adaptation or even someone famous for narrative filmmaking. Rather, in 1973, the first interview that the then young journal published was the following piece on filmmaker and critic Jonas Mekas. Discussing what he refers to as "non-narrative film" (suspect as he is of terms like "avant-garde" and "experimental"), Mekas begins the interview with Gerald Barrett by telling him about the two meanings of the term New American Cinema, or N.A.C.: one, a descriptor of a moment in American cinema history, referring to filmmakers like John Cassavetes and Richard Leacock (as well as Mekas himself); and two, a reference to a filmmaking collective that Mekas helped initiate. After this opening discussion, Mekas compares the development of narrative film against that of non-narrative before moving into some specific aspects of his own films. For instance, he considers editing in non-narrative films, which he regards as requiring "a much more personal, intuitive and automatic kind of editing" that can be done "only during the shooting." At the same time, Mekas reflects frequently on his role as a critic and criticism in general, citing the problems that most reviewers have with non-narrative cinema (though he is hopeful, he admits, that those problems will be resolved over time). He discusses his regular column at the time in *The Village Voice*, and he defends the importance of a broad-based knowledge of the history of cinema combined with a deep passion for the medium, citing his tendency to "write only about films I like." Mekas nods toward adaptations late in the interview—he says he is "against adaptations of plays and novels," though he cites some he admires—and ends by listing some of the best non-narrative films of the 1950s and 1960s.

What will likely fascinate many readers of this interview is Mekas's willingness to include so many seemingly disparate forms of filmmaking under the rubric of non-narrative films. Stan Brakhage, Andy Warhol, Richard Leacock, and Mekas himself—quite different filmmakers—all fall under this term. In this way, while the interview is now over thirty years old, it perhaps has a great deal to teach scholars and enthusiasts of cinema about the limitations and possibilities inherent in any generic terms. Indeed, in general, Mekas's reflections on these issues and others still seem as provocative today as they undoubtedly were in the second issue of *Literature/Film Quarterly*.

Interview by Gerald Barrett
Originally published as "Jonas Mekas Interview: October 10, 1972," Litertature/Film Quarterly *1, no. 2 (April 1973): 103–12.*

BARRETT: Dwight Macdonald has called you "the patron saint of the New American Cinema." What is the New American Cinema?

MEKAS: The term, the New American Cinema (or NAC), was, mainly, taken from the title of an article I wrote in *Film Culture* in 1962. It was a survey of certain films made during the previous decade, and in it I discussed tendencies and individual artists such as Cassavetes, Leacock, Vanderbeek, and Brakhage; indicating, stressing those directions which were new. And I thought that there was a definite break with the traditional cinema in techniques and forms, in content and feeling, and I called all of this the New American Cinema. So, when people began referring to the things I said, the filmmakers I referred to, they usually used the term, the New American Cinema. Then, later, I myself started using the term for the same purpose. You call someone "Peter" or "Stan," and you know who you are talking about. But the name the New American Cinema has also another origin. In 1960 I got together some of the independent filmmakers, those who were working in the avant-garde film (at that time, called the "experimental film") and those who were working in the low-budget, semi-commercial area, and we decided to create some kind of an organization to produce films, to distribute films, to fight censorship, and to promote our films; and we called ourselves the New American Cinema Group. We wanted to avoid terms like "experimental or "personal" or "avant-garde." We simply wanted to call our movement "new," which we thought it was.

BARRETT: Was the group interested in creating a new feature film movement?

MEKAS: Some of us wanted to move in that direction. Some members of the group were interested in feature narrative films in the cinéma-vérité style, and I felt, and still feel, that that was new and was a contribution to the narrative film tradition. The work of Ricky Leacock and the Maysles brothers at the beginning—and the later branches, Andy Warhol, the first two films by Norman Mailer (not *Maidstone* [1970])—those films were made by men who went directly into a life situation and stuck with a protagonist, like the Maysles' *Salesman* [1968]: and in that sense those films were narrative and dramatic. Other filmmakers, like Warhol, imposed artificial situations that non-actors had to go through, and it is here that Mailer's first two films are important. Of course, Mailer is not an actor: but he has such a great ego-personality that, just as in his writing, he had to be at the center of his films. An actor would work within certain conventions to give us the idea of a cop, but when Mailer plays the cop in *Beyond the Law* [1968], his imagination and his temperament lead him into very strange and unconventional fantasies and meditations on a cop. I can't think of a modern novel or a film in which the cop has come out as such a complex and interesting personality. Mailer actually makes us feel what it's like to be a cop.

However, all of the narrative films referred to thus far are quite conventional, even if they are part of the New American Cinema. To talk about the really *new* in the modern narrative film, we have to turn somewhere else. There is another kind of narrative film, much less known than all the others, a film that deals with myth, such as Brakhage's *Dog Star Man* [1962] and Markopoulos's *Twice a Man* [1964]. It's here that the real revolution took place. These films explode the conventional narrative form and bring to the narrative film an intensity and complexity not known to cinema before.

BARRETT: But most of the contributions of the NAC are in the area of shorter, non-narrative films?

MEKAS: Yes. Much of the achievement in the last ten years or so is in the non-narrative form. But this is because the narrative form in the last sixty years of cinema has been developed much further than the non-narrative forms. By 1960, the narrative film had been explored on almost every level. But the non-narrative film was only at its beginning. That's why, although the achievements of the avant-garde narrative (or, perhaps more exactly, "mythopoetic film," to borrow P. Adams Sitney's term) are very monumental, it is still correct to say that the main achievement of the sixties was the working out of the language, techniques, vocabulary, and forms of the non-narrative film.

BARRETT: Let's go back to Macdonald's statement for a moment. While it's clear that your work was seminal to the NAC, I have always had the feeling that he was being a bit sarcastic in calling you the "patron saint" of the movement. Macdonald has never taken the non-narrative films of the NAC very seriously, and he has

been joined by other critics such as Pauline Kael, John Simon, and Stanley Kauffmann.

MEKAS: Yes, and these people have seen relatively few non-narrative, avant-garde
films. They refuse to see them, but they like talking about them; they're not interested in them. It is easy to be sarcastic about things you don't know. They're
more interested in producing entertaining copy—Pauline Kael, John Simon and
Macdonald are always great fun to read—than in providing the correct information on things they are writing about.

BARRETT: They refer to those films in such terms as "undisciplined," "amateur-
ish," "confusing."

MEKAS: They take the same kind of stance as a Stalinist social realist attacking Picasso, or the Nazis attacking the German Expressionist artists. They say things like
"Your camera shakes," or "You don't know what you are doing," or "You're
sloppy," or "Any child could do it." They're not really carrying on a serious discussion.

BARRETT: Does your film *Reminiscences of a Journey to Lithuania* [1972], screened
the other evening at the New York Film Festival, offer us some examples of this
critical problem?

MEKAS: Let's take, for example, the exposure of my film. I did not eliminate shots
on the basis of under- or over-exposure. I cut out shots because I did not like the
way they looked, what they said. Because the question of under- or over-exposure
is no longer that simple as it used to be in cinema's infancy. The modern film aes-
thetics have thrown out such conventional textbook ideas as the "normal" exposure, or "normal" focus, or "normal" this or that. Now, we say that the exposure
can be from complete white to complete dark, and you choose what you need according to what you are doing—it all depends on the feeling, on the mood, on
one's style, on the rhythm, etc., etc. The same with speeds—you can film from
fastest to slowest. And the same is true with every cinema technique. Of course, in
other arts this has been true for many decades, or many centuries. Is there a "normal" color scale in painting? Must all trees be green? A certain green? Such ideas
have been thrown out.

BARRETT: Similarly, you generally edit in the camera, don't you?

MEKAS: I edit most of my footage in the camera. Post-editing on the table is
more a matter of eliminating what didn't work. Where I failed in my editing during the shooting, where I missed the feeling, the rhythm of the scene, where I
didn't get to the essence, at least as I feel it when I'm looking at it later, then I
cut it out. I cut out the badly written "paragraphs." But I don't usually touch what
I leave in. Thus, my editing technique is different from the classical, the traditional idea of editing. But this is only because our ideas of what editing is have
been based until now on the narrative film requirements and practices only. Non-

narrative forms require a much more personal, intuitive and automatic kind of editing, and this can be done only during the shooting. This is not to say that there is no editing of any kind during the shooting of a conventional narrative film. Besides the editing in the editing rooms, there is also the editing or structuring within the shot, during the shooting. The shot is structured by how the actors move within the frame, by the placement of the lights, by how the sound travels, by the pacing and the movements of the camera. All of this takes place during the shooting. Narrative directors have to be concerned with that: Antonioni, Hitchcock, Rossellini. So, there is always that kind of structuring during the shooting. So that the conception and practices of editing differ in the different forms of the same art: how you organize the smallest elements into the total structure.

BARRETT: So, critics such as Macdonald, Kael, Simon, and Kauffmann are unable to properly evaluate new narrative and non-narrative films because they're using invalid criteria.

MEKAS: Really, what they're saying is: "Why does Blake write those fourteener lines? Can't he write a novel? Can't he write something serious?" They wouldn't, of course, say that about literature, because they know that there are certain conventions in poetry that differ from those in the novel. But in cinema, the differing traditions of narrative and non-narrative films do not exist for 99% of the reviewers. To them, cinema is what comes from Hollywood or from the European "art" film centers. This is even the case with Andrew Sarris. If you ask Sarris to define cinema, he comes up with something like this: "Cinema is that thing which people refer to when they say 'Let's go to movies.'" If we would take that kind of attitude with respect to literature, we would end up with nothing but "best sellers." No art other than cinema is so lacking in valid methods of evaluating work in various forms. But things are beginning to change—mostly, I think, through universities and other learning institutions. We're beginning to develop an acceptance of different forms in cinema.

BARRETT: Is *Reminiscences of a Journey to Lithuania* an example of a different cinematic form?

MEKAS: Yes, it's like most of my work of the last ten years: it's created in the form of a diary, or an autobiography. It's a comparatively new form. Cinema has been going into various directions in the last fifteen or twenty years. Even within the existing forms of narrative films, various forms of diary began to appear. First, there were films that were quite fictitious, like Stanton Kaye's *Georg* [1964]. He created a fictional diary. The script was written out and the seemingly real events were actually staged. Of course, you could consider Bresson's *Diary of a Country Priest* [1951] as another example: an adaptation of a novelistic diary-notebook by Georges Bernanos. Such forms were in existence prior to the work of the last decade. More recently, filmmakers began directly shooting material dealing with their actual lives, their day-to-day lives, their friends; and after they shot the footage, the material was structured, organized, and issued in the form of film notebooks. I have here in mind work of Warren Sonbert, Andrew Noren, Gerard Malanga, Michael Stewart, Bob Branaman, Taylor Mead, Stan Brakhage (particularly in *Songs*), and of a good number of others. The diary, of course, is a variety of the narrative film: there are protagonists, the filmmaker himself, his friends. My first completed work in this form was *Diaries, Notes & Sketches* [1969], and it contained day-to-day footage taken with my Bolex during the years 1965-1968. The three-hour-long "volume" consisted of my daily camera " notes." Regarding *Reminiscences of a Journey to Lithuania*, in August of 1971, I went to Lithuania where I come from and I visited there my brothers, my mother, and I kept a camera notebook as I was staying there for two weeks. When I brought the material back to this country, I structured it into a film of three parts. In the first part, I used some of the material shot when I first came to this country in the early fifties. Then, I have the Lithuania footage. Part three consists of my visit to Austria, to my friend, Peter Kubelka. And each part serves a different function; each part touches on a different aspect of the ideas of "home," "culture," "displaced person," "roots," "homelessness."

Barrett: Did you feel that the particular film genre you were working in was considered by those who viewed it at the New York Film Festival?

Mekas: Well, Professor Gerald O'Grady presented the film to the audience as a film made in the form of a diary, an autobiography, and there were objections: "What are you talking about? A film is a film. What is this division . . . diary . . . autobiography?" It's like saying, "Anything that has two wings and two legs and flies is a bird. A bird is a bird." But we know there are differences. Everything that flies and has two wings and two legs is not a pigeon. Those interested in birds have to go into categories to make meaningful distinctions, and it's the same with cinema.

Barrett: Let's suppose that we have a critic who has made the proper distinctions in his mind and sets out to criticize a particular contemporary American avant-garde film. . . .

Mekas: That is only developing. That is only beginning. Proper criticism, during the beginning years, was very difficult. In the beginning, and, of course, I am speaking here about the early sixties, the period of NAC—with so many good films being made in such a short period of time, I could not act as critic. I was really a mid-wife. I was excited and wanted everyone to see the work of people such as Brakhage, Jack Smith, Markopoulos, and the others. But periods of great creativity do not last forever. Now, things are slowing down. Now, we have a body of works and the beginnings of an avant-garde film tradition.

Barrett: Which brings me to your writing in *The Village Voice*. What will happen when you switch from your role as mid-wife to a more critical posture? Will your critical views be accepted by those who believe that some of your previous comments exaggerated the worth of certain films? You didn't criticize the films, you simply praised them.

MEKAS: That was enough, at the time.

BARRETT: But you seldom offered the viewer a method of evaluating the films or of validating your praises.

MEKAS: That cannot be helped. First, there is only the artist and his work. Then, there are his friends. The work, at first, grows through and with the artist alone, and his close friends. It cannot start from the other end, from the museum. Furthermore, the artist doesn't have to explain: it's enough that he did it. Explanations and analyses begin when the work goes to the people. No new art movement begins with a history; new art movements make history. The stage of serious criticism in cinema is only coming now. Again, I am speaking not about cinema in general but about the avant-garde film, specifically. There are three or four people who are beginning to write, to discuss, to organize a critical position. Some very intelligent writers on the avant-garde film are beginning to come out of universities. The first really serious book on the avant-garde film will be coming out next spring, P. Adams Sitney's *The Visionary Film-Makers* [published as *Visionary Film:The American Avant-Garde*, Oxford University Press, 1974], a monumental work. My own book, *Movie Journal* [Macmillan, 1972], just serves to introduce it. It's not really a book of criticism; it's just a history of the period. The histories, dialogues, and various viewpoints that are common to an understanding of literature and the literary tradition are only beginning in the avant-garde film. But there is progress. In the early sixties the only critical source was *Film Culture* magazine. Certain films were discussed there, and you would have some criteria for evaluation. The next stage came about through the anthologies. Gregory Battcock's anthology of writings, *The New American Cinema* [Dutton, 1967]. Then, Sheldon Renan's book, *An Introduction to the American Underground Film* [Dutton, 1967]. Limited as it was, it did give an overview of the history of the movement. Then, there was P. Adams Sitney's *Film Culture Reader* [Praeger, 1970]. Now, it's becoming more complicated. With Parker Tyler's book *Underground Film* [Grove Press, 1971], we have an alternate stand; a different view of the same films is presented and now we can see a number of the early films from two sides. And then, there is *Artforum* magazine, which, under the editorship of Annette Michelson, has become a source of some of the most intelligent writing on film. A dialogue is beginning. In literature, of course, dialogues have been going on for centuries. So, now, all of these writers are discussing the avant-garde film, and they have certain disagreements. Anyone who is intelligent enough can begin to guide himself. New books on the subject are being written and published in England and on mainland Europe. If one still rents avant-garde films blindly today, all that I can say is that he is a fool.

BARRETT: In your 17 August column in *The Village Voice*, you write that you avoid commenting upon commercial films because your critical standards cannot be applied to them because they are not serious enough.

MEKAS: Sometimes I go to catch up on those that are discussed in the press. I sit and I relax and I have a nice evening. But also, I find myself forgiving so many things, relaxing all my standards. I would never approach any of the avant-garde films that I respect in this way. When I look at an avant-garde film, I measure it from the very beginning, moment by moment. And when a film begins to fail, even for a moment, how can we excuse it? One asks for a certain totality, a certain level of achievement throughout. The level of achievement in the commercial narrative film during the last decade has been very, very low when compared with the achievement in the non-narrative or the new narrative film (for example, *Chelsea Girls* [1966]).

BARRETT: But there are some films that are not avant-garde and are not commercial, there are some fiction feature films that have reached a high level of achievement. For example, at your theater in New York, at Anthology Film Archives, you show films by Renoir, Ozu, Bresson, and other non-avant-garde moderns. You wouldn't term Bresson avant-garde, would you?

MEKAS: To tell the truth, we don't divide that much; at Anthology, we don't use those terms. There is a great danger in dividing films in terms of avant-garde and non-avant-garde, of commercial and non-commercial. Is there a set number, how many people must see a film before it becomes "commercial"? Brakhage has told me that his *Dog Star Man* has been seen by over one million people. Does that make *Dog Star Man* a commercial film? I'm willing to dismiss that kind of terminology. The only distinction I can accept is non-narrative and narrative. Even there, there are complications. So that, at the very end, we can speak only about the individual artists.

BARRETT: Can we say that there are good films and bad films?

MEKAS: That I can accept. One can speak in those terms. That's legitimate. Or in terms of different forms, or genres.

BARRETT: Well, what kinds of distinctions can be made about the difference between a good film and a bad film?

MEKAS: It finally comes down to the passion of the critic toward a particular film. But, of course, on what is that passion based? First, he should see many, many films and be passionate about cinema in general. Then, all of the critic's background comes into play, that is, all of the aspects of cinema come into play: the history of cinema, the theory of cinema, the techniques of cinema, the forms of cinema, the contemporary examples of cinematic works, the individual creators. Think of a film as a chair. How does one decide if a particular chair is well made? By comparing it with other chairs, by memories of all the chairs in which you sat. And even so, you may discover that you are wrong about that particular chair unless you sat in it for a few weeks. Only many, many viewings of a particular film can finally establish its superiority to others. However you live, whatever you do, you make choices, you make decisions. So, in cinema if you are in a position to show your friends some films, you choose the films you show to them: you don't pick them at random. You want them to see the most beautiful films, those that gave you pleasure and continue to give you pleasure. And you want to share that experience. So you begin to compare films in order to show your friends the best.

BARRETT: I agree. An evaluation of a particular film is based upon the critic's intimate and extensive knowledge of all the aspects of cinematic art as well as his unique tastes and predilections. Do you think that such an evaluation can be validated in the space of a short column? Say your column in *The Village Voice*?

MEKAS: If I trust somebody's judgment, he doesn't have to go into lengthy backings of his recommendations. One word is enough. In other words, either one trusts my taste or not. Of course, my space doesn't permit me any lengthy analyses. I can express my feelings about a film, that's about all. That's why I write only about films I like. When I like them, I can express my enthusiasm in that one short column. But to be negative, to put something down, to attack some bad film that my colleagues are raving about—that's something else. To seriously attack something, you have to prove, you have to discuss. The next stage after passion is analysis. You have to discuss the film on aesthetic grounds, on social grounds, on technical grounds, on historical grounds; you have to place the film in a proper perspective and explain yourself. I have done this in a few cases, but I have done very little of that. It's the people like P. Adams Sitney, Ken Kelman or Annette Michelson who can write ninety pages on *Dog Star Man*, whom you must look to.

BARRETT: Of course, analytic criticism would take time away from your filmmaking.

MEKAS: That's true. I'm involved with the Film-Makers' Cooperative, the Anthology Film Archives, Film Culture, my own films. So, I don't feel guilty about my non-analytic writing. I'm not a critic! Really. I'm not a critic! The furthest I can go is to say that I'm a mid-wife. And that's about it. Or, if I'm thought of as a critic, I'm as much a critic as Baudelaire was, or Apollinaire; that is, those artists who have written on art and artists in a way similar to mine. None of them wrote studies, analyses. They were practicing a very personal kind of criticism.

BARRETT: Since the form of your films in the last ten years, the diary form, is a literary convention, I wonder if you have any thoughts about the subject of films derived from specific literary works? Do you ever look at a film in that way: how well it cinematically accomplishes what has previously been accomplished in words?

MEKAS: I saw Gregory Markopoulos' *Psyche* [1948], and for years after I was not aware of the source, the novel by Pierre Louÿs. It was Gregory's film, and it had no relation to literature. And then I saw *Himself as Herself* [1967], his film based on Balzac's *Seraphita*, and it didn't look at all like it was based on a literary work.

These are the true adaptations. Actually, they're not adaptations, they're something else. Gregory used the literary works for inspiration. And then he completely transformed the sources to turn his films into something else. But as far as direct adaptations are concerned, are there any successful adaptations? Of course. Bresson's *Diary of a Country Priest*. Actually, I'm against adaptations of plays and novels. I'm for original film sources.

BARRETT: Why is that?

MEKAS: Well. I should say that I'm not against adaptations if the film is based on a bad novel or play. Then it's simply material to be used; you can be very free with it. But if you are working from a great literary work? It's legitimate to take some aspect of, say, *Moby Dick*, for your inspiration, but to make an adaptation of it? What can you add to it? What insights can you add to a book like that? What other new angle can you reveal? It's all there. You can only simplify, banalize, distort. But, of course, when you deal with a bad novel, which is like a script to begin with, you know that the film can be better.

BARRETT: Why do you think so many directors do it? Russell's *Women in Love* [1969], Richardson's *Tom Jones* [1963], Visconti's *Death in Venice* [1971]?

MEKAS: Because the producers want it. The director has to play the game to assure the producer of his built-in financial returns.

BARRETT: Can you conceive of a good director seriously setting out to cinematically reproduce a great literary work?

MEKAS: Eisenstein considered filming Joyce's *Ulysses*.

BARRETT: He even wrote a script for *An American Tragedy*. Murnau, of course, did *Faust* [1926] and *Tartuffe* [1926].

MEKAS: Of course, I haven't resolved for myself the contradictions involved in the subject of adaptations. For instance, I find it different with silent films. One thing that's legitimate is to illustrate books. Illustrations are decorative and a filmmaker can add something to *Faust*, like Doré did with his illustrations of *Paradise Lost*. There is that tradition. That doesn't insult me at all. Silent films based on great literary works could be looked at in that way. The characters don't open their mouths to vulgarize authors' lines. And, of course, in painting, every line of the Bible has been painted over and over all over the walls of the Western Civilization and, of course, some of these works are as great as the Bible itself.

BARRETT: What about Dreyer's *Gertrud* [1964]?

MEKAS: Dreyer always comes in as an example. But, there, he's dealing with a classic on the level, say, of Arthur Miller. It's a classic that is local, so I don't know how Danes look at it. To us, the literary source doesn't exist in *Gertrud*. We don't know the play. And with Dreyer, I would bet and swear that Dreyer is a ten-times better artist than the man who wrote the play.

BARRETT: One reason I asked you about your feelings on the subject is that when you describe your editing practices you sometimes use literary analogies.

MEKAS: There was a time when cinema was young that filmmakers tried to avoid any terms or analogies that would suggest relationships with other forms of art. They wanted to emphasize their individuality, their originality and the uniqueness of their cinema art. But I think that cinema does not have to have that kind of inferiority complex anymore. We know what it can do. We know that it can do something original and unique. So now, at this point, we can begin to see the comparative area. To understand what cinema is, it is sometimes very useful to make use of the terminology, the means of expression, even the techniques found in other arts. All arts overlap. In all arts, you find similar forms. We have an arabesque in music; we have an arabesque in art and sculpture; we have an arabesque in cinema. Very often, I invite those who are seeing avant-garde films for the first time and object to certain aspects to think about other art forms they are more familiar with and find points of similarity. It helps.

BARRETT: Talking about points of similarity, I'm surprised that so few avant-garde filmmakers have tried to do anything with transforming personal lyrical poems to film. There seems to be a meaningful overlap there.

MEKAS: The problem here is the same as with the adaptations of novels; you just can't add anything to a good poem. And if a poem is bad, why bother with it? On the other hand, as the non-narrative forms developed, they began on their own, and in their own terms (that is, in terms of cinema) to touch and draw inspiration from the same inner sources from which the greatest of the written poems have emerged. So that very naturally, and very organically, a form or, rather, forms of cinema have developed that correspond to those of poetry in literature. And it's here that we find some of the true glories of the American cinema of the last two decades. I have in mind works such as Brakhage's *The Dead* [1960], *Sirius Remembered* [1959], or *Prelude* [1961]; Anger's *Eaux d'Artifice* [1953] and *Fireworks* [1947]; Broughton's *Mothers Day* [1948] and *This Is It* [1971]; Baillie's *Castro Street* [1966], *Mass* [1964], and *All My Life* [1966]; Bruce Conner's *A Movie* [1958] and *Report* [1967]; Belson's *Samadhi* [1967] and *Chakra* [1972]; Jack Smith's *Flaming Creatures* [1963]; Robert Breer's *Eyewash* [1959] and *Fist Fight* [1964]; and etc., etc.—all works without any recourse to any literary sources; works ecstatically rich with poetic feeling and form. These works are expanding the medium of cinema for the expression of the poetic content in cinema.

William Friedkin

The *life* of a film exists because the audience is willing to take it away
with them.

$\mathcal{I}$n 2000, William Friedkin's director's cut of *The Exorcist* (1973) was released,
having been re-mastered into surround sound and including several scenes cut
from the original theatrical release. *The Exorcist* inspired two sequels as well as two
versions of a prequel, none of which approach Friedkin's original *or* director's cut
box office success: when adjusted for inflation, *The Exorcist* remains in the top ten
grossing films of all time at the American box office.[1] Although he is still making films, Friedkin remains best known for *The French Connection* (1971) along
with *The Exorcist*, both of which are discussed in detail throughout this interview
by Gerald R. Barrett. However, this comparatively lengthy interview goes far beyond discussing particular films to establishing a fascinating portrait of the director and his self-fashioning.

Friedkin establishes a dichotomy between "arthouse" and commercial cinema,
although he acknowledges their ironic interdependence as well, saying "There
wouldn't be a *Mean Streets* [1973] without an *Exorcist*." He describes his own work
as being "for entertainment," primarily driven by profit imperatives rather than
artistic pretension (he even ironically reveals that the sound accompanying the famous revolving head sequences in *The Exorcist* is that of his own wallet). Yet, Friedkin's *auteur*ist emphasis on controlling all aspects of his film production (including
casting, scriptwriting, virtually all aspects of production design, promotion, *and* distribution); the analogy he makes between a process of montage "within the frame"
in *The French Connection* and Picasso's cubist paintings; his own dedication to creating foreign language versions of *The Exorcist* rather than moving on to other feature films; and his numerous references to other directors as well as film critics belie the detachment in his ultimate emphasis on filmmaking as business.

14

Here, Friedkin also reveals himself as exceptionally equivocal: insisting on the audience's necessary interpretive role (refusing to answer some questions on the meaning behind his films), yet insistent that as filmmaker he must be deliberately *"shaping* audience response in a certain direction"; condemning Pauline Kael's influence on audiences (perhaps most famously with the example of *Bonnie and Clyde* (1967), yet admiring of her anti-sycophantic film criticism; dismissive of contemporary reviews and film criticism in general, yet nostalgically adulatory of James Agee's work; ostensibly against "the *auteur* stuff" (by Andrew Sarris and others), yet clearly establishing himself in alignment with what the term *auteur* connotes in terms of his relative control and overseeing vision. He positions his own self-conscious, intertextual work in relation to canonical films as well as other *auteurs*, including some who are also represented in this collection: Franco Zeffirelli, Frank Capra, and Federico Fellini.

Interview by Gerald R. Barrett
Originally published as "William Friedkin Interview," Literature/Film Quarterly *3, no. 4 (October 1975): 334–62.*

William Friedkin was born in Chicago in 1939. He grew up in Chicago and took a job in the mail room of a local television station at the age of 16. Before he turned 18 he found himself directing live television, a career that lasted through eight years and thousands of live shows. A shoestring film documentary, *The People vs. Paul Crump* (1962), won an award at the San Francisco Film Festival and led to a job with David L. Wolper, the documentary producer. Another low-budget film, this time a feature (*Good Times,* 1966) started Friedkin on his present career of feature-length fiction films: *The Birthday Party* (1968), *The Night They Raided Minsky's* (1968), *The Boys in the Band* (1970), *The French Connection* (1971), and *The Exorcist* (1973). Thanks go to George Stewart, Ray Leonard, and Ron Cailahan for their aid during this interview (September 1974).

BARRETT: I want to say at the outset that I'll try not to duplicate questions and discussions the reader could find in your other interviews.

FRIEDKIN: Well, it's hard not to repeat yourself, there are only so many things one knows and can talk about.

BARRETT: I have a few things to talk about that I don't think you have previously discussed in an interview.

FRIEDKIN: Good. And I have a couple of new things I want to talk about.

BARRETT: What are they?

FRIEDKIN: I'm sure they'll come out naturally during our conversation.

BARRETT: How is *The Exorcist* doing these days?

FRIEDKIN: *The Exorcist* is right now, after eight months of release, the fourth highest grossing film of all time. It will eventually be the all-time top grossing film. In America, so far, it has grossed sixty-five million in profits, and the estimate for the foreign market is another forty to fifty million.

BARRETT: What are you doing these days?

FRIEDKIN: I've worked on *The Exorcist* from beginning to end, and it took three years. The end was last week. I just finished doing all of the foreign versions of the film. I did the Italian, German, and French dubbed versions and supervised all the subtitled versions too . . . Japanese . . . Spanish. . . .

BARRETT: Sounds tedious.

FRIEDKIN: I don't mind when I see the checks! That kind of thing is the hard work of direction that people don't think about.

BARRETT: What's the most important part of direction?

FRIEDKIN: It changes at different points in the making of the film. Initially, the most important decision you make is to decide what story you're going to tell. There's no decision more important than that. Because the commercial cinema, in which I work, is a storytelling medium. It's not necessarily a medium for . . . well, it isn't *at all* a medium for documentary purposes, for educational purposes, for experimental purposes. It's strictly a medium of entertainment. And the other aspects of it, if there are any, come as a kind of by-product of the audience experiencing the story. So, the most important decision I make as a filmmaker is to decide what story I'm going to do. There's nothing more important than that . . . ever.

BARRETT: And after you select your story?

FRIEDKIN: Once that's decided, it then becomes a matter of translating the story into details; it becomes a matter of how I'm going to tell it. And the next most important elements are the casting and the people who are going to work on the film.

BARRETT: What's the relationship between you, your cast, and your script?

FRIEDKIN: After I know who's going to act in the film and who's going to work on it, I pretty much take things by osmosis. The way I work is pretty well set. I don't change my style of work from one film to another. I prepare very carefully. I communicate what I have in mind to everybody on the picture, immediately. Either with diagrams, drawings, or written explanations of everything that I have in mind. While I'm shooting I constantly try to achieve as much spontaneity as possible. Which is to say, I try to work with actors who are free to throw away the script. [Actors] who, like me, work on a script as hard as they need to, and then disregard it and just *become* the character[s].

BARRETT: How do you get your cast to *become* the characters they play?

FRIEDKIN: I try to cast people based on one inherent quality: intelligence. I don't care how good an actor is, or how good his performances have been, when I talk to him, in my initial meetings up front. I try to gauge intelligence. And I don't mean bullshit artists. I don't mean a guy who's going to tell me what I want to hear, but real intelligence and the ability to understand what the story's about on very deep levels so that one can disregard all of those levels and not have to play them.

BARRETT: I'm not sure I follow that.

FRIEDKIN: Take, for example, the Vincent Price horror films. Everything is played on the surface level. Personality, behavioral, thematic facets are so *clearly* understood by those people that they try to play every level and leave none to the imagination. That's why all the looks are arch, that's why everything is overemphasized. I try to deemphasize all of that *old* theatrical stuff, because you find that the camera has a tendency to reflect further than the mirror does. The camera has the tendency to magnify facets of human behavior and to suggest many more things than are there. It's like putting a pebble into the water, and from it flow all of the many waves. So, I cast people who are capable of understanding and then disregarding all of the very deep levels. I also believe in casting to physical types in the sense that if I'm doing a film, let's say, about a boxer, I'm not going to have the part played by someone who slouches around and looks like he's never been in a gym.

BARRETT: You say that your actors are free to throw away the script?

FRIEDKIN: I work on the scripts [a] very long [time] and very carefully and, by the time I get onto the floor, I never use them. I throw them out, just throw them out, and the actors do the same. I will rehearse extensively with actors on a scene, and then I'll say. "Do you remember all that stuff? Ok, now throw it all out, and do it *your* way!" Then we start messing around with it. Around ninety-eight percent of all the dialogue in the last two pictures was the actors' invention. Occasionally, someone in the writing process comes up with a line that is, shall we say, comparably memorable. And so we'll keep that particular line. Because it seems to be a good button on the scene, or a good way to come into the scene; but in the middle of a scene, all of the stuff is the actors living out their roles. And then I work as a kind of road guide, a tourist guide, making sure that they don't wander off onto byways that will lead them nowhere. Because the main thing you have to know as a director is where the hell you're going with this thing. Whereas, the actor may not; the actor comes in and does piecework, really; he has no real knowledge of how his performance is going to be ultimately used, nor control over the ultimate use of his effort.

BARRETT: What about the others who work on the film?

FRIEDKIN: Same is true for all of the other creative people who contribute. Camera, sound, lighting, wardrobe, whatever. Film is probably the most collaborative medium of communication there is. They all have their ideas about what their particular area should contribute, but none of them really know, ultimately, not only *how* it is going to be used, toward what end, but *what's* going to be used of what they've done. So they're all out there giving 100 percent all of the time. Whereas, I may have in the back of my mind, let's say, that I might not even make use of wardrobe detail for somebody who's in the background in a scene. And I might not even use the scene! I shoot a lot of scenes, you know, that never get into the picture. Sometimes I'll say, "Don't worry about that detail," and the person in charge of wardrobe will say, "What do you mean?" I'll say, "It's ok, don't worry about that." And the people who know me, who have worked with me more than once, know what that means by now. Whereas, at another time, I'll be a *total* stickler for authenticity, because I have a gut feeling at the time that that particular shot or scene has *got* to find its way into the ultimate picture. But I do encourage everybody to cut loose once I'm convinced that they share my vision about what the hell we're supposed to be doing.

BARRETT: Do you give your cameraman and the various technicians the same freedom to improvise on the floor as you do your actors?

FRIEDKIN: No. But one of the things I would suggest to anyone who wanted to make films is that you should visualize the entire film in your head before you make it. You've got to see the entire film in your head. Once you can do that, then you can go out and start changing it. If you've ever seen Picasso paint, as I have, or if you look carefully at his finished work, you see that he constantly alters the image. Somewhere in his head he knows what he wants. Meanwhile, he gets on the canvas and starts transposing, and scratching out, and drawing over, and painting over. You can do that if you have a clear vision of what you want to achieve. You can't do that if you're out there just messing around. You can't go out there on the floor with a crew and start improvising with technicians unless you're independently wealthy and you're financing the project yourself. You certainly can decide that this angle is better than that angle, or that you should be twenty feet closer instead of further away, or that you should be on a long lens rather than a wide lens; but, at the *time*, you can't change *everything* and say, "We should be pointing that way instead of this way." Or, everybody shows up at seven in the morning to shoot the scene and you say, "This should be a night scene, what the hell are we doing here? I'm going back to bed, see you tonight at eight." That kind of improvisation is just masturbatory. But within the give and take of selecting the frame, choosing just the right kind of light, selecting what should be excluded or emphasized in the frame, what details should be pointed up from in the background, all of that has a great element of improvisation to it; and it's very collaborative in the sense that others you are working with are contributing to it. Very often the script girl or the cameraman or whomever will say, "What would happen if you did this?" There are a lot of things in films that I have directed that were provided by people I worked with. With respect to my cameraman and soundman, I encourage them to go off and be very interpretive while always remembering that the important thing is to tell the story. Everybody has to realize that what we're all there for is not to jerk off, you know, or to experiment, to find a new form, but to tell the story as simply as possible. And that, strangely, is one of the toughest things there is to do, to make oneself tell the story simply. Because, when you first start out and learn that you can handle the camera, you know what the lenses can do, you know what different microphones are capable of, you know what you can do with different lights, light used either as a sidelight or a backlight, or a full front light, or whatever; at the beginning, when you're learning these technical things, the tendency is to demonstrate your knowledge of them and to put them up front in a film. That's something I still haven't mastered; it's a very strenuous task to keep technique totally absent from the storytelling.

BARRETT: How long has it taken you to master the techniques of the medium, itself?

FRIEDKIN: It wasn't until I was making *Boys in the Band* that I really knew *what* I was doing with the film. I had no real idea about technique or how to really use the medium until something happened that sparked my thinking: I was in New York making *Boys* and I wandered into an exhibit of cubist painters at the Museum of Modern Art. I was really struck by the quality of those early paintings. I had not previously read anything about the cubists . . . I later did. I was struck by how those painters, working in a two-dimensional medium, were able to suggest an object in motion and an object seen from all sides at once. I was really struck by this notion of attempting to break free from what was essentially a restriction of the art form. And it occurred to me that this was a challenge offered by the motion picture medium too, where, again, you could only show height and width. And the secret of using the camera is to create the *illusion* of depth where there really is *no* depth. For example, most scenes shot by most beginning directors are shot pretty flat. The audience observes the scene pretty much as if it were watching actors on the stage, in profile, talking to each other, with very little suggestion of depth. It occurred to me that I was not really using the medium in my films to that point. *The French Connection* was the very first film in which I was able to try out my ideas. Take something as simple as showing a car in motion. The standard method might be to cut from one angle to another to show the progress of the car. But it occurred to me that it might be extraordinarily more interesting to show person and object head-on, coming toward the camera, and let the camera pan them as they move laterally past so that we have a side view, and then let the camera hold and continue to show the object as it continues in the distance and we see it from the rear. Just that simple use of montage within the frame, itself, which is possible *only* in the film medium, is something that was never taught and never learned except by a kind of osmosis while observing the cubist paintings. I tried out such notions in *The French Connection* and I feel that it's the first film I made where I really used the medium. And that was quite recent, in 1971. I've only made one film since so my ideas are very much formulative. Every picture I've made has been both an adventure *and* an education. I've not only learned more about the use of the medium, but I've learned about subjects I've come in contact with that I wouldn't have known about if I weren't a filmmaker.

BARRETT: Getting back to the idea of creative collaboration, how much freedom do you give to your editor?

FRIEDKIN: None, really. I go into the room and edit the film. I mark up the stuff on my own and then the editor goes in and does the actual physical work. My recent editor was allowed to edit a trailer on his own, but that's the farthest I've gone. To me, editing is more exciting, more interesting, more discovery-prone, more important, than any other facet of filmmaking. You can, literally, blow a good film in the cutting room, or make a film better than it is, or ruin stuff that was well-shot to begin with; you can just ruin it. I find that the attitude in the cutting room that works best for me is to be *merciless*. I've reached the point now where I don't have to psyche myself to do it: I just view the stuff as total *shit*, I divorce myself from the guy who directed it. I become another person, in effect. You literally have to split yourself in two at that point. And you have to forget about all of the troubles that you had getting that shot, all the difficulties you had in achieving that performance in take 28, or whatever it was, and say, "This doesn't work! This doesn't make it! And not only doesn't it make it, but it's holding up the flow of the stuff that does, and it has to go!" So all of the beautiful sunsets go, and everything else. But more than that, you know, not just great shots, but whole sequences that you thought were crucial, if not vital, to the film. When the editing process begins and takes on a life of its own, the footage becomes another film. And all of the planning and preparation, everything that you did leading up to that, is so much grist for the mill. Editing is the most exciting part of filmmaking for me. I would be an editor full-time if I could make as much money at it, if I could live the same life-style, as I do by directing.

BARRETT: I've read that quite a bit of the Iraq footage in *The Exorcist* had to go. What are you going to do with it?

FRIEDKIN: Nothing. I have hours of great stuff, but I won't be able to do anything with it. Same with *The French Connection*. I went to Marseilles and shot a great deal of footage and then got back to the cutting room and woke up. I said, "What is this shit?" Then I cut it to the bone and threw out the rest. I seem to want to begin my films with a documentary; I guess it goes back to my documentary days with Wolper, when I first came to Hollywood.

BARRETT: Since we're on the subject of cutting, did you have final cut on *The French Connection* and *The Exorcist*?

FRIEDKIN: Mm-hmm. Which isn't to say that I didn't solicit opinion and advice from a variety of people. I did, and I had a lot of very helpful advice. But I've never had a film, except for *The Night They Raided Minsky's*, that ever went out in any way except the way I cut it. The first film I made was *Good Times* with Sonny and Cher. I'm not advertising it; it had been quietly put to rest some seven years ago, and now television has brought it back from the dead. But right from the very first film, when I didn't have it contractually at all, as imperfect, shall we say . . . my choice of adjectives . . . as imperfect as *Good Times* is, it's all my cut. I did it.

BARRETT: Well . . . Let me ask you this: Why do *you* have final cut and so many directors do not?

FRIEDKIN: First of all, because I know what I'm doing in the cutting room, and many other directors don't know and don't care. It's a place they don't want to go; it has great mysteries. And some people have built careers on directing films and never chancing to investigate the mysteries of editing. And I love editing, as I said. Secondly, if you make a film that goes out and works in its initial engagements, nobody comes around and tries to recut it. It's when you make a film like *Isadora* [1968], the biography of Isadora Duncan . . .

BARRETT: The Reisz film?

FRIEDKIN: Karel Reisz directed it, and I thought it was terrific at the time. It went out and died; so, immediately, a committee at Universal took it over and re-cut it by the numbers. One said, "I saw eight people yawn at this part," and another said, "I saw fourteen people fall asleep at that part," so they *yank* that out and they continue to recut it. Recutting, generally, *generally* speaking, happens when a film goes out and bombs in its initial engagements. There are other situations, of course, where the guys running the studio are so egomaniacal that they say, "I'm going to cut this picture." But now, myself and others have it in our contracts that those guys . . . For example, when I make a film, I deliver a can of film to the studio. I have nothing to do with the studio. They don't see the rushes, they don't talk to me, advise me, buy me a cup of coffee, discuss the sports pages with me . . . *nothing*. We make a deal, I go out and make a movie, I hand them a can of film, they say, "Thank you very much."

BARRETT: But you're unlike many directors in that you get involved in distribution.

FRIEDKIN: I give my advice on that but I don't get in too deeply in their bailiwick, although I have turned a lot of ad campaigns around, as well as a little bit of distribution. And on the first-run engagements of *The Exorcist*, I *literally* checked the theaters where the film was going to play. The projection equipment, the sound equipment, everything. And then, that's it. Then I go off and do something else. I must say, however, that if *The Exorcist* had gone out and bombed it would have been recut. There would have been nothing I could do about it.

BARRETT: In spite of your contract which gives you final cut?

FRIEDKIN: Sure! I would have sued them, but so what? Who wants to sue somebody in the United States today? I don't advise it. You can't win; it's a lawyer's world. Everytime you say, "I'm going to sue somebody," eight million lawyers around the world feel the vibes and smile and say "Oh, God! Oh, I can't believe it! It's happening again!" Nobody benefits in a law suit. The bottom line of what I'm telling is that, creatively, the product is the director's; but, actually, it belongs to the guys who put up the money. On a legal basis, they own it. Whatever director you admire—Kubrick, Fellini, whoever—somebody put up the money for their pictures and holds the rights. And even if the director holds the rights. Right now, Fellini's new movie, *Amarcord* [1973], is in Hollywood being recut by Roger Corman.

BARRETT: Oh, God!

FRIEDKIN: I've seen it uncut and I think it's just beautiful! It's a lovely film and Roger Corman's company is distributing it in the United States and there are certain things they don't like about it. So those things are going out. And they're dubbing a version, and a part of the pleasure of seeing the film, as many probably will never see it, is to hear the original Italian voices do it. So, now, Roger Corman will have a lot of people doing "DA DICK-EH AK-CENTS!" But Fellini sold Corman the rights. Corman *owns* it.

BARRETT: Well, Fellini can't complain if he sold Corman such rights.

FRIEDKIN: The only other alternative for a Fellini, or any director, is to not sell the rights, and do one of two things. Either not have the movie shown in America, or to come here, himself, or set up a company here, and engage in the distribution of the film in America. This is not something that many filmmakers care to do. Now I know you're going to ask me about Pauline Kael's recent comments . . .

BARRETT: I'm saving that for later . . .

FRIEDKIN: . . . about directors starting their own company for distribution purposes.

BARRETT: Yes, go on.

FRIEDKIN: This is one of the worst ideas imaginable for commercial filmmakers. Most of the people she encourages to do that are the least equipped to engage in the vagaries of American business. You can really get killed! I'm involved to an enormous extent in distribution, and if I was involved to any greater extent, I would be able to direct, maybe, one picture every three years, which is what has happened with *The Exorcist*. Of course, I made a lot of money on the film, but I could have made three times as much money if I had done all of the other pictures offered to me since the picture came out. But I chose to stay with the distribution of the film; I became obsessive about it, but only because I felt that the people involved in its distribution did not know as much about the audience as I did.

BARRETT: You're part owner of a film company, too, aren't you?

FRIEDKIN: Yes, the Director's Company, but it's a production company; Warner's does the distribution. I'm in it with Peter Bogdanovich and Francis Coppola. I have yet to make a film through the company. Coppola did *The Conversation* [1974] and Bogdanovich did *Paper Moon* [1973] and *Daisy Miller* [1974]. *Daisy Miller* has proved to be a bomb at the box office. We'll be lucky if it gets back its one million production cost, not to mention its one million advertising budget and another million spent on prints, legal fees, and the like.

BARRETT: Now that's one aspect of the system that puzzles me. How can some directors make one expensive bomb after another and still continue to make films? For example, take Robert Altman and Ken Russell. I enjoyed *McCabe & Mrs. Miller* [1971], *Images* [1972], *The Savage Messiah* [1972], and *The Music Lovers* [1970], but the mass public didn't. In fact, except for *McCabe*, neither did the critics. How are such filmmakers allowed to continue to lose money?

FRIEDKIN: The trick is to make a smash film and get someone to sign you to a long-term contract. Altman made *M*A*S*H* [1970] and Russell made *Women in Love* [1969]. That, incidentally, is the way some think Otto Preminger has spun out his career.

BARRETT: Do you think that the technical and financial problems that we've been discussing limit film as an art form? What I mean is this: You're making films to get large masses of people into the theater to entertain them, to give them their money's worth. But there are other directors who, let's say, have a more personal statement to make. Do you think that such directors are at a disadvantage in the sense that once the film is in the can they don't have much control over its presentation?

FRIEDKIN: Well, all you have to do to reach a point of total frustration is to go to some place like Wilmington, Delaware, or Milan, Italy, or Thailand, or Tasmania, and see your film projected in a theater. You recall the days, the *months* spent in laboratories trying to achieve perfect color balance, a perfect print. And all the care you took not to have, for example, any wires at all in the levitation scene in *The Exorcist*. We had this enormous piece of magnet built to create the levitation, and now you see it on the screen and there are 800 scratches, 800 wires, running through the *whole* print! Because of the state of the art, you can't make a print that will stay new any longer than two screenings, so this business of control over your art is a myth, a fantasy; it's out of our hands! You can achieve a *large measure* of control, maybe 50 percent, but the state of the art, itself, is such that the best film stock in existence fades in two years. The colors that you strove for are gone! The minute you begin to print from CRTs instead of the original negative, you begin to get color distortion. And an original negative in color will only give you fifty good prints, everything after the first fifty prints becomes secondary prints. And the colors distort, and the whole thing softens up, and loses definition, and light and dark areas become gray areas. All of this is part of creation.

There's a wonderful cartoon in the latest *New Yorker*. Two people are in a bar and one is saying to the other, "Do you think life is a writer's medium or a director's medium?" It's neither a writer's medium nor a director's medium; there are certain limitations to the state of life and the state of the art that restrict and limit one's power to control. The most you can do and the best you can do is to *reach* people in some way. *Touch* them emotionally . . . in some way. Even, with the imperfection of the art, itself. But anyone who is working in American film, *commercial American* film . . . I'm not talking about Jonas Mekas and the underground cinema which, to a great extent, I admire. They're not in the commercial cinema. For example, Ed Emshwiller's work is of great interest to me on any number of levels, and I think his work is very influential, and very moving, and always interesting, but it isn't commercial, let's face it. It's an acquired taste. It's folly to ask, "why doesn't Warner Brothers finance Ed Emshwiller?" Because they're a publicly held company that wants to see a return on their investment. Believe me, if there was suddenly a public run on Ed Emshwiller or Maya Deren, Warner Brothers would be doing the same number, going crazy, that they do on me or whomever. Million dollar contracts! It's a business! One of the things I try not to do, with some success, is to deceive myself. It's a business and if it doesn't make money there will be no film in this country for mass audiences. There wouldn't be a *Mean Streets* without an *Exorcist*. The studios need box office hits to take chances with the smaller, more personal films. And I've financed some work of non-box office filmmakers, myself. Bob Downey, for example, is a good friend of mine and a guy whose work I respect and love, and I put money into Bob's pictures. I don't *care* if they make money; I think they should be *made*. I wish that they were more widely appreciated; which is to say, make money. But believe me, if I wasn't in a financial position to do that along with Jack Nicholson and others who finance Bob, Bob wouldn't make movies.

BARRETT: You're a trustee of the American Film Institute; do you consider the AFI to be of help to filmmakers?

FRIEDKIN: In addition to its archival activities and its other work that develops a realization of American films as an art form, an entertainment medium, and a communications medium, the film school, which is in California, is by far the best I've seen, and I've seen a lot of them: MIT, UCLA, NYU, whatever. I think it has the best film school in the country! Also, it's the most practical, because they're teaching film to men and women in a manner which allows them to go out and use it professionally. And I have a feeling that that's probably the most important reason to go to school in America, to find a profession out of what you're assimilating. It's not just for aesthetic or personal use, it's to practice it. Unfortunately, the tentative note in my voice is due to a *tremendous* internal crisis at the AFI that resulted in the resignation of the dean, Frank Daniel, who was really the guiding educational force at the school. I'm working rather closely with the fellows of the AFI to restore Daniel; and, if not, to reform the AFI . . . *totally*. It became a political football in which the fellows had nothing whatever to say about the retention of the dean or the establishment of a permanent charter, or various other internal problems that contributed to the . . . *fucking up* of the school, frankly, in the last six months. But in the last few years the AFI has produced an incredible number of working men and women who have contributed to creative filmmaking. A number of directors like Terry Malick, who directed *Badlands* [1973], John Hancock, who did *Bang the Drum Slowly* [1973], and Oscar Williams, who did a movie called *Five on the Black Hand Side* [1973]. They all came out of the AFI program, and there are others.

BARRETT: It seems that the AFI's had problems since its inception.

FRIEDKIN: Well, it's out in the open, now. It was really the creation of one man: George Stevens, Jr. and he's a fellow who has made, like, one sculpture in his life, and that's it. You know of the Watts towers, made by one man who worked for 45 years collecting scrap from the railroad tracks: junk, tin cans, whatever, and he made these incredible twin towers that are nothing more than monuments to the spirit of the man, Simon Rodilla, and of humankind. Like Simon Rodilla, George Stevens, Jr. has made one sculpture, the AFI, and that's it. And he tends to be very paternalistic and he tends to use the AFI for his own personal purposes. And initially, when the AFI was forming, he was its guiding force and he brought all of the elements together, and did that very well. Now, it doesn't work that well; now, he's got fifty fellows up there, men and women who are making *films*, and they all have different input, and they all have different goals, and he's completely unmindful of the interests of the fellows.

BARRETT: Talking about different interests, what do you think about video as an inexpensive alternative to film? I know some young filmmakers are considering that possibility these days.

FRIEDKIN: So far, the results I've seen are not good for big-screen projection. I think that's coming. I have a feeling that television tape could replace film stock. *Could*, I say; I don't know that it will. But right now, it is to film stock what the Polaroid SX-70 is to what goes into your Pentax. It just *ain't* good enough, not for a professional. But it's good enough for the small screen, and for television. They've tried, recently, to make some films on video tape for transfer onto film stock, and it isn't there, yet, if the quality of the image means anything at all. Now, I'm going just the other way; I'm going to the biggest screen in the world, the IMAX which I'm about to become a partner in, along with Universal Pictures. It's a screen that's *ninety* feet wide by *eighty-five* feet high. Initially, we're adapting theaters, but we'll build theaters so that audience seating, instead of going back on a slight slope as it does in a normal theater, will go upwards on something like a straight line parallel to the screen. The film runs horizontally through both the camera and the projector, and the frame size is almost the size of a postcard. It's specially made Eastman stock. There are two such screens in existence now; one is in Toronto (it's a Canadian development), and the other is in Spokane at the World's Fair. It's incredible! You could stand six feet away from the screen, you could stand *three* feet away from it, and see the image in perfect focus. It's virtually three-dimensional, more so than all the 3-D processes. The only thing that has stood between widescreen process and public acceptance in the past has been that no one has been able to come up with a good story. It's always a documentary, a travelogue: going down the Ganges, in Cinerama. I have a story for this process which is very top secret. Only because it will deal with a subject that has never been treated on the screen before and, if I mention it, somewhere somebody will rip it off. Which I won't mind . . . after I've got mine shot. I also plan to use a dynamic frame; I'm not going to use that big screen constantly. But the IMAX is two years away, maybe three. Of course we'll change the name of the process to something a little more romantic. "IMAX": It sounds like a tailor in the Bronx.

BARRETT: What will you be doing in the meantime?

FRIEDKIN: I'm going to be working on an action-adventure-suspense film in South America. Kind of a combination of *The Wild Bunch* [1969] and *The Helstrom Chronicle* [1971]. And Universal's given me the rights to make a horror film compilation on the order of *That's Entertainment!* [1974]. I'll use Universal's original *Phantom of the Opera* set [for Arthur Lubin's film of 1943] and add a new stereo soundtrack.

BARRETT: Sounds like you'll be keeping busy. You've been quoted as saying that once a director has seven or eight years of giving the public what it wants, he burns out. Do you still feel that way?

FRIEDKIN: I didn't state that as an accepted fact, it was just a personal observation. With today's filmmakers, it's very difficult to stay current. The scene is changing so rapidly. It's true in fashion, it's true in music, it's true in all the popular art forms. Popular artists burn out so fast. Who remembers Jan and Dean anymore? 1953 is a drop in the bucket of history; when one looks back on the difference between 1953 and 1974, it won't be all that great. And yet, we realize that *The Band Wagon* was the most popular film of 1953, with music by Dietz and Schwartz. Now, who are they? Fred Astaire was dancing then, and who the hell is dancing today? And the *popular* music of today is, in my opinion, the reason there are no movie musicals being made. It does not lend itself to choreography or to romance, which is the *staple* of the musical film. It's hard to do a musical to the Rolling Stones.

BARRETT: One director has said that directing is a job for a young man or woman because it's so demanding . . .

FRIEDKIN: Physically, yeah.

BARRETT: You're constantly faced with so many problems and so many people to deal with. But at the same time, there are some directors who seem to have had really long careers, but they're often not the directors who are appealing to the large mass audience. I'm thinking of people like Luis Buñuel, for example.

FRIEDKIN: You can name a number of filmmakers who are old men or who have had long careers and not take into account that for each one of them there are fifty or 100 people who have disappeared off the face of the earth. At the time that Capra and Wyler and Stevens and others were so successful and popular, there were guys much bigger than them. Gregory La Cava, Fred Niblo, the man who did the original *Ben-Hur* [1925],[2] people like that who fell out of fashion in about eight years. This is the *only* reason why I continue to go to colleges. The *only* reason is to get some small semblance of an idea of what young people are thinking. Most people who make films and become successful immediately isolate themselves. I know all my friends and contemporaries do. They all live up on the hill and they're totally surrounded by yes-men and yes-women. They don't ride the subways, they don't have to buy gas for themselves anymore, or go to the grocery store, or do *anything*. They have people do that. And pretty soon they start making *personal* films, because that's all they know anything about. They don't know *what's* happening in the streets, so they make a personal film. And if that personal film doesn't catch fire in the audience, it's all over. Of course there are *geniuses* like Fellini, but there are no American Fellinis. The American culture is not good grass for that kind of *filmmaker*. Our entire culture, our literature, our art, is literal. It's basic. It's the reason there was a French New Wave and not an American New Wave. Those kinds of films that were so admired here by the American filmmakers in the sixties were *unproducible* in this country. They were particularly French just as Frank Capra's films were so intrinsically American. At the time! And yet, they are so intrinsically un-American today. Today, a Capra film is a reactionary film. What was once patriotism is now reactionaryism. All of these film movements generally come out of the culture that produces them. The American culture is generally a literal, earthbound, storytelling culture. Basic stories are the staple item of filmmaking in this country. Stories where people can get behind the characters and care about the people on the screen, whatever the hell the film is, whether it's *American Graffiti* [1973], or *Return of the Dragon* [1972], or *Duddy Kravitz* [*The Apprenticeship of Duddy Kravitz*, 1974]. If people can get behind what's on the screen, it's going to work. The only reason the people are into *The Exorcist* is because they believe the characters. Forty million have seen *The Exorcist*, and not because of the hype.

BARRETT: Some have suggested that your treatment of the characters in *The French Connection* and *The Exorcist is* hype.

FRIEDKIN: You know, there are many ways to do a *French Connection* or an *Exorcist*. One could have directed *The Exorcist*, for example, without ever showing any symptoms of literal possession. One could have made it as strictly a horror story, a *Turn of the Screw*. I didn't do that, frankly, because I don't think anyone gives a *damn* about *Turn of the Screw*. Not in the movies. The literary experience is one thing, but the people who go to movies in this *world*, you know what I mean, not this *country*, but this *world*, on a mass level . . . I didn't always think this way, but I learned the hard way . . . You make movies for large groups of people, all over the world. And you don't make them for the most intelligent, the elite part of the audience. You make them, literally, for people in Thailand who will never have subtitles. When they see the film they won't see a dubbed version. What they have in Thailand and in many parts of the world is a man or a woman who stands alongside of the screen. Every five minutes or so, when too much stuff has happened for the audience to digest, they stop the film and this person explains what has gone on for the last five or ten minutes. I've seen this! So, what you try to do is make a film that will have them stop the projection the least number of times in Thailand. *The French Connection* was such a film; it had so little language in it. And that, to me, is the ideal movie. The ideal *kind* of movie. I don't mean that *The French Connection* is a great movie. I mean that it's the ideal kind of movie for me to direct. On the other hand, *The Boys in the Band* was *terrible*. They stopped that every thirty seconds in Thailand. It's not a good movie. It's a good story and a good play; it worked brilliantly on stage; it works far less well on film.

My experience with audiences all over the world, audiences that pay *money* to see a film, audiences *everywhere*, is that they don't want to hear dialogue. They want to see images. And the people who understood this the best are the people who made Walt Disney cartoons in the early days. These were guys who had to realize that they were making movies for children, and everything that they drew into that frame they put into it by clear choice. It wasn't there to begin with, it was a blank cell. It wasn't like taking a camera outside to shoot two people, and you pretty much like what's in the background so you shoot it without realizing that there are a number of things in the background that work against your scene. So many well-known filmmakers today, guys with major reputations, have no *idea* what's in the frame, and very often there are things in the frame that work against suspense, or comedy, or whatever the emotion is; there are often things in the frame that don't *make it*! This is particularly true with color; color has such an impact on what the eye and then the mind is instantly experiencing. The people who made those Disney cartoons only put in what was relevant to tell the story, frame by frame. And if they had a scene that was supposed to be terrifying, only those shadows and colors that sold that idea were in that frame. They even went so far as to have the characters that they drew shaped in such a way that their form told the audience what the hell the characters represented. And when I say "audience," I don't mean some hip kids from New Haven, I mean the *world*. That's ideal movie making to me. That's what the movies is *all* about.

PART II

BARRETT: I'd like to summarize central portions of Pauline Kael's *New Yorker* article of August 5, 1974, because so much of it seems to be about you. She writes about "slam-bang" films that appeal to illiterate audiences in underdeveloped countries, "visceral" pictures that numb an audience and prevent a mass response to true film artists who are less blatant. She claims that people get "pummeled and deafened" by *The French Connection*, and *The Exorcist* is a "debauch" that delivers in much the same way as a porn flick. Such films, she feels, debase the viewer with their "philosophical nihilism" and leave them soiled. She goes on to claim that saturation publicity and the producer's treatment of a film as a piece of goods leads the mass audience to believe that best-selling junk is better than less publicized poor-selling works of film art. She asserts that film students are being taught to worship the director who makes the buck and suggests that directors should take over the business end of their films. She says that the industry's worship of films that are "crude and insensitive" could kill film as an art form. She believes that films such as *The French Connection* and *The Exorcist* indicate a lack of belief in the good taste of the audience. She concludes by pointing to you and George Roy Hill as directors who can work within the system and feels that "the system works for those who don't have any needs or aspirations that are in conflict with it, but for the others—and they're the ones who are making movies—the system doesn't work anymore and it's not going to." What is your response to all of this?

FRIEDKIN: Well, number one, I read the article because I was asked to respond to it by the *Los Angeles Times*. That was why I read it. As an article, I found it thick, and muddle-headed, and almost impossible to plow through. For somebody in the field, its conclusions are both simpleminded and wrongheaded. As a practical matter, the person who wrote it has an *enormous* contempt for the audience. The person who wrote it condemns the audience out of hand for what they choose as opposed to what they do not choose and is contemptuous of the audience for choosing X instead of Y, for choosing a hot dog sandwich instead of a cheese soufflé or a beef Wellington. This is, you know, fair enough—anyone can do this. If you have access to print, or any medium of communication, you can impose your taste on other people, and if they're watching, or reading, or listening, they have to pay attention. This is the case with Kael's piece. But I know a couple of things about her that are not apparent to the people who read her. First of all, she tried to do an interview with me on three occasions, and I refused to do so because I feel that the *New Yorker* is an elitist magazine and it is trying to foster an idea about the medium in which I work that is contrary to the facts about that medium. And she did a book on Orson Welles's *Citizen Kane* [1941] in which she attempted to discredit Welles's contribution to it and to say, without ever bothering to interview Orson Welles, that he didn't write the script, that somebody else did. And I did an interview in New York at the time of the book's publication, with Johnny Carson or somebody like that, wherein I brought this out. I pointed out that she only interviewed anyone with an anti-Welles point of view and so attempted to discredit him. So there is a personal history that I have with her.

The other thing is people *never* attend a movie in such numbers as when they go to see a hit because they hate the picture. There is only one reason that a movie becomes a hit, one reason only. It's not publicity, it's not hype, it's not advertising, because I can give you example after example of films like *Lost Horizon* [Frank Capra, 1937] that were heavily advertised, two or three times the advertising budget of *The Sting* [George Roy Hill, 1973] and *The Exorcist*, that didn't even return the negative costs. The only thing that causes people to go to the movies is word of mouth. People come out and say whatever they say. They could say, "I hated the thing, but you've got to see it!" or "it's disgusting, it's the most disgusting thing I've ever seen!" And this *causes* you to go. But generally, I must say, take your own experience, do you generally go to something that somebody tells you is "disgusting" and "horrible"? Not me! If somebody told me that there was a ten-car crash outside, I, personally, wouldn't feel called upon to go out and see it. If somebody came in here and said, "Fifteen bodies are sprawled on the street," I wouldn't be interested, I wouldn't *want* to see it. So, I don't for a minute believe that people go to see *The Exorcist* because they hear it's disgusting. *The Exorcist*, which is, right now, the third [*sic.*] all-time moneymaking film in only seven months in release, is third because people want to see it. Now, you can say, if you don't like the film, you can then say that those people who do are "stupid, cheap, low-brow, and prefer hot dogs to beef Wellington; they're idiots!" And to a large extent you'd be right! But you could never work for the audience and feel that way. Where I take exception to Pauline Kael is that I don't draw the line between chamber music and Guy Lombardo. I don't prefer Guy Lombardo's music at all. I don't listen to it, but I don't condemn it out of hand. I don't say that, because I find it sterile and simplistic and crude, it's wrong! And I don't accuse Guy Lombardo of being a fascist or a racist or a purveyor of *shit*! I honestly believe that he's doing the best he can, and he's doing it because people are into it! And if they weren't into it and *loving* it, he wouldn't be out doing it [. . .]

It's difficult to explain this, but a large part of what people like Kael do is to do, to a large extent, what I attempt to do, and that's move people emotionally. And very often by overstating the case. I am not saying that there is nothing valid in Kael's piece. I am saying that working in the field, as I do, I find nothing valid in it, personally. I find that her suggestion that the filmmakers named in the article should band together and form a distribution co-op is addressed to filmmakers who, with rare exceptions, have never had a successful film. Bob Altman has had one successful film out of ten and he goes public with his works the same as I do. For example, take *California Split* [1974], it opened at the same theater *The*

Exorcist did, with the *same* amount of advertising, no more, no less, and the people took their choice. Now, you can say, "Well, the people are idiots!" Well, that's possible, but I just don't believe that people go to see a movie because they hate it. I do not, as Miss Kael does, *reject* those audiences that do not respond to the same things I do. I *disagree* with them, but I don't reject them or condemn them. I don't feel that Kael is a very good film critic or a very good person. A good film critic, like James Agee, who was a *great* critic, *never* denounced something that he didn't like. He either chose not to write about it, or he criticized it in a way in which the criticism was always positive and optimistic. He never condemned out of hand the people who made the film. Such an attitude is humanistic. The film journalism that prevails today is antihumanistic, it's the kind of film journalism where you condemn those people you disagree with. If you don't like his films, Peckinpah is a fascist! So-and-so a racist! This kind of character assassination does far more harm than any of Sam Peckinpah's movies. His movies are dealing with fictional people in fictional circumstances. When Kael called Peckinpah a fascist, she was dealing with a *real* person and a *real* reputation. And whatever else Peckinpah may be, he is not a fascist. And he had no response to her at all. As I have said, you can't sue, you can't get equal time, you can't get equal space. As Willy Loman said in *Death of a Salesman*, "It comes with the territory." Any kind of success, to whatever degree, fosters an extraordinary amount of criticism. On the other hand, I must admit that I prefer this kind of adversary journalism to the kind of ass-kissing crap that goes on. More people get away with murder in the press, be they politicians or filmmakers, because of mindless praise. And you get more junk stuff being praised because of this cult business, which I totally discourage and don't believe in. I'd rather see something like Kael's piece than the *auteur* stuff. I think it's much more interesting and provocative. I wish there was more of it.

BARRETT: I can understand that the problem of negative criticism would get to be a drag for the director, but most critics are locked into deadlines and in too many cases are forced to review films they don't like. Andrew Sarris, the *auteurist*, has talked to this. He sometimes has a choice, either to be negative or not write and not get paid.

FRIEDKIN: Well, I don't respect Sarris. I've gotten good reviews from him, but he writes for such a *small* intellectual elite and he has misinterpreted everything I've ever done. *Totally* destroyed it. Sarris, you know, bends everything through the prism of his own demi-consciousness, and whoever reads him is *stuck* with him. I really don't want to talk about it because I don't want to encourage it.

There are two schools of film criticism. One is represented by the kind of mindless person who sits and types out a summary of the film, usually incorrect, as a factual résumé of what's in the story. It's like reducing *Hamlet* to its plot; it becomes soap opera. Take a guy like Archer Winston writing for the *New York*

Post. His whole review will be a summary of the plot. Why bother to see the movie? The other kind, like Kael or Sarris, take a film that somebody has written, photographed, directed, whatever, and they use it as a springboard for their own ideas on the film industry, the state of the world, the crisis in the sugarcane industry. And their ideas have nothing to do with the film. The art of film criticism has declined to minus ten since James Agee's death. One only has to read the collected reviews of Agee to see what I mean. Occasionally, someone comes in from outside, like Norman Mailer has, and writes a really *fantastic* piece of film criticism. But I haven't really read film reviews in three or four years, so I don't know what's going on at present.

Barrett: A few new critics are coming into their own: Molly Haskell, for example.

Friedkin: Molly Haskell is, to me, no better and no worse than any of the rest of them. The same with Judith Crist, whom I know very well; she's a close personal friend, but we never talk about films, ever. Because . . . I frankly think she doesn't know a *god-damned* thing about films! There are no reviewers whom I respect today. Based on what the public relations people tell me, every film that I made got between 70 and 80 percent good reviews. But I don't read them. I gave up reading reviews when I realized that there was nothing to learn from them. The reviewers were not telling me anything that I could use to improve my work or my ability to communicate with audiences. And that's all I really care about.

Barrett: Have you ever been interviewed by Rex Reed?

Friedkin: Several times.

Barrett: I might have known, but I've never read his books.

Friedkin: Neither have I, so I don't know if they're there or not.

Barrett: He seems like a nice enough guy, but I don't think he knows much about film reviewing. Would you agree?

Friedkin: Rex Reed has his peculiarities, but he's ok. I particularly like someone like Charles Champlin, who is in the Agee tradition, someone who concentrates on the films he likes and writes about them. But, as I said, I question the value of the whole business. I know that some critics like me and they'll always write a good review and some don't like me and they'll write a bad review no matter *what* I do. Hostile journalists are depressing. I particularly remember this one person who came in with an axe to grind and was abrasive from the very beginning. I insisted that she get a tape recorder, record the interview, and give me the tape for my information. She did so reluctantly. Later, she called up and quickly read the interview to me over the phone. It was like another world; she distorted what I had said into something that meshed with her imaginative view of me that had led to her initial hostility. I called up her publisher and played the interview for him and he killed the piece.

BARRETT: That's a real waste; being forced to spend your time killing distortions.

FRIEDKIN: I don't usually worry about interviews; they'll distort you if they want to and you can't do much about it. But this was so obvious that I had to do something about it.

BARRETT: Getting back to your comment that reviewers base their opinion of a given film on their attitude toward the director, Sarris claims that critics do have favorites, and films by favorites become pawns in battles between the reviewers. Andrew Sarris writes on the *auteur* director, Pauline Kael puts him down for it, and John Simon denigrates them both.

FRIEDKIN: And people are fed up with it all. Canby's in trouble at the *New York Times* for his reviews. Readers are complaining. The *Times* has gotten rid of a number of critics because they lose touch with films the people are going to see and spend time with obscure Japanese films that *no one* wants to go to. Roger Greenspun went last year, and before that, Renata Adler, and before that, Bosley Crowther.

BARRETT: I wouldn't put Crowther in the same class with Greenspun and Adler. Adler was a good writer learning about film while on the job, and Greenspun may have liked the underground too much for the *Times*, but Crowther was middlebrow all the way.

FRIEDKIN: Yeah, okay. He just kept missing the boat on the films that people liked.

BARRETT: His problem was that he didn't know what to do with any kind of modernist storytelling. Elliptical narrative was too much for him.

FRIEDKIN: The last straw was his review of *Bonnie and Clyde*. He gave it a negative review and everyone else was praising it to the skies. Personally, I thought *Bonnie and Clyde* was a drag, a real fucking bore. There were great sections in which nothing was happening. Why was it such a big hit?

BARRETT: For one reason, it appealed to the sensibilities of the time. Those were the years of the *Time*-hype, the New American Cinema. We had *The Graduate* [1967], *Bonnie and Clyde*, *Easy Rider* [1969], and *The Wild Bunch*, films with anti-establishment content, ironic tone, and anti-traditional uses of the genre conventions. Those films appealed to the college film generation which, at the time, was very much involved in peace marches, campus strikes, and political movements such as the SDS.

FRIEDKIN: The only group I belonged to in high school was the SHPH.

BARRETT: What's that? I never heard of it.

FRIEDKIN: "Students for a Half-Pound Hamburger." We figured, what was the sense of fighting for greater flexibility in the democratic process if we couldn't even get a basic half-pound hamburger?

BARRETT: I'm glad I asked! What did you think about the decision to give the Academy Award for Best Picture of 1973 to *The Sting* rather than to *The Exorcist*?

FRIEDKIN: Naturally, I was disappointed for a few days. But I do believe in the Academy Awards as a standard, as the best prevailing standard, that the motion picture industry has to honor those films that it believes are meritorious. Now, they don't always make the right decision, but you'll generally find over the years . . . generally, that those films that have won the Academy Awards are those films that have appealed to most of the audience and most of the critics.

BARRETT: How would you compare *The Exorcist* with Bergman's *Cries and Whispers* [*Viskningar och rop*, 1972], which was also nominated for Best Picture?

FRIEDKIN: Nothing makes *The Exorcist* any better than *Cries and Whispers*. All I can say is at the time that particular group voted for *The Sting*. That's all it means; it only means that a majority of the Academy felt that *The Sting* was the best picture of the year. It is not carved on a rock somewhere; it is not on Mt. Rushmore; it doesn't even mean that *The Sting* can hold a candle to *Cries and Whispers*, or *Herbie Rides Again* [1974], or anything else. The voters were a specific group at a specific time in history; the same group of people voting at another time on the same group of films might have thought differently. I don't believe that it's possible to rule out *The Sting*, or *The Exorcist*, or *Cries and Whispers*. I think that the movie-going public wants a diet of all. They want the diet of *The Sting* and *The Exorcist* all over the world, to an extent. Now, I don't know why, I can't answer why, but I can tell you that it's a fact that they do.

BARRETT: So your films reflect rather than improve public taste?

FRIEDKIN: I don't think I'm capable of improving public taste, to be very honest with you. I don't know who is or who has. It's a very noble idea. But, you see, one question I have to ask myself is not whether or not I'm capable enough or should or should not improve public taste, but what is the public there for in the first place? Why do you think they go to movies? I *personally* think that they go to the movies to be entertained, not to have their taste rearranged. You have to realize, and I think I do realize, that there is no such thing as an amorphous mass of people; the audience is a great many people of different age groups and educational levels. And even though 70 percent of the people in this country who go to movies regularly are the young, the educated, and the affluent, that doesn't mean that I am going to get all 70 percent. That doesn't mean that I'm going to get all of the people who see my film who think as I do. That means I'm going to get a lot of people who are *dumber* than me, and a lot of people who are quite a bit *smarter* than me. And in other countries I'm going to get a lot of people who don't even speak my language. And I have to try to make a film that will not insult them, that will not insult the intelligent or be over the heads of the less intelligent. There is no way, if you work in the commercial cinema, as I do, to not be conscious of public taste. If I were to say that most movies are trash and the public just wants hot dogs and fudge Sundays . . . First of all, I don't believe that and, secondly, I don't have that cynical an attitude about the public. I have never made a film that wasn't my own taste; but I would never make a film that wasn't something that the audience wanted to see. I will only undertake to do a subject that I think the audience will respond to. I then set out to do it to the absolute *best* of my ability, given all of my limitations, and to draw the best work out of all of the people working with me on the film, whatever the cost. And I wouldn't do this unless I believed that the film would be successful.

BARRETT: Given your definition of success, it's ironic that you started out directing films by making a version of Pinter's *The Birthday Party* [1968]. How did that come about?

FRIEDKIN: I think I was twenty-five at the time. I had never directed a play on the stage and I had no reputation and no real background as a motion picture maker. I had a background in television and I went to Harold Pinter who was, then, better known than he is now; and now he's known as one of the influential playwrights in the contemporary English-speaking theater. And he's a very private man. He doesn't go out in public, he doesn't socialize, he has nothing to do with business; he just doesn't care. And I got to Harold and convinced him, I don't know how, that a film should be made of *The Birthday Party* and that I should do it.

BARRETT: How did you get to speak to Pinter?

FRIEDKIN: Most people who have made it in the arts are surrounded by a great wall of protection. Almost anybody can reach me, with anything, because I'm not embarrassed in giving a quick answer about whether I'm interested in it or not. I got to him through mutual friends; if there wasn't somebody who knew him, I probably would never have gotten the rights to *The Birthday Party* at the time. Also, you really have to know what you want to do with what you want. The way in which I presented my ideas to Pinter, for example, was refreshing to him. I didn't want to use big stars; and he had just been through a meeting in which some producer wanted to do *The Homecoming* and use Elizabeth Taylor and Richard Burton and, I don't know, Albert Einstein!, whoever was a big name at the time. And Pinter was outraged. So, we were in essential agreement on the way to do it: that it should be made in England and that there should be some exteriors to establish the kind of life within which it was set; that it should be done *totally* realistically and not the way Pinter is commonly interpreted as being symbolic or allegorical or not really being about its storyline, its plot line. The key to Pinter is his plot. The behavior of those people is only strange because it may not be the way you or I would carry on; but these are real people, and all that he did was not give you a whole set of prefabricated facts about them before you meet them. He presents them whole, very much the way life is presented to people. I walk into a new situation and I don't know anybody and nobody knows me, and what is immediately presented to me is the strangeness of these new people. I see someone with a neck brace and I think of the most bizarre reasons for the neck brace; and I think that's the way human nature works and that's what Pinter has in his plays. The fact that you can get four or five people in a room and one of them says something that absolutely terrifies you, and I think it's funny, and somebody else in the room pays no attention to it, whatever. The irrational fears of people are what all of Pinter's plays are about. *The Birthday Party*, especially. Irrational fear is a quality that, for some reason, interests me tremendously.

BARRETT: Do you find that when you make a film out of a work of literature, something that you have done on several occasions . . .

FRIEDKIN: I just did *The Birthday Party* and *Boys in the Band*, that was the only so-called literature I worked with.

BARRETT: How about [William Peter] Blatty's *The Exorcist*?

FRIEDKIN: That's not literature, it's a commercial book: Billy Blatty wrote it to write a bestseller, and he did.

BARRETT: Okay, so what do you do differently with a work of literature as opposed to a prose entertainment? What . . .

FRIEDKIN: I wouldn't take a work of literature and put it on film; I don't think it belongs there. It works so well in its own medium. The books that have excited me the most . . . let's take Proust's work. Something that is so "cinematic" on paper would not be at all "cinematic" on film. Because it becomes a *reductio ad absurdum*. You can't *do* Proust on film. What you can do is a kind of semblance of Proust. You can, perhaps, capture the tone of *Swann's Way*: you can go to the places and do a kind of interpretation, a kind of impression, but you can't do *Swann's Way*. Why not *Friedkin's Way* or *Barrett's Way*? The point is, why take somebody else's classic and bastardize it? That's the conclusion I've reached.

BARRETT: Are you saying that you'll never again make a film based on a work of literature?

FRIEDKIN: Absolutely.

BARRETT: But you may make films based on prose entertainments?

FRIEDKIN: Trash makes the best movies.

BARRETT: Why is that so?

FRIEDKIN: Because, first of all, you're not protecting a reputation. Nobody is ever going to come out of a theater and say, "Jesus Christ! Did they ever screw up *I, The Jury!*" You'd be surprised what a factor that is in the cinema, people getting outraged over what you've done to an accepted classic. There's no way, for instance, that you can come off doing Shakespeare. No way. For example, the *Romeo and Juliet* [1968] that Zeffirelli did was a beautiful film, but it wasn't Shakespeare. It was the essence of *Romeo and Juliet*, but so was *West Side Story* [1961] in a funny kind of way. It was essentially *Romeo and Juliet*, but, God knows, it wasn't, and neither was Zeffirelli's. He butchered the language, and Shakespeare is language more than anything. If it's anything at all, it's language because, reduced to plot, the plays are absurd. For instance, the plot of *Hamlet* is totally absurd and unconvincing. And *Macbeth*, too. I was recently asked to direct a production of *Macbeth* in Los Angeles. I researched it for two months and I gave it up because I realized that everything I wanted to do with it was contrary to what Shakespeare had written. I became very familiar with witchcraft, especially eleventh-century Scottish witchcraft. I became totally familiar with the witchcraft rituals that go back that far, and I realized that the rituals of witchcraft that were practiced in the eleventh century, that were accessible to Shakespeare, that he chose not to use, were *far* more interesting, *far* more vivid, *far* more *terrifying* than anything in his play, which is God-damned silly! Shakespeare was obviously a man who had no *belief* in witchcraft: he had no *interest* in it. He wrote *Macbeth* on a commission from King James I, and King James I was interested in witchcraft; he had written a celebrated book on witchcraft and, in the King James version of the Bible, put in a lot of references to witches where there were none before. Shakespeare was really writing to please the king, and he threw in a lot of stuff about witches that he really didn't know about or care about. And the witches' scenes in *Macbeth* are *travesties* of witchcraft as it was practiced in the eleventh century in Scotland. They were ludicrous; and I say to you they are bad literature and bad playwrighting. Better stuff exists in those old books, in Scott's *Demonology*, for example. And I was throwing all the Shakespeare stuff out and putting in authentic material; and I suddenly said to myself, "Hey, what the . . . This is not Shakespeare's *Macbeth*." And I had around $25,000 in the production, already; and Charlton Heston and Vanessa Redgrave were going to play it. It would have been a fantastic production. I had laser beam projections; I had parabolic displacement to project living ghosts right out onto the stage and into the audience. They were wired so that they could talk, and move, and float around; they were, literally, three-dimensional people offstage being projected by means of a parabolic mirror. It was going to be a fantastic production, but I abandoned it only because I realized that I didn't like the play. I'm not going to take something like an acknowledged masterpiece . . . My interpretation of it was fair enough; it wouldn't have bothered me to interpret it differently, but to rewrite something is totally different. I found myself rewriting *Macbeth* and that was terrible. You have to ask yourself, "why do it?"

BARRETT: If good literature is untranslatable into film . . .

FRIEDKIN: I'm speaking very personally, you understand.

BARRETT: Yes, okay . . . Why do so many directors do it and why are there audiences for this kind of film?

FRIEDKIN: I can't speak to anyone else's motivation, but as Cecil B. DeMille said when someone asked why he made the Bible over and over again, "Why should I let two thousand years of publicity go to waste?" Advertise a movie called *Julius Caesar* and everyone says, "Oh, right!"; but advertise a movie called *Fred Weintraub*. *Fred Weintraub*? Classic literature is accessible, it's public domain, you don't have to pay for the rights and it's the easy way out. It's a cop-out. It's much more difficult to do an original film for the cinema, like *Citizen Kane* which, for me, is the greatest movie I have ever seen. Possibly it's the greatest film I ever will see. It's the yardstick by which I measure my own work and the work of others and I find us all coming out wanting. It's an original work for the cinema. Drawing, you know, on many other influences; but it was not, first of all, a novel, or a play, or an essay, or a painting, or whatever . . . a piece of music, like *Alice's Restaurant* [1969]. It was a . . . *film*. And it's terribly successful as a film. And I don't mean financially, because it was never financially successful, as a matter of fact. It's just a great movie for me; and it's a quarry for filmmakers, just as Joyce's *Ulysses* is a quarry for writers.

BARRETT: Hitchcock, in a way, is a quarry for filmmakers, too. I was thinking about the Hitchcock MacGuffin, the trick where he gets the audience interested in discovering an inconsequential fact, inconsequential with respect to Hitchcock's intentions, but something that keeps the plot going and the audience guessing.

FRIEDKIN: Yeh.

BARRETT: Well, you had a MacGuffin, a MacFriedkin, if you will, at the end of *The French Connection*: the gunshot at the end of the film. You have claimed that it was put in because a film becomes more interesting to a mass audience if it contains a pointed problem of interpretation that no one seems to be able to answer satisfactorily. You have said that such questions stimulate conversation about the film at cocktail parties and the like.

FRIEDKIN: That's an oversimplification. The gunshot at the end of *The French Connection* has any number of resonances, the resonances that are suggested by that gunshot lead to an examination of other resonances in the more complicated layers of the film. But because nobody is really sure of what that gunshot means, they begin to speculate about it, about possible meanings, and this is what a film should do to an audience. No film should *dictate* a response; a film should *provoke* discussion, but not lead to final or ultimate conclusions. Nobody with any sense of whimsy at all, no one at my age, let's say, can have any ultimate conclusions about life.

BARRETT: In other words, the gunshot is not a frivolous thing that you put in for a joke?

FRIEDKIN: Nothing that I put into a picture is frivolous, believe me.

BARRETT: You have been quoted as saying that you simply wanted to end the film with a bang.

FRIEDKIN: Well, that's partially *true*.

BARRETT: But that has nothing to do with the film; it's a detached pun.

FRIEDKIN: But I can also, when pushed, give two or three reasons for the gunshot, but none of them would be . . . I don't believe that film has any *real* life off the confines of the frame except in the minds of the viewers. I don't want to suggest what the possible meaning is because it isn't up there. And the fact that the film does, indeed, end with a *bang*, which is a shorthand way of saying how it ends, doesn't mean that it was there *just* for that reason. It is there to provoke discussion and to provoke response, and, indeed, it does. What I object to, and rather resent, and am very sad about, is that wherever I go throughout the country people interested in film will ask me, "What does the gunshot mean at the end of *The French Connection?*" That's the most *common* question I'm asked. And reviewers and writers and interviewers always ask this, which is why I've *stopped* doing all of this stuff! Really cut it off, except on a few rare occasions such as this. The questions are all so simplistic! "What does the gunshot mean?" I don't know what the hell it *means*! I don't know what it means; I do know why it's there and it seems to me to be obvious. People want you to do their thinking for them.

BARRETT: Robert Frost had a great answer to that.

FRIEDKIN: Did he know what the gunshot meant?

BARRETT: Ha, ha! When he was asked about the meaning of one of his poems, "Stopping by Woods," he answered, "Anything you want it to mean." I think that's a good response for any artist; it's not his business to interpret what he created. I don't think that it's your business as the director of *The French Connection* to tell me what it means.

FRIEDKIN: I don't know if I'd go that far: "Anything you want it to mean." Certainly, any filmmaker is shaping an audience response; certainly, any work of art is *shaping* audience response in a certain direction. You're trying to carry the audience with you; and they're pretty hip, they know which way you're leading them. What I'm saying is that the *life* of a film exists because the audience is willing to take it away with them. But nobody is going to take some kind of pat conclusion that places everything in a neat pigeonhole. For example, what I've found happen on the last two films I've directed is that, to a large extent, people get furious about them. There are so many people who, for personal reasons, are unwilling to accept the possibility of literal possession.

BARRETT: Thinking of *The Exorcist*, is the medal . . .

FRIEDKIN: I don't know what the hell the medal is!

BARRETT: I think of the medal as the gunshot, the MacFriedkin of *The Exorcist*.

FRIEDKIN: In a sense, yeah. There's always something like that. There's always something in your life that keeps popping up, a talisman of good or evil, but you don't know whether it is a talisman. The medal in *The Exorcist* is a talisman of good or evil.

BARRETT: The problem with that is it doesn't make literal sense in the film.

FRIEDKIN: What does?

BARRETT: The travel of the medal through time and space . . .

FRIEDKIN: Nothing makes literal sense. The progress of mankind doesn't make literal sense to me.

BARRETT: So, in a way . . .

FRIEDKIN: . . . Why the hell we have inherited this earthly paradise and have proceeded to *burn* it, to defecate on it, blow it up, where's the sense in that?

BARRETT: But that's questioning the absurdity of man, it's not questioning the ability of a physical object to transcend . . .

FRIEDKIN: Every good film questions the absurdity of man in some way. Any film that you take away from the screen questions the absurdity of man in some way. The films that you tend to remember make you question your own life and man's in general, and they take a special place in your consciousness. Very often, they're quite personal to you; there are a lot of films, now, where a small minority, but an increasingly significant minority, are finding a shared experience. Like *King of Hearts* [1966]. When it first came out it didn't say much to the audience at the time, but it's now finding an audience because of the way the world's gone. At the time of its initial distribution the progress of the protagonist through those situations seemed strange to people. Now, I put it to you, it's not quite as absurd as it was.

BARRETT: Will the same thing happen some day with the medal traveling through time and space?

FRIEDKIN: There are a lot of ideas that I had in mind about that. For example, I was playing with the notion of time warp. That some literal object that is found in the ground in Iraq turns up in somebody's dream 7,000 miles away and six months later.

BARRETT: I really liked the idea of the medal falling in space.

FRIEDKIN: A lot of things in dreams are suspended like that.

BARRETT: I thought that was really fine.

FRIEDKIN: I like the dream sequence in *The Exorcist* very much.

BARRETT: I do too.

FRIEDKIN: Dream sequences are very hard to bring off. And the one in *The Exorcist*, I think, works very well. It wasn't pushed too far like in so many dream sequences.

BARRETT: I also liked the lab scene where the girl was getting a . . . What was it?

FRIEDKIN: An arterialgram.

BARRETT: I thought the relationship there between sound and image was very exciting.

FRIEDKIN: It was all literal sound. Part of the excitement of directing a movie as opposed to, say, writing one, is that it heightens your powers of perception. You become conscious of everyday sounds and images that most people who are not trained to look through a camera or listen through earphones will not perceive. When I'm not making a film I'm very often turned off to such things, but when I start thinking about making a film, I start being more responsive, again.

BARRETT: What questions have you yet to answer about solutions to the technical problems you encountered while making *The Exorcist*?

FRIEDKIN: So many people have asked me how the little girl's head revolved and I've dodged the question. But since I just finished my last job on *The Exorcist*, I said, "what the hell!" and I've been talking about it, so I'll tell you. We bent the girl's head around 360 degrees!

BARRETT: Ha, ha!

FRIEDKIN: No, that's a life-sized dummy, a dummy that was remote-control operated so that we could also make breath come out of it. We were pumping cigarette smoke out to show breath, and we had separate controls for the dummy's hands, and the head could turn 360 degrees at any speed. I never really used it as fully as I might have because I thought that people would *never* believe it. So the head doesn't ever do a full 360; I let it do about 280 or 300. And the sound of the bones cracking as the neck was turning was done by bending my wallet, here, with the credit cards, and *highly* amplified. Since Linda's face was partly foam and false hair, her look could easily be duplicated on the dummy. It was all designed by a genius of a makeup artist named Dick Smith, who also did Marlon Brando's makeup in *The Godfather* [1972], Dustin Hoffman in *Little Big Man* [1970], and Hal Holbrook's Mark Twain [*Mark Twain Tonight!*, a television biography of 1967].

BARRETT: Earlier, we talked about a number of female critics. Are there any female directors whose work interests you?

FRIEDKIN: There's a woman named Karen Spurling. I don't think any of her work has been released commercially. She's made a couple of films that have had trouble getting released that I think are terrific.

BARRETT: How about the woman who did *Wanda* [1970]?

FRIEDKIN: Barbara Loden. I haven't seen the film but I want to. I haven't seen Susan Sontag's films, either, but I know Susan. Susan is really a wonderful person.

BARRETT: What do you think of her as a film critic?

FRIEDKIN: Boring! Boring, thick, labored! Susan, herself, is not!

BARRETT: Have you read her essay on Jean-Luc Godard's *My Life to Live* [*Vivre sa vie*, 1962]?

FRIEDKIN: No! I haven't! The best way to be disappointed in the films of Godard is to read something about them. You're looking for stuff that isn't on the screen! But Susan is terrific, bright, intelligent; and I tried to read her stuff and I can't. She wrote a *marvelous* essay about *The French Connection* and she sent it to me and I couldn't *read* it! I thought it was going to be about *The French Connection* but it turned out to be about the crisis in the sugarcane industry. It was all too thick for me. I'm not into that. Film criticism has declined to such an extent that I can't look at it.

BARRETT: How about actresses; are there any new interesting actresses?

FRIEDKIN: I'm interested in why there aren't more stories about women. I don't understand it, and it's not because there are more male directors, there always were. There used to be *great* films about women, and the actresses were *fabulous*. And now there are none. There are no interesting women in American films; there are some in French and Italian films, in Japanese films. One thing that has hit women harder than men, for some reason, is the homogenization of the culture. Up until the sixties there was a tremendous separatism in the culture that encouraged differences between people so that somebody with a strange quirk or a funny accent or a different kind of walk was encouraged. Today, largely because of television, our accents are becoming homogenized. Wherever you go in this country, people *sound* the same, *dress* the same, *look* the same, and . . . *think* . . . the same. All of America looks alike with Gino's and Howard Johnson's. In New York City, Robert Moses with his housing program tore out a culture and replaced it with bland skyscrapers that are insults to the people living inside them. Take hair styles. Students seem to have two kinds, one for men and one for women, and they're both the same. That's wrong! That's bad! That's terrible! And films produce few prophets. The filmmakers simply reflect the blandness of the culture.

BARRETT: Aren't you contradicting yourself?

FRIEDKIN: I sometimes do that.

BARRETT: You're against blandness, but wouldn't you have to be making bland films to appeal to such a mass audience?

FRIEDKIN: Not at all. The central characters in my last two films are hardly representatives of a bland lifestyle. They're very unusual; they're individuals in a faceless society, and that's what I think the audience finds attractive about them. That's the reason my last two films are so popular.

NOTES

1. "Domestic Grosses: Adjusted for Ticket Price Inflation," *Box Office Mojo, LLC* (Burbank, California), http://www.boxofficemojo.com/alltime/adjusted.htm (August 1, 2007).

2. A short silent version of *Ben-Hur* was made in 1907, directed by Sidney Olcott, Frank Oakes Rose, H. Temple, and Harry T. Morey.

Andrzej Wajda

Art thrives on both great and miserable moments.

$\mathcal{O}$ne of the most telling words to crop up in the opening exchanges of Krystyna Korvin Przybylska's interview with Polish director Andrzej Wajda is "accident"— once, in reference to the theater (and, by extension, life itself); the other time, in reference to *Hamlet* (which Wajda characterizes as "an accidental play"). That Wajda should be so keenly fixated on chance as it affects art and life is no doubt a reflection of his particular place in history in postwar Poland; as Przybylska points out in her excellent introduction, "Wajda perceives Polish history as the victim of elemental forces spawned by destiny in a country allotted an unfortunate geography." One wonders if Wajda would feel the same way today, given the most recent history of both his country and the world (and given his involvement in Polish politics). Regardless, it is clear that for this filmmaker, the relationships among art, history, and life call for constant reflection, both on and off the screen.

Interestingly, this interview begins not with cinema but with theater. Wajda had just taken a position as "headship of the Krakow 'Stary' Theatre," as Przybylska notes, and so much of the initial interview concerns itself with Wajda's views on theater, with frequent digressions on the differences between theater and film. This discussion leads into some consideration of acting—again, both in theater and film—before Wajda moves to reflections on the relative position of the director in cinema, here commenting on the effects of *auteur*ism by stating quite bluntly, "what bothers me lately in film is just this tendency to promote the work of director into dangerously exaggerated proportions." Again, Wajda returns to the aleatory and art ("I think that every piece of art is an accident"), critiquing Pop art and postmodern aesthetic tendencies more broadly considered. After this, the interview turns to Wajda's peers, as he offers opinions on Luis Buñuel, Roman Polanski, and Francis Ford Coppola; finally, Wajda reflects on America as

44

well as the humanist aims he has pursued in his work from the beginning: "Man is given life to live it. Only respect for other human life creates social norms. If we break this principle, we break ourselves—we cut our own throats. Art cannot serve the self-annihilating instincts, even if the reward is success and great films."

Interview by Krystyna Korvin Przybylska
Originally published as "An Interview with Andrzej Wajda," Literature/Film Quarterly *5, no. 1 (January 1977): 2–16.*

Andrzej Wajda is the most quintessential director of the so-called Polish School of filmmaking. In 1956, when he was thirty, he directed *Kanal* [1957] a film based upon a tragic passage of Polish patriots through the slimy sewers of Nazi-occupied Warsaw. Screened at the Cannes Film Festival, this movie earned Wajda a directing award and, subsequently, conspicuous recognition both in Europe and America. Two years later, his next film, *Ashes and Diamonds* [*Popiół i diament*, 1958], an account of a day following the end of the war but full of its horrors, catapulted Wajda into a prominence equal to that of the major cineastes working in Eastern Europe.

Wajda's cinema began and has remained a cinema of collision, a dialectic of courage (or its futility) set against a recognizably social matrix. The crucial point of Wajda's cinematic oeuvre is the dramatization of Polish national ethos. Most of his films focus on individuals entangled in historical circumstances: the eighteenth-century partitions of the Polish land; forced participation of Polish legions at Samosierra in Napoleon's Spanish campaign; the Warsaw Rising of August 1944 against the German occupants; the rebuilding of the nation from the ashes left by war.

Creating a mode that could be defined as historical tragedy, Wajda perceives Polish history as the victim of elemental forces spawned by destiny in a country allotted an unfortunate geography. With the notion that a man is an actor in a play not wholly of his making, Wajda's characters act out their prearranged dramatic destinies. But they act them out with heroic gesture. Though desperate, they are not besmirched, bitter but not cynical. They have to make a good job out of a bad situation. Thwarted in a vain attempt to keep faith in the national cause, Wajda's heroes, handsome and magnetic, often purify themselves in undeserved death. His heroines, on the other hand, are but self-liberating helpmates offering males the sweetness of love before fate runs through its cycle. Wajda's point of view is totally masculine; his only authentic heroine is history.

Once Wajda has found an actor to his taste, an impersonator of his own ego, he stays with him. The first memorable lead was Zbyszek Cybulski, who during his lifetime became a legend, an idol of Polish existential unrest in the postwar years. His silhouette as a young man in battle dress and sun glasses "marked" for tragedy, as depicted in *Ashes and Diamonds*, stirred the imagination of Polish youth in the late 1950s and after. Cybulski himself died tragically in an accident when running for a train, for which he was, as usual, late. One of Wajda's best films about the postwar decade. *Everything for Sale* [*Wszystko na sprzedaz*, 1969], is commemorated to Cybulski's death. Like Truffaut's *Day for Night* [1973], which it predates by several years, it is a film about making a film. The plot concerns the search for an actor who has disappeared during the shooting of a film. This absent actor represents the dead Cybulski. His friends, still alive, portray the director and fellow actors who look for the traces left by the hero while continuing to shoot other episodes of the film in progress. At the end, the moviemakers find the body of the lost actor dead from a train accident. The script and leading role have to be recast. In this movie Wajda also pays tribute to a hero representative of his own generation, born before the German invasion of Poland in 1939, who matured during the occupation and the embittered years immediately after the war. A victim of politics and an incarnation of a social myth, the dead Cybulski is replaced at the end of *Everything for Sale* by a younger and saner character, Olbrychski. He puts on Cybulski's army jacket, only to take it off as unfitting. In its place he dons a track suit, and the movie closes with a long, stunningly beautiful sequence of Olbrychski running, intermittently cross-cut to a herd of galloping horses—life, it seems, does not accept defeat.

With *Everything for Sale* Wajda's films become less rhetorical. The sense of history is flavored with a touch of irony. The favorite Wajda-esque symbol from the past, a defeated character singing his swan song of pathos, like the flute player in *Kanal*, now assumes a different shape. In *Everything for Sale* an actor playing the violin against the picturesque Warsaw panorama proves to be no more than a shot from a film in the making. Though martyrology of the Polish school gets softened and the approach becomes more epic than lyrical, at base there remains the dilemma of a character in an impossible and uncontrollable situation. In this respect, Wajda's idiom does not change. *Landscape after the Battle* [*Krajobraz po bitwie*], made in 1970, includes an elongated sequence of prisoners in striped uniforms being released from Auschwitz after the liberation of the camp by invading forces. Shot from a zooming camera, which makes their silhouettes practically motionless, the lines of prisoners are spread along the whole width of the screen, as if strutting from out of the tangles of the camp's wires. Their move toward freedom, toward normality, is but a mirage. Now, physically free, they remain spiritually unfree, unable to embrace freedom after years and ages of sequestration. Thus another running sequence pinpoints Wajda's sense of man's aimless universal motion.

Wajda's excesses—labeled by Western critics as "baroque" or else expressionistic—his overstatement and a high-pitched coloring are, in fact, his personal style. The "Wajda frame" offers a forceful and overdrawn picture of reality. Stylistically, he combines the romantic symbolism of the Polish literary tradition with a penchant for visual intensity. A constant of his technique is visual shock. Though brutal at times, even his brutality is aesthetic. His violence may be awesome, but never hideous or unjustified. His screen design (often he is the designer for his films) nearly acts. His settings exploit the world of art, suggesting careful and personalized research.

For his theatrical adaptation of Dostoevsky's *The Possessed* at the Yale Repertory of Drama in 1974, Wajda used a stage-size projection of the famous Polish painting by Chelmonski, "Horse Quaterion." Against this background of a carriage of four horses galloping across vast, uninhabited plains, his actors portray impotent people being gnawed by the jaws of the Russian Revolution. (Horses are for Wajda a personal symbol. As a child he witnessed cavalry charges from the barracks in which his father, a professional officer, was stationed.) Generally, "horsescape" fills Wajda's films and the white mare "acts" in *Lotna*.

Wajda has always been sensitive to symbolic props: a cross, a half-buried corpse before a burning city, snow laced with blood (like the white and the red of the Polish flag), uhlans confronting German tanks with sabers, a retreat of an endangered battalion into Dantesque sewers. *Ashes and Diamonds* comments on the defeated and demented Polish intelligentsia through the metaphor of song and dance—they shuffle across the floor at dawn in a traditional Polish polonaise, like some somnambulistic carnival clowns.

With all his passion for tragedy, Wajda is no defeatist. Under the surface of his refined, pictorial taste, there lurks a strong, organically affirmative, even peasant-like approach to reality. He can err in taste (much in the style of Ken Russell), the overdoing of the scene, the superfluous and flashy nouvelle-vagueish effect, the opaque dialogue, awkward and torpid, spoken theatrically rather than dramatically. But he compensates on this with the enormous energy of a social-minded statement, relentlessly and selflessly probing the so-called Polish question.

In a typically Polish way, Wajda believes that no personal story is for sale. History will decide what you are, according to the contour and the color of your behavior within the confines and pressures of time.

PRZYBYLSKA: After twenty years in a directorial career you have begun to share your film life with theater, even by accepting a headship of the Krakow "Stary" Theatre. How did this come about? Is your enthusiasm for the theater a sign of disenchantment with the film reel?

WAJDA: Like much in life, my first work for the theater came about as a pure accident. In 1958, one of the Warsaw theaters wanted to stage Gazzo's American hit, *A Hatful of Rain*. Since the leading role was given to an actor with whom I had worked extensively in the movies, someone suggested that I direct the play. It was a pioneering work—we knew very little then of how to deal with a strictly naturalistic play. The theatrical devices of the Kazan School of Acting were virtually unknown in our country. No one, for example, perceived that running water could be used as a valid performing effect. Our theater, highly academic and formalized, has always catered to the intellectual-philosophical tradition. It has capitalized on the perfection of gesture and articulation. Our conservative and literate audiences expected well-delivered, discursive texts. Consequently, we had to dust off tradition, and rather stand it on its head. Our leading star, Zbyszek Cybulski, was made the medium of that transformation. He delivered texts in an incomprehensible and intensified Brando mutter, rarely facing his audience. To this he added his personal stamp. One evening, while an eager and expectant crowd awaited the rise of a first-night curtain, a roaring motorcycle was heard arriving at the main entrance. Cybulski, his helmet still on, entered and walked down the aisle to the curtain. Pulling it apart, he began his performance. With this type of entrance, he made the spectators feel he was one of them; each was entitled to enter the stage as he did and to act as he acted.

PRZYBYLSKA: Is it not true that you were responding to the impossibly academic and emphasized way of acting in Poland, and largely, even in Eastern Europe, where actors are born in the theater, not like in America where because born in the movies they learned how to act naturally and casually?

WAJDA: My resentment to the academic theater seems to have intensified with my second theater experience, the direction of *Hamlet*. The greatness of the play is that it has been maimed. Having been copied numerous times, several authentic pages have been lost. *Hamlet* is in effect an accidental play, an enigma. And like most enigmas, a masterpiece. What must a director do in order to direct a play? First he has to skeletonize it. It usually comprises one train of thought. Then he has to direct within this conceptual frame since he cannot direct all of those ideas. But *Hamlet* is so diverse that you cannot choose a segment for emphasis. When you read the play it makes for the whole world. When you see it on the stage there is just a conception—of Orson Welles, of Laurence Olivier, etc. *Hamlet* itself remains untouched, too good to reproduce or improve on.

PRZYBYLSKA: It is the filmic thinking that interested you most in the theater?

WAJDA: There was one thing that drove me mad in the theater when I began. Trained in filmmaking, accustomed to deciding how much to show in a single frame and thus image after image leading viewer through my selection of visuals, I was bothered that every viewer saw something different because of his seat, one in the first row, another in the corner of the first balcony, etc. It seemed to me uncontrolled and chaotic. To get rid of my obsession with "chaos," I decided to emphasize it. When in 1959 I directed my third play, Gibson's *Two for the Seesaw*, I made the actors perform among the audience. We thus created the first Polish theater in the round. It appeased me that the accidental nature of "frame" perceptions in the theater was now enhanced in that the spectators saw even less of the frontality, and therefore—saw more.

PRZYBYLSKA: I remember a striking scene from Dostoevsky's *The Possessed*, as directed by you and performed at the Yale Repertory Theatre in the fall of 1974. You grouped the revolutionaries, in a conspiratorial meeting deep down the stage, as if a camera's long shot. Were you also "thinking film" then?

WAJDA: Not really. When arranging my actors for that episode I was thinking about how small and defenseless they seemed on the big, empty stage, the world. I tried to put this visually.

Europe has a courtly tradition, but every epoch has had its own theater as well, by which I mean a public theater, like Greek Theatre, or like Molière's, for that matter. We have been accustomed to experience the theater through literature, through the word. We know that mysteries preceded Greek dramatic texts. But when we think of the theater we think about those texts. What is so exciting about modern theater recently, as with Grotowski, is its return to the essence of theater, to the ritual. To make a good spectacle, two elements are necessary—the actor and the spectator, the addressor and the addressee. The author is less necessary. An actor may become an author while acting and the audience may become actors. Today's theater does not wait so much for authors as for theater people.

What is beautiful about both theater and film is that a group of people finds a leader. I am not the director in a group because I am called "director," but because the group considers me to be stronger, brighter, and wants me to lead them. This phenomenon did not exist before in the theater or film. In the past, the author supplied the text, the director engineered it, and the actors performed it. It was a distinct hierarchy. In the theater of the twentieth century, to the extent we can talk about it, there is a spectacle-happening instead of textual interpretation. I, personally, work with texts, but I try to convert them into a symbiosis of image and word, without favoring the language.

PRZYBYLSKA: The ephemeral, vanishing quality of the theater as a one-time spectacle certainly contributes to the uniqueness of the genre; theater performance in its full beauty and impact cannot be preserved on tape or record. Modern technology makes possible the possession of your own film, a reel, but it does not recapture the spectacle of film-in-the-making (nor is film-in-the-making more than a fabrication). Is not the process of the shooting of a film a form of theater?

WAJDA: Yes. And this unique experience is, like theater, a one-time experience. Whereas after some time you view a film again, it seems like an act of profanation, as if those not supposed to see it, suddenly have been allowed to. There is something ambiguous about this. Of course, there are some old films that one can still accept today. Accept—even while suspecting an ambiguity. There seems no use in recording at all. In this respect theater is superior to film, and that is why filmed theater performances are fiascos. What is left is a museum piece, and a museum piece of the most bizarre kind. This is for a very simple reason: the quintessence of the film is the actor. As theater styles undergo considerable change, acting is most affected. A new form of acting signifies a change in atmosphere toward a new epoch. Take the case of James Dean. When you see him on the screen, you do not know whether he is standing, lying, or hanging, or scratching himself. In the past, an actor was supposed to take on some kind of posture. Good manners were obligatory. Not so with the James Dean generation. His appearance on the screen marked an entry of a completely new behavior. This is what actors do from time to time. They break through an obligatory pattern of behavior.

There is an essential difference between acting in the theater and acting in film. In the theater, two basic steps are needed. You create an expression for what you want to say, and then you make it last, so that you do not have to repeat it the next day. Every "theater night" this expression has to be voiced with the same intensity. Spectators cannot be discriminated against according to whether they attend the premiere or the hundredth performance. You have to be honest with your audience. Each night you have to treat them with an equal aliveness emanating from your inner resourcefulness; each time equally powerful, equally genuine. Each night an actor has to turn his psychic energy into real and not mechanical gestures. When preparing for his role he awaits the moment when he achieves this top emotion. Then he has to memorize this emotion, analyzing it in such a way that he can renew it. He begins on the stage where he would stop in the film. By contrast, in the film once an actor achieves an apogee of expression, the camera records and preserves it for him.

PRZYBYLSKA: Are you suggesting that the film has sanctified fake surprises, that, in a way, it denies us the real although latent desire that something should actually happen?

WAJDA: There is always the possibility of going overboard in the theater, which is erased from tapes and records. As is known, amateurs can play in movies but are little used in the theater. In film nearly every actor, whether professional or amateur, can reach a certain level of excitement before the camera. Once achieved, he need not repeat this particular sensation. For an actor on stage, this is a continually renewable motion, having semblance to real life.

Take a live dialogue. It includes a potential accident, a slip, essential parts of life-art. Nowadays, the dialogue has somehow been lost. People drive cars, watch TV, make dialogue. The art of storytelling practically disappeared from modern lives. Contrast this with certain Arabic countries when you still must, by custom, haggle over the price of merchandise. A friend told me once, how on a trip in Egypt, he instantaneously paid the requested sum to the owner of a stand at the town market. The man threw the money back. He did not want remuneration as much as dialogue. He thought it unfair for him to come to the market, a human gathering, all the way from his distant village and then—not engage in human dialogue. The weeks of arduous travel with his merchandise should be compensated. Theater can still offer this kind of exchange. The film in comparison seems ready-made, precooked. It is true that film compensates for this by creating a powerful illusion of reality and pulling the viewers in as if on giant cogs. But everything that forces is in the end weaker. Pressure is not a lasting thing. For this reason a handful of poems will survive, and some literature, and some painting.

PRZYBYLSKA: What do you think is the role of a film director? And speaking of forcing people, why is it necessary to stigmatize the people working under him? I mean by that why do we more and more talk about the *auteur* films, the "collected works" of a Bergman or a Fellini, as if no others are creatively involved in these productions?

WAJDA: Yes, what bothers me lately in film is just this tendency to promote the work of director into dangerously exaggerated proportions. The persona of the director has replaced the prestige of the novelist. The screen provides what used to be the domain of the novel; it informs about new modes of being, new fashions and behaviors. And as the world of Balzac differs from that of Dostoevsky, so the personal vision of Fellini is impossible to imitate. He alone can create the Fellini world. The actors cannot create it for him. And yet, there are only a few Fellinis. Other film directors take advantage of the fact that a small group of great directors have inflated the prestige of this profession. What results is a tyranny of directors who brutally dominate all others engaged in film. It seems that a basic decency has been violated. Film directors seem not to know what is their place. Even if the director is superb, it is not he who lends his face to the crowds of people. Someone else emits the light, exposes his body and soul. The actor. I am fully aware that everything I want to say on the screen has to be filtered through someone else's individuality, somebody else's character and nature. Take an example. When we want to set the light needed for shooting an episode, we use the actor's eyes as a target. Why? Because when looking at a film sequence, a viewer first notices the actor's eyes. What you are interested in is whether the eyes tell the truth or a lie. Only afterwards do you notice other elements, compositional arrangement, decor, in a word, what is generally called mise-en-scène. No matter how Mr. Eisenstein wanted film to be a painting that with its whole surface emanates to the viewers (which is the key to the mystery of real painting—you always perceive and comprehend a painting as a totality), the viewer of a film first notes the face of an actor, then in that face he notes the actor's eyes, and he wants to know whether these eyes speak the truth or a lie.

PRZYBYLSKA: You seemed to be concerned about the just treatment of your actors and collaborators. How much, in fact, do you direct them and how much do you leave to chance, or to "controlled change"? We know that there are basically two schools of directors, the disciplinarians and the improvisers, with old Hitch being an apostle of the former. In which are you?

WAJDA: I think that every piece of art is an accident. Film direction is to me like strategic war action. Do not forget that we work with living material. It is not enough that I have a company of soldiers at my disposal and that it is up to me what I do with my section and my regiment. All I know is that I have this regiment. What I cannot know, and therefore cannot fully control, are the forces of other regiments, although I may have information as to how they are positioned. I may collect all possible information and be convinced that I am capable of defeating my enemy. But what happens in action? All kinds of surprises. For example, I employ an actor whose potential I am absolutely sure of because he played a soldier in a former battle film of mine and he was magnificent. But then he suddenly panics and, an actor on whom I counted the least, proves to be a mystery; the means at my disposal also prove mysterious. Different forces than those which I started have come into focus. Therefore, I cannot react automatically. I have to fortify whatever force does not serve me well, and I have to save what is letting me down. In this changing situation, certain roles are suddenly rising, while others are sinking. My work is of accidental nature, although I know the direction in which I am going. People do not become through me what they do through a painter's brush or a sculptor's chisel—a piece of canvas or stone. I sculpt in living people. And people usually are different today than they were yesterday. Yesterday they may have been obedient to my wishes and desires; today they have perhaps outgrown me and no longer trust me, or they have become enfeebled and cannot perform according to my demands.

PRZYBYLSKA: But the paint and the brush can also be disobedient, can they not?

WAJDA: Yes, they can, but only to those who do not know how to use them. Like words that are disobedient to a poor poet. If an artist knows what he is doing, then his achievement lies between the poet and the words, between the painter and the paint. Between my imagination and its result, there is something living. A being—an actor—whom I cannot totally mold. Molding people is dangerous. We have seen millions of the movies in which actors are utterly subordinated to directors. Take Hitchcock. Although his reputation rests on the preconceived well-planned scene, accident is unavoidable. When he shot *The Birds* [1963], some of them were bound to fly slower on one day than the day before. What he then had to do was select the version that was closest to his prediction. Of course he could eliminate accident by shooting in the atelier, by having his equipment, lighting, and other instruments work without error. But he could not absolutely separate himself from all accident. If I, on the other hand, decide to shoot a number of scenes in a chaotic way, by cutting I can achieve the same result; namely I can obtain order out of chaos.

PRZYBYLSKA: The arts have often sought to catch up with the sciences, as for example Surrealism and Cubism. Some artists have even anticipated or foreshadowed our future technology and civilization. Do you believe that the art of filmmaking is capable of anticipating the future?

WAJDA: Yes. And it is our principal aim. In my opinion it is not true that art today formulates a viewpoint. It is still a heritage of the nineteenth century to think that artists and writers want to express certain ideas about what reality is. In our life the flow of events is so fast, the pulse of things so feverish, that art serves to give us signals of what is coming. From art we learn what is gathering, what is taking shape. Not because it is fashionable.

Not because someone has been talking about it. No, nothing is phrased, no one knows anything yet; but suddenly there is a feeling, a premonition. Let me go back to my favorite example. An actor with whom I worked both in the theater and in the movies, the late Zbyszek Cybulski, started his acting career very early. He happened to be myopic and had to wear corrective lenses when off the stage. Then he got a pair of tinted big glasses and insisted on wearing them on screen as well. Something compelled him to hide behind his sunglasses. He no longer wanted the spectator to see his eyes and to learn whether they told the truth or a lie. We do not know whether James Dean hangs or sits or stands. He talks with lowered head, is hardly audible or articulate. But you know that he is under serious stress and in great doubt. To me, the phenomenon of James Dean in America or Cybulski in Poland is like a revelation in religion.

PRZYBYLSKA: Before you joined the Lodz Film School, you studied painting at the Krakow Academy of Arts. Have you kept up this interest? If so, how do you respond to such late achievements as Pop Art? Do you think this art, an expression of fascination in as well as a deprecation of American culture, is serious or else ironic?

WAJDA: There is no doubt about it. Pop art is ironic. Why else would it be enlarged, intensified in color, etc.? When I enter a store and look at the shelf full of cans, the sheer number frightens me. But when I enter an exhibition and see an enormous painting of a can of Campbell's soup, I am no more afraid. It makes me grin. It does not, however, make me reluctant to buy. There is no doubt that more and more people will participate in universal prosperity. There is no other road for mankind than for a greater amount of people to obtain a greater amount of everything, so that the production of goods must grow. The standard that an average American enjoys was once possible only for the others. Nowadays, while producing for the others, people also produce for themselves.

Art has become not only popular, but very eclectic. I do not like it at all. We feed on other epochs. We make notes on the margins of books that have already been written. Poetry becomes a discussion with other poetry, and film becomes a discussion with other film. A spectator who lives apart from the intellectual currents and comes to see a certain film does not know with whom the film is conversing. Whenever art lives on art it can perhaps achieve its summits, but it also displays certain fatigue.

The processes that once took ages, now become diabolically quick. Someone who painted, for example, had the possibility of a slow and harmonious development. He evolved his theme, his model, and materialized it slowly and painstakingly during the cycle of his life. Picasso, for example, planned to his very end. Today artists use themselves up quickly. At the point that you succeed in opening your first one-man show, people already want you to become someone else. But you cannot become someone else. Still, nowadays people are anxious to receive a shock of "otherness." If we see one thing, we then want to see something else. We need another shot. In film this process is even more rapid. Every new film applies stronger and stronger devices to force the spectator to look at what he is being shown. These devices are not even relevant to the general subject matter; they become a necessity in themselves. The strength of an erotic scene or a brutal display of physical power defeats itself. All these flashy effects are soon used up, so that the effects that come have to surpass in sheer brutality, in violence or in eroticism. The massacres in *Bonnie and Clyde* [1967] were a flash of novelty—now they are insufficient. What happens to a director nowadays who wants to show brutal death on the screen? To apply these effects is impossible. It will be taken as untrue and inauthentic—we are all aiming at a greater truth, always more precise and exact than before. It is impossible to return to pastoral, bucolic style. When I showed my film, *Kanal*, to the Cannes Film Festival in 1957, critics accused me of violence, although I showed a real, if not understated, experience of the Polish underground during the Warsaw uprising. The critics complained that they had not come to Cannes to view such atrocities. Today, they are unhappy with the violence of *Kanal* because it is too sentimental. There was an unjust war, and I wanted to show that people should resist it, even as they did. For this reason I had to show the war in its real character—as murderous and awesome. Every exaggeration could be justified in such a situation, because it was synonymous with protest. Now, nobody cares about protest. Now, you are given scenes in which a policeman scatters someone's brains around, but the story defends neither the victim nor the policeman. The scene is an end in itself. It serves no deeper purpose. Violence acts as the attracting energy. Buñuel once said that it is immoral to shoot a man with a gun. All it shows is that it is easy to kill; you shoot a man and he falls. That is all. What should be shown on the screen, said Buñuel, is the agony of death. The dying man is suffering but the killer suffers, too. Only this mutual torment can lead to a catharsis. This is how I portrayed the death of Cybulski on the dump in *Ashes and Diamonds*. Now killing has become a device, a secondary thing. I am afraid that it is difficult to stop this process.

PRZYBYLSKA: You have taken a stand against superfluous violence in movies. In this respect, what is your opinion about a master of the gothic, your émigré compatriot, Roman Polanski?

WAJDA: It seems to me that Roman has always dreamed of becoming a Hollywood director. His whole life has been devoted to that goal, and in his latest picture, *Chinatown* [1974], he achieved it. Having achieved this purpose, he stopped being Polanski. His strength lay always in being able to shoot an American picture and branding it with his unique, idiosyncratic approach. I do not believe he can be frozen in a classification and I expect something completely new from him in the future. After his last big and gory production, *Macbeth* [1971], he embarked upon a youthful search, *What?* [1972], a film that could have been directed by a teenager just out of a film school. I understand why someone who seeks perfection, as Roman does, has to come to work in America. When Antonioni made *Zabriskie Point* [1970] he committed a mistake that Polanski has cleverly avoided. Antonioni said in his movie what *he* thought about America—that does not interest anybody. People are interested in America, not in what Antonioni thinks about it. They are interested in Antonioni as an Italian director, so long as he serves the history of cinema. The fact that the great Antonioni deigns to bend over America is ridiculous, because America is bigger than he.

PRZYBYLSKA: What is your favorite American film by an American director?

WAJDA: Recently I have been fascinated with Coppola's *The Conversation* [1974]. It seems that this film has taken over what has always been happening in music, and what happened to theater in the fifties, namely employing a single idea and extending it. As in a sonata or a fugue, there is one leitmotif that is woven and then rewoven in various shapes and tonalities. *The Conversation* tells you to spy on someone else is impossible in a world of incessant motion. When you look at the glass walls of modern buildings, you see the whole world, reflected human faces, cars, etc. They all flow. Everything is reflected in something else and this something else is a reflection as well. In this infinite flowing motion, it is difficult to see what we are looking for. Personally, I consider *The Conversation* more a filmic movie than the action films that take pride in rejecting everything for the sake of the so-called pure cinema.

PRZYBYLSKA: You have complained about the scarcity of scenarios and literary texts in present-day Poland. Have you been thinking about composing your own films scripts?

WAJDA: The difficulty is that most of our young writers complicate their texts enormously. They apparently look for meaning in the language itself. In contrast, in Western countries there are scriptwriters of what I would call "useful" texts. Literature does not have to be beautiful. Poland has [a] peculiar tradition that a writer must be a prophet, a guiding conscience of the nation. Tonality thus becomes ponderous. After the partitions of Poland, more than one hundred and fifty years ago, our country continued to exist, thanks to a handful of books. Thanks to those several books read and cultivated by certain families clandestinely, the Polish people succeeded in remaining Polish. These few books became a bridge between the moment at which we lost our political independence and the moment we regained it. In the intervening years we lived with those texts like the Jewish people lived with the Old Testament. For this reason Polish writers came to the conclusion that their duties were much broader than those of their Western colleagues. Since in those years of national deprivation there was no government, no political and social life, books had to fill the vacuum. Books had to replace national events. Mickiewicz, our renowned Romantic poet, is a symptomatic example. He taught German to one of his daughters. During one of the lessons, while translating Schiller for her, he realized that he was transferring the German verse automatically into Polish verse (he composed verse that easily). At that point he closed his book. He became frightened that words flowed from him like sounds from a pipe organ and he felt this was a ridiculous occupation for an adult. So he took to politics. He created a Polish legion in Turkey and took a "real" part in history. This reaction would be impossible for a Western writer, who would instead choose to develop his ability into mastery. If he found himself speaking verse he would immediately record it. As for myself, I have become tired of my own versatility.

PRZYBYLSKA: Do you mean you are tired of fictitious creations? When did this occur?

WAJDA: This feeling possesses a man when he approaches his forties. At this age you can see a sum of your certain achievements. You realize that you will not do certain things. You are short of breath and, yet, a big portion of life is ahead of you. Note that forty-year-old men often volunteer for war operations. The first army volunteers tend to be sixteen-year[s]-old (my father joined the army when he was sixteen); the next the forty-year-old[s]. They find security in giving themselves over, in being told what to do, thus ridding themselves of the responsibility for their own fates. They shoot, they sleep, and they march forward. They participate in something valid, but at the same time are released from it. At least they do not pay their own bills. The job of a filmmaker also seems to be very attractive. It combines physical with mental work; concrete action with inspiration; influence upon and independence from others. Yet, there is something infantile about it as well. Like playing with toy soldiers. This first occurred to me when I was directing a battle scene. It was as if I were maneuvering tin soldiers, a children's game. I had a similar feeling while directing erotic episodes—as if I were trespassing into someone's intimate experience. Obviously, like all work, your satisfaction depends on the success you achieve.

Despite what you call exhaustion, your films continue to show what is called "meaningful human action." Your characters are never fully and finally defeated; at least not with respect to internal human valor and energy. They are never sick. Man is given life to live it. Only respect for other human life creates social norms. If we break this principle, we break ourselves—we cut our own throats. Art cannot serve the self-annihilating instincts, even if the reward is success and great films. The tendency of sickness in art will have to be reversed. How it will reverse itself I do not know. It is extremely hard to tell what the masses for whom we create are really like. What kind of audience do we have? Take Americans. Are they stupid people or clever? Do they go to see *The Exorcist* [1973] because there are no better alternatives or because it suits their taste? Certainly, there was no need for this type of trashy production in the years when Americans felt they were building the country, the civilization. They were modest people, attending church. They surely had a devil within them then as now (the devil is always the same, whatever the circumstances). In more pioneering days there was no need to portray strong people; it was enough to scalp or to be scalped. Life demanded strenuousness. In my opinion, it is the monotony of suburban and provincial life in America today that creates the need for some electric blow-off, so to speak. Out of necessity it has become not heroic, but dwarfish.

Distrusting the arts as created by professionals, young people nowadays seem to create their own form of spectacle. They simply go into the streets, offices and schools dressed as the Vietnam "veterans," postmasters, painters. They sneer at everything, disguise themselves in all possible ways. Do you consider this a symptom of coming crisis, a dance on the volcano?

This exciting dance on the ruins of the world's empires should not please us much. The actors in this show will have to pay for it. I saw it all happening, originally, when I traveled to London in the sixties. You have to remember that England created an elite that ruled over the British empire. And what remained of that splendor were four Liverpool boys playing guitars. The teenagers who imitated them broke all existing norms of style and behavior. Before, when you dreamed of wearing a uniform, you had to pass the entrance examinations for cadet school. Now, when you look at English boys parading the streets in jackets of royal guards, with jeans beneath, you realize they have it both ways: they are the royal guards, and they make fools of the royal guards. They prove superior to the real guys standing before the Palace, the guys who took pains to get that colorful and privileged job. Those boys with the jackets and jeans are acting out the fall of the British empire. On ruins you are entitled to utmost licentiousness; there are no limits. Art thrives on both great and miserable moments. When we think of Roman architecture we have a well-defined idea—that of beauty and precision. Once, in a town on the Yugoslav coast I saw the remains of a splendid Roman city—splendid walls capped with a cupola. Probably during a long span of time that city was destroyed and forgotten. What was preserved were only the enormous Roman pillars. When building started again, the big lumps of those Roman pillars were brought over, piled one on another, coated with lime, and made into a wall. The builders were not even smart enough to turn the more elaborate, relief side of the pilaster toward the front of the wall. They have hidden it forever from human sight. This gave me a lot to think about. Probably after the next total war, if we have that misfortune, a downed military plane will be an object equivalent to that Roman rotunda. The survivors will stretch a piece of canvas between the wings of the destroyed plane and make a tent to live in. Of course, by that time nobody will know about the origin of the objects serving as a frame for this construction—planes will no longer fly. This will be the architecture of the new era.

PRZYBYLSKA: How do you see the United States in this context?

WAJDA: If you look at Manhattan and you treat it as a piece of America, you get the impression of the end of the world. You cannot lift yourself higher nor sink lower. But if you drive out fifty miles to all those wooden houses painted with white oil paint, you pass into another epoch. They are not the same people. And if you drive through the woods for hours and hours, American ecological complaints become ridiculous. What can congested Europe say, or Japan which is not able to build other than on the ocean? Americans do tend to crowd on the East coast and enjoy a pseudo-decadence, but fortunately there is no serious obstacle to their stretching themselves into other areas. The land is there. In this context, we cannot talk about the end of the American empire, even though we would love to fantasize about it.

Marcel Ophüls

Whenever people try to censor a filmmaker, they never admit that
what they are talking about are political issues, because this would be
extremely primitive and extremely unsophisticated. They always find
other issues. They will tell you that your film is boring or unstructured or too long or too this or too that. Because they know that as
soon as they admit that they have political priorities, you can then
pounce on them.

$\mathscr{T}$he story of a filmmaker whose film is taken from his or her hands, only to be
lost, destroyed, buried in a studio's archives, or, perhaps worst of all, recut and ex-
hibited in a form which the original filmmaker never intended, is unfortunately
all too familiar to students of film history; Erich von Stroheim's *Greed* (1924), Orson Welles's *The Magnificent Ambersons* (1942), and Sergei Eisenstein's *¡Que Viva
Mexico!* (1932) are some of the most famous examples. While there are certainly
alternative narratives of lesser filmmakers saved by more talented editors and producers, the romantic narrative of the artist struggling against the powers that be,
and losing, still has a powerful effect on even the most jaded of film scholars and
enthusiasts. And yet, when we encounter this narrative not as some fabled lore in
the back of a dusty film magazine but as the raw confession of a director who has
been badly wronged by financiers, the story grips us not for the mythos of the
downtrodden artist but simply for the insidious ways in which a group of people,
perhaps with the best of intentions, dismantle the work of a talented person and,
in the case of this piece, badly distort the overall trajectory of the film, if not history itself.

In the following interview, the documentary filmmaker Marcel Ophüls
leads interviewer Frank Manchel through the step-by-step process by which
Ophüls's film *The Memory of Justice* (1976) was taken from his hands, re-edited,

and presented in such a way as to run counter, almost completely, to Ophüls's original vision. Part of the problem, as Ophüls relates, is that his original intentions changed as the film was being made, but as he puts it, "This is one of the interesting things about documentary filmmaking. If you develop techniques of letting reality come to you, then there is the process of change and hopefully a process of growth in yourself." Unfortunately for Ophüls, his financial backers had an idea of the film they wanted well before Ophüls had even started filming, as he himself learned all too late. Throughout the interview, Ophüls soberly reflects on the years following the film's release, ending with a fear that he is simply too drained from the experience to move on. Responding to Manchel's question of if he will begin a new project, Ophüls simply repeats the phrase, "I don't think I can, I don't think I can." While he was eventually able to make other films, Ophüls's interview is likely to make even the most detached readers saddened, angry, and shocked at the decisions made by those in power—people Ophüls, incidentally, has no trouble citing by name.

Interview by Frank Manchel
Originally published as "A War Over Justice: An Interview with Marcel Ophüls,"
Literature/Film Quarterly *6, no. 1 (January 1978): 26–47.*

It's easy to see why Marcel Ophüls is such a controversial filmmaker. He is an artist who refuses to sacrifice principle for profit or popularity. Starting with *The Sorrow and the Pity*, which, in 1972, established him as one of the world's foremost documentarians, Ophüls began asking unpleasant questions about our society. He wanted to know, for example, what was the truth about the Nazi occupation of France during World War II. While the movie itself angered the French mythmakers, *New Republic* critic Stanley Kauffmann summed up the superb critical reaction by stating that the film "looks at the past," makes us "understand a little more of both the sorrow and the pity," warns us to "be careful of feeling superior to others," and, "rather chillingly, leaves the future to us." That same year in *A Sense of Loss*, Ophüls explored the complex problems in feud-ridden Northern Ireland. Rather than provide easy answers to complex issues, he chose to disturb audiences with his profoundly humanistic images of an apparently hopeless conflict. Ophüls's commitment to objectivity and his refusal to be compromised by unpopular opinions prompted *Time*'s critic Jay Cocks to pronounce him "the Orwell of the cinema."

Then, in 1976, after four years of personal agony and court battles with his European producers, Ophüls unveiled *The Memory of Justice*. The title, attributed to Plato's conviction that mortals in a less than perfect world must be governed by the primeval memory of Justice and Virtue, acted as a guide to Ophüls's investigation about the nature of war crimes. Once again the director became embroiled in controversy. Critics, scholars, and the general public have taken strong stands over the people interviewed in the film, the editing techniques, and the various interpretations resulting from worldwide screenings. Within recent months, the film itself has almost disappeared from public view. Paramount Pictures and New Line Cinema, distributors of the 35mm and 16mm prints respectively, appear to have had little success in getting the film circulated. The questions surrounding the reception of *The Memory of Justice* are disturbing.

Thus when Marcel Ophüls visited the University of Vermont during the week of April 11, 1977, I persuaded him to present his side of the story. What follows is an edited transcript of his feelings about the controversy.

MANCHEL: When did the idea for doing *The Memory of Justice* first begin with you?

OPHÜLS: Well, Frank, for the sake of honesty, I feel I should throw a bucket of cold water on the idea that filmmakers always have pet projects, and that they are in a position to realize these pet projects, and that is what they consecrate their lives to. In fact, what happened is that after having made a film in Northern Ireland [*A Sense of Loss*, 1972] and being once again out of work, I was approached by the BBC, who had had a great deal of success with their showing of *The Sorrow and the Pity* in England. They wanted to have another four-and-a-half-hour movie, more or less along the same lines. And so the logical and natural inclination for all of us in this connection, once the BBC put up the seed money, was to say, "Well, what about the chronological follow-up to *The Sorrow and the Pity?*" This essentially meant the first three or four years after the war in Western Europe. That original project I used to characterize by saying, "Society falling back on its rotten feet." Sometimes I wish we could have stuck to that original idea. I still think it was a good project. We would have concentrated on France after the war, General Charles de Gaulle, Pierre Mendes-France, Albert Camus, Jean-Paul Sartre, the liberation, the trials of Pierre Laval and Marshal Philippe Pétain, the Labour Party taking over from Winston Churchill in England, the Germans trying to find their way through the ruins, discovering Hemingway, Faulkner, and the beginning of the Cold War. The Nuremberg Trials would have been just one chapter in that original project. And while I was researching for that film, I met Telford Taylor. I had read his book called *Nuremberg and Vietnam: An American Tragedy* [1970]. I had also found out from a French journalist that there were fifteen hours of footage done by the United States Army Signal Corps during the Nuremberg Trials, which had been used in various documentary films since the war but never with synchronized sound and picture. Then something happened, which I don't want to go into, and I had to go to the BBC and to my sponsors and say, "Well look, I think this film about postwar France is being done by others and maybe we should do something else." In fact, my meeting with Taylor in New York had suggested a new possibility. And I said, "Well, let's do a film about the Nuremberg Trials." My sponsors at the time were more enthusiastic about the new project than I was, and it is only with hindsight that I have come to understand their enthusiasm.

MANCHEL: When you say your sponsors, you're talking about the BBC, Polytel International, a television packaging company, and Visual Programmes Systems Ltd., a British production company.

OPHÜLS: Yes. They came in at different times. First there was the BBC; then the man who was the head of purchase programs at the BBC and who was my well-wishing sponsor at the time got in touch with the subsidiary of Phillips in Hamburg, a very powerful German production company called Polytel. There were a series of contracts signed. All of this is part of my life and it's very dreary for me and for anybody else. Then they involved a private English firm whose principal stockholder is Evelyn Rothschild.

MANCHEL: Is that Visual Programmes Systems Ltd.?

OPHÜLS: Yes. A man called David Puttnam. Another man called Sanford Lieberson. They make films like Alan Parker's *Bugsy Malone* (1976), Ken Russell's *Mahler* (1974), and Lutz Becker's *Swastika* (1973). I had had earlier contacts with these people because they had asked me to do a fictionalized version of Albert Speer's memoirs, which they had acquired.

MANCHEL: How significant was the connection between the proposed Speer film and the current problems you were facing with the sequel to *The Sorrow and the Pity*?

OPHÜLS: It is only a sideline and a dead end. I would have to go into the motivations for wanting to make a picture about Speer's memoirs and about our conversations at that time. I think it would take us too far afield. Anyway, my trying to rescue the project, the original project and the seed money and the groceries, was to suddenly come out with an idea that originally was only supposed to be a chapter. The plan was now to expand the chapter into a whole film, including, of course, the implications in the postwar world of the Nuremberg Trials. The idea, with hindsight, met with a suspicious amount of enthusiasm. When I say that the amount of enthusiasm seemed to be suspicious, with hindsight, what I mean is that I should have been bright enough and analytical enough to understand that a commercial alliance between German co-producers and trendy Wardour Street, young English producers who were aiming for the American market, should have made me aware enough politically and sensitive enough politically to understand what these people saw in the Nuremberg Trials. With a hindsight of thirty years, it was to them an opportunity of relativizing history and of appealing to what they assumed German prejudices to be. In other words, the idea of getting off the hook by demonstrating that evil is not confined to the Third Reich. On the one hand, this would be for the German television audience; on the other hand, this would be appealing to radical chic conceptions, or what they assumed to be radical chic conceptions on the American market. To put it another way, those people, because they very sincerely took very adamant positions against the Vietnam War, would have a tendency growing out of their experiences to equate or to compare My Lai to the crimes committed by the Third Reich which led to the Nazi Holocaust. This, I think, was an attempt to cash in on what the Marxist would call an "objective alliance." The idea would be to attempt to cash in on what these people suppose, wrongly I think, to be the positions of the kind of people in America who would go and see documentary films, left of center, and the German television audience of people who would be glad to find out that there is some connection between My Lai and crimes committed by the Germans during World War II. I have to confess quite openly that because of my naiveté or my innocence or my good faith or whatever you want to call it, I did not perceive this from the very beginning. Or perhaps I did not choose to perceive it, because when you have to make a living in any one profession you have a tendency to discard signs that go against your interest, because your immediate interest is in making a film.

MANCHEL: I want to clarify one point. In Jay Cocks's *Time* essay concerning *The Memory of Justice*, when he wrote about the internal struggles over the film's evolution, he stated that "Ophüls set out to explore the contested—some would say outrageous—theory that Nazi genocide and tragedies like My Lai are somehow comparable, an idea that had widespread currency a few years ago."[1] What I want to clarify is whose idea was it to make the film a Nuremberg Vietnam comparison: yours or the various producing groups?

OPHÜLS: I guess that when I started out researching the original project, the relative, the historical priorities, in my own mind, were perhaps closer to the product which the producers and co-producers expected of me than finally turned out to be the case. This is one of the interesting things about documentary filmmaking. If you develop techniques of letting reality come to you, then there is the process of change and hopefully a process of growth in yourself. And therefore, you can then shift positions during the process of the filmmaking. That certainly happened in *The Memory of Justice*, and I'm perfectly willing to say that. In that way, the producers, who fired me at one point, do have some semblance of a case. Because in the preliminary discussions, my own positions were perhaps closer to what they hoped the film would be.

MANCHEL: We're talking about events in 1973?

OPHÜLS: Yes, this was 1973. In the course of filming, I wrote memoranda to them which stated, as honestly as I could, the shift in my positions.

MANCHEL: For example?

OPHÜLS: Well, for example, the fact that by the time that I came to America I no longer wished to confront men like McNamara or Westmoreland or Bundy or Rostow with the question, "Are you, sir, a war criminal?" This had a lot to do with a sense of proportions and a sense of humility which I had acquired by my research and my work concerning Germany and the German connection and the Nazi connection to Nuremberg. It was in fact a shift in emphasis. And since there was that shift in emphasis, I thought my producers should know about it, and I wrote them a memorandum which stated that shift as clearly as I could.

MANCHEL: Can you be more specific about the shift in your attitudes toward Germany's connection to the Nuremberg Trials?

OPHÜLS: Well, I just mean that the longer I was confronted by the task I had chosen for myself, the more aware I became that I had no right to substitute myself for trial by law. Since this was ostensibly a film about justice and about the difficulty of judgment and about the ways in which society tries to deal with this, it became more and more apparent to me that any individual, including any individual who has the privilege of having access to the mass media, is not entitled to substitute his own subjective judgments for trial by law. The shift in emphasis, therefore, meant that the theme I assigned to myself had to enable me to talk to people who had been convicted of crimes; that I couldn't cross-cut this with people who my own subjective views, my own political priorities, made me assume were potential war criminals; that this kind of cross-cutting would be detrimental, not only to the film, not only to what I was trying to say, but also to political priorities and to historical priorities in general.

MANCHEL: What is the chronology of these events? You began the contract negotiations and the research for the film in 1973. Later in the year you come to America, and the shift in emphasis plus the memoranda between you and your producers begins in 1974?

OPHÜLS: The filming started in November 1973. By spring of the following year, while at Princeton, I began editing the film. Then during the early summer of 1974, I started writing the memoranda. Shortly afterwards, still in the summer of 1974, I returned to London to complete the editing and the film project itself. And then I was fired from my own film. To be quite accurate, I wasn't fired from the film. The film was confiscated from me. It was a blatant power squeeze that took place on December 22, 1974, after what is known in the trade as the rough-cut screening.

MANCHEL: Before we go into the film's being confiscated, let's clarify the state of the film before December 22. How much of *The Memory of Justice* was completed?

OPHÜLS: It was a four hour, thirty-eight-and-a-half-minute film which was not absolutely identical with the four hour, thirty-eight-and-a-half-minute film which Paramount is now distributing. But for all practical purposes, it was identical. My contract provided for a film of a minimum length of three-and-a-half hours and a maximum length of four-and-a-half hours. It was the BBC who insisted on having the four-and-a-half-hour length. In other words, I was eight-

and-a-half minutes above the length stipulated in my contract. My argument at that time, which went on for days, was that I was asking for the privilege—I was asking to be indulged in my caprice of mixing and dubbing those eight-and-a-half minutes. Then, if in the judgment of my producers and co-producers, after the film was dubbed and mixed, they found the additional eight-and-a-half minutes a breach of contract, I would remove the excess footage. I was being a realist. Having a lot of experience in this profession, I was not about to let myself be put into a breach of contract on a matter of length.

MANCHEL: Then in point of fact people are unfair when they typecast you as a person who only makes four-and-a-half-hour films. The length of this film was dictated by the BBC.

OPHÜLS: Absolutely! The length of *The Memory of Justice* was determined by the BBC. It resulted from the format they had chosen for the subject matter they wanted filmed. I repeat. This was the BBC's initiative, not mine.

MANCHEL: How much footage had you shot prior to the editing stage?

OPHÜLS: Ninety hours.

MANCHEL: And you then proceeded during the summer and fall of 1974 to cut it down to a four hour and thirty-eight-and-a-half-minute film. How was the rough-cut organized?

OPHÜLS: The first part was called, and is still called, "Nuremberg and the Germans." The second part is called "Nuremberg and Other Places." I must confess again that this is cheating. The second part still has an awful lot to do with Nuremberg and the Germans, and only in the very last third of the film do you get to Nuremberg and other places. This is important because it has to do with what my sense of proportions came to be after the end of my inquiry. Let me now pick up that beautiful Christmas of 1974 in London. The Ritz Bar in London. After the rough-cut screening we met there. The representative of the BBC was present and the representative of the German co-producers was present for a while and then had to catch his plane back to Hamburg, and of course, the two hot shots were present.

MANCHEL: The hot shots being . . .

OPHÜLS: Sandy Lieberson and David Puttnam. There seems to be some sort of community between Wardour Street and Carnaby Street. They were, let me tell you, anything but leftists; in their professional policies, in their methods of hiring and firing, in their personal views about the role of capitalism in a market society, they were anything but leftists. But they were leftists about their assessment of how they could make money on the American market with that kind of film. Oh yeah. . . . There were three issues discussed at the meeting at the Ritz Bar. The eight-and-a-half minutes, which they refused to have dubbed and mixed; there was, of course, a lot of discussion about that and a sort of standstill. By that time I knew pretty thoroughly what the real issues were. I think I knew. I still think I know. One thing we should all understand is that, in political films, whenever a conflict arises, people never admit that the conflict is political. Whenever people try to censor a filmmaker, they never admit that what they are talking about are political issues, because this would be extremely primitive and extremely unsophisticated. They always find other issues. They will tell you that your film is boring or unstructured or too long or too this or too that. Because they know that as soon as they admit that they have political priorities, you can then pounce on them. You can make a public issue on it, and then you can rally support to your side. They are not about to do that. All right, so the conversation at the Ritz Bar, which lasted I think two-and-a-half hours, was mostly about those eight-and-a-half minutes. There were three issues. The first was on the eight-and-a-half minutes, which I did not refuse to take out of the film but simply asked for the privilege of mixing and dubbing, so that they could make up their own minds. The second issue had to do with frontal, would you believe it, with frontal nudity. The representative of the BBC—the man who had been my original patron, who had put up the seed money—was by that time, for reasons of his own, a hundred percent accomplice. He was later overruled by the hierarchy of the BBC, which finally did telecast my film and made a public commitment to telecast my film or no film.

MANCHEL: This man's name was . . .

OPHÜLS: Gunnar Rugheimer. There are rumors that he is about to quit the BBC to become an employee of Polytel Incorporated International. Whatever that means, he's a former agent of MCA. An interesting man, a very clever man, and a man whom I still have a debt to, because he did support me for a long time. And he is a wheeler-dealer and he is a go-getter with all the advantages and disadvantages that that sort of thing has. As to the frontal nudity, Gunnar was saying that the BBC has codes of standard for, you know, prime hour broadcasting and youth and general audiences and that sort of thing, which made it imperative that frontal nudity not be shown during prime telecasting hours. I knew this to be bullshit because I have seen the BBC things and the BBC is much, much less Puritan than, for instance, American commercial networks are. They have shown frontal nudity over and over again when they showed *Hearts and Minds* [1974], for instance, but I wasn't about to quibble at that stage and I said, "Well listen, Gunnar, I'm all in favor of respecting family standards, and if the BBC has certain standards about frontal nudity, I will eliminate frontal nudity for the BBC, but I will do that in the print destined for the BBC. I don't think that you as a representative of the BBC have a right to demand that I cut it in the negative. Because this would indeed be censorship and I understand very well, dear Gunnar, what your problem is. Your problem is that if the film is going to be presented at the New York Film Festival with the sequence that had frontal nudity, and then is to be presented later on at the BBC with that particular sequence censored, you will then be responsible to answer certain questions asked by discerning journalists. But if you have good reasons and good guidelines for the stand that you are taking, then you must be prepared to answer those questions to those journalists."

MANCHEL: Fair enough.

OPHÜLS: Fair enough. Whereupon my Wardour Street hustler said, "Well that, Marcel, is not the question, because we also request you to cut this in the negative." And then I said, "No." In fact, all of this, of course, is what Truman used to call a red herring, because by that time they were trying to wave a red cloth in front of the bull so that I would charge out of the arena. They had long ago (or short ago) decided, for reasons of their own, that I was not willing to play their game and they, therefore, wanted to have another man to recut the film, and they were waiting for me to walk out. As it turns out, the issue of the frontal nudity was later settled very, very fast because the program controller of BBC (who had refused to arbitrate when the fight was taking place in Wardour Street, where all he had to do was to take a cab at Christmas time to drive five miles down from Television Center—and who later had to fly 5,000 miles to New York to see the print of the film) reversed the decision of the BBC and said, "We'll take the film, the Ophüls film, or nothing, including the frontal nudity." He felt that was a ridiculous pretext. He is a man by the name of Aubrey Singer. So in the end, the BBC did show my film, including the frontal nudity.

MANCHEL: Without any problems?

OPHÜLS: Without any problems! The third issue had to do with Russians. The German co-producers wanted me to include a dissident Russian in the film, although they were in no way entitled to do this by contract. Their reasons for wanting to have this in the film, I think, are very obvious. They wanted to lull the German television public into the intellectual comfort of being able to compare German extermination camps with Russian Gulag Archipelago. The intention seems so obvious that it doesn't need much editorializing. I was not unwilling to do this, because I do happen to think that Stalinism is one of the atrocities of modern times, and while I question the motives of my German co-producers, I have no great doubts about the iniquities of the Gulag Archipelago. So I did try to get Solzhenitsyn. I did not succeed. For some reasons of his own, which I think are not too difficult to analyze either. At that time, Solzhenitsyn had just come out of Soviet Russia. He had stayed in Germany, and then gone to Zurich. Perhaps Solzhenitsyn, a genius and obviously a very intelligent man, was afraid of being annexed by the kind of political skullduggery that we are talking about and, therefore, was reluctant to be within the framework of a film on the Nuremberg Trials. So he refused. If I had a tape of the Ritz Bar, those people who have hairs on their head, which I don't happen to have, their hairs would stand up straight, because Mr. Gunnar Rugheimer, the representative of the BBC at that particular conference was saying at one point: "Well, Marcel, you didn't get Solzhenitsyn, so why don't you satisfy our German co-producers by going into a white Russian bar and interviewing some gypsy violinist?" I am quoting textually, "Our German co-producers are unhappy because you have not come up with a Russian dissident. So why don't you give them their Russian dissident under any terms?" And I was trying to explain to them that unless it is Solzhenitsyn, or unless it is Sakharov, who happens to live in Moscow and who is unavailable, it did not seem to me to make a great deal of sense. I also tried to explain to them that Stalinist war crimes and Stalinist crimes against humanity were touched upon in the film, and that as far as my sense of proportion was concerned, this seemed to me to be adequate. I also tried to explain to them that the motives of the German co-producers seemed to me to be so transparent as to be a major turnoff. Furthermore, I had no contractual obligation to do this, because there was nothing in my contract that obligated me to furnish one interview rather than another. Finally, I said, "Well listen, if you are willing to give me another ten minutes over and above the four-and-a-half hours that we already have, then I will try to cash in on the contacts that we have made with Daniel . . . the Russian dissident in Paris. [A very interesting man who was available in Paris.] But I will not do it to the detriment of the four hours thirty-eight-and-a-half minutes that I have now, because it seems to me that [the] four hours thirty-eight-and-a-half minutes that I have now are more to the point and more pertinent to what I want to say than a Russian dissident whom the German co-producers feel should be in the film." At that point, David Puttnam, who I think is 32 years old, suddenly said, "Listen, Marcel, I'm getting very tired of this. We've been arguing about these things for two-and-a-half hours." And I said, "I've been working on this for two-and-a-half years. I don't mind arguing about it for two-and-a-half hours." He said, "Yes, but I have other things to do. And I'll tell you this right now, our intention is to cut up the film in any way, shape, length, or form that our American clients would judge to be adequate." Whereupon I said very quietly, "David, if you do that you will be in breach of contract." Whereupon David said to me, "Marcel, that may well be, but you'll have to take us to court and by the time that the judgment is given in court, we will have recouped, hopefully, our money." Whereupon I said, "I think this is morally perverted." Whereupon he said, "I don't know how someone who has breached his contract in terms of budget and scheduling has any right to question our morals, because I think that you are morally degenerate."

MANCHEL: This was Christmas time.

OPHÜLS: This is the 22nd of December. Whereupon I got up and said, "Gentlemen, I think I have seen enough of you," and walked out of the Ritz Bar in London. Twenty-five minutes later they went to the cutting room and told the editors that I had walked out of the film and that they were justified, therefore, in taking custody of the work print. On the very next day, which was the 23rd of December, and a Sunday, it was very difficult to get a British solicitor to give me advice. So even before I could get that advice, I sat down and wrote a letter to them by registered mail pointing out the difference between walking out of a meeting and walking out of a film. And I said that there was no clause in my contract which obligated me to suffer their physical presence. There is no clause in any contract as far as I know between filmmakers and producers which obligates either party to ever suffer the physical presence of the other party. You can correspond by mail, by lawyers, or by telephone. This is not a breach of contract. They chose to interpret it as such. They chose to interpret it as such not only on legal grounds but simply on power grounds, because they assumed, quite rightly, that I would not be able to afford to sue them. Okay, so after trying to get out an injunction against them, after trying to rouse the British unions to blackball the work in the lab, unsuccessfully, but with a lot of support from people like Lindsey Anderson, Robert Boles, Stanley Kubrick, I left England and went back to Princeton, which was at that time my only job, and more or less gave up on the whole thing because they were right. I could not afford the services at that time of lawyers and lawsuits. So they proceeded to have the film recut—

MANCHEL: By Lutz Becker.

OPHÜLS: He was the one who did *Swastika* and *Double-Headed Eagle* (1973). Now the proof of the pie is in the eating, and their denial that they had political motivations in confiscating the film from me is totally ludicrous once you have seen the Becker version, which they took five months to do and which was broadcast on German television. I will try to confine myself to a couple of examples. In the Dresden sequence, I question former Wing Commander Rose about whether he would have accepted to go to Nuremberg if the London charter had been different and had included allied war crimes and if "Bomber" Harris had been in the dock. In the interview with him, Wing Commander Rose, who had just testified to the fact that he, as the Chief of British Air Force Intelligence, had given very, very solid information to the Allied High Command and to the American and to the British Air Force to the effect that Dresden was not a military target. And, therefore, should not be bombed. The American General Spaatz, who was in charge of strategic bombing, thereupon reacted by saying, "Well, if the British agree not to bomb Dresden, we will not bomb Dresden." Whereupon Jim Rose, who is now a publisher of Penguin Books, incidentally called up his own chief at headquarters, Air Marshal Saunby, and told about the information that he had from totally reliable German intelligence sources, that the S.S. Panzer divisions were joining the Eastern Front northeast of Prague, a hundred miles from Dresden. "Bomber" Harris's second-in-command said, "Well, that makes no difference to us. We are going to bomb Dresden." Whereupon at the end of the Dresden sequence in *The Memory of Justice*, I ask Wing Commander Rose, "Well, if the London charter had not excluded allied war crimes from the deliberations in Nuremberg would you have accepted to go to Nuremberg and testify about what you knew?" He says, "Yes, of course." And being an Englishman, and a decent Englishman, he then immediately adds, "but I would have had to listen to what the defense had to say, because perhaps I did not have the whole picture. But as far as I know, Dresden was a war crime." Then there was a pause and I asked, "And in the twenty-eight years since, have you ever heard of anything that would make you change that assessment?" And he hesitates for a fraction of a second and he says, "No." And then he smiles. All of that was cut from the Becker version. So much for British suscepti-bilities! What was also cut from the Becker version were things like Albert Speer showing his home movies, including meetings with the economic bosses of the Third Reich (people like Porsche, who designed the Volkswagen) and then re-marking quite casually that these people got back into top jobs after the war and took over German industry. That was cut from the film. For reasons of length? In-teresting question, isn't it? You think it's length?

MANCHEL: No.

OPHÜLS: No. In the interview with Admiral Karl Doenitz, my question about his having made an anti-Semitic speech and whether he sees any connection be-tween that anti-Semitic speech and the extermination camps has been cut from the Becker version. Do you think this is for reasons of length?

MANCHEL: No.

OPHÜLS: I'm sorry I'm using you as a patsy. I do not think that it's for reasons of length. But the most flagrant thing, when we talk about the proof of the pie be-ing in the eating, is something that I came across very late when I was waging a lawsuit against the German co-producers and against German television, because they had programmed the Becker version in contradiction to our agreements and had left my name on the film. In a way, I suppose it is flattering that they should have thought that it was in their interest to keep my name on that truncated ver-sion. So, there had been an injunction in a German law court two weeks before the thing was supposed to go on the air on German television. Meanwhile, I was seeking evidence for that lawsuit. Very late one night, my assistant Ana Carrigan stumbled across a passage in the transcript of the Becker version, and all of a sud-den she said, "Hey, Marcel, here is something on page 3." This was in the very first minutes of the Becker version. "Look at this." I then looked at something which later became known as the Telford Taylor distortion. My own film starts with the montage of the defendants of the Nuremberg Trial . . . "*Nicht Schuldig . . . Nicht Schuldig . . . Nicht Schuldig!*"—pleading *not guilty, not guilty, not guilty, not guilty*. The Becker version, interestingly enough, starts with atrocity footage from the Vietnam War. Burning of a village, hutches, napalm bombings. This is then followed by the testimony of Colonel Tony Herbert, which also is included in my film, but only in the very last reels, saying that when he first discovered the atrocities being committed in Vietnam, he thought that these were field incidents, that once he got back to Saigon, he would be able to clear them up. He then pro-ceeded to report them in Saigon and discovered that various Saigon generals were interested in the cover-up and were accomplices to these acts. Then he thought that when he got back to Washington he would be able to clear it up, and he found that once he was back in Washington, it went all the way up to West- moreland. Herbert finally had to resign from the Army. This is placed in the first 60 seconds of Lutz Becker's film, long before you ever get to see Göring, Hess, and the other defendants in Nuremberg. Before you ever see anything about the Nuremberg Trials. You see how emphasis can change things. And the third seg- ment, within the first three minutes of the film, was a statement by Telford Tay- lor. He was Chief U.S. Counsel at Nuremberg and led the follow-up trials, and he was the chief assistant to Justice Jackson at the main Nuremberg Trial. And he is made to say in the German version that was put on German television and was seen by millions of Germans—he, chief of the former prosecutors of the Nuremberg Trials—was made to say the following thing, and now I quote, liter- ally: "It would seem to suggest that American forces at Vietnam had been guilty of the same crimes and to the same degree as the Nazis that we had convicted in Nuremberg." Quote, unquote. This is the passage which Ana Carrigan, very late one night in the editing room in London, had suddenly discovered in the Becker transcript. She called me over and I looked at it. My first reaction was to say, "They must have used an actor," or "They must have used false sync. This is not possible." I mean, if you know Telford Taylor, if you have read his book, and if you know his extremely complex attitude toward his own past, toward his own involvement in Nuremberg and his anti-Vietnam stands, then you know that he could not possibly have said anything of the kind. He, incidentally, is as close as anyone to being my spokesman in the film. It sounds arrogant for me to say that, because Telford Taylor is very much more than my own spokesman; he is Telford Taylor, a great, great man. I thought: "Wait a minute, now, this is not possible." Then I said, "Well, let's look through the transcripts of his original interview," and it took us about an hour and a half to find the passage in the transcript of the original interview. I must tell you that the original interview was five or six or seven hours long, I remember. I finally found that in the earlier reels of the in- terview with Telford Taylor (those reels were where I was trying to break the ice with him) I had asked a series of questions about the paperback editions of his book, *Nuremberg and Vietnam: An American Tragedy*, because I had discovered quite by accident that the first edition, the first paperback edition, had on its cover an American flag with a swastika superimposed upon it. And that in subsequent edi- tions of the paperback that swastika had been eliminated. Only the American flag was left on the cover. And, since by the time I was doing the interview with Tay- lor, I had a pretty good idea about what Taylor's political ideas were—I said, "Telford, tell me, why is this? Why is there the swastika on the American flag in the first editions and then it disappears?" I already had a pretty good idea of what the answer would be. Then he said, "Well, I guess a lot of people objected" and so on. Then there are another two pages of transcript where I try to pin him down. He was still quibbling a little, being a lawyer, and finally, I got him into the position where he says, "Yes, well I guess I was the one who was instrumental in getting the editors to remove the swastika from the American flag." This was, of course, the one moment I was waiting for and said, "Why?" My question was "Why?" And the answer was, "Because it did seem to suggest that American forces in Vietnam had been guilty of the same crime and to the same degree as the Nazis that we condemned in Nuremberg and I don't believe that is so." Quote, unquote.

MANCHEL: This was a very fine editing job that they had done.

OPHÜLS: Isn't it though? The proof of the pie is in the eating. If ever there was any doubt about the difference in political priorities and the difference in political opinion and the difference in political assessment between my original sponsors and me, this example that I just quoted at great length seems to me to be absolute proof that by the time we came to the Ritz Bar, my suspicions were justified, because this is indeed the version that they wanted to put on German television, a version that had the chief American prosecutor making that statement, which was the absolute opposite of what he had originally said. It's like cutting the word "not" out of a statement. When I discovered that, I telephoned Telford Taylor, and I said, "Telford, I think that the time has come for you to join my injunction in a Hamburg courtroom, because your case is even clearer than mine." And he did. Now, incredibly enough, it took German television and my German co-producers another six months to remove that statement. And there even came a time when my new sponsors, the people who had got me back into control of my own film, called up Telford Taylor one night and said, "General or Professor, this guy Ophüls, he's crazy! In his own interest and the interest in getting his film out, please remove your injunction from that Hamburg courtroom. Because until you remove that injunction from the Hamburg courtroom, the German co-producers will not give way, and therefore, the film will never come out. And therefore, in the interest of the film, in the interest of our investment, please remove your injunction from that Hamburg courtroom." And Telford being the man that he is, and that I expect him to be, said, "I'm sorry, I can't give you any promises and I have to talk to Marcel about the conversation that we just had." He then picked up the phone, called me and told me about it. And I said, "Telford, please don't remove the injunction."

MANCHEL: With the lawsuits in process, you then had the film taken over by Paramount?

OPHÜLS: Yes. Paramount and Max Palevsky, who is the man I just talked about. He is and has been a friend of mine, and he quite spontaneously and quite voluntarily, when there were the articles in the American press, called me and said, "Marcel, can I help you? How much money will it take to buy these other people out so that you can finish your own film?" And life, being as ambiguous as it is, he is also the man who then called up Telford Taylor one year later to tell him that I was crazy and that he should remove his injunction.

MANCHEL: Nevertheless, the film was then released and was put on the list of many critics' best 10 films of the year in 1976.

OPHÜLS: Twelve of them.

MANCHEL: Twelve of them. And much to your surprise and many others' when the Academy Award nominations were announced, *The Memory of Justice* was not even among one of the five documentary films nominated.

OPHÜLS: We even got a headline in *Variety*. I was off in Switzerland trying to get the first chapter of my book written, and I was so foolishly confident about there being no problem about the nomination that I wasn't even in touch either with Max or with Paramount or with anybody else about it, because I thought that there might be some problems about the Oscar, but there certainly couldn't be any problems about the nomination. So I was off in a remote corner in Switzerland doing some skiing and doing some writing.

MANCHEL: Various circles have speculated about the possible reasons for your film's not being nominated and its subsequent poor distribution and trouble at the box office. You are, of course, aware of those speculations.

OPHÜLS: You bet I am, Frank. But you are now in the realm of speculation, and we must be careful about what is and is not true.

MANCHEL: Nevertheless, can you comment, agreed that we're in the area of speculation, about what it is that bothers certain people and groups about your attitude toward the Nuremberg Trials?

OPHÜLS: It is not only ironic, it is traumatic. It's the sort of thing that can land you in the booby-hatch and that has landed me in the booby-hatch. To devote four years of your life to fighting the sort of thing that I am trying to convey to you, and then find that some supercilious bastards on the pedestal of their own granite self-righteousness will attack the film for equating My Lai with Auschwitz—when I had just gone through four years of hell endangering my own future and that of my family, fighting against that idea. And, therefore, I say that these people are supercilious, self-righteous, insensitive bastards.

Now when you talk about the Academy Award nominations, I'm not talking about the Oscar. I haven't seen *Harlan County U.S.A.* [1976] and I certainly haven't any quarrel, not having seen *Off the Edge* [1976], not having seen *Hollywood on Trial* [1976], not having seen *People of the Wind* [1976], and not having seen *Volcano* [1976]. I have no quarrel at all with the idea that the majority of the Academy Award members may prefer these films that I have just named to my own film. I mean that's part of show business and that's part of the things that I have to contend with, and I am perfectly willing to play the game. But there does seem to be a discrepancy between a documentary being the only non-fiction film to be on the ten best lists of a majority of the most important American critics, of having received honorable mentions by the New York Film Critics, by the National Board of Film Critics, and not even being one of five films nominated for the Academy Awards. There does seem to be some sort of discrepancy there. And if we bother to talk about it, it has to do with the importance of the film, not only with the importance of the subject matter, but also, quite concretely with the importance that the judgment of one's, quote, "peers," unquote, has for one's own professional future. What happened? I don't know what happened. One thing is certainly detrimental to *The Memory of Justice*: the Academy, which is supposed to be the judgment of one's peers, does not have compulsory attendance to the screenings. I'm perfectly willing to have people vote by their feet at the box office. Again, this is part of the reality of show business. But I'm certainly not willing to accept the judgment of my peers, except on the basis of compulsory attendance. And certainly not when I make a four-and-a-half-hour film and am then forced to compete with one-and-a-half-hour films. I'm not willing to admit to the validity of the judgment of out-of-work actors on that basis.

MANCHEL: Let me bring you back to the issue, though, of the criticism leveled against the film.

OPHÜLS: There is a suspicion that you have, Frank, and that I may or may not share, that certain Jewish. . . . Let me start from another angle. *The Sorrow and the Pity* had what I have become accustomed to call "the Jewish Seal of Good Housekeeping." And therefore, part of the commercial American success of *The Sorrow and the Pity*, even though it was also a four-and-a-half-hour movie of "talking heads," was to a very great extent predicated on attendance in New York and other places where live a very large percentage of the Jewish community. However, I think artists have an obligation to react against what they feel are the misunderstandings on which their previous successes have been predicated. It's one of these mysterious obligations that I think we have. And therefore, I quite consciously and openly confronted certain issues in *The Memory of Justice* which I feel have to do with good conscience on false grounds. Therefore, I courted and eventually obtained the opposition of a certain segment of Jewish opinion in this country, which I would characterize as a neo-conservative segment of Jewish opinion, which one should further try to define as being middle-aged. We don't want to go too far into this point of view because it would take too much time. I understand their motives. I sympathize with some of their motives.

MANCHEL: We both do.

OPHÜLS: We both do. I feel some solidarity in this realm.

MANCHEL: Again, we both do.

OPHÜLS: I think that Auschwitz was unique. I think that the Holocaust of World War II, in its proportions, in its premeditation, in its ideology, in the fantastic support that this ideology obtained with the majority of the German people is unique. I agree with that and I agree with the solidarity with Israel, when Israel is in trouble. So I can understand how people, who in their youth had certain radical-liberal ideas, which made them sympathize with radical-liberal causes, discovered in the process of aging, what the clichés were, what the pitfalls were, what the traps were. They re-examined the causes which they had formally subscribed to and were brought, because of Israel, because of the Holocaust, to revise their positions. But having said that I understand that, I must also add that I think that using the millions of victims of the Holocaust to give you a perpetual raincheck on good conscience to take whatever political attitudes you care to choose concerning Nixon, for instance, or concerning the Vietnam War, then I cannot think of anything more indecent or more obscene for a Jew to indulge in.

MANCHEL: Now let's be clear on this so that there can be no misunderstanding. There is an attempt to put *The Memory of Justice* in the same category as Louis Malle's *Lacombe, Lucien* [1974], or Lina Wertmüller's *Seven Beauties* [1975].

OPHÜLS: Yes. Yes, because these people have chosen certain positions for their own reasons, which, I repeat, I understand: American power is what does, in fact, guarantee the survival of Israel. And therefore, I can understand that some people would come to adopt certain positions on Vietnam which I personally happen to believe that Jews, because of their experience, should not adopt when it comes to trying to assess who is the oppressor and who is the victim. But I can understand how this can come about. But to then use the monument of evil that Auschwitz and the Holocaust represent to vindicate their own [opinions] about Vietnam and about Israel, I repeat, in my opinion, is indecent and obscene, and *The Memory of Justice*, in comparison to that kind of attitude is, whatever else it may be, a decent film. I don't know if it is a good film. I don't know that it's a successful film. But I know that in comparison with that attitude, it is, on the purely humane level, a decent film.

MANCHEL: And you agree with Bruno Bettelheim and his criticism of *Seven Beauties*?[2]

OPHÜLS: Most emphatically.

MANCHEL: And you object strongly to the comparison between *Lacombe, Lucien* and *The Memory of Justice*?

OPHÜLS: Most emphatically.

MANCHEL: Now, two other points which are important to bring up. First is the question that Harold Rosenberg raises in *The New York Review of Books*,[3] when he refers to a book by Bradley F. Smith, entitled *Reaching Judgment at Nuremberg* (Basic Books, 1976). Rosenberg claims that you make a factual error. You read the Smith book after it came out. What was your analysis of the Smith book, following your review of the book?

OPHÜLS: Do you think we should go into that? To explain what Bradley Smith says . . . ?

MANCHEL: The point that Harold Rosenberg makes in his "Shadow of the Furies" is that Smith's book argues that Roosevelt and Churchill agreed on the summary execution of Nazi leaders, along with Stalin. You and the film make the statement, or the statement is made in the film, that only Stalin was responsible. Although Rosenberg admits that you didn't have access to the book at the time of your film, is it nevertheless true that your film presents inaccuracies?

OPHÜLS: Yes. I mean this is the only example of fair play that he displays in his whole article. He does say that I obviously did not have access to the book, because the book was published after the film was made. I thank him for his fairness.

MANCHEL: But since then you have read the book. Is Rosenberg right?

OPHÜLS: Let me try to explain. After having read the Rosenberg article, I couldn't read the Smith book because I was in Switzerland at that time. But as soon as I returned to Princeton, I got the book and read it. Now, here's the interesting thing as far as I can see. The statement in the film was made by Lord Hartley Shawcross, who was very much closer to sources of power at the time of the Second World War than any professional historian can be, including Bradley F. Smith, both on the basis of his position and the basis of his age. Lord Shawcross was Attorney General of the government at the end of the war and at the time of Potsdam. But the fact is that having read Mr. Smith's book, I find that there is no contradiction between the information that Smith had access to, and the statement that is made by Lord Shawcross in the film. Let me try to explain that as briefly as I can. In wartime, people, including the leaders of states, have a tendency to use the fury and the justified anger vis-à-vis the enemy in a certain way at the beginning of the war and then, as the peace draws closer and closer, that tendency will gradually be amended by various other considerations. This is one of the facts of life, of politics. And what Smith is talking about in his book which Rosenberg, fair play or no fair play, fails to mention, is in connection with the early stages of the war, the Quebec Conference between Roosevelt and Churchill. There is no contradiction, in fact, between my film and the new book whatever—these were all, of course, secret conferences. Bradley Smith, who is a very competent historian, had access to the diaries of a man called Biddle, who was a judge at Nuremberg and a very highly placed man in Roosevelt's brain trust during the war. And of course, all these were secret conferences, but the Quebec Conference between Churchill and Roosevelt, happened rather early in the war. I think 1942, if my memory serves me. And the Yalta Conference, which is what Shawcross talks about in the film, came two years later. So it is quite possible, and psychologically not at all unlikely, that by that time Churchill and Roosevelt had come to have other priorities, because the necessity of creating a just, democratic, peaceful society in the postwar world was at that time high in the order of priorities of sincere and dedicated democrats, which I believe both Churchill and

Roosevelt were in their own way. And by that time a totalitarian ideologue and, as we now know, butcher and criminal like Stalin would not have had the same positions in Yalta, that by that time I assumed Roosevelt and Churchill could have adopted. So there is really no real contradiction, and Rosenberg's ingenuous attempt to rally Churchill and Roosevelt to what he thinks should have taken place after the war, namely summary executions, is extremely disingenuous, because it has to do with Biddle's diaries about Churchill's and Roosevelt's rage and commitment and dedication in the beginning of the war, before they actually confronted the necessities and the priorities of what are we going to do with the Nazi leaders after the war.

MANCHEL: Your defense of the film against the critics might lead some people to believe that you don't admit to any errors or misjudgments in the film. In point of fact, didn't Professor Raoul Hilberg, author of *The Destruction of the European Jews* [1961] point out to you that you made a serious omission in your questioning of Albert Speer?

OPHÜLS: Yes. This was—my visit here with you—this was a very unhappy moment for me. After my lecture and during a question and answer period, a middle-aged man who was obviously not a student, whom I therefore assumed to be a professor, but who did not identify himself, pointed out in the course of his comments and his question, the existence of a correspondence between Speer and a man called Pole, who was in charge of the construction of the concentration camps and the extermination camps. In the course of that correspondence, Speer apparently pleaded for harder measures and more ruthless measures to get the concentration camp inmates to aid in the construction of their own camps.

MANCHEL: More primitive conditions.

OPHÜLS: Yes. Well, more ruthless conditions to get them to do the work. And the fact is that I was not aware of that correspondence, and that in my attempt as a movie-making amateur to do my homework and my research prior to making the film, I did not come across the correspondence, for whatever reason. And it then later turned out that the man who had made that comment during the question and answer period is Professor Raoul Hilberg, who has written a very famous book on the Holocaust called *The Destruction of the European Jews*, which I indeed had read, or at least I had thought I had read, during my research. As a matter of fact, if I hadn't read it I would have been extremely remiss, because it is an extremely important book, but I guess I didn't read it thoroughly enough. It's like students preparing for an exam. You read some books, page by page, and chapter for chapter, and some books you read one chapter or two chapters and then you put them aside and read another book, and somehow you get into a process where after having read 30 or 40 books you don't remember which ones you have read, page by page, and which ones you have glanced at, and you just take them all back to the library. And the fact is that I missed that particular thing, and this is a major sin of omission, because this is as far as I can ascertain a real down to earth objective fact. Had I been aware of that, it would have been certainly my job, as a journalist and as a filmmaker, to confront Speer in the course of the very long interview I did with him, with that particular piece of evidence and get his reaction to it. Had I done my homework properly and exhaustively, I certainly would have done that. There would have been no reason why I shouldn't have done that, and I certainly would have done that and, therefore, I feel very guilty and very responsible about this, because while there are a great number of journalists who have had and are still having access to Speer, still I am one of maybe fifty or a hundred. And in not very many years Speer will be dead and I will be dead and Professor Hilberg will be dead and then nobody will have asked Speer that question.

MANCHEL: One final question after four years of hardship and agony, and now this severe critical attack from a certain element in society—where do you go with *The Memory of Justice*? Is it over? Do you walk away from it, or "Fight on"?

OPHÜLS: My mood shifts from one moment to the other, because it's an albatross hanging around my neck. I have obligations to my own family and to myself and to my own life and also to what I have learned from my father to be the priorities of show business, to go on being creative and productive as long as I possibly can, and *The Memory of Justice* in this time of my life is preventing me from doing that. Therefore, [I] very much wish to get away from it. I don't think I can. I don't think I can.

NOTES

1. Jay Cocks, "A Battle over Justice," *Time* (May 12, 1975), 77.

2. Bruno Bettelheim, "Reflections: Surviving," *The New Yorker* (August 2, 1976), 31–36, 38–39, 42–52.

3. Harold Rosenberg, "The Shadow of the Furies," *The New York Review of Books* (January 20, 1977), 47–49. See also Ophüls's and other responses in "*The Memory of Justice*: An Exchange," *The New York Review of Books* (March 17, 1977), 43–46.

John Schlesinger

I think there's a lot of rubbish talked about the *auteur* theory.

*T*he original title of this interview was "I both hate and love what I do," and it's an appropriate way to introduce this lively conversation between Michael M. Riley and his subject, the late British director John Schlesinger, a conversation that took place in 1977, when Schlesinger, as Riley notes, "was directing Sir John Gielgud in a production of *Julius Caesar* at the National Theatre." At many points in the conversation, Schlesinger reflects on various oppositions, whether it is in the interview's original title (a tongue-in-cheek answer to one of Riley's questions, but clearly one he also puts weight in); what he calls "a kind of fantasy/reality theme" running through his work; a related tension between the narrative films he has chosen to make and his background in documentary; and the resistance that novelists sometimes put up when faced with the process of adaptation, though even here, Schlesinger qualifies his answer, saying that his own experiences with "adaptors of their own work" have been met "not unhappily on either occasion." Indeed, part of what makes this interview and so many others in this volume fascinating is that the subject here is actually considering the questions as though he is hearing them for the first time, and in a sense, he is. After all, one of Schlesinger's heroes is the photographer Henri Cartier-Bresson, someone who was interested in "the catching of life as you see it." It's that immediacy that here stands Schlesinger "in good stead" (a phrase he uses in the interview), and while readers will be interested in the anecdotes they may have heard before (including the original casting of Joe Buck, along with Schlesinger's witty commentary), they will likely be gratified that the director has taken such care with each answer, a lesson learned, perhaps from Cartier-Bresson, in the genuine care and patience Schlesinger takes to consider each question anew.

Interview by Michael M. Riley
Originally published as "'I Both Hate and Love What I Do': An Interview with John Schlesinger," Literature/Film Quarterly 6, no. 2 (April 1978): 104–15.

British film director John Schlesinger was interviewed at his London home on January 24, 1977, by Michael M. Riley of Claremont Men's College. Mr. Schlesinger's films include *A Kind of Loving* (1962), *Billy Liar* (1963), *Darling* (1965), *Far From the Madding Crowd* (1967), *Midnight Cowboy* (1969), for which he won an Academy Award, *Sunday Bloody Sunday* (1971), *The Day of the Locust* (1975), and *Marathon Man* (1976). At the time of the interview, Mr. Schlesinger was directing Sir John Gielgud in a production of *Julius Caesar* at the National Theatre.

RILEY: As a director you have often dealt with characters who are caught between their illusions about themselves or what they could make of their lives and the reality of what life is really like.

SCHLESINGER: Well, I think one of the things that I've often been attracted to is a kind of fantasy/reality theme. That, for example, is one of the things that attracted me to *Midnight Cowboy*. I liked the notion of a fantasy about what New York was like to somebody who was really naive and the reality of the experience of going there in order to be a hustler, to make it. What drew me to the book finally, though, was its humanistic terms, the underlying seriousness of the theme of loneliness, the need for some kind of commitment from another human being. I felt there was a terrific movie there.

RILEY: You've said in the past that you were interested in doing a film of *Midnight Cowboy* from the time you first read the book but that because of various obstacles some time passed before you could actually do it.

SCHLESINGER: We went through a very long process not just to get it financed but to try and get it written. I didn't feel that Jim Herlihy [author of the novel] was the man to do it. We talked to several writers about it. We talked to Gore Vidal, who laughed at us. He was charming, very funny and witty about it. He said, "It's ridiculous; it's a silly book. I've dealt with it all before in *The City and the Pillar* [Vidal's third novel, published in 1948]; let's just have a nice amiable lunch." We finally chose Jack Gelber to do the screenplay, and Jack had a couple of goes at it and fought Jerry Hellman, the producer, and myself violently over the question of making Ratso a cripple and making this coldwater flat what it was. He said it didn't exist, it was sentimental. Altogether he tended to resist the things I rather liked in the book. Anyhow, we eventually parted company, and Waldo Salt came in. I'd never met him before, but after a number of very lengthy conversations and much correspondence, we finally agreed to go ahead with it and do another draft. There were more meetings and another script that Waldo started. Then we stopped and went back to square one because by that time I was living in America and seeing all sorts of things around me that I felt would be useful to the film.

RILEY: Once you began working with Waldo Salt, what was the general direction of the development of the script? What were you trying to close in on as you revised it?

SCHLESINGER: Apart from structural questions, I suppose the thing we were closing in on was an overall style of film that showed the fantasy/reality that echoed all round. We were sharpening all the ways of dealing with it. First of all, how to make the journey work in terms of reinforcing that journey with positive things that made Joe Buck say, "Yes, it's okay. I'm doing the right thing." There was a kind of free association of his memories that he had to feel in that bus going to New York. Then when he arrives in New York, there had to be the reality of the city plus the nightmarish quality of trying to find someone and feeling closed in, hemmed in—hence that sequence in the subway. We wanted to convey the constant feeling of nightmare fantasy that anybody can feel in a city like New York that is strange to them and in a culture where you are offered so much "promise" all the time. The "promise" on television alone is extraordinary. That poodle wig-maker, for example, was a real image. I actually was sitting in California looking at a television talk show, and there came this incredible creature, this woman, and this funny man in a toupee who had this poodle. I rang up Waldo and said, "Listen, Channel Seven! Look at it now, this minute! We could use it!" And we did. Joe Buck is confronted by it, sits in the bath and sees it. The fantasy, the offer. This is the madness of it all. Even the fantasy of the drug addict with a mouse; I saw that. I use such things constantly.

That's one of the nice things about being a filmmaker. I started life as an observer in a sense. I was a still photographer, and I've always been interested in the work of somebody like Cartier-Bresson, the catching of life as you see it. I've always rather enjoyed going through an immediate experience—as opposed to an intellectual experience—observing and seeing and noting down the strangest happenings and places and using them. I've done that constantly. Sometimes successfully, sometimes they seem stuck in, and I've been criticized for it—rightly or wrongly. But sometimes they do stand one in good stead.

RILEY: I suppose that's related to your background of making documentary films. Certainly in *Midnight Cowboy* that kind of detail is important to the way the film makes one feel the presence of New York. In fact, that strikes me as one of the ways in which the film changes the novel or at least modifies it. It's true that in the novel New York is where much of the action takes place, and various things happen there that might not happen in the same way somewhere else. But in the film the city is more insistent; it seems to press in more on the story of Joe Buck. It really becomes almost a character in the film.

SCHLESINGER: Well, New York itself is of course the whole fantasy and the reality as well. The whole thing is about someone going to New York and what he thinks it can be and what the reality of it is. That reality is so strong. It's the most extraordinary city in the world. You can stand on any street corner, and something infinitely worse than you could ever imagine, or more extreme, more extraordinary, is going on just out of vision. That's what's always amazed me about New York. It's the one city in the world where I've been and seen things that leave me feeling that I cannot believe my eyes and ears. I've often said that if we put that in a film people wouldn't believe it. So New York is indeed a character in *Midnight Cowboy*; it can't help being so.

RILEY: You said that you didn't think that Herlihy was the right man to do the screenplay.

SCHLESINGER: Well, I don't often think the novelist is. Why I say that in this particular instance, I don't quite know except that a conversation with him early on before we even bought the rights to the novel made me question whether he would be flexible in terms of viewing his material in a totally different light. I've only worked twice with adaptors of their own work, not unhappily on either occasion, but by and large I think a fresh mind is sometimes a very good idea. The problem is that when one has gone through the experience of writing a novel one sometimes finds it very difficult to think of it in a totally different way, particularly when the construction is complex. And the structure of *Midnight Cowboy* presented some difficult problems. We tried it every which way. I remember that one character we kept trying to get in was that strangely menacing fellow who was after Joe Buck, the one who took him to the whorehouse. That particular scene was something that we always wanted to have in, but we never could make it work. It was in and out of the script constantly.

RILEY: Were there many changes in the script after you began production?

SCHLESINGER: Yes, there was quite a lot of that. The opening scene didn't come to us until very late in the shooting. It's not in the script; at least it's not in the working script. It wasn't written until August [1968], and we started the film the previous May.

RILEY: That's a very effective opening where you begin with a white screen and the camera pulls back to reveal that it's the screen of a drive-in movie theater in the daytime. It establishes one of the most important sources of Joe's illusions or fantasies.

SCHLESINGER: The opening was constantly being changed in the script. Those pages were written in a motel in Texas, in fact. The whole journey was continually rewritten, and that opening came finally out of desperation. It grew out of an idea of my assistant, who said, "Why don't you open with a night scene of Joe

Buck as a child playing while Sally Buck is sitting there watching television and there's a cowboy picture on the screen?" It was a big night scene, but suddenly it occurred to me that we could do the whole thing much more effectively by day with just that one simple image.

RILEY: What do you think is the most important difference between the film and the novel?

SCHLESINGER: I think the film was perhaps more ironic than the novel, which I felt might actually have been a bit sentimental in places. I don't think the film is sentimental, although some people may have found it so. The notices, if you look back at them, were by no means all raves. Some were good, of course, but we got some really quite bad notices, too. But the public response was enormous.

RILEY: When I've shown the film to students, they have very mixed feelings about the ending. How do you see that? What is that moment to Joe? Is it affirmative, or is it despairing?

SCHLESINGER: I don't see it as a despairing ending. I feel that it's a catharsis to the whole film. It's a catharsis of a boy who has been lost and who has these strange memories of being picked out for sexual prowess and how important that seemed to him. He has this whole experience of going to New York and finding that the fantasy is total bullshit and that the reality of life there is one of eking out some kind of existence, and then he finds the relationship that he strikes up with Ratso. Some people have said it's a homosexual relationship, but it really isn't per se. It's about the need of one human being for another. I daresay that Ratso—if anybody had found him attractive, man, woman, or dog—would have been anxious to express it physically perhaps. That's why he was so hostile toward it all. But I think that having made a commitment to Ratso, Joe realized the whole ludicrousness of the situation. On the bus he ruminates about the possibilities of what he's going to do, and I think in the back of his mind his taking Ratso to Miami is a kind of gesture. I think he knows it's hopeless. That's what I remember discussing with Jon Voight, that Joe knows they aren't going there for a life together in the future. He knows that Ratso's probably not going to survive the journey. At the end when he sits there with Ratso, I don't think Joe's saying, "Now what am I going to do? I'm lost." I think he's already released himself from the fantasy, he already knows that he's going to be okay.

It certainly never struck me as we were doing it that we were making something that was meant to send the audience out in deep depression feeling that Joe Buck is totally lost, because I don't think he is.

RILEY: As a matter of fact, he's saved.

SCHLESINGER: Yes, and I think he's saved by that relationship, by discovering something about the possibilities of a human relationship in the midst of this very unlikely one. That's exactly what attracted me to the material.

RILEY: Besides *Midnight Cowboy* you have made several films that were based upon novels. I find it interesting that your film *Sunday Bloody Sunday*, which isn't based upon a novel, is one of the most novelistic films I've ever seen.

SCHLESINGER: Some people do think that, perhaps because it was so literate. It was written in such a literate style. We were dealing with very civilized people in a rather controlled, contemplative way, which is why it gives that impression. It's less dramatic, or at least less obviously dramatic. And it's an internal film rather than an external film, which may give one the feeling of reading, the same kind of sense you would get from reading a novel. I think that's possible. But a film is not a novel.

RILEY: I think that's my favorite of all your films.

SCHLESINGER: Yes, it's mine too. Probably the best thing I've ever done. It's also the most personal. The story was very personal to me. I knew all those people extremely well. I gave Penelope Gilliatt the essential outline, and she reworked it totally in her own terms. Then I came in with her, and we worked a couple of years developing the script through four drafts before we had something that was shootable.

RILEY: How do you feel about the suggestion that the Glenda Jackson and Peter Finch characters are so much more interesting people. . . .

SCHLESINGER: Than the boy. I think it's my criticism of the film. In real life the boy who was the basis for the character who is at the center of it all was enchanting, funny, outrageous in many ways—in terms of selfish behavior—but a thoroughly entertaining, intelligent human being. I don't think that's what we got from either the script or the performance of Murray Head. I realized, of course, that the character in the film was by no means the same as the original boy. He was quite attractive, I suppose, but he was so extremely selfish. Some people have said that that was the strength of the film. Here were these two extraordinary people wasting time over someone who was really not worth it, but, you know, "beauty is in the eye of the beholder." I suppose you could say that it worked because of that. People do waste time over the most unlikely people whom others deem to be valueless but in whom they have found something they needed or wanted. Well, that's fine; I'll take it. If I had my life to do over again, though, I would have liked to have seen that central character much more interestingly done. I think the film would have been improved by a more vital force in the center of it. Maybe it would even have been more commercially successful, because I think some people who didn't like it—and there were those that didn't, a large public that stayed away in droves—couldn't understand the predicament. If they had found the boy interesting and entertaining, perhaps they would have understood it more.

RILEY: When I think of that last speech by Peter Finch when he turns and looks directly at the camera and reflects upon it all, it seems to me that much of what the film was saying was that whether the boy was worth it or not was almost beside the point. These two people loved him; they wanted him.

SCHLESINGER: Yes, I'm not suggesting that the character should have been some sort of superman. That would have unbalanced it. What I'm saying is that it would have been better if there had been a glimmer that he was really a quite interesting person. I remember that Penelope Gilliatt and I had endless discussions about that character. She wanted him rather like a chameleon, and I always felt that I would like someone in the center with a little more individuality but who behaved in such a way that people would say, "You're well rid of him." That was the point of the last speech: people say too easily, "Well, you know, it was never going to work out; therefore, why bother?" It's true that it wasn't going to work out, but the Peter Finch character said, in effect: you mustn't judge; sometimes the experience itself is enough; sometimes half a loaf is better than no bread. That is something I firmly believe. I think so many relationships founder because people have a kind of ideal and when things aren't ideal they are quite incapable of making the adjustment necessary to see that there are both pluses and minuses. Instead of evaluating what there are of these two, they throw the whole thing out without giving it the necessary patience and tolerance and understanding.

RILEY: We have referred to the last speech by Peter Finch. In terms of film style or conventions, it's unusual for a character to address the camera directly.

SCHLESINGER: It was not my idea; I must say that. It was in the first draft script, and although there was a lot wrong with the first draft, I realized as soon as I read it that the last speech was a superb idea. It was a marvelous idea that he should address the camera and send the audience out with an attitude, so to speak. It was also good because the audience became the doctor and he the patient. And it worked wonderfully. Although it's understated, I think it's a bold film, in a sense. I don't want to make great claims for it, but it's something that gave me a great deal of satisfaction in seeing it again, the feeling that we had all collaborated on something that was in its time a good film to have made.

RILEY: Speaking of looking back upon one's films, you once remarked in an interview with Alexander Walker [film critic for the London *Evening Standard*] that you had liked making *Darling* and were pleased with it at the time but that in retrospect you were less satisfied with it. What is it about *Darling* that does not hold up as you look back upon it?

SCHLESINGER: Well, I don't want to knock the film totally, because it was in many ways very successful. There was a lovely performance by Julie Christie and a wonderful performance by Dirk Bogarde. I thought all the performances were very good, but looking at it years later, I thought it was a film that seemed altogether too pleased with itself. I think part of that is in the dialogue, in the kind of knowingness of that clever, clever dialogue—which is a sort of hallmark of Freddie Raphael—brittle, unreal dialogue like Larry Harvey's scene with Julie on the steps of the gambling club where he comments upon everybody. I don't think people quite talk like that in such an epigrammatic way. Now it just seems to stick out like a sore thumb. It made me wince the last time I saw the film. When we were doing it, we were all sort of wild with enthusiasm about that game they played, and I think it was our idea about how the other half lives, having never really played silly games in brothels. Altogether, I think it was our fantasy, and, frankly, it rang false in time. There are moments in it, though, that don't ring false at all. There are moments that are even rather stylized which I still love—like those with the sister and brother-in-law. But I find our vision of the high life a bit suspect.

RILEY: What do you see as recurring themes in your work?

SCHLESINGER: In several of my films I've dealt with this idea of the "if only," of somebody wanting to be other than they are. You know, if he weren't a cripple, what would he do; if he were attractive, what would happen; the idea that if he were an operator, a really smart operator, he would do something else. It's the Miami fantasy in *Midnight Cowboy* or the dwarf in *The Day of the Locust*. "I want to be a big man"—hence the cockfight. That scene isn't about a cockfight at all. It's about that little man wanting to be treated as a normal-sized human being. That was the underlying theme of that scene to me, and I'm perfectly certain that's what it was in West's novel—the subtext of the scene, if you will. The subtext is something which not only interests me but which I think is essential to all drama.

RILEY: Speaking of *The Day of the Locust*, I would think there was a danger that Nathanael West's rather stylized vision might become pure caricature in a film.

SCHLESINGER: I agree. That was a problem, but I don't think it did become caricature. I labored for four years on *Day of the Locust*, trying to lick a very difficult novella into a film, but I loved making it. It almost gave me more pleasure to make than anything else I've ever done. That had a long history of being offered by a producer who had absolutely no muscle to get it off the ground; I had no muscle as a director then either. I remember reading it and thinking what a terrific story or subject. I could see the ironies even though I didn't yet know Hollywood. I thought it might make a very good film, but there seemed to be no way we could get it done. So it was shelved. I later went to Hollywood and lived there for a bit and could see the truth of the novella all around me. After the success of *Midnight Cowboy*, Warner Brothers asked me what I'd like to make, and I said, "Well, I'd like to make *The Day of the Locust*," whereupon they bought an option on it and said, "We've got it for you." I said straightaway that Waldo should do the screenplay, and we started conversations about it. Then suddenly Warners said they saw this as a twelve-week picture costing a particular amount, and I said, "I don't think that's sufficient. Let's, for God's sake, have our heads about us." But Warners got panicked and tried to dump the project, which they couldn't contractually do at the time. So the script went forward over a long period. In the meantime I grew very depressed, having just had *Hadrian VII* cancelled on me after the commercial failure of *Bloody Sunday*. I was in the doldrums for a year, and I could suddenly see *Day of the Locust* going out the window. I was in a very depressed and negative state about it. I said, "The script is no good, Waldo. The whole thing's ridiculous. Don't let's even try." By this time I was associated with another producer, and I told him that I didn't think it was going to work, that it wasn't even worth trying. He quite rightly said that I hadn't given Waldo a chance. So Waldo came over here, and very reluctantly I worked with him for a month. Yet during that month my juices started to go, and I got more and more excited about the possibilities. We produced a script that was certainly better than the first two, but it was rejected. Later I gave the script to Jerry Hellman, and he said, "I think it's terrific, but I don't think it's right yet." Finally we persuaded Paramount to get slightly interested. They gave us a stage and some money to test some actors, and we gradually amassed a package and a much better script. Paramount finally gave us the go-ahead, and we felt like a couple of right mavericks of Hollywood making this picture with everybody shaking their heads. And we loved making it. We had a ball doing it. I suppose the fact that we were in a sense winning a battle pleased us more than anything else.

RILEY: It seems to me that the film differs from the book in terms of scale. Not just in the sense that it's a small book, a novella, but it's highly compressed, whereas the film takes a larger scaled approach to the material. The picture is painted on a larger canvas, if you will.

SCHLESINGER: Well, I don't know that it is a larger scale. I think it's larger scaled only in that it's connected. There's a sense in which the novel is unconnected. For example, West could simply describe the whole business of walking through set after set until you suddenly come upon the disaster of Waterloo. Or he could describe all those secretaries dressed as sailors and everybody not seeming what they are and the houses not being what they are, and in a brief space in a wonderful piece of writing you've got Hollywood. Now, we had to do it dramatically; everything had to be led up to dramatically. That's a great deal of what gave us such terrible problems with the script. If you talk about adaptations, *Day of the Locust* was the most difficult one of all. It was really very tough trying to develop it into a story with characters of flesh and blood and a dramatic thrust to the whole thing. When I saw the first cut of the film, I knew it was going to be controversial, but I was very proud of it—and still am, incidentally. I realized that maybe the casting of Karen Black as Faye was fatal, but I felt that we had a really interesting and extraordinary film which by no means was going to be popular.

RILEY: Why did you decide to cast Karen Black rather than a younger actress?

SCHLESINGER: First of all, I think for any girl to fantasize effectively, to have that kind of affectation without seeming really rather ridiculous demands a little more experience than a seventeen-year-old would have. We auditioned endless young actresses and indeed tested some, and none of them had the kind of energy and imagination, the sheer feel for playacting that was convincing. It demands a certain amount of sophistication to be able to be that affected without seeming just merely silly and childish. It was fine for West to talk about this young girl of seventeen who was gorgeous and a nymphet who's really rather charming with her affectations, but in fact when you got a girl of that age to do it—well, all I can say is that we failed to find anybody. Maybe we should have gone with—I don't know who—Tuesday Weld perhaps. I think the problem with Karen Black is that she actually isn't physically very attractive, and I think we failed there. As a matter of fact, I worked for an entire afternoon with Raquel Welch, who did a very good series of workouts on it. We nearly went with her, but something made us say she's too good to be true. She would succeed. There's something about Karen Black, excellent actress though she is, that convinces you she wouldn't succeed.

RILEY: Why did you choose William Atherton, who was largely unknown, for the role of Tod?

SCHLESINGER: Well, I almost always go for somebody unknown on every picture I make. I thought there should be somebody to make the voyage who was an innocent virgin, so to speak, to the audience so that he could take them with him. It was like casting Jon Voight in *Midnight Cowboy*. Somehow seeing Warren Beatty fail as a hustler on Forty-Second Street would be sort of ludicrous, though he wanted to play Joe Buck.

RILEY: Earlier you were talking about the subtext of the cockfight scene. Isn't there a risk in such a scene that the visual reality will be so vivid, such a bloody thing to see, that it will throw the whole thing out of balance dramatically? In other words, the physical impact of the cockfight may simply override the subtext, which is why you want the scene to start with.

SCHLESINGER: The scene is so extraordinary in the book, but I suppose that when you actually see blood, see that little man licking blood out of an eye or suckling the beak, it is just too much for a lot of people. We had a problem of that sort in *Marathon Man*. There was a scene with Dustin Hoffman when his brother dies in his arms. We had a moment when Hoffman is kind of stunned, and it was a moment he played beautifully. But the blood was coming out on the carpet, and the audience at a preview were turning off the emotion of the scene and on to the totally different emotion of a horror of blood. So the moment had to go. But I felt the cockfight was quite justified. I am fascinated by people who are in a situation where there is a heightened tension which pushes them to do things which make people say, "Oh, my god!" Dramatically that's very interesting to me. Thus, the cockfight never seemed to me to be too much, though I know it was to a lot of people.

RILEY: When you speak of the process of making films, you often refer to "we." What do you think of the notion of the film director as *auteur*?

SCHLESINGER: I think there's a lot of rubbish talked about the *auteur* theory. If you are the sole writer, the sole author of the film in terms of being the writer and the director, yes. A director who goes through the process of fashioning a script with a writer is an author in a sense, but not the sole author. I do think it's a collaboration; however, I think it's a director's medium. I don't think a film is primarily written unless you take something like *Network* [1976], which I think is clearly a written film. I don't feel the presence of Sidney Lumet [the film's director] very strongly within it; I feel the presence all over it of Paddy Chayefsky wagging his finger very firmly. I think there is a difference. But the process of working with a writer is so extraordinarily complex. A writer may very often think of a totally visual idea which kicks off an entire way of shooting a scene, or a director may think of the content, saying we need a scene in which so-and-so happens. I've many times improvised a scene with a writer, but I would never claim that I am the sole *auteur* of a film. Absolutely not.

RILEY: What do you think of your fate at the hands of the critics?

SCHLESINGER: I've often been dismissed; I still am largely by a certain kind of critic. I think that some of them feel uncomfortable because they have never been able to put me into a nice little slot; they haven't been able to place me. But I long since ceased to lose sleep over that. They've got their job to do, and I've got mine.

RILEY: Speaking of your job, how do you feel about it? How do you feel about your career at this point?

SCHLESINGER: One thing I regret is that I've never actually made a comedy. I love to laugh, and I adore comedy. I'd like to do something that was just very funny, and I never have. I always seem to want to give people something to think about rather than something just to say wasn't that fun. It has to have something that is going to put people through a special experience. I've always chosen material that has somehow got something more, maybe because I find the process of making a film so intensely, personally involving and very difficult. It drains me, and it makes great demands. I expect it to make great demands and in a sense want it to. I both hate and love what I do; I get my knickers into a terrible twist during it. I need a lot of bolstering up, and I lose courage and confidence many times during the process of making something, panicked and nervous, but I do really love it finally.

Billy Wilder

Involve the audience in the game you're playing.

*J*ohn Allyn's short interview with Billy Wilder, one of the most celebrated classical Hollywood directors, is primarily concerned with *Double Indemnity* (1944), a film in which stylistic and thematic concerns now commonly associated with *noir* are so fully actualized, and seemingly self-consciously presented, as to belie the fact that the generic label came years after the film. The inclusion of this interview is partly inspired by the recent wave of films which may be, at least stylistically, classified as neo-*noir*: *Memento* (2000), *The Man Who Wasn't There* (2001), *Brick* (2005), and *The Black Dahlia* (2006) and *The Good German* (2006). Each of these films represents forms of psychological disturbance, social malaise, and ironic disillusionment associated with *noir* (and typified by *Double Indemnity*). *The Man Who Wasn't There* stands out for literalizing the darkly ironic shock of Wilder's original gas chamber ending for *Double Indemnity* (an ending that was shot but which has never been released). In this interview, Wilder discusses his rationale for changing the ending and emphasizes the importance of "the love story between two men" (Walter and Keyes) that is surely at the heart of the film; the fatalism of *Double Indemnity* is perhaps counterbalanced with the optimism inherent in privileging such an on-screen relationship. Here, Wilder also discusses the "fun" of working around the Production Code through emphasizing the importance of subtle suggestion (demanding active audience discernment) as well as the process of making the film: from adapting James M. Cain's novel to designing and shooting particular scenes.

We have edited John Allyn's original introduction to this interview because it mostly summarizes the plot of Wilder's well-known film in relation to its source-text. Allyn especially emphasizes the impact of the film's ending (a "washed-up" Walter dictating his murder confessions, denied a run for the border by Keyes) in relation to Cain's original ending. In Cain's text "the insurance company allows the murderers to escape, but on the boat to Mexico they feel they have been spotted and decide to jump overboard in a suicide pact reminiscent of some of the plays of Chikamatsu for the classical Japanese puppet theater" (116).

Interview by John Allyn
Originally published as "Double Indemnity: A Policy That Paid Off," Literature/Film Quarterly, 6, no. 2 (April 1978): 116–24.

My comparison of [Wilder's *Double Indemnity*] to the original novel left me impressed with the magnitude of the changes wrought by Wilder [and Raymond] Chandler, but left me with some questions about their motivations. For example, was the change in the ending made primarily to conform to the Production Code of the day? How did Billy Wilder happen to be teamed with Raymond Chandler on the script and how did they approach this assignment? What influenced the visual style of the film? And lastly, what was James M. Cain's reaction to the adaptation of his novel?

I was fortunate enough to obtain an interview with Billy Wilder, conducted in his bungalow at Universal Studio on February 25, 1976 [. . .] Our discussion was limited to the adaptation of *Double Indemnity*. Mr. Wilder answered all my questions forthrightly and with vigor (pacing a lot) and I pass along his words as added insight into the art of adaptation by one of its masters.

WILDER: I'm sure that in your research you found out that Mr. Cain, a very, very nice man, and at that time a very sought after writer, had written that enormously successful *The Postman Always Rings Twice* [1934]. And then in the wake of it he wrote *Double Indemnity* in installments for *Liberty* magazine. It was a bit of a copy, or in the same vein of *Postman*. And a producer, he's dead now, by the name of Joe Sistrom, had read the story and had brought it to the attention of the studio and to *my* attention. By the way, he was the producer, but they only wanted to give him associate producer credit and he refused it; he didn't want to take any credit at all. I said sure I would do it but for that particular picture Mr. Brackett, my usual collaborator at that time, was working on something else so I sort of took a leave of absence. I wanted Cain himself as a collaborator, but he was busy working at Fox. I think he was doing *Western Union* [1941], a picture that Fritz Lang directed. So Joe Sistrom said there is another writer who is dealing with Southern California and that was the beginning of Chandler. He brought Chandler in and Chandler and I sat down and wrote the script.

ALLYN: I'm very interested in learning what inspired the radical changes in the ending.

WILDER: If I remember correctly, the novel was very complex and also there was a slight duplication. He does all that very careful planning to have an alibi when they do away with the husband . . . Now you would have to go through a similar setup again when he establishes his second alibi. And in this way you would not have the big confrontation scene between him and Mrs. Dietrichson—Phyllis. You needed a scene between the two. Otherwise you would have had the man shot in the park from out of nowhere, we don't know by whom, and then you learn what happened later.

ALLYN: From the conversation in the hospital, which is undramatic.

WILDER: Yes, which is undramatic . . . We also shot, I would like you to know, an epilogue. Where he was being executed in the gas chamber.

ALLYN: I've heard about that. Was it actually shot?

WILDER: It was shot—I thought it was very good film. I had the warden come down from San Quentin and the doctor, and it was all done *minutely*, with the stethoscope to the glass and the bucket under the seat and the pellet. And I had a scene between him being gassed and Keyes watching him. I shot that, but then I did the narration thing into the dictaphone and I came to the very end where Keyes says, "Where are you going?," and he says, "I'm going across the border," and Keyes says, "You won't even make the elevator," and in the distance you heard the siren of the police car or ambulance and the two guys looked at each other. That was the ending. I already had the exchange of looks and striking of the match so any more would have been just repeating.

I always find, you know, in writing movies or directing movies, I find that with all the experience you gain, you don't know it but you very often tell the same thing four or five times. The audience is so far ahead of you. Nowadays even farther because their eyes and their ears have been so sharpened by all the television they see. They have become much smarter, so don't spell it out that clearly—let them add two and two together. You have to stimulate their minds and you have to make them work *with* you and once you do that, that's fine. If you make them lazy, if you just do it in the banal way, you don't *involve* the audience in the game you're playing. And if you're not smart enough to make them participate in the game that is going on, you *lose*. They don't want to sit there like animals. They would like to play the game *with* you.

ALLYN: There's always been the question in my mind as to what was your starting point when you began to adapt it.

WILDER: The idea was to write a love story between the two men and a sexual involvement with the woman, to see whether we could dramatize it—that even the most normal of men can fall prey to a sexual attraction. And, ultimately, the guy shows an element of decency by confessing so that the innocent boyfriend of Lola won't go to the gas chamber.

ALLYN: So you were accomplishing two objectives at the same time. You were making it a better story and also making Walter more acceptable.

WILDER: I hope it's better. I just wanted the audience to go with Walter, to make him a murderer all right, but with redeeming features. The Keyes relationship and ultimately the gesture of letting the innocent man off the hook. If he confesses, then it has to be motivated by him, by his sense of justice. Perhaps he'd done it, but within that murderous act there is still an element of compassion and decency.

ALLYN: Were there Production Code objections at any stage?

WILDER: Well, there was Production Code. Naturally, we could not have overt sex, so we did it kind of by innuendo. When she comes to his apartment . . .

ALLYN: Dissolves . . .

WILDER: But we had no problem with the Production Code. This was when it was more fun, you know, because we did this very subtly. We did *not* see a man choking somebody to death. We were on her face as she was driving and we knew that offstage it was happening. Sex was happening offstage. All of those nasty things. And even now I don't do them, *not* because the Code has been relaxed; I'm just not trying to use gratuitously dirty words. But it was a shocker for its time.

ALLYN: Well, then, that raises a question about style. It seems to me that your style of directing and the style of the acting were deliberately underplayed, whereas the lighting and music are highly dramatic. And *that* is what makes up *film noir*, so-called.

WILDER: Yes, I remember, those things come back to me now. The cameraman was Seitz, with whom I have made many pictures. John Seitz was the original cameraman for Valentino, to show you how far back he goes. And the film was in black and white, which is much more difficult to shoot than color. Black and white is a very difficult medium because you have to create your own values and shadings, whereas in color it's much easier. However, I told him what I would like to get on the screen—you know sometimes when the sun kind of slants through the windows of those old crappy Spanish houses, and the house is not too well kept, you see the dust in the air. And he invented a sort of an aluminum powder which we blew into the air just before we started shooting . . .

And another tiny episode that may be of some interest. The murder is committed and they put the body on the tracks and now they're waiting. I did the waiting in the car in the studio, everything else I did outside. And we were shooting just before lunch and Walter came into the scene and said "Let's go" and off they drive. And then, lunch. And I'm on my way to get into my car—I had a date with somebody. And my car wouldn't start. And suddenly I said "What is that!" and I rushed back and said "Don't touch a thing! I'm going to do it again—I'm going to do it differently!" And that's when I did that thing with the battery giving out.

ALLYN: You know what reaction I get in my classroom now to that scene? The girls say you're trying to show the superiority of the man.

WILDER: Why?

ALLYN: Because he can start it and she can't.

WILDER: No, it's got nothing to do with . . . It's just that . . .

ALLYN: In the script it explains that he pushes the starter and then . . .

WILDER: Yes, because he is a little smarter than she is, and maybe a better mechanic. But I wanted to get the element of suspense, "Oh, my god, now they're stuck . . . " In other words, since he obviously is older and has been in cars more often, he knows that you have to pump up the gas a little bit and then at the same time you have to switch it on . . .

ALLYN: Yes, there were so many fine additions that did build suspense, like the whole scene where Phyllis comes to the insurance office is not in the book at all. The whole scene where Keyes offers Walter the job as assistant claims manager is not in the original story.

WILDER: Yes, there's a lot of stuff that we actually improved.

ALLYN: Yes, I think you did.

WILDER: Then there's another thing. I don't know whether you caught my boo-boo, but I did it deliberately. I knew there was no other way out. And that is when . . .

ALLYN: The door.

WILDER: The apartment door opened the wrong way.

ALLYN: I didn't catch it, some of my students did . . . You know, the big talk now is *film noir*. I suppose you've read these articles?

WILDER: Yes, people come around, yes.

ALLYN: Naturally people making films at that time didn't say, "Let's go out and make a *film noir*." But what were the influences on you at that time?

WILDER: I don't think there were any pictures in that vein, you know, because that sort of started off with Chandler . . . But I imagine one influence was, subconsciously, *M* [1931] by Fritz Lang.

ALLYN: Offscreen murder.

WILDER: Yes, I don't know, and maybe this will sound very pompous, but possibly a kind of deep-seated influence from having read a lot of Dostoevsky when I went to school.

ALLYN: When you were working with Mr. Chandler, was your system of working with him much like you worked with the others? He was hardly a man of the theater or films.

WILDER: Yes, it was very tough with him because it was the first time he'd ever been inside a studio. He'd never worked on pictures—he had no idea what a script looked like. As a matter of fact, in a book on him he said that I was a son-of-a-bitch, but all he learned about pictures he learned from me. He was a weird man and he was then in the throes of being on the wagon. He was a very heavy drinker, but he was on the wagon then. And he was actually a very mean guy, you know, bitter and suspicious, but by god he wrote like an angel. We worked well together, except that being the first picture he ever wrote in his life he was kind of playing in Yankee Stadium . . . But . . . I was trying to use his descriptive power, you know . . .

ALLYN: Some of that was used in the dialogue.

WILDER: And in the narration, yes. But, funnily enough, I got into that rhythm and a lot of the dialogue is mine. You would say "What a Chandler line" but it was my imitation of a Chandler line. Like, for instance, "What's your name?" and she says, "Phyllis—you like it?" And he says, "Well, let me drive it around the block a couple of times." That sounds like Chandler. But it didn't matter—we worked well together.

And then I got a very high compliment. The picture was previewed at the Fox Theatre in Westwood and there standing in the lobby was Cain, and he put his arms around me and he said that this is the first time that somebody did a decent job with any of my . . . and he was very, very happy with it. You know, when Cain says that I did justice to his story, although it was changed a lot, or when somebody sends me an interview with the now deceased Agatha Christie and she says the only good picture ever made out of any of her books was *Witness for the Prosecution* [1957], those are the things that count much more for me than a review in *Esquire* or *Time* magazine. When the original author says, "Hey, that's a good job," or "that's the way I visualized it," or "you did it even better than what I had in mind when I wrote it."

Robert Wise

I think a movie should primarily grab hold of an audience, involve
an audience from very, very early on, and never let go of them.

*I*n 1978, director Robert Wise sat down with Bruce Austin to talk about his
career and filmmaking in general. Wise has a somewhat unusual vantage point for
a director in that he was successful in classical Hollywood but was also successful
in the waning years of the studio system, throughout the period we now know
as New Hollywood, and even in the early stages of what the film and entertainment industry looks like today. Wise, however, is less likely to consider the differences among these periods than he is to discuss his larger ideas about directing,
no matter what the historical context. Indeed, although he often reflects on various autobiographical anecdotes, historical moments, and technological developments, at its heart this interview is about Wise's approach to filmmaking and what
he feels is central to the cinematic experience.

Austin begins the interview by asking Wise about Val Lewton, Wise's first
producer, with Wise acknowledging that he still feels Lewton's influence, even 40
years later. After more reflection on the studio system and the relative amount of
power that directors had in that era, Wise shifts to the present, discussing the idea
of final cuts and what happens to one's films when they are screened on television. Noting his tendency to work in several genres, Wise confesses to films he
regrets making (though he only names films made "apart from Lewton at RKO,"
B-movies with titles such as *Criminal Court* [1946] and *Mystery in Mexico* [1948]).
From here, Austin asks Wise to discuss several innovations in the filmgoing experience as well as the relative importance of visual and aural aspects of cinema.
After covering historical dramatizations and location versus studio shooting, Wise
spends much of the latter part of the interview discussing various aspects of
working with actors, including improvisation, Method acting, and child actors.

Finally, Wise cites what he feels threatens the film industry before making, at the end, a plea that might strike some readers as unusual, given Wise's larger scale films: the idea of federal subsidization for the film industry as well as "grant-making for independent filmmakers."

Interview by Bruce Austin
Originally published as "An Interview with Robert Wise," Literature/Film Quarterly *6, no. 4 (October 1978): 295–313.*

Born 10 September 1914 in Winchester, Indiana, Robert Wise entered the industry in 1933 with help from his brother, David, an RKO accountant. He began as a cutting department messenger for that studio and by 1935 was an assistant cutter working on such films as George Stevens's *Alice Adams*. In 1939 he became chief editor for RKO and his credits included *The Story of Vernon and Irene Castle* (H. C. Potter, 1939), *My Favorite Wife* (Garson Kanin, 1940), *Citizen Kane* and *The Magnificent Ambersons* (Orson Welles, 1941 and '42, respectively), and *All That Money Can Buy* (William Dieterle, 1941). Wise's directorial debut occurred during the shooting of *Magnificent Ambersons* when the U.S. Government asked Welles to do a film in South America as part of the Good Neighbor Policy. Because of this fortuitous interruption, Wise had the opportunity to direct several scenes for *Ambersons*. To date, he has been honored with the Irving G. Thalberg award as well as four Academy Awards for Best Picture and Best Director (two apiece for *West Side Story* (1961) and *The Sound of Music* (1965)). A self-effacing individual who eschews anything even remotely smacking of ostentatiousness, Wise punctuates his remarks with soft table thumps and hand gestures. In March he was firming up a deal with Paramount for a science-fiction film (which at the time he was not at liberty to name) and negotiating with Columbia about a comedy-drama. A few weeks after our discussion Wise wrote me confirming that the Paramount deal had been settled. He begins shooting *Star Trek* (1979) in early August.

AUSTIN: Early in your career you worked very closely with Val Lewton at RKO. Would you expand upon this—what he meant to your career, what he did in terms of what you are today and when you began work in the industry?

WISE: Val was my first producer, a creative, marvelous man. As you know, he made a series of small, low-budget, class horror pictures in the early and mid-forties. He brought a new kind of horror film—the psychological horror film—to the screen. He was a very, very creative man. He had been a writer and had published quite a number of swash-buckler adventure stories before he was 20. He was a reporter on the New York *World*. Then he became a story editor for [David O.] Selznick and from that position he was hired to come to RKO to become a producer of these lower budget films. He was a highly educated, well-read man. He always contributed very much to his films. He drew on the old masters, painters, for character types, costumes, and sets. He worked on scripts with writers very often. He did much of the writing—final writing—on scripts, although he never took any credit until, I think, *The Body Snatcher* [1945], when they made him take the credit. So he took a pen name. He was very involved with the look of the picture, with the way the sets came off, the costumes, the casting, the whole thing. Yet he was so supportive of the director. He never, in any sense, tried to take over from the director or second-guess him. He was a real gentleman and was nothing but supportive to all of us who were then starting as directors—Mark Robson, Jacques Tourneur, and others. He always acted as kind of the buffer between the front office and the directors on the stage. We were making these films in 16, 18, 19 days and had to move fast. Occasionally, we would get a little behind schedule and they would put the heat on Val. Val would come down to the stage and say, "Well, they told me to tell you to pick it up. Now I've told you, go ahead and make your picture." He'd give you a pat on the back and away you'd go. He was one of those who, in a sense, was the star of his own pictures, and got to be that because the series of these quite marvelously done small films were so much his. He created a special niche for himself in the business and was recognized nationally by some of the major magazines.

AUSTIN: Is his touch upon you still felt?

WISE: I don't know. I suppose sometimes, particularly when I do things like *The Haunting* (1963), which was rather a return for me to the days of the Lewton pictures and some of his concepts. He always said the greatest fear is the fear of the unknown, that that's what frightens people more than anything else, and I kept remembering that when I did his kind of film. And, I suppose, certain approaches to camerawork, lighting, that kind of thing. I can't think of any specific thing that hangs on from him.

AUSTIN: You explained to me earlier that you had started college [Franklin College in Indiana, about 18 miles south of Indianapolis] but had to drop out and then you came out to Hollywood.

WISE: A Depression college dropout, yes.

AUSTIN: And I recall reading that you were given your first opportunity to direct when Gunther Fritsch was drafted into the Army. Was this how you broke into directing?

WISE: Well, that isn't quite what happened. I was cutting the picture [*The Curse of the Cat People*, 1944] and it was Gunther's first feature film as director. Gunther had made a number of documentaries that had caught Lewton's eye. He was assigned to direct this film, which I was editing. Gunther was a lovely guy and doing a good job but very, very slowly. He couldn't seem to pick his pace up. Really, what finally happened was that he got so far behind and they couldn't seem to make him go faster—these were limited budget films. They finally just had to take him off. They told me on a Saturday noon they wanted me to direct Monday morning. I showed some reluctance to do this because it was awkward. I was working with the man. As a matter of fact, I was scheduled to go back that Saturday night to work with Gunther on the set, and I felt awkward about going back knowing that I was going to be taking over for him on Monday. I expressed this reluctance to Lewton and Sid Rogell, who was executive producer of the RKO B-picture unit. They said, "Listen, somebody else is going to be on that stage directing Monday. Now it could be you or it could be Joe Blow, but it's not going to be Gunther. What do you want to do?" And since I had been at them to give me the chance to direct, I had to take it. [This was in September 1943.]

I had done a little directing: second units on two or three films that I was the editor on. I had made new scenes, added scenes after previews on a couple of films. I did some scenes for *Fallen Sparrow* [1942, directed by Richard Wallace] that I had edited, and some for *Magnificent Ambersons*. So I had a taste of it. When this chance came along and when they explained the circumstances to me, I obviously had to go ahead and do it.

AUSTIN: When you began in the picture industry, the studio system was still in force.

WISE: Very much.

AUSTIN: At the time of the studio system there were a number of constraints placed upon directors. What about now? Within what parameters do you have to work?

WISE: It's far different now. Of course when one has been in the business, as I have, directing now for 35 years this fall, my position is different. When I started, and for the average director—I'm not talking about the guys who were top names like Ford or Wyler—you had restrictions. You had much more supervision from the front office and much more input and orders from the front office about the final cut of the picture, how it should look, what should be done—or attempts at that anyway. Now, at least for someone in my position, there's much less of that, much less interference.

Some of us, not too many, have in our contracts that we have final editing rights, both for theatrical release and television. TV is very important because they do butcher our films on commercial television. We have far less interference and control from the front office, the studios, the money people. Usually what they want to have is, first, approval of the script. Obviously, if they're going to put X millions in on the project, they want to be able to say, "Yeah, we want to go with this script." The budget has to be within certain parameters, and they demand consultation and approval of the casting of maybe the first two or three major roles.

Once you get these all agreed on, from there on it's pretty much your own ball-game.

Another thing, very often they'll want to have some kind of limitations on the length. In other words, they don't want you to deliver to them a picture that's two hours and forty-five minutes. But it's much better for the individual film-maker to have his creative controls and do his own thing without undue outside interference or controls.

AUSTIN: What are some complaints you have about working in and with the industry today?

WISE: I don't have any undue complaints today as compared to years ago because I have so many of the creative controls I didn't have before. One of the complaints I would have, and I can understand why it has developed, is that there seems to be less range of types of stories we can do now as compared to the old days. These are the realities of the business. The competition of television and the feeling of needing to give the audience something on the movie screen—something they can't get on the TV set—starts to limit the range of material we can do in films. Any number of times I'll have a script come through, or a property, that some-body brings to my attention, and, I'll read it, like it, and think it will make a good film, but know that it belongs on television. I feel I won't be able to go out and sell it to any company as a feature film because they will say it doesn't have enough of the ingredients—or hoped-for surefire ingredients—to bring in people in suf-ficient numbers to pay the film off. This happens all the time. So that would be my biggest complaint. I think it's something I can't blame the companies for com-pletely because they're looking to ensure that they get enough money back to keep in business. If the indications are that certain kinds of smaller, quieter, more per-sonal films are not going to do business, they are going to go the other way. Now there's a break in that because we've had some smaller films that have done really good business this last year—not *Star Wars* [1977] business—but certainly damn good commercial business and I think that's a hopeful sign. Maybe there will be a breakthrough and we'll be able to get into more things.

AUSTIN: You have final cut rights on your films. Would you expand on that and what you spoke of regarding television "butchering" pictures?

WISE: I have had final cut ever since *Andromeda Strain* [1971] and on all of them since. I'm talking to another studio about a picture now and they know I'm af-ter final cut. We haven't resolved any differences we might have on it. I think it's very important that, if possible, the guy who directs the film should have the right to have his version shown. This is one of the common complaints that directors have in the business. I know a lot about this because I was president of the Di-rector's Guild from '70 to '74, and I know the things that hurt. One of them is when a studio or a producer will take over a film from a director and change it—change it completely, change the continuity, recut it, and turn it all inside-out until the director says, "This is not my work. This does not represent what I did." We feel this is a danger because a man is valued by the work he's done. And if his work, in his estimation, is bastardized by something out of his control, then it's not fair to him—it's not a fair representation of his work. Often you wind up in lawsuits.

Another complaint, the even stronger complaint from the directors, is about what happens to their films when they go on television. Not only just the commercial interruptions and the number of them, but cutting to fit a time slot. Cutting down, chopping down. I decided to make a stand on that and when Universal came to me with *Andromeda Strain,* I liked it very much, but I had my agent make a condition that I had not only final cut for the theatrical but for television as well. Except for having to make cuts for broadcast standard, which I had to give them, they could not cut or change or do anything with my film without my okay.

AUSTIN: So it was your okay as opposed to you going in there and actually re-cutting it for them.

WISE: Right. They can't cut it down, can't do anything to it without my okay. All they can do is put in the commercials. I tried to make my editing control, my editing rights on TV, extend to *where* the commercials were going to go and *how many* there were going to be. But I just couldn't lick that. I would have had to take it to court. They claimed that that was not part of my rights clause, so I finally gave in on that. I did have a meeting with them about where they would place the commercials and I think I suggested a couple of better places for them to put the spots than where they were planning. But other than that they couldn't alter it, except for putting in the commercials, without an okay from me. Now of course there's a limit to that, Bruce. That's only valid. I can only really police it when the picture's on networks. Once it goes out in syndication, I have no way of policing it. So we do the best we can.

AUSTIN: To what extent do you see the artistic integrity of a film destroyed when televised? What particularly irks you about a film of yours, let's say, broadcast on TV?

WISE: The thing that I dislike most is that theatrical films are not built to have all those commercials cut in. I realize TV is a reality of our lives, though, and we have to face it. We're going to get bigger screens, projection television on the wall, the five-by-seven or seven-by-nine format, and cable and I'll have to settle for that. To the studios and the people who put the money up for films, television sales are very important. But speaking just artistically, obviously it's terrible to have those commercials put in there every few minutes that stop the whole show. That's why cable television is much preferable because at least you get to see the film without those commercials. You don't have the film cut and changed; you don't have the interruptions. It's the way the filmmaker made it and that's the way it ought to go up there. Another thing is what I just mentioned a moment ago about brutally cutting the picture to fit into a time slot. To commercial TV it's just so much product; they brutally cut, do away with scenes and continuity and feeling altogether. Of course basically I think *any* of us would rather see our films up on the big screen of the theater. That's what they're really meant for. That's where you get the full satisfaction from them.

AUSTIN: What about the concept of resolution? Television is a low-resolution medium whereas film—in the theater, up on the screen—is a high-resolution medium. How does that affect or destroy, if at all, the televised film?

WISE: The film's not as effective visually or aurally. It doesn't come off either way—visually or aurally—to its maximum, by any means, on television. But this is the way it is and we have to accept it. We have only to hope that there will be more advances which will come in the improvement of the resolution. I'm sure the sound will get better—that stereo sound will develop. There will be more and more cable television so that eventually we'll have fewer films in theaters but always, I hope, theaters will be around for the best films that come along.

AUSTIN: So you view television as something that must reluctantly be accepted.

WISE: I'm afraid so, yes. *Maybe* it's possible to make pictures these days with a stipulation that they are not to go on television. I think it would be hard to find the money people to go along with that. Someone like Gadge Kazan, for instance, has accomplished this. For several years now he has actually owned *Baby Doll* [1956]; it's his negative. The networks have been after him to show it, but they want to cut it. He could get a million dollars for it but he won't let them cut it. More power to him.

AUSTIN: You've made films in quite a few genres. Do you like to work on a particular one?

WISE: I don't really. I would put it in another context. There are a couple of genres that I would not do again, haven't done in years, and never read scripts that are related to that genre. One is westerns. I haven't made a western since '55. I think the scene's been overdone. There have been so many hundreds of them—thousands of them—made over the years. I just don't particularly enjoy doing westerns. The other genre is spectacle. My only venture into that was *Helen of Troy* [1956] years ago for Warner Brothers. It turned out not too badly for what it was intended, but it was a genre I found I did not particularly enjoy once I got into making it. Rather than say what my favorite is, I'd have to say my unfavorite are those two. Beyond that, any genre that comes along that happens to strike me as a good project I'll go for. I don't think I like musicals any more than supernatural or science fiction or comedy.

AUSTIN: Artistically, which of all the films you've made is a personal favorite?

WISE: I've been asked many times what my favorite film is and I've had to say each time that I didn't have one favorite—maybe six or eight. But when you put it "artistically," I suppose *West Side Story*: what its challenges were, what it took to do it in the artistic sense.

AUSTIN: Are there any films you regret making?

WISE: Oh, I think so. Those particularly that you have hopes for that don't come off, especially those that don't pay back their costs to the studios. I think you regret that as much for the money that was lost as your own personal reasons. In another context, there are films that I made when I was under contract that I wasn't completely enthusiastic about doing. Some were the B pictures that I made apart from Lewton at RKO: *Criminal Court,* which was kind of nothing, and *Mystery in Mexico.* Any of us that have been under contract to the studios have made films sort of half-reluctantly.

AUSTIN: What is the Filmmakers Group?

WISE: The Filmmakers Group *was*, because it's not in existence—or we're not working through it anymore, a producing company. Mark Robson, who's an old friend from back in the editing days, and I formed a company with Bernard Donnenfeld. Bernie had been an executive at Paramount for a number of years. He left Paramount, and Mark and I had been talking about forming an independent company. We had both met him [Donnenfeld] when we had been on the negotiating committee for the Director's Guild and we liked him very much. When we saw that Bernie was leaving Paramount, we immediately contacted him to see if he would be interested in joining up as the third partner—to be our executive, our operating officer. We formed the Filmmakers Group with the hope, at that time, of maybe attracting another director or two to join us. But we never really got it rolling enough to make the concept that attractive to anyone else. We formed it hoping that we could get together some independent financing for our films and not have to be tied to the studios. But that turned out to be more of a dream. We got money, but the people with the money wanted so much of a piece of the company that we felt we were better off going back to the studios to make our deals with them. Under that company Mark made *Happy Birthday, Wanda June* [1971] and I made *Two People* [1973]. Then he made *Earthquake* [1974] and I made *Hindenburg* [1975]. Of course the one big winner out of it was *Earthquake*.

AUSTIN: Since you began your career as a sound editor, would you consider the verbal and the visual as equal partners in a film or does, or perhaps *should*, one outweigh the other?

WISE: I suppose that coming up through editing as I did, using and knowing sound, music and background values, I consider them fairly equal in importance. However, I have to keep reminding myself, and I think everyone should remember, that it is a visual medium and if there is a leaning a little bit to one side rather than the other, it would be to the visual rather than the sound. I think impressions are more readily made and have more impact visually. What you strive for is the exactly right combination of the two.

AUSTIN: How then do you perceive innovations such as Sens-Surround?

WISE: Well, I think that's interesting but that it's kind of a stunt. I thought it was effective for what it was. I don't think anything should take away from what you put up there on the screen in the way of your drama. Now there's talk of new sound systems that are going to put the sound all over the theater, and clear out in the middle of it, and this and that. I think all those are interesting and can be effective. However, I have a concern that maybe they will overpower, take away from, what an audience needs, which is full concentration on the screen and what's coming off that screen. I remember when they were playing around with 3-D pictures years ago, some of them had the sound whiz by you and go all over the theater. I found myself looking away from the screen and trying to follow where it was coming from. And that was very detrimental, basically, to the drama on the screen. All these sound innovations, improvements, and advancements, which I'm sure are going to be effective and are certainly worthwhile, I think they have to be very carefully used as they relate to the story you're telling and the drama you want. The paramount challenge of the director in making his film is to hook the audience with what he's putting up on that screen, and hook them as early as possible and keep them hooked all the way through the film. I just would hope that the sound developments would not be so innovative and become so much of a character themselves that they detract from the concentration of the audience on the story and those actors up there.

AUSTIN: What other sorts of "hooks" do you see? We talked about sound, how about plot and narrative structure?

WISE: Well, yes, I'm thinking of that even more than sound in terms of hooking the audience. I think the way you open your film, the effectiveness of the visuals you open with, wherever you are in the plot, and what you're doing with your characters—all these should make it as interesting, intriguing, and captivating for an audience as possible, both visually and aurally.

AUSTIN: What is your criteria for a "good" movie?

WISE: I think a movie should primarily grab hold of an audience, involve an audience from very, very early on, and never let go of them. The really good movie is one that totally involves an audience from beginning to end so that they forget where they are. I don't think there's necessarily a contradiction between a good movie artistically and a good movie commercially. Hopefully, the artistically successful movie will also be a movie that involves the audience. That's the combination, to me, that's the best because I think that's what we're into. I am very much a believer in not catering to the audience, not to say, "Hey, what do they want? Let's give it to them," like television does so much, but you must consider the audience very, very much when you're making the story you want to make and realize that it is being made not just for your own subjective, personal taste but for millions of people out there. It seems to me the more appeal the movie has to the great mass of people, without sacrificing artistic quality, the more effect your theme will have. If you make it so personal, so to yourself, so special that very few people go to see it, then you really haven't punched over what you have to say. The potency of the theme of your film is only as good as the number of people who see it.

AUSTIN: Richard Lester has said of the director's role that it "is to be an absolute dictator and produce a personal vision on a subject that he has chosen. He must be absolutely ruthless in producing an accurate vision." Would you care to comment on this?

WISE: I'm not sure if I know quite what he means by "ruthless." That's a word I don't like to hear or use too much. I think his idea, his thought, of that personal vision is a very good one. However, I would think that my version would be that one should be absolutely *dedicated* to getting that vision but not so ruthless as to the exclusion of everybody else contributing ideas and thoughts and creativeness to that vision. If you receive suggestions and ideas from others, I don't think it's any less personal. Now maybe that's not what he meant by "ruthless," that you would cut out anyone else's ideas. I wouldn't quite see it that way.

AUSTIN: So then you're fairly open to suggestions while in production?

WISE: Yeah, I'm open! Maybe a lot of times I don't accept what people suggest, but I think you very often deny yourself a lot by not listening to others. I elicit contributions from actors. Actors bring the scene to life, and very often they will find clinkers in dialogue, or come up with a marvelous idea of how to revamp it a little bit and change it, make it better, make it truer. I usually accept those ideas. Now sometimes they will come up with poor ideas, and you'll say, "Thanks a lot but no thanks, let's just do it the way it is."

For instance, when I was working with Orson Welles, people would say, "How do you work with him? He is such an autonomous kind of big-ego fellow." I said, "Well, I haven't had any problems with him." And I didn't. Orson would always listen to my suggestions—he might not have taken nine out of ten of them—but I never felt I could not make a suggestion to him. Sometimes he'd take them and improve on them. I think most directors, or at least most directors I know, are receptive to ideas on the set from other people. Occasionally you get somebody on the set who becomes a pest; he just wants to come in, come in, come in constantly. You have to turn people like that off because it gets to be trying to be nagged.

AUSTIN: Could you describe your style of filmmaking, perhaps as distinguished from other directors? How do you approach a motion picture?

WISE: That's awfully hard, it seems to me, for the individual director to do, Bruce. Especially since you don't know how the other fellows approach their work.

I could speak to one basic thing—improvisation. There are marvelously fine, talented directors—more Europeans than Americans, but Altman comes to mind—who like to have things not too set, who like to wing their scenes, maybe not have the scenes fully written out, have the actors improvise their dialogue. They feel, I guess, that this makes for a greater sense of credibility, reality, spontaneity. I admire that but it's not the way I could work. I'm from the other school which is one that believes very strongly in a tremendous amount of preproduction preparation and planning, both as to the script and the physical aspects of the film—getting everything set and as planned, organized, coordinated, and anticipated as possible. I storyboard, generally, all of my film so I know where I'm going and where I *want* to go, not the way I end up every time, but where I want to go at the start at least. I go in on the set with all this done which, I feel, makes it easier. The set is less tense and it gives me more time to work with the actors; to get better performances and better scenes on the screen for everybody. Now this doesn't mean that I'm so hard and fast that if I've got a sequence sketched a certain way, and it doesn't want to go that way when I get the actors and cameraman on the set that I can't break away—I don't stay married to the sketches.

On *Audrey Rose* [1977] we had one scene, a big argument scene between John Beck and Marsha Mason, which we had rehearsed, but when it came to filming that scene, it somehow didn't feel right. Frank [DeFelitta, the scriptwriter and co-producer] said, "Why don't we let John and Marsha just go at it. They're aware of where we are in the story and they know the characters." They did and really got at each other. We had a tape recorder there, and Frank went back to work and took dialogue out of that. We shaped it a bit, and the scene in the film is based on their improvisation. It's a much better scene than was in the script—one of the strongest in the picture. I like to give the actors their head once we've agreed early on about the character they're playing, the story, the plot, the whole body of the film. Mine is a *prepared* approach with ample room for improvising as we go along.

AUSTIN: *The Hindenburg* was a dramatization of an historical event. With *Audrey Rose*, the popular literature is chock-full of how-to and "cook" books on reincarnation and related occult themes. Regarding research then, how much of that do you do for your films?

WISE: I get very deeply involved in it on all of my films. As a matter of fact, this is one of the things that I always say is so much fun. One of the special pleasures about making and directing films is that it's a learning experience. Every time you go onto a new project, or practically every time, you are into a new subject matter and you learn so much about whatever the subject is. *The Hindenburg* you mentioned. I'm probably one of the world's great authorities on lighter-than-air ships now because of all the research I did. I went through the Smithsonian in Washington and the National Archives for stills. I read books; I flew to Germany with my art director [Ed Carfagno] and went to various archives there looking for stills and written material. I went to the big museum in Munich, flew down to Frederikshoffen where the Hindenburg was built and where they have a small lighter-than-air museum. We picked up material wherever we could. We had to build the Hindenburg from bits and pieces, here and there, because all her blue-prints had been lost or destroyed in the war.

On *Audrey Rose*, what I did there, more than anything else, was simply to read a number of the books that had been written about psychic experiences and people going into hypnotic regression and this kind of thing. I even went to a mass hypnotic regression session one day outside of Santa Monica which I didn't find very impressive.

Andromeda Strain was an exciting experience of getting into the science world of today. I got in touch with the Jet Propulsion Lab in Pasadena, and they contacted some scientists from different departments there, and I ended up with four of them who became my team of technical advisors. That way I got into the lab, got exposed to the world of computers as it was then—this was 1970—and all the technology they had. Also, all the equipment we used on the set was real (like those mechanical hands that the fellows worked with). It was a fascinating, marvelous learning experience.

AUSTIN: Interestingly, you mentioned earlier the notion of the editor who becomes a director and who, because of this, tries to be more frugal when shooting—and that this isn't always the case. Some directors maintain that they mentally see their film—have a vision if you will—*prior* to the actual filming itself. Still others hold that their film is discovered in the editing room, that they've found nuances that perhaps went by unnoticed while on the set which they could now plug into and enhance the film. Without necessarily limiting yourself to either of these two pots, where do you see yourself?

WISE: I would say I'd place myself in the first pot primarily although you will, sometimes, find little looks, little qualities, in the film that you've overlooked. I would assign myself pretty much to the first category—not too many surprises.

AUSTIN: You would attribute this to your meticulous preplanning?

WISE: I would say to a certain extent, yeah. Also, I have a very good memory for film. I wonder if it goes back to my days as an editor.

AUSTIN: Do you have a partiality for film format, in other words, Cinemascope versus the three by four ratio?

WISE: No, I really don't. I think, like most directors who worked for a number of years on the old three by four, before they came in with Cinemascope, Pana-vision, and the wide screen, we had difficulty with the new format and rather re-sented it. But I think we've come to use it and know how to use it pretty well over the years. What I try to do is study each project and see which format I think is best for a given project. For instance, *The Hindenburg* was almost built-in for wide screen because of the shape of the dirigible itself. On the other hand, when

I did *Audrey Rose*, a more personal story, I wanted a smaller screen. I think it depends on your project.

AUSTIN: When you get into the film, once you begin shooting, do you have a preference for location versus studio shooting?

WISE: What I try to do, and the rest of us too, is go in the direction that's the very best for a given project. Some directors prefer location shooting. I, and maybe a majority of fellow directors, in a sense prefer studio shooting only because you have things under control. When you're on location you're always at the mercy of the uncontrollable or unpredictable. And most of us have been clobbered badly by weather and conditions we had no control over.

Weather is your biggest problem when you're on location. And weather could be any kind of thing: rain, wind, tides, any of the physical elements can screw you up. When I did *The Sand Pebbles* [1966] in Taiwan, our main set was about 20 miles out of town in a little fishing village. We used to go out, sometimes with six or seven different calls depending upon whether the sun was out, or it was cloudy, or if it was raining, which *direction* the wind was coming from. Because if the wind was coming from one direction, we'd shoot a certain set of scenes; if it was coming from another, we'd shoot the other set of scenes. Also, whether the tide was in or out was important because if the tide was out, my boat was sitting on her flat bottom in the middle of a sandbar that was supposed to be the river. I used to literally go to location in the morning not knowing if I could start with call sheet number one or if at 10:00 the weather might have changed around and we'd have to shift into other scenes, change wardrobe, get new actors. It kept us jumping and hopping and twisting endlessly.

So it's always with a sense of relief for most of us to get the location work done and get back inside the studio where you can really control things. You go on location when it's right and the only way. *Andromeda Strain*, for instance, I knew I'd have to get out to location for that little town in the opening of the film. But I also knew the big part of the story, in the underground facility, would have to be done in a big studio stage. *Two People*, which I did with Lindsay Wagner in Morocco and Paris, was all shot on actual, real location; I didn't shoot a foot in the studio because the picture seemed to call for that kind of documentary treatment.

AUSTIN: During the nose cone fire sequence in *The Hindenburg* you used, I believe I've read, twelve cameras to shoot that particular scene. Do you use multiple cameras often?

WISE: In some action scenes or dance numbers I've done it. In *West Side Story* I occasionally used three—usually two. The reason I used twelve for *The Hindenburg* was that it was a one-shot thing. Once we set it off [the fire], boom, that was it. We felt we had to place a camera at every conceivable place we could to get the best coverage. We put in as many cameras as we could beg, borrow, and steal.

Most of them were working on remote. A couple of them were old, not very valuable IMOs that we just put in the middle of the cone so if we lost them we didn't lose much. I don't think we lost any of them, though. But I don't use two or three cameras as a regular thing—it eats up a lot of film for one and causes lighting problems.

AUSTIN: How closely do you attend to previews of your pictures?

WISE: Very closely. I'm very keen on both kinds of reactions. We usually have preview cards for people to write their comments on and check how they liked the film, the scenes they liked best, and the scenes they disliked. But I don't think any of us give a major consideration to those in terms of what we do. Most of what we end up doing in terms of changing the film after the sneak preview is what we sense and feel from the audience as to how it played. However, if the cards come in and a great number of cards single out a particular thing, we might take a double look at that to see what's causing so many people to become annoyed or bothered or confused about something. I think our major reaction, though, is simply how the film plays: whether it holds the audience or if the people are restless—if they're going out to go to the bathroom, get candy. For some reason, somebody talked me into not taking along preview cards on *The Hindenburg* and I thought, "Oh, fine." But I missed them. I missed having the cards that sort of pinpoint problems for us.

AUSTIN: How did you go about learning to work with actors?

WISE: Coming into directing as I did, suddenly in the middle of a picture, I had to learn it on the job. I had never done any acting myself. When I was involved in school and college plays, I was always the behind-the-scenes guy. Of course, I watched other directors as they worked with actors. I spent plenty of time on the sets visiting. Also Garson Kanin had come out to Hollywood and begun directing. I stood by with him on the set when he did *My Favorite Wife* [1940]. But I had to feel my way when I was working on *Curse of the Cat People* (and my next picture) on how to approach actors, how to get to them, how to get the best out of them.

AUSTIN: How *do* you go about getting the best out of an actor?

WISE: I first start with a meeting of the minds—an understanding—with the actor about his character, the role he's playing, and how, basically, this character fits into the whole story to be sure we're not seeing it differently in any way. Once I get on the stage and we start to rehearse and I give them the general thrust of the character, I let them go with the scene. I work with them on changes, variations and adaptations. Gradually, between us, we build the scene. I don't come in and lay down a lot of restrictions on the actors when we go into a scene. I try to find out what they can bring to it. If you come down too hard on the actors you're inhibiting them. You're not finding out what they can generate and bring to the scene unless you give them a free hand.

AUSTIN: How much rehearsal time do you spend before filming begins?

WISE: I like to have a period of rehearsal before we start shooting. On *Audrey Rose* we had a week. If it's possible I'd like to have a couple of weeks for rehearsal. But on many pictures you can't do it because of the logistics. Once you start an actor in rehearsal he's on salary. Now, if he doesn't appear until the middle of the picture, you're paying him several weeks for nothing. When you don't have rehearsal time before you shoot, then you simply have to take it day by day, scene by scene, and use whatever time it takes to rehearse the sequence you're going to do. Sometimes it goes fast—might take a half an hour or so—other times you might spend all morning on a scene before you start to light and shoot.

AUSTIN: Is there a style of acting you find difficult to work with? For instance, some directors will say Method actors cause them to gnash their teeth and wring their hands.

WISE: No, I've never had any problem with the Method actors I've worked with.

AUSTIN: Is it more laborious in terms of explaining motivation and so forth?

WISE: Yes, sometimes they want to talk it to death, to find out the motivation behind the motivation and all levels and depths behind the characters. Sometimes, there is a tendency to want to analyze, I think, overly. There is one particular star whom I've done a couple of films with and like and respect very much. I found that if he got an idea in his head about something in the scene—either an attitude or an action or a line—if I talked him out of it the idea would just keep bugging him. So I found it was simpler in the long run just to let him try it, whatever it was. I might not have thought it was right, but I'd tell him, "Go ahead, try and see." He would, and very often, maybe three out of four times, it wouldn't be right and he'd forget it and go ahead and do the scene. But at least it was out of his craw. Of course, sometimes what he'd try was good and we'd use it. But other than maybe over-analyzing the character and digging a little too much, I don't find Method actors a problem.

AUSTIN: In quite a number of your pictures you've had children playing a leading role. As far back as your first film, *The Curse of the Cat People*, there was seven-year-old Ann Carter; in *The Sound of Music* you had several children. . . .

WISE: A lot of children.

AUSTIN: And most recently Susan Swift, an eleven year old, played the title character in *Audrey Rose*. What's your method for dealing with and directing child actors as opposed to adults?

WISE: I have always had a good, easy relationship with children. I work on their level. I try to put things easily and simply and don't come on with any big director bit. I try to approach them just as directly, as easily, and as off-handedly as I possibly can. I don't try to make any big thing out of it. The main key to working with kids is to establish a rapport with them as quickly and as early as you can. I try to gain their confidence and lessen their nervousness, queasiness, or anything they might have. I try to make things as simpatico as possible and to have a lot of fun.

AUSTIN: Are there any special problems involved with working with children?

WISE: Yes, limited time. Here in California, depending upon the age, some can only work three hours a day. The rest of the time they have to go to school. You have to plan your shooting very carefully because at a certain time you're going to lose them for a while, and you have to have another scene you can go into. For instance, with *The Sound of Music*, I had to take a teacher from here to Austria—to Salzburg—so those kids could go to school over there the same as here. Because it was a California-based company, the state insisted that their rules would apply. This gives you a budgeting and scheduling problem on the film. Also, it breaks the continuity. Maybe you're going along well with your scene with a kid, and suddenly you realize that they haven't had their three hours [of tutoring] in by four o'clock. So right in the middle of things they have to be taken away from you. It's always a bothersome problem. Another problem with kids is to keep them concentrated without making it *too* heavy on them. I remember one time, speaking of the kids on *The Sound of Music*, they got a little rambunctious and they weren't paying attention enough. They were a nice bunch of kids, and fortunately got along very well, but they were over there in a foreign country and on their days off they were doing sightseeing, experiencing new things, and so forth. So I was having to really bring them in line. Finally I had to go to the parents and call a caucus (there had to be a parent or guardian over there for each one). I told them, "Look, you've got to talk to the kids and tell them that we're aware they're not paying attention and that they'll have to get on the ball and stop horsing around when we're working. I don't care what they do away from the set." And I talked to the kids, too. I said, "You'll have to toe the mark better because you're not doing the job."

AUSTIN: In a recent interview, when asked about directing kids again, François Truffaut exclaimed, "No more films about children!" Have you reached that point?

WISE: No. Of course, he's done a lot of films with kids—more than I have. With *Small Change* [1976], though, I can understand that after a siege where you have nonpro's—little, little kids—it can drive you right out of your mind. I would say that for myself it depends upon the story—the property. If it has something with a child in it and it's right, and it's something I want to do, that would be fine.

AUSTIN: Joan Darling is an accomplished actress, director (*First Love* [1977]), and has worked with Norman Lear. What was her function on *Audrey Rose*?

WISE: To work with Susan Swift. I always felt, even before the part was cast, that because of the importance of such a pivotal role in which you had to believe so strongly that this little girl was really going through what she was experiencing, I needed somebody special to work with this little girl—whoever it was and no matter how much professional background she'd had. I wanted someone to help turn the key and get this girl to understand, to get her responses up and get her as positive as possible. I felt all of this even before I had made any tests—that I would be helped by a coach. And I always felt it should be a woman. It seemed to me that a woman would be able to make a better contact with the little girl in the areas that we needed. I tested four girls: Susan from Houston, a little girl from New York [Brooke Shields], one from San Francisco's ACT Theatre, and one from here [Los Angeles]. We liked Susan best, but we were a little bit concerned, not about the dramatic scenes so much, but her bread and butter, everyday scenes. By this time I had started to examine the possibility of getting someone to work with her. Several people suggested Joan, whom I had not known. I talked to Joan about it, and she said she'd be very interested in doing it. We wanted to get Susan back to test her in a couple of additional scenes just to be sure. At that point I asked Joan to work with her. They got along beautifully, and Susan just *loved* her, thought she was marvelous. So I asked Joan to help me on the picture. She wasn't around on the whole picture, but she did work with Susan on her scenes, made her ready for them, and when she could, she was on the set when we were shooting.

AUSTIN: Throughout the film medium's brief history, there have been a number of challenges to it: radio in the early part of the century, television around 1950. What about today? What do you see as the biggest threat, or challenge, to the film industry?

WISE: Part of it is the increasing number of entertainment sources that people are getting: more things to do, more trips to take, more *kinds* of things to do, more participations. I don't think there's any one single threat. Television is continuously threatening. It's a big competitor in terms of the audience's viewing time and how much they'll give to films vis-à-vis television. However, we are getting ancillary values out of that because our films are shown on television. The biggest threat is probably the increasing number of alternative leisure things for people to do: boating, motor homing, flying, travel clubs, and all of this. There's a lot of competition there.

AUSTIN: What are your feelings about federal subsidization of motion pictures as some European governments do?

WISE: I think that would be lovely. Taking a realistic look at it, though, I don't think there's much chance. Whenever anything like this comes up, as I recall, there's a lot of hue and cry about the special interest thing. I think there would be a tremendous amount of opposition to it in Congress. It's awfully hard for people in a position to pass on legislation like this to relate *Star Wars* or *Jaws* [1975] doing 200 million dollars in film rental and a business needing subsidy. But that's only a part of the picture. I'm afraid that the image is one of a business that's rolling in wealth.

AUSTIN: What about the American Film Institute? Do you think they could be instrumental in helping?

WISE: I would hope so. But they're always strapped themselves for money. I think if they had the means to get more and do more in the granting agency area, they would. It's just that their funds are spread pretty thin. And while they do some grant-making to independent filmmakers, it's not *nearly* as much as is needed. I don't see any chance of that improving remarkably unless there is a lot more money found someplace in the government for the AFI. The Small Business Administration is just now getting into film financing. This has just happened in the last few months. I don't know all the details, and this isn't addressed exactly to the small filmmaker, but it is another aspect of the government doing something in the area of film financing.

Jean-Charles Tacchella

There is always someone who dies in my films. That's because I love life too much.

*W*hile transcript alone will suffice for many excellent interviews with film-makers, often the circumstances surrounding the interview can illustrate the grand—or, in other cases, unassuming—ways that directors live their lives when they are not going about their art. Those same circumstances also sometimes pay tribute to the serendipitous path by which an interviewer comes to know his or her subject. Such is the case here, when Robert M. Hammond's collection of shooting scripts led him to contact French director Jean-Charles Tacchella, a relationship that developed over time "and passed from the formal to the familiar." Eventually, Hammond decided to interview Tacchella about his work and his attitudes toward filmmaking and scripts. This interview took place in 1977, and although Tacchella's most recent film at the time was *Le Pays bleu* [*Blue Country*], made a year prior, the film to which the interview returns most is *Cousin, cousine* (1975), no doubt because the director was heading to New York to produce a stage version of the film on Broadway.

The conversation begins with Hammond's suggesting there is a "'Roussillon School' of film," given the number of French filmmakers who have ended up in the French village where Tacchella resides. But, as Tacchella is quick to respond, "I don't believe that there are any *schools* or groups," citing the *Cahiers du Cinéma* as an example. Such an observation is unusual, given that most people *do* tend to think of the *Cahiers* journal as a quite cohesive group, at least in terms of their collective support of the *auteur* policy. And yet, it is precisely the willingness of Tacchella to challenge such received wisdom in both obvious and subtle ways that makes this interview so engaging.

114

After discussing the *Cahiers* and his friendship with André Bazin, Tacchella recounts his own history as a critic as well as his early work in cinema as a gag writer, scenarist, and, eventually, director. In regards to the scenario and its relative importance, Tacchella explains his sense of the relative "primacy" of that part of the filmmaking process, digressing that "someone should write a history of the scenario." The interview continues with discussions of various subjects, including actors, improvisation, the idea of "evolution" in cinema history, the film *Cousin, Cousine* (at several points in the interview), and a comparison of French versus American audiences. Hammond closes by asking Tacchella to sum up his credo, to which Tacchella responds with not just one but several, choosing, in the end, to allow one of his critics to speak for him—"Roland Duval situates me 'between Labiche and Lubitsch, with a touch of Erasmus'"—only to offer, wryly, "I don't know if that's true, but I like it."

Interview by Robert M. Hammond
Originally published as "A Chat with the Father of Cousin, Cousine*: Jean-Charles Tacchella,"* Literature/Film Quarterly 7, no. 1 (January 1979): 2–10.

In the summer of 1977, Jean-Charles Tacchella, the director of *Cousin, Cousine*, was staying in Roussillon, a little village made known to many Americans a decade ago by Lawrence Wylie's book, *A Village in Vaucluse*.

I first met Jean-Charles in June, while collecting French shooting scripts. My collection of over two hundred scripts grows piecemeal since I often must bear duplicating expenses myself, except on those rare occasions when I find actors, *régisseurs*, writers, directors, or producers who have a spare copy to donate. I phoned from a café on the square in Roussillon, only to discover that Tacchella's house was nearby. We chatted briefly in his study, and eventually became friends. We ate meals and raised glasses together and passed from the formal to the familiar.

After xeroxing three scripts Tacchella had donated (*Cousin, cousine*, *Le Pays bleu*, and *Voyage en Grande Tartarie* [*Voyage to Grand Tartarie*, 1974]), it dawned on me that perhaps he would be interested in an interview where he might say things he had not touched on in other interviews in the United States. I had learned from his friend Jean Dewever that he had evolved into directing after many years as a writer, even as Dewever had evolved on an opposite course, from directing to writing. So I asked him if he could say a few things about the importance of the scenario for the success of a film. The result was the interview which followed.

Those who have met him know that he is an easy-going, friendly man, who has the aspect of the serious and the aloof school-boy until he starts to speak. He appears far younger than his years, attributable perhaps to the fact that, as he says, he loves life. He is a busy man, working on a close schedule, but he has none of the jumpy or distracted air that, especially in France, usually characterizes such a personality. Instead, he gives the impression of a man of quiet vitality. "We're fortunate," he says, "to meet just at this time. It's about the only time in the coming year that I'll have time to breathe." In October 1977 he is to be in New York to work out details for the adaptation of *Cousin, cousine* as a musical for Broadway.

HAMMOND: You have a house in the village of Roussillon, and it also happens that Colpi, Dewever and Vaneck and Jacques Becker's daughter all live there, too. Is there a "Roussillon School" of film?

TACCHELLA: Oh, a lot of people live in Roussillon and nearby. Some came on my account, like Henri Colpi, Jean Dewever, and Maurice Ronet. They're all film directors, anyway, among other things. There are also the director of photography, Andre Debreuil and the designer, George Lévy. They came because they saw where I was living and they fell in love with the area, too. Then there are others who discovered the place by other means: Edmond Fress, Marcel Jullian (director of Channel II TV, who lives in nearby Lacoste), Pierre Vaneck and Michel Drach (who lives over in Gordes). Then there is Alain Jessua, who is a frequent visitor.

But Roussillon is more a pleasure spot than a working place. In any case, I don't believe that there are any *schools* or groups. Seen from afar, from a foreign shore, you always think so. There are sometimes, of course, people who get along well with each other. For instance: *Les Cahiers du Cinéma*. There, there was no directive, no manifesto. There was no leader. Bazin was, though, a sort of spiritual guide. He was very indulgent. His attitude was, "Put yourself in the director's place—that's where to begin—before you start your criticism." I feel he was right. That's the valid way of criticizing. (By the way, when I answered questions of cinema students in Texas, they said many of my answers sounded like "pure Bazin.")

Bazin and I were very close. He and I were eager, after the war, to see the American directors when they came to France, like Wyler and Welles. Welles had never seen the definitive copy of his *Magnificent Ambersons* [1942]. We showed it for him. He was furious.

HAMMOND: You were a critic at first, weren't you? Which reviews did you write for?

TACCHELLA: I was film critic from 1945 to 1953 for *L'Ecran Français, Ciné Digest* and others. Then there was *Objectif 49* that I co-founded with André Bazin, Alexandre Astruc, Doniol-Valcroze, Pierre Kast, François Chalais, Claude Mauriac, and others. Jean Cocteau was our president. Our goal was to present all the *films maudit*, films which had never been commercially successful. We had two festivals at Biarritz.

HAMMOND: While you were a critic, you became a scenarist and adaptor. What was your first film? What are the most important ones and who were the directors?

TACCHELLA: I must say I had always wanted to make films, but it was Pierre Braunberger who got me into film in 1950 when I worked as a gag writer. In 1952 I worked in Rome with Léonide Moguy on two scenarios. In 1953 I collaborated on the adaptation of Moguy's *Les Enfants de l'amour* [*Children of Love*].

From 1954 to 1962, I was a scenarist. I did the adaptation of Yves Ciampi's *Les Héros sont fatigues* [*The Heroes Are Tired*] in 1955, and the original scenario for his *Typhon sur Nagasaki* [*Typhoon over Nagasaki*] in 1956. In 1957 I co-authored (with Jacques Emmanuel) Christian-Jacque's *La Loi c'est la loi* [*The Law Is the Law*]. In 1958, for Yves Ciampi, I wrote the original scenario for *Le Vent se lève* [*Time Bomb*] and for Claude Barma I collaborated with Jacques Emmanuel again on the original scenario for *Croquemitoufle* [1959].

I was adaptor (with Gérard Oury and Annette Wademant) for Michel Boisrond's *Voulez-vous danser avec moi?* [*Do You Want to Dance with Me?*] in 1958, and in the same year did the original scenario as well as the adaptation (in collaboration with Oury and Jean-Claude Pichon) for Oury's *La Main chaude* [*The Itchy Palm*].

As a scenarist I had only one aim: to help the director realize his intentions. I never considered the scenario as a personal expression. And then, as you perhaps noticed, all the work I've mentioned is adaptation and scenario. They always took the writing away from me once that was done, and called in a dialoguist. Only one of the directors I worked with before 1963 had me do dialogues as well. That was Jean Dewever, for whom I was also first assistant on *Les Honneurs de la guerre* (*The Honors of War*, 1960).

In 1962, I did two more films: the adaptation for *Liberté I* (Yves Ciampi, 1962) and the original scenario for *Le Crime ne paie pas* [*Crime Does Not Pay*] (Gerard Oury). There was one last film I wrote for, in 1963. That was Jean Valère's *Le Gros coup* [1964].

Then I decided to try to direct my own films. There were three scenarios that I had done before 1963 that were shot later by other directors. Maurice Ronet did my *Le Voleur du Tibidabo* [*The Thief of Tibidabo*] in 1964; Alexandre Astruc did *La Longue marche* [*Long March*] in 1965; and Jean Dewever did something I had called *César Grandblaise*, but which came out under the title of *Les Jambes en l'air*. That was 1971.

Of all these films, only one is like me; that's *Les Honneurs de la guerre*, for which I wrote both dialogue and scenario. It was the story about one day during the liberation of France in a little town: the story of the same day seen by the French and by the Germans. I'm sentimentally very attached to that film.

HAMMOND: And so now you turn out to be a director. How did you begin, finally?

TACCHELLA: It was hard for me to get started. I had several projects, the most important being *Tous les jours dimanche* [*Seven Sundays*]. I had the advance from the Centre National de la Cinématographie, but even with that promised funding no one would touch my film. The ways to finance a film in France are by an advance from the Centre, or an arrangement with the distributors in advance by means of "name" actors. Often you actually have to become a producer yourself if you want to direct your film.

So from 1965 to 1970 I wrote serials for French TV, of which the best known was a serial directed by Joseph Drimel called *Vive la vie*. I also tried my hand at the theater and had three plays produced at the Théâtre Mouffetard in 1973.

I had wanted all my life to be a director and even before I was a critic . . . but I didn't feel I wanted to go through the classic channels, being apprentice, assistant, and so forth. In the end, I decided to shoot a twenty-three-minute film with thirty actors, *Les Derniers hivers* (*The Last Winters*, 1970). I had gotten a little money from the Centre for the film, I had found a producer, Dimka, who would finance it in part, and I myself was co-producer for about half of it.

The film got the Prix Jean Vigo in 1971; was put on in the United States—especially in the universities; got the Silver Hugo at the Chicago Festival and Diplôme d'Honneur at the Krakow Festival (short subjects) in Poland.

As a result of the film's success, I was able to do—thanks again to the Centre—my first feature film: *Voyage en Grande Tartarie*.

HAMMOND: Since you've been writer and scenarist, I suppose that you give priority to the scenario of the film. Or do you find that there are some films where the scenario plays the dominant role and others where it remains secondary?

TACCHELLA: That's easy to answer, at least on the surface, because I like to do everything in the film. Until now I've never signed a contract until the last minute, until everything is decided, just so I will be sure of having complete control. I've told the producer: "I do the whole thing myself or not at all." I've always liked to be completely free (so far as money allows, that is). Therefore, I've also done my own scripts. They let me get away with this kind of thing more, now, because they feel that I've established my reputation.

So yes, for me the scenario has primacy, but it's not all that simple. This primacy exists only to a certain degree. When you do the writing, you write with a certain intention. Shooting is a different matter. If you hold to the same aims as you did in writing, you find yourself underscoring certain themes and you emphasize the obvious.

I find that I become a sort of duality. I write, but then the director acts on the material. It even happened once that I wrote a scenario and was quite pleased with it as a scenarist. But not as a director. I decided not to film it.

The director, with his different optic, can't do the same thing as the writer did. The intention of the scenarist should not be visible, since that's how you make the public feel it has discovered something.

You know, someone should write a history of the scenario. A lot has been written on the history of the cinema. Some attempt has been made at writing a history of directing. But nothing has ever been done for the scenario. Of course, it's very complicated. Critics are often hard put to know who has done what, who is responsible for a certain gesture, a certain detail. Everything on the screen can be attributed to three possible sources. Was it from the scenario? Was it the director who told the actor? Was it the actor who thought of it?

HAMMOND: Do you make an effort to create ellipses where the writer may have expressed things at greater length?

TACCHELLA: I love the elliptical. I cut brutally, before the spectator realizes what was happening in the scene; but I have already written these cuts into my own shooting scripts. For me the unexpected must be on the screen, not in the camera angles. Dreyer said you should "use the camera to eliminate the camera."

HAMMOND: How long did you work on the scenario of *Cousin, cousine*?

TACCHELLA: I wrote that in one month. I like to write quickly. Perhaps it's a hangover from my days as a critic. Perhaps from my TV experience. One year I wrote forty hours of film for television.

HAMMOND: How would you circumscribe the respective duties of scenarist and director?

TACCHELLA: I can't tell you about other people's experiences. All I can do is to tell you how I go about it myself, since I have been, since 1970, the only scenarist and dialoguist and director of my films, at one and the same time.

I write the scenario scene by scene, directly, with the dialogues, but it is not yet a shooting script. There are no technical directions.

Then I contact the producers, I choose the actors, I get better acquainted with them, and then I write the shooting script, taking into account each actor's personality. Then, when I have found the location for each scene, I sketch out the camera placements on a floor-plan. Often, the night before filming a scene, I look over these sketches and I change certain things—frequently as a function of what the actors have done in the preceding scenes.

HAMMOND: Do you work with the actors together before shooting the film? Or one at a time?

TACCHELLA: I don't like to work collectively. I work with each actor separately. Oh, I have them meet each other. They should know each other. But I like to observe the actors, live with them, to be able to use them to the maximum. I also use certain details of their real life and insert them into my shooting script. For example, Marie-Christine Barrault was talking to me one day and she said, "You know, when I'm in love with a man, I just adore cutting his toe-nails." So I wrote a toe-nail cutting scene in *Cousin, cousine*. I had Victor Lanoux let his toe-nails grow . . . not cut them for some time. What happened was that during the film

Marie-Christine was so carried away by cutting Victor's nails that she kept doing it between takes. I had to tell her to stop or there wouldn't be anything left to cut in the next take! It's the kind of thing that makes the actor more at home in his role.

Like the day I called Victor Lanoux to ask him to play the role. His wife answered the phone and said she'd get him, that he had a new motorcycle that he was trying out around the block. It turned out he had a passion for motorcycles, especially for the one he'd just bought, so I put it in the film. And then I had a problem. Since it was a special model, very difficult to find, I was scared to death all through the shooting that someone would steal it. As it happened, it *was* stolen . . . but just the evening of the last day of filming. In a way, it was *the* motorcycle for *that* film.

HAMMOND: How much improvisation do you allow yourself during the filming?

TACCHELLA: I don't like the idea of improvisation per se, because when actors improvise you're liable to lose the rhythm of the film. However, I like the illusion of improvisation. I try to get this by my work with the actors. On the stage I don't alter my shooting script much, except if, of course, I find improvements that appear obvious to me. And then, on a stage there are so many unexpected things that can happen. A change in the weather, a car parked on the opposite side of the street, forcing the placement of characters to change. That kind of thing. Sometimes good, sometimes bad. Aside from these unavoidable things, I keep everything as planned.

On the other hand, within the limits of that plan, I allow a certain amount of improvisation because I like to be surprised by the actors. I never rehearse lines, only the blocking. Sometimes, for a scene with two people, I like to see what they want to do, so I let the actors play it themselves and I adapt to their acting.

Ordinarily I shoot at a very low ratio. Only two or three takes. Often, if the first take is good, I don't need to make a second. I use very little film stock.

HAMMOND: It's rather rare for a director to be his own scenarist and dialoguist, isn't it?

TACCHELLA: Yes, but I think that the director of the modern day should be able to do everything. If he doesn't know how to write, he should certainly learn. Many directors in France *think* they know how to write a scenario, but they don't know anything about dramatic construction. The director should know about the problems of this structure. They think they have an intriguing story; but it turns out to be a boring one simply because it isn't dramatically valid. Or else, a director who is not a writer will frequently be dissatisfied with his scenarist, because he feels he is not getting what he wants. In those cases, he'll frequently ask for other writers and still other writers. . . .

HAMMOND: A possible evolution exists in recent cinema, starting with the so-called *auteur* cinema (the director considered as author, *à la* Bazin), the New Wave, philosophical cinema (concerning the critical theories of semiology, phenomenology and structuralism), writer's cinema (Robbe-Grillet, Duras, Sagan, e.g.) and . . . what others?

TACCHELLA: I don't know that you can establish a clear evolution. Those trends existed or still exist, but are perhaps out of the main stream of film history.

Of course, there is much to be said for Bazin's idea of the style of a director, of the identification of the director by the films he worked on. On the other hand, the New Wave wasn't an aesthetic school; it was the revolt against the system. Because in the French cinema, between 1950 and 1958, it was impossible for a director to start out, unless he had been assistant director for a long time. Claude Chabrol, by financing his films—films which were hits, by the way—was the first to make a dent in the system. That was the beginning of the New Wave, which coincided with the appearance of more sensitive film stock which permitted more economical filming.

As for the philosophical current; that exists, too, and not only in film criticism. There are people that make films which constitute the criticism of the film itself. I'm against this kind of filmmaking, because I find it a negative concept. Film for me is a popular art. I like for the cinematographic expression to be direct and effective.

HAMMOND: Having begun as a critic you must be well placed to say something about the periodicals devoted to film in France. Cinema students in the United States know the *Cahiers du Cinéma* particularly. But you also have *Positif* and the one you wrote for: *L'Écran Français.*

TACCHELLA: Those are the three best—and have been over thirty years, no doubt about that. *L'Écran Français* was born of the Resistance, and went on from 1945 to 1953. It was slightly to the left and was finally taken over by the communists in 1949. It was a weekly, and it refused to take any ads. To give you an idea of its stature, just think of some of the writers who wrote for it! There was, besides myself, Alexandre Astruc, Jacques Sigurd, Nino Frank, Claude Martinez, André Bazin, Georges Sadoul, Charles Spaak, Pierre Laroche, Roger Vitrac, Henri Robillot, Roger Boussinot, Jacques Krier and Jean Thévenet (both now in TV), Roger Thérond (now head of *Paris-Match*), Pierre Kast, Jean Vidal, Jacques Becker, Jean Grémillon, and more.

La Revue de Cinéma had been edited by Jean-Georges Auriol at the beginning of the sound era. It came out again after the war, but it was commercially unsuccessful. It finally re-emerged in 1951 as the *Cahiers du Cinéma.* It was a monthly and knew its *grande époque* from 1953 to 1963, with such writers as François Truffaut, Georges Sadoul, André Bazin, Jacques Rivette, Eric Rohmer, Jean-Luc Godard, Claude Chabrol. Bazin asked me to join in, but I was already involved in script writing. *Cahiers* [has] now become more political than cinematographic.

Positif is also a monthly, and started in 1953. It has the most interesting film articles. It has very good studies of the great directors. Other monthlies are *Écran 77* (now in its sixth year), *Cinéma 77* (more political and toward the left, and the organ of the Ciné-Clubs), *La Revue du Cinéma* (journal of the Fédération Jean Vigo), and *Lumière* (which is now more oriented toward photography than criticism).

HAMMOND: Getting back to *Cousin, cousine* . . . how do you judge it compared to your other films?

TACCHELLA: I'm not able to judge that. Some say *Voyage en Grande Tartarie* is the best; some say *Le Pays bleu*. If the public can't agree, I can't very well, either. I've made all of my films with a hundred percent free hand; I mean, as I said, I demand complete control. (Of course, I can't say that *financing* was unlimited. I've always filmed with very little money. On the other hand, I always keep my eye on the budget so that I can know when I can afford to shift funds within the budget itself.)

HAMMOND: I understand that *Cousin, cousine* has been more successful in the United States than in France.

TACCHELLA: I beg to differ. *Cousin, cousine* was a hit in Paris and in France. It was a commercial and also critical success since the film got the Prix Louis Delluc, given by the critics to the best film of 1975. I don't know where this idea comes from. Perhaps it's because there are so few French films that are hits in the United States.

HAMMOND: Is the success abroad greater than *A Man and a Woman* [1966], or *Z* [1969], for example?

TACCHELLA: On the commercial level, receipts for *Cousin, cousine* have already come to more than receipts for *A Man and a Woman*, and will soon be more than *Z*'s.

HAMMOND: In your judgment, what are the qualities that the Americans seem to like, which might not appeal to the Frenchman?

TACCHELLA: It seems to me that there are three things that account for the success in America: Firstly, there is the vitality of the film. I like life to burst out on the screen, and not be the simple result of the story or of the dramatic action. I like the spectator to be surprised by life more than the plot. I refuse to have anything to do with anything that looks like cinema. I like to use dramatic devices as they appear in our own lives: Love, problems of everyday life, death. And especially death as it happens in our existence. Now, you rarely die on the screen the way you do in life. In film, revolver shots are more frequent than cancers or heart ailments. There is always someone who dies in my films. That's because I love life too much.

Secondly, the film seems to be very French. I think that Americans have the impression that they are living in France when they see the film. But at the same time the rhythm isn't the usual rhythm of French films. The rhythm is closer to the American cinema's. I've always considered American cinema as first in the world in the whole history of cinema. And its number one quality for me is its rhythm.

Thirdly, it's a film which lies outside of today's styles. I'm completely disinterested in the *latest thing*. I make films that I dreamed of making twenty years ago. That may make my films fall outside of schools or waves or cliques. And in any case, I don't think we should follow such things. Besides, especially in the United States, with its sex films and films of violence, it was a welcome change.

HAMMOND: Could you state your credo in more positive terms; that is, not just in terms of the absence of sex and violence?

TACCHELLA: Well, I feel that to make a film you have to have a lot of reserve and naiveté. Without reserve, the style of a director can't be any good; it can't be true. Without naiveté, he can't be effective. There are a number of directors I esteem for their moral honesty: Ozu, Grémillon, Rossellini, Rohmer, Epstein, Renoir, Vigo and Tati, among others.

I like a certain number of things about our times, but I'm repelled by Manichaeism (the "good guys" and the "bad guys"), and I try to say what I have to say subtly, through life. I don't want to be a fist-swinging subversive. I hate violence. On the other hand, I like what Labiche said to Zola: "I've never been able to take man seriously." That could be my motto. So, although I feel that there are some qualities that you have the right to ridicule (such as stupidity and selfishness), you have no right to ridicule others (suffering or illness, e.g.). Roland Duval situates me "between Labiche and Lubitsch, with a touch of Erasmus."

I don't know if that's true, but I like it.

Louis Malle

I like for the audience to be self-conscious of themselves as voyeurs
because they are! After all, they have paid to see someone else's dream!

$\mathcal{F}$rench director Louis Malle had already made his reputation by 1978, and
when he sat down with Andrew Horton for the following interview, the filmmaker had just completed his first American production, *Pretty Baby* (1978), a
film about a twelve-year-old prostitute in a New Orleans brothel, her mother,
and the real-life photographer E. J. Bellocq. Although the film was somewhat
controversial for its casting of a young Brooke Shields as a prostitute, it preceded
a decade of some of Malle's best known work: *Atlantic City* (1980), *My Dinner
with André* (1982), and, perhaps one of his most well regarded films, *Au revoir, les
enfants* (1987). Here, in the discussion that follows, Malle shows his ability to
move rapidly through—and recall a great deal in—film after film in his oeuvre,
always returning to *Pretty Baby* to underscore further aspects of the production he
has just completed. Horton begins by citing a frequent subject of Malle's work,
youth, to which Malle immediately shows his own sense of humor about himself
by noting, "It's getting a bit obsessive!" Such exchanges are common in this lively
interview, where Malle also considers the relationship between documentary and
fiction; the creation of soundtracks, including Miles Davis's work on *Ascenseur
pour l'échafaud* (1958) (or, as it is known in what Malle calls "its ridiculous English title," *Frantic*); Polly Platt's collaboration on *Pretty Baby*; Bellocq's photographs; and Luis Buñuel. But perhaps the most poignant anecdote is saved for the
end, where Malle recounts a Jewish classmate, during the Occupation, being
taken by the Gestapo. "Let me tell you," he says, "that this is the kind of experience you don't forget." Malle died in 1995, and readers will likely find themselves
seeking out the director's work, including *Pretty Baby*, after reading his thoughtful, intelligent, and often quite candid reflections.

124

Interview by Andrew Horton
Originally published as "'Creating a Reality That Doesn't Exist': An Interview with
Louis Malle," Literature/Film Quarterly 7, no. 2 (April 1979): 86–98.

Louis Malle's *Pretty Baby*, the story of a twelve-year-old prostitute and a with-drawn French photographer in a New Orleans whorehouse in 1917, is the latest film in a distinguished and varied career that began in 1956 when the then very young French director worked with Jacques Cousteau to make *The Silent World*. His films since then include *Ascenseur pour l'échafaud* (*Frantic*, 1957), *Les Amants* (*The Lovers*, 1958), *Zazie dans le métro* (1960), *Vie privée* (*A Very Private Affair*, 1961), *Le Feu follet* (*The Fire Within*, 1963), *Viva Maria!* (1965), *Le Voleur* (*The Thief of Paris*, 1966), *Calcutta* (1969), *L'Inde fantôme* (*Phantom India*, 1969), *Le Souffle au coeur* (*Murmur of the Heart*, 1971), *Humain, trop humain* (*A Human Condition*, 1974), *Lacombe, Lucien* (1974), and *Black Moon* (1975).

The interview took place in Mr. Malle's office in the Paramount Pictures of-fices in New York, on April 23, 1978. The interviewer was Andrew Horton, As-sistant Professor of English at the University of New Orleans.

HORTON: A number of your films focus on youth: *Zazie dans le métro, Le Souffle au coeur, Lacombe, Lucien, Black Moon, Pretty Baby*. Why?

MALLE: I don't know really. Maybe I should do something else now. It's getting a bit obsessive! I'm not doing it on purpose. It is true, however. And even *Black Moon* was a sort of a variation on the theme of the rites of passage. You could even say this about some of my earlier films in the sixties, such as *Le Feu follet*, which finally is about a man who commits suicide because he refuses to become an adult.

Probably I was terribly impressed myself at that age with the difficulties and trauma of entering the world of adults. This is sort of the moment of truth. It is *the* one of a lifetime. And I see a lot of children at that age have a moment of to-tal lucidity. But the moment you become part of this world of adults, you are just one of them. You start cheating and lying: there is a vast difference between what we say and what we do. All of this compromise. *Lacombe, Lucien* was very obvi-ously about such corruption.

HORTON: In *Lacombe, Lucien* we see a progression in the young peasant boy's cor-ruption as he moves from killing birds, chickens, and rabbits to killing people as a Nazi collaborator. But in *Pretty Baby*, Violet seems to already be there: as one reviewer put it, she has no innocence to lose. Is this correct?

MALLE: I'm not sure about that because innocence is not so easy to explain. One of the things that impressed me about the Al Rose book, *Storyville* [University of Alabama Press, 1978], was that in an interview a woman said that when she was five years old she knew everything there was to know. This is terrifying, but still I don't really believe that innocence is just the lack of information. Violet is a part of the world around her but she is still very much a child. What makes the character so interesting is that she is graduating into corruption at a very early age, but at the same time I have a strong suspicion that she has managed to save a lot of values of what it is to be a child.

It seems the more I get into the things I really care about, and the theme of *Pretty Baby* I really cared about doing for a long time, the more there are contradictions and unanswered questions. But the reason I got interested in the whole situation is because I don't have the answers.

And I certainly don't believe that it is by making a picture that you find answers. The first time I felt very concerned about something, and I felt that the only way to cope with it was to make it into a movie, was when I made *Le Feu follet*. I was worried about the question of suicide since the story more or less happened to a friend of mine. I was very emotional about it and the picture, once it was shot and shown, was more sentimental than the films I make today. It looks like I have been cleaning up my act a little bit concerning this!

But I didn't find the "answers" with *Le Feu follet*. I remember that I did not want it to open because it was a little too personal. There were a lot of very confusing things about the film. And I also made those documentaries of India which were something like seven hours long to prove that I did not understand anything about India!

HORTON: You seem to emphasize, as witnessed by your documentaries for Cousteau and about India, a "documentary" approach to your subjects, yet the result is to uncover the unusual or "fictional." Could you comment on the relationship between documentary and fiction in your work?

MALLE: I don't mean to say that documentary and fiction are the same, but as I have found out more about both aspects of filmmaking I have realized you could, for instance, speak about the fictional aspects of documentary. And I believe strongly that documentary filmmakers who pretend to be objective are just dishonest. It's absolute bullshit. You're much more subjective and personal in documentaries because you are supposedly just filming what you see that you didn't create. But obviously the way you film shapes what you get.

There is more said, for instance, in *Pretty Baby* in the way the picture is filmed than in its content or in the script. Because I think what is disturbing to many people about the film is—and I don't mean to say it is my best film because it is not, but it is advancing in a direction that I am interested in—what is disturbing is that I try to address the sense—rather than the intellect. I want, through visuals and sound, to create a world almost tactile. I feel this very strongly. In

Pretty Baby there is something very seductive and corruptive in the way the film is narrated. And it is probably most shocking for people in this country that sin is presented as absolutely exquisite! Which it is!

HORTON: You have worked with Robert Bresson as assistant director on *Un condamné à mort s'est échappé* [*A Condemned Man Escapes*, 1956]. Is he an influence on your work? I am thinking particularly of *Mouchette* [1967].

MALLE: It's interesting that you mention *Mouchette*. I'm still an enormous admirer of Bresson, and I think I'm the only filmmaker that he cares to see, and we've kept up a very good relationship. Bresson is supposed to be a very austere filmmaker, but I feel *Mouchette* is a very sensual film. The end of the film where she is rolling down the hill to her death made me cry. I literally cried, and I very rarely cry when filmmakers want me to cry. And *Balthazar* [1966] was also very much about an experience of the senses. That's what I admire about Bresson: that he has managed to create these sensual moments. When I worked with him on *A Condemned Man Escapes*, Bresson was interested in me because I came from documentaries. He asked me to take care of all of the details such as the spoon with which the prisoner was digging—all of these details which had to do with the escape. I was very impressed with all of his close-ups of such details and with his concern to show a sense of touch.

The soundtrack for the film was also remarkable. I saw it again recently and it is extraordinary. He manages to create a world of sensation that he conveys. In that sense I feel very close to him.

HORTON: The same seems true of your work. While one is first struck by your distinct visual style, it seems you have also paid, especially in *Pretty Baby*, close attention to your soundtrack. There is something always happening—off-screen songs, children talking, cars passing—even if nothing is happening on screen.

MALLE: We spent a lot of time on the soundtrack in this picture. The paradox is that we shot in New Orleans, and you don't see anything of New Orleans! We found this incredible house in the city which no set could have done justice to. In a way the house was more important—along with Brooke Shields—than the script! But the soundtrack was meant to suggest the world outside the house since they are like prisoners.

I worked with my editor, Susanne Baron, whom I usually work with, and we felt we should evoke the outside world as if we were in a cell. And there was also a lot of use of the sound as counterpoint—the sound of children, for instance. Sound was very important also to give a distance. One scene in particular I am very proud of because I think it is one of the most interesting things in the film. In one scene Bellocq is photographing Hattie in the room during the afternoon and the piano is playing in the background. The music disappears and then comes back. Floyd is supposedly rehearsing a "Jelly Roll" Morton song, "King Porter's Stomp," and it stops and goes, and it works incredibly well with the scene. I remember that

Jerry Wexler, our musical supervisor, was against this idea, wanting us to play the song straight through. But I said "NO!" It's much more interesting to have him stop and play. And it gives a distance.

HORTON: Could you comment on the importance of music in your films since each film features some particular kind of music? In *Lacombe, Lucien*, for instance, you have the opening scene set to a bouncy tune by Django Reinhardt.

MALLE: First I must say that I am very shocked by the way music is usually used in films. It's one of the most efficient ways to manipulate audiences, as you know; a kind of Pavlovian response. And it works so well it is frightening! Myself I am not prejudiced against scores, but in recent years I have been working with *source* music. And so the music is already a part of the scene. But I try to use it more as counterpoint—not to reinforce a situation, but to work against a situation. But basically music is important in my films because music is important in my life.

For instance, the music in *Le Feu follet* came as an absolutely natural thing. I was in that kind of a mood, that kind of a situation, and that was when I was listening to Erik Satie. And so very naturally this music entered the film and became the score. In my first film, which has the ridiculous English title *Frantic*, with Jeanne Moreau, I used Miles Davis. When we were shooting the film we were all crazy about Miles Davis, and I was in the middle of sound editing without knowing what to use. I was thinking perhaps of using some records. But then I found out that Miles Davis was going to be in Paris to play in a club. Then I spent five or six nights trying to convince him to come and see the picture and to accept to do what he finally did, which was to improvise! We finally ended up in a sound studio for one night where I showed the film to him several times and then he made up a remarkable score. It really made the picture look much better than it was!

That's the way I've always worked, though some of my films, like *The Thief of Paris*, have no music. Recently I used Charlie Parker in *Murmur of the Heart*. Actually the film opens with the boy stealing a record from a record shop: it is a Charlie Parker record!

HORTON: You worked on the screenplay to *Pretty Baby* with Polly Platt. How was your collaboration?

MALLE: It was a real collaboration. I felt she was a good choice because I wanted a woman for a woman's point of view, and I needed to work with someone who was very much a part of the American cinema tradition. And Polly was very helpful because of her connection with Peter Bogdanovich (former husband) and John Ford. She was indispensable. She was very "American," though I don't know what being an American means, but I felt she helped me respond to the culture. So when I met with her I already had an outline that I had had with me for over a year. Then first she did a great job researching the film. With her background in production design, she was very good at that, particularly since it was a period film. We found a number of interesting things, for instance, the unpublished memoirs of a "Madam"!

HORTON: What about Bellocq's photographs? Did you find many of them?

MALLE: Yes, but what is interesting is that at the time they were made, people did not even know there was a photographer named Bellocq. They had the plates, not the photos, and they did not know who to attribute them to. Then they sort of invented him! But it's much more complicated than that. The book of his portraits is not accurate because even though they put together lots of interviews, it is clear that he was not very well remembered! All they really know is that for the last thirty years of his life he worked as a commercial photographer and also, for a while, at a shipping company. . . . They say he was a hydrocephalic and a cripple and that he was like Toulouse-Lautrec. But I don't think this is a very good comparison, because if you look at the photographs and at Lautrec's paintings, you see that they were two different kinds of men. We knew Bellocq best through the photographs. Polly and I spent hours and hours looking at the photographs with magnifying glasses. Actually a friend who works in a museum in Paris once told me that Bellocq's pictures are fakes, but if you look carefully you see that this cannot be so because there are too many little stupid details that cannot be faked.

HORTON: Each of your films very successfully evokes an accurate atmosphere and mood of a particular period: turn-of-the-century French Society in *The Thief of Paris*, for instance. And yet one reviewer has said in reference to your work that art has no necessity to be faithful to historical accuracy. Do you feel this remark is correct or do you find it important to try and be faithful to a sense of history?

MALLE: I work very hard to be accurate. What do I do finally? I re-create a world and then once it is properly re-created, I like to forget about the fact that it is a period. In my way of filming I don't emphasize the period. I try to film my pictures as if they are something I have just encountered. Maybe this is the influence of documentaries. But, yes, the period has to be as accurate as possible because then it gives you the freedom not to think about it and to look at the characters just as they are. But this means, of course, that you have a lot of homework to do in order to get to that stage. And I like to do this work. It's interesting and troubling to sort of re-invent the past. It was especially interesting in *Pretty Baby* because those places were so incredible.

HORTON: Your vision of a New Orleans whorehouse in 1917 is spoken of by Vincent Canby as a non-romantic kind of "romanticism." You de-emphasize sexuality and brutality in order to present "sin" as "exquisite," as you say, or simply quite ordinary. What would you say to those critics who complain that you have left out the seedy side of prostitution?

MALLE: I'm not really quite aware of that. People seem to have been totally taken by the photography. By the way, one amusing aspect of the photography is that Sven Nykvist did not actually film all of the scenes. I just read one critic who writes, "Again Nykvist takes over for the filming of the picnic scene," but Sven wasn't there to shoot the picnic scene! That is nice! Sven is such a great artist he does not even have to be near me!

But the photography in this film is not flashy. For instance, Sven practically never used backlighting in the film. Which is unusual, especially for a period film. And the set is remarkable, but it's not the usual image of a whorehouse. Usually you think of colors such as red and gold, which are richer. But we tried to tone down the colors. I don't know. I don't see that the film is so visually stylized myself. Again I would say that I didn't really mean to do it in such a way. I guess I could have shown more squalor but it just didn't happen that way. There are, however, one or two moments when you have a feeling of it. But basically I felt that, dealing with that subject and theme, it might be more disturbing if everything looked so easy and so nice. One American friend saw it before it was finished and said she found the film particularly terrible and beautiful and seductive at the same time. That's what I wanted people to feel. I don't think it would have helped to show more rats. I love to show rats because I love rats, but they didn't need to be in this film.

HORTON: Let me ask about Bellocq: he is so elusive as a character, and yet his relationship with Violet is touching.

MALLE: I must tell you something about the Bellocq-Violet relationship. When I was shooting the picture I suddenly felt the little I knew of Bellocq was me. There was a part I could identify with. And I got to identify with him very, very much. Especially as the character was played by Keith Carradine, but of course it goes both ways because I also felt close to Keith. There was something in him I responded to, and I had been considering lots of other actors. We were very much like brothers. We had a kind of intimate communication. And I felt in the middle of shooting, especially during those difficult scenes in Bellocq's house where Violet is supposed to come and stay with him—I started asking myself, if I had been Bellocq and considering that Bellocq was not terribly interested in sex, you could very well imagine the relationship without sex. Which probably would have been my attitude. After all, this child is a child. That would definitely be my interpretation.

If you used your imagination you could imagine a lot of things taking place between them. But obviously this big sexual fantasy, hang-up, of the child molesters who enjoy child prostitution or child pornography has to do with the fantasy of incest and perhaps also the fantasy of rape: there's something violent about it. It's about penetration; it's brutal. And it's repressed. But it seems to be such a strong fantasy that I think that's why it's so big today in this country, for instance. But you can also imagine another kind of relationship between a child and an adult, one like Violet's and Bellocq's.

And in this relation I must tell you that I thought a lot about Lewis Carroll. He was a fascinating man who used to photograph nude little girls, pictures that have been published. He was a clergyman but I have no idea what was going through his mind! Yet he never did anything. He was just interested in little girls, and so he wrote *Alice in Wonderland*. But his photographs are remarkable.

This fascination with children is something I certainly share. You could say that the human body starts decaying at the age of sixteen. There is nothing more moving or beautiful than the body of a child. It's one of the things I find fascinating with my own children, for instance. I always feel like hugging them and touching them because they are so. . . . But I have so many troubles with such a film because people talk about nudity. For me, nudity is not taboo because it is not obscene. But a lot of people bring in their own fantasies, and that's why they get so emotional and outraged. I see it completely differently.

HORTON: You have two artists in the film. Floyd has his music, which is background for the business and life of the house. He's a professional who moves on to Chicago when the house closes, yet he is also human as witnessed by his reactions to Violet's tribulations. Bellocq with his photographs intrudes into the house and ultimately, into Violet's life, bringing art and life together in an unusual way. Do these two examples reflect your views of art and reality?

MALLE: The scene where Bellocq brings a picture of Hattie which the other girls gather around and admire and notice for the first time how beautiful they can be is a strong comment on my work. That scene was my scene. The girls are surprised: they have to see a photograph in order to understand that Hattie is beautiful. And then at the end of the scene when they ask him, "How did you do that?" and he says, "Magic! It only takes one second!" is a good line. You know I showed the picture to Susan Sontag when she was just finishing her book on photography, and she was fascinated by that line. That scene is essential to an understanding of what art is about: creating a reality that doesn't exist. And that would be my answer to many critics because of course *Pretty Baby* is about a world that doesn't exist. Yet it is very realistic in a way. I think I'm very much of a realist, but there is, on the other hand, a certain interpretation of reality that is somewhat stylized, but I create style in a way that is a little bit "wicked"!

HORTON: Perhaps your term "wicked" embraces your sly sense of humor. You have, after all, been compared to some degree with Luis Buñuel and the way he presents a "realistic" picture that can at any moment become humorous, absurd, surreal.

MALLE: I love Buñuel! I love the filmmaker and the man. But Buñuel is often made into something that he is not. I find his so-called "surrealism" is his least interesting feature. The secret of Buñuel is his childhood, that he came from a middle-class Spanish family. Probably his best film is *Tristana* [1970] which is an adaptation of the novel by Galdós, a kind of Spanish Dickens. This film is the real Buñuel into which he puts a lot of humor and self-parody. He is very, very funny. I like his irony and I like his style and I feel very close to him in that way. He's austere and his technique is to have the most outrageous situations in his script and to film them in the most realistic way, and it works wonders! It's astonishing! Those who try to imitate Buñuel don't understand that style is what the person is about. People make the mistake to think that something is Buñuelian because it is bizarre. But the opposite is true.

I'm often amazed that people will tell you a lot about character and theme and motivation in a film, but they don't realize that it's the way a picture is filmed that is much more important. Perhaps they are unconsciously aware of it. Because if someone else took the script of *Pretty Baby* they could have done an entirely different film.

HORTON: You seem to work quite often with non-professional actors such as Brooke Shields in *Pretty Baby* and Pierre Blaise in *Lacombe, Lucien* and to keep your actors off balance while shooting by changing scenes or tactics at the last moment. Is this an effort to maintain spontaneity and sincerity?

MALLE: It's an effort to fight the essential weakness of filmmaking which is that it is so slow and technically so heavy. And you lose that innocence very quickly. I try to "reinvent" it. Everything is so slow. And don't forget that a filmmaker has to make a film three or four times: you have to write the script, then shoot it, edit it, and then when it opens there's the fact that you have to talk about it! So to keep a freshness, especially for the actors, you have to find new ways.

HORTON: I'm interested in how much altering or improvising you do in a film. For instance, the effective auctioning scene during which we momentarily see the reaction shots of the men gathered around watching, especially Floyd, with a mixture of sadness and nostalgia. Was that in the script?

MALLE: No. Actually the script was a lot more complicated, and I cut out some during the shooting and even more during the editing. The reaction shots are something I added as a sort of introduction to the scene. And I added the long close-up of Floyd which becomes an important moment. That scene is quite different from the way it appeared in the script. For instance, I had Brooke look straight into the camera because I wanted the audience to feel ill at ease. I wanted the audience involved, to be a part of the action. I like for the audience to be self-conscious of themselves as voyeurs because they are! After all, they have paid to see someone else's dream! That's what cinema is: in the dark, isolated, it becomes a voyeuristic medium. Which is not true in theater where another kind of ritual communication is important. But film leaves you alone in the dark with your own fantasies.

I've always had the theory that the spectator is a very important part of the film. The same film viewed by two different viewers is not the same film. The spectator is a creative part of the process.

HORTON: Was the ending of the film a problem when you were writing/shooting? We see clearly that she is a child as she tries to get Bellocq to come off to St. Louis with her and her "parents," and yet she is heading from a whorehouse and a child-marriage into a pure bourgeois life.

MALLE: I thought it was very ironic in a way to have what was supposedly, from a moralistic point of view, a "happy ending." But in fact it is completely heartbreaking. I've always had a problem with ending my films because my films are about certain extreme situations in which the characters are more important than the outcome. In *Lacombe, Lucien*, for instance, this totally obscure peasant with no past and no future who for accidental reasons for three months has a life where he is in a position that should not have happened to him—to be a Nazi—but it lasts for three months and what happens to him after is very incidental.

In *Pretty Baby* I was interested in Storyville and Violet because it is obviously the end of something. For most of the characters it's the end of an era, and for Violet it is a time to become an adult. She might become respectable and bourgeois as in the true story, or she could become a prostitute again. But either way it doesn't make the characters different.

HORTON: What happened to the "real" Violet?

MALLE: The original story is with a sort of an old housewife with grandchildren in the suburbs of New Orleans, and she told how she was born in a whorehouse on Basin St. and started working at twelve. And then at sixteen or seventeen she married one of her customers and became very respectable.

HORTON: Your attitude toward society, that is, bourgeois society, seems to be similar to that of Buñuel in many ways. On the one hand, you point up the shortcomings of that society, yet on the other hand, you seem to have a certain affection or at least acceptance of it with all of its faults.

MALLE: There's a beautiful line in *The Thief of Paris* that says something to the effect that the thief is the moon of the honest man, meaning he is the fantasy or other half of the same person. But, of course, the whole idea of that film was that the thief and the honest man became incorporated when he (Belmondo) became a *successful* thief, so thus he was quite bourgeois!

I feel a lot like that as a filmmaker. I probably started making films out of rebellion, protesting the system of values, but the moment you become successful there are lots of temptations to join the Establishment. It was after *Thief of Paris* that I went to India because I felt the danger of such a situation. I've reached a point now where it doesn't worry me much. I know that we live in a world of compromise, and filmmaking especially has a lot to do with compromise, but I consider myself as one of a very small group of directors who have not been compromising very much. Like Buñuel, like Bresson.

At the same time you know the price you have to pay. Sometimes you have to be polite to people you want to throw out of the window. But that's not terribly important. What's important is what you do with your film. And I don't compromise as far as the films themselves are concerned.

And it's important to be able to drop out at any moment—which I might very well do now, for instance. Especially since *Pretty Baby* is doing well. That's my reaction to success!

HORTON: You have been classified by some as part of the French New Wave, but in earlier interviews, you have disowned such a classification. How do you see it now?

MALLE: I never knew exactly what it meant. There was the whole group at *Cahiers du Cinéma*, and I was not a part of that. In that sense I am not technically part of the group of Truffaut, Godard, Rivette, Chabrol, Rohmer. But we all had something in common for we were a generation that learned everything through seeing films. We were all complete film freaks. But I myself also learned from music and art and other interests. While someone like Truffaut was and has remained a film maniac. Any town he would go to he would check the papers to see what film he could see that night.

HORTON: *Holocaust* [1978] has recently been shown on American television. Mixing melodrama and documentary, it covers the Nazi atrocities. In many ways, however, your film *Lacombe, Lucien* was perhaps even more successful than *Holocaust* in helping audiences understand how an individual could become a fascist killer. Do you view your film as a political film about the Nazi period?

MALLE: I saw part of *Holocaust*, and I was absolutely shocked. It is probably a good idea to show that this horror existed, but the way that it was shown was so heavy and simplified. Exactly the opposite of *Lacombe, Lucien*. Every film can be considered a political film, but there was a certain political idea built into the film that was very controversial because it suggested that collaboration happened so often. You know, because the old attitude was that collaborators were very few and that they were just monsters. But this is not a very serious approach, of course. Actually I could demonstrate fairly convincingly that *Lacombe, Lucien* is a Marxist film. Because it's Marx's idea that the general proletariat could be an objective support of fascism, and of the ruling class, because they are not politically aware and so they become the tools of others in order to survive. And we see this occurring in every guerrilla war. When I was in Algeria I saw a lot of Algerians collaborating with the French. And they were very much from that poor background where they had to do anything to eat.

HORTON: To what degree was *Lacombe* based on your memories of the war?

MALLE: The period was very vivid in my memory. I was eleven years old and went to a religious school and the Gestapo came to the school one morning in January 1944 looking for children hidden under false names. It was a completely traumatic event. They took the children and the head of the school, all of whom had been turned in by a young servant who was working in the kitchen. He had been caught stealing from the school and they threw him out, and for revenge he went to the Nazis. He was just a kid, a little like *Lacombe, Lucien*. Actually, my first story was like the true story, but it was too close to me, too emotional so I changed it to what it became.

But I wanted to use that starting scene where he went to the Gestapo and denounced the boys. There was one in my class whose name was Bonet, which is a very French name, and I remember this little guy from the Gestapo in civilian clothes opening the door and asking for a boy with a name that was very obviously a Jewish name like Silverstein or something. And we saw our friend standing up, and he went around the room and shook hands with every one of us. Let me tell you that this is the kind of experience you don't forget.

Yes, to return to the point, I feel that *Lacombe* is very political because it implies that evil is not only committed by monsters. It would make life easier if this were so. But again I have been fascinated with the subject because I have known some of these people. In Algeria I knew a little fellow who was very nice. He's probably married now and living in the suburbs with two cars, and yet in those days he was torturing people. He was what they called an OR, Information Officer. But I spent an evening with him, and he seemed so average, so normal. And that's where the danger comes in because you begin to understand that everybody could become a fascist. Maybe that's a pessimistic view, but I believe that 90% of any population could become fascist.

HORTON: How do you feel about cinema today? Has television taken over, leaving film as a kind of aristocratic art form?

MALLE: Well, I would say that the industry seems to be in good shape. But the price they have to pay for this seems to me to be too great! I don't know. I feel that this religion of the blockbuster is very unhealthy.

Frank Capra

There is no higher calling in the world than being a director.

*I*n the following interview with Frank Capra, the director is candid about his primary focus on making money, notwithstanding the vicissitudes of working within the classical Hollywood studio system. Despite becoming a major asset to Columbia Pictures when the studio was "very small," Capra famously also co-created the independent production company, Liberty Films (so-named in 1945), through which he produced and directed what is now widely regarded as his masterpiece: *It's a Wonderful Life* (1946), starring James Stewart. Ironically, the comparative box office disappointment of *It's a Wonderful Life* was among several reasons for the demise of Liberty Films. The film has since been named by the American Film Institute as the most inspiring of all time.[1] The humanism of *It's a Wonderful Life*, its primary focus on the face (the uniqueness of Stewart's in particular), is echoed by the humanist philosophy that Capra espouses here.

This interview is a fascinating window into the transition from silent to sound production in Hollywood (as witnessed by Capra); the director's rise within the filmmaking business; his work with various personnel within the industry (including Barbara Stanwyck, whom he directed in her first feature film, *Ladies of Leisure*, 1930); his belief in unobtrusive direction because, in his words, the machinery "must never be seen." The interview foregrounds Capra's primary concern with appealing to an audience through "credibility," strictly classical continuity, emotionally immediate and actor-focused storytelling, and emphasis on entertainment (because the "message will come out" without laboring it). The unabashed idealism of Capra, along with his candor (including his frank description of wrongly rising to accept an Academy Award for *Lady for a Day*, 1933), makes a striking contrast with the press-junket processed, more guarded statements often made in interviews with filmmakers working today.

Interview transcribed by Harry A. Hargrave (on behalf of three students)
Originally published as "Interview with Frank Capra," Literature/Film Quarterly *9,
no. 3 (July 1981): 189–204.*

Born in 1897 near Palermo, Sicily, Frank Capra emigrated to America at the age
of six. While his father labored in a small vineyard near Sierra Madre, Frank
worked his way through school. Graduating in 1918 with a degree in chemical
engineering from California Institute of Technology, he joined the Army and
taught math in San Francisco until the Armistice was signed. In San Francisco he
"backed" into a movie career. Knowing nothing about movies, he talked his way
into directing a one-reel picture, *Fulta Fisher's Boarding House* [1922]. In Hollywood he wrote gags, first for Hal Roach, then for Mack Sennett. Sennett assigned
Capra to create a character for Harry Langdon. The collaboration was successful,
and Langdon hired Capra. *The Strong Man* [1926] and *Long Pants* [1927] followed.
The two parted, and in 1928, Capra joined Harry Cohen at Columbia Pictures
in a partnership which was to be one of the most profitable in the history of the
movie business. After a good start with *That Certain Thing* [1928], the new Columbia director made eight silents in two years before graduating to sound with
three Jack Holt "talkies."

In 1930, he directed his first big hit, *Ladies of Leisure*, which made a star out
of Barbara Stanwyck. Other early successes with Columbia included *Dirigible*
[1931]; *Platinum Blonde* [1931], with Loretta Young, Robert Williams, and Jean
Harlow; and *American Madness* [1932], with Walter Huston. In 1932, Frank Capra
directed one of his favorites, *The Bitter Tea of General Yen* [1933], with Barbara
Stanwyck and Miles Astor. Capra followed with a box office smash hit, *Lady for
a Day*, which netted Academy Award nominations for Best Actress (Mae Robe-
son), Best Director, Best Picture, and Best Script. But it was to be the next film
for which Capra would receive the first of his four Oscars. The year was 1934
and the picture *It Happened One Night*. No other movie had then ever won Oscars for Best Picture, Best Director, Best Actor (Clark Gable), Best Actress
(Claudette Colbert), and Best Screenplay (Robert Riskin). This was the first of
many successful collaborations between Riskin and Capra.

Broadway Bill [1934] came next. In 1936, he won a second Oscar for *Mr.
Deeds Goes to Town*, with Gary Cooper, and one of Capra's favorite actresses, Jean
Arthur. In 1937, Capra created Shangri-La for *Lost Horizon*, with Ronald Col-
man, Jane Wyatt, and Sam Jaffe. A third Oscar was awarded Mr. Capra in 1938
for *You Can't Take It with You*, pairing Jimmy Stewart and Jean Arthur as young
lovers, with Lionel Barrymore and Edward Arnold as their fathers. *Mr. Smith Goes
to Washington* [1939] brought Jimmy Stewart and Claude Rains face-to-face in a

Senate battle. It is a film that affirmed Capra's faith in democracy and the innate dignity of man.

In 1941, *Meet John Doe*, starring Gary Cooper, proved to be one of the hardest-hitting films of Capra and screenwriter Robert Riskin. Before entering World War II, Mr. Capra finished *Arsenic and Old Lace*, released in 1944, starring Cary Grant. He joined the Army shortly after Pearl Harbor and began the seven films of the *Why We Fight* series. Those are considered classics in the documentary field. For them he won another Oscar and received medals from General Marshall.

In late 1945, Capra formed his own production company, Liberty Films. For the new company he made what has come to be his favorite film, *It's a Wonderful Life*, again with Jimmy Stewart. It ran nip and tuck with William Wyler's *The Best Years of Our Lives* for Best Picture of 1946. Katharine Hepburn and Spencer Tracy were the stars of Capra's screen version of *State of the Union* in 1948. After selling Liberty Films to Paramount, Mr. Capra made two films with Bing Crosby for Paramount: *Riding High* in 1950 and *Here Comes the Groom* the following year. Between pictures Capra made a series of four hour-long television shows on science for the Bell Telephone Company, before teaming with Frank Sinatra in 1958 for *A Hole in the Head*.

Capra's most recent feature is *A Pocketful of Miracles*, made in 1961 with Glenn Ford, Peter Falk, and Bette Davis. In 1964, he directed a documentary film on space travel for the New York World's Fair. And in 1971 he wrote his autobiography, *The Name Above the Title*. During the last few years Mr. Capra has lectured and held film seminars in over 50 American and Canadian schools, sharing his film experience with thousands of students and faculty members. The following interview between Mr. Capra and three interested students was taped on March 24, 1976, on the campus of North Carolina State University.

Capra's visit to North Carolina State University was made possible by grants from the National Endowment for the Arts and the Film Institute of the University. During his stay, March 15–24, 1976, he met with film classes, talked with individuals interested in the movies or in film careers, and lectured nightly to students and the general public after screenings of his major works.

QUESTION: Could you tell us about the silent era in films? What was it like directing in the silent era?

CAPRA: Well, the principal difference between the silents and, let's say, sound, was that we didn't use scripts. We had a thing called a scenario—at least some of the very expensive films did have a scenario of some sort—very thin. Just with titles as to the kind of story. But Mack Sennett in the comedy department never wrote anything; nothing was written in Mack Sennett's studio. He didn't like books; and if you brought in a book, he'd throw you out. "No gags in books," he'd say. He had been a water boy to an Irish section hand, and this Irish foreman became his idol. He wished he could be just like him: strong and positive.

There were never books around there, and he just thought that visual humor couldn't be found in books; and he was right. There were no word jokes; there were visual jokes. They were visual things; and these you had to think up without any paper. And we just discussed the sequences and what would come next in a two-reel comedy. The plot was quite simple, and what we'd try to do was to get two gag-men teams. And they would work on that. Now you would tell the routines that you thought up to Mr. Sennett. If he liked them, and of course he was a great audience, you could hear him laugh for two blocks; he'd just open his mouth and guffaw. I guess his strength was what he liked and what he laughed at was pretty surely what the audience would laugh at. So he was sort of an audience barometer. If he liked the routine he'd work on it too, but he was not an inventive man himself. He'd try to tell a joke and even forget the punch line; he was not funny in himself. But he was a great audience. And if he liked your routine, you were allowed to go and tell the director the routine; and if the director liked it, he'd shoot it; if he didn't like it, he wouldn't shoot it.

QUESTION: Wasn't there an occasion where you thought of an idea, and he didn't like it? What happened then?

CAPRA: Yes, there was an occasion. There were occasions when he didn't like the idea. I had an occasion once about a wheel with Ben Turpin, the guy with the crossed eyes. He was making love to a girl. He had taken her out in the moonlight in his buggy, and he tried to get amorous, and she didn't want any part of it. Every time he'd get amorous, the wheel would almost slip off because his rival had unscrewed the wheel from the axle, so this wheel would almost go off. But when she pushed him back, she'd be saved for the wheel would move back over, too. But finally, of course, the wheel came off, and he fell down. Well, that's a running gag. You can use it and get a routine out of it. And he said, "No, that isn't funny." Well, I thought it was very funny; and so I told it to an actor who was working on the Ben Turpin show, and he thought it was funny; and I said, "Why don't you tell it to the director?" So he went around and told the director. The director loved it, and he shot it. Then Mr. Sennett went into the projection room to see the rushes, and here was this gag.

QUESTION: Why didn't Mack Sennett like it?

CAPRA: He didn't think it was funny. That was his right. He always said, "Whose name is over the gate?" "Yours Mr. Sennett." He raised heck about that gag, and he said, "All right, we'll leave it in. I want to teach you a lesson. But I'm taking you to the preview. I'm going to prove to you that it's not funny." Well, we did go to the thing, and it was very funny. And boy, I came out to raves and everything else. I came out rubbing my hands, and he says, "You're fired."

QUESTION: What did you do then?

CAPRA: Being fired by Sennett was not all that serious because if you came back and walked in front of the gate and looked penitent, with your old clothes on, and he saw you walking in front of that gate when he came in his big car and when he went out in his big car (you had to be there all the time), he'd see you doing penance in front of that gate with his name on it. Well, in about three days he'd let you in. You'd get your job, and that was Sennett.

QUESTION: How did he compare with Hal Roach? Did they work along the same lines?

CAPRA: No. Hal Roach was more of a structured person. He was not quite as slap happy as Sennett. He was more structured to the thing. It was more of an assembly-line proposition. At Sennett it was a happy go lucky, free for all thing—anything went.

QUESTION: How long did you wait before you started working with Harry Langdon?

CAPRA: I was there about a year before I started working with Harry Langdon.

QUESTION: Did he hire you? I mean did he see your work and say, "Hey, I want that man to direct?"

CAPRA: I just was a gag man for Harry Langdon for about another year. I just wrote his material. I didn't direct Harry Langdon until he left Sennett and went on to make feature pictures, and I became his director on the film we saw the other day, *The Strong Man*.

QUESTION: Did Harry Langdon do his own stunt work?

CAPRA: No, you can't let the star of your show do stuntwork. If he breaks a leg, then the whole thing goes to pieces. No, you use doubles all the time.

QUESTION: A lot of people didn't make the transition to sound. They didn't survive. How did you survive?

CAPRA: It was just a period of transition. You were still in the business of telling a story. That's the business of entertainment, that's really not such a new business. Except that we were dealing in words now as well as in pictures. The transition was not that difficult. Almost anybody who knew anything about films, silent films, survived into sound. It was not a great change for people to make. It was a great change physically for the studios. They had to soundproof the stages, spend a lot of money, build new stages in many cases. They had to get a tremendous amount of new equipment they didn't have before. The recording equipment was very, very expensive. But oddly enough very little production was stopped because of the change. They just kept on making silents and sound, and then gradually changed over to sound without losing stride.

QUESTION: Mr. Capra, what film do you think first fulfilled your aims or purpose as a director?

CAPRA: My purpose as a director was to make money. So I was very happy when the audience liked the very first one I made because that was my aim. At that time we got very little money; at Mack Sennett's I got $35 a week. When I started directing for Harry Langdon, I got $600 a week, which was quite a jump. That was our main thrust—money.

QUESTION: Did you not have your own film company, was it Liberty Films?

CAPRA: That was almost 30 years later.

QUESTION: Whom did you form it with?

CAPRA: I had been in the army; and when we got out of the army, I formed it with people who had been in the army: William Wyler, George Stevens, and a businessman named Sam Briscuit. There were three directors and a businessman.

QUESTION: Did this company have any purpose as such?

CAPRA: Yes, we wanted to make independent films, not make films for a studio, just make them for ourselves.

QUESTION: Did you use any star, or did you . . . ?

CAPRA: We used whatever people we could get. We hired for each film. We'd expand for making a film, and contract. Expand and contract; that way we didn't have any great overhead to carry.

QUESTION: You went from gag writer to director. Did you ever think about going any further than director into some other . . .

CAPRA: There is no higher calling in the world than being a director. What more can you want than to be a filmmaker?

QUESTION: All your life you believed in the motto: "One Man, One Film."

CAPRA: Yes, I knew nothing about the stage, and I knew nothing about anything else really when I started in this business. I graduated from Cal. Tech. as a chemical engineer, and that was what I was going to be. I couldn't get a job. I sold apples on the street until I got into filmmaking. That's all there was to it. I had an opportunity to get a job with a film company, and that was what started me. The first film I made was a little one-reeler. I did the whole thing because nobody else knew anything about it, and everybody knew less than I did, and I knew nothing. So, you can see how we were the blind leading the blind. Anyhow, there's when I started with this "One Man, One Film" idea. I could not understand how anybody else could write the material for you and then you'd shoot it; and then you'd give it to an editor, and the editor would put it together the way he wanted it; and then the producer would do it up. I just didn't understand how all of this could happen and yet produce an art form. This was a committee. Everybody would give their own interpretation to that film. And naturally, when a committee dabbles in art, they don't come up with much. You've heard that a camel is a horse made by a committee. I thought that if this is an art form at all, it's the guy that makes the show. The so-called artist should have control, not the actors, not the wardrobe people, or the song people, or the photography people. I was able to put that idea into execution at Columbia Studios, a very small studio down on Poverty Row where I became the big fish in a very small pond; therefore I could ask for things that I couldn't get any other place. And the first thing I asked for was to have complete control of what I was doing. Since they needed me and the films I made for them made money, that was very fine with them. And they could fire me at any time. That's the way I did inaugurate this "One Man, One Film" idea. I was the first hired director to be able to do that. Of course, if you owned your own company, you [could] do anything you wanted to. But I didn't own my own company. A man like DeMille owned his own company; therefore he could put his name where he wanted to, and he could really control his material. And today it is practically "One Man, One Film" all over the world.

QUESTION: Could you choose your own technical people then?

CAPRA: Right, you have to choose as much as you can. I mean, you just can't choose at will. People who are working some other place won't stop there to come to work for you.

QUESTION: How did you begin working with Robert Riskin? Was that by accident?

CAPRA: No, Robert Riskin came out when Columbia hired a lot of young playwrights. He came with the bunch. There were about six or seven. He came out with that bunch. And we worked together on our first film, which was *Platinum Blonde*; and we became very good friends, and we started vibrating to the same tuning fork, and then we worked together on about twelve films.

QUESTION: Also Dimitri Tiomkin did a lot of your musical scores.

CAPRA: Yes, Tiomkin scored a lot of films. He was a Russian. He emigrated to Paris, and began to speak French with a Russian accent, and knew German with a Russian accent. He began to speak English with a Russian accent, and finally he began to speak Russian with no accent or with an odd accent. So he's a man who can't speak any language anymore without an accent. But he's a wonderful musician. I gave him the first opportunity he had to score a film which was *Lost Horizon*, and that was the most expensive thing Columbia had ever made, and to give it to an outside man who had never had any experience in scoring a film was really something that the studio thought was absolutely crazy. But I wanted something new and different, and I thought that this man could give that Russian-Asian quality to the music that I thought the picture ought to have.

QUESTION: When did you decide to put music behind them?

CAPRA: Music is another tool which you are able to use in telling a story, as you use sound, as you use color. These are all tools. Your principal tools, of course, are the actors. The others are all accessories to your storytelling. So you use them as you think the story should be colored by music, or by sound, or by color, or by photography, to advance the mood or the style of the scene that you're shooting.

QUESTION: Could you tell us what happened at the Academy Award dinner for *Lady for a Day*?

CAPRA: Well, I thought I'd made films that merited at least the attention of the Academy, of course everybody thinks that. But I thought it very strongly. *American Madness, Platinum Blonde, Dirigible*—films like that have been mentioned at least. But since we were a very small studio, we didn't have many votes, probably not more than two votes in the whole studio. When *Lady for a Day* came along, it was a very big hit in theaters, with the public as well as with the press and the critics. And it also was a big hit with the Academy voters because it was nominated for four categories: Best Picture, Best Actress, Best Writing, Best Directing. It was a tremendous thing for me. I looked up the records and no film had ever won four major Oscars, and I thought here's a chance to make a sweep, this is probably the best picture for the whole year; and anybody who votes for anything else is out of his mind. So I was really sure that we'd get at least four awards. I became impossible to live with. We moved in from the beach; I rented a big house in Beverly Hills to be seen around; I gave parties; I went to restaurants and stood around so they'd see me, and I got a tuxedo made by a tailor, expecting surely to be seen; and I rehearsed speeches, I wrote lots of acceptance speeches; and I practiced them before a mirror so my voice would break in just the right place. My wife was in her ninth month of pregnancy, and she just locked the door and thought I'd lost my mind. And I had! So I went to the Academy Dinner at the Biltmore, and Will Rogers was the master of ceremonies. He was giving out the awards. The first celebrity I ever knew was Will Rogers. I thought this was a good omen. I had invited about ten friends. The first was the writing award, and I thought Bob Riskin's going to win this, and I'm going to win the next one. It was not *Lady for a Day*; it was for *Little Women* [1933]. Victor Herrman and Sarah Mason were called up to the stand, and I thought Oh, my goodness. Well, I said, okay, I'll settle for three. The next one was mine, and Will Rogers began talking. It was dark, and I had this crumbled up little speech in my hand, and I unrolled it and tried to look at it, and I couldn't, and he said: "The envelope," and he looked at it and he said, "It couldn't happen to a nicer kid than this, and I've known him for such a long time, and he came from nothing"; and every word spelled me, of course, and finally he said, "come up and get it, Frank." Well, everybody at my table leaped in the air, and it was a long walk to the dance floor. I went around people's tables saying, "Excuse me, excuse me," etc. And I got to the dance floor, and the spot-light was going around, and I was saying, "Here I am! Over here!" And finally the spot light goes over and stops and picks up another guy on the other side of the dance floor, and it's Frank Lloyd, the director of *Cavalcade* [1933]. I was actually aghast and astonished standing there in the dark, and Will Rogers embraces him and everything else, and finally somebody said "Down in front!" right behind me, and I moved. And that long walk back with everybody yelling "down in front" was the most miserable thing I've ever had happen to me. And I was so mad at the Academy I said that if they ever, ever, ever give me one, I won't accept it. Well, the next film was *It Happened One Night* . . .

QUESTION: Where you won everything?

CAPRA: I was there.

QUESTION: And you accepted?

CAPRA: I accepted.

QUESTION: While you were at Columbia, Joseph Walker was the director of photography for most of your films. Could you tell us about this collaboration? How did his style affect your style in motion pictures?

CAPRA: Well, he had no particular style. What he was interested in was trying to figure out what you wanted. But he was innovative. He wouldn't be stopped by anything; you couldn't really stop him. If you had something difficult you wanted to get, some kind of a mood, he'd do it. He knew how to get it. We did a lot of experimenting together with the use of lenses and with the use of masks and with the use of gauze, and things like that.

QUESTION: Although you feel that the camera in its relation to the movie should be as unobtrusive as possible, how do you feel about unique camera angles and expressionistic lighting in respect to creating or in helping to emphasize a mood? Would you think it's all right as long as it's used in that . . .

CAPRA: If it's trying to emphasize a mood, yes. But if you see the machinery, the story's going out the window. It is not a machinery-to-the-people medium. It's a people-to-people medium. The actors are telling the story. You can only involve the audience in the lives of the actors and characters that the actors are playing. You can't involve them in machinery. They don't give a darn about a sunset, or a fast moving camera, or a hand-held camera, or anything like that. These are ego-massaging, little, egocentric things that directors indulge in, and we indulge in for ourselves and for each other. But audiences are bored with that.

QUESTION: Maybe I've just seen old prints, but I'm wondering do you use a soft focus effect to create a romantic or nostalgic mood. I noticed in *It Happened One Night* in some of the shots of Claudette Colbert it seemed that she was in soft focus to suggest her romantic interest in Clark Gable.

CAPRA: Well, it's not just to suggest her interest in Clark Gable. You want her to look very nice at that moment, and that's done with long focus lenses where the focus will become very narrow; and if you focus on the person's eyes and nose, everything back of their head gets soft because it goes out of focus. So you get a feeling of a kind of softness about the whole scene which transmits itself into the mood of the girl if she's in a soft mood. We did a lot of that kind of stuff—a lot of work with four-inch lenses, even six-inch lenses.

QUESTION: How about deep focus? Do you use that in *American Madness* to dehumanize a mob, or did you use it in other aspects?

CAPRA: We used that mostly to widen the focus so that more people would be in focus, and that's when you use a wide-angle lens, and you get great depth of focus with that. And you get a very short depth of focus with the larger lenses, the three- and four-inch and the six-inch lenses. So we'd use, let's say a 35mm or a 25mm lens on the wide shots where everybody would be in focus even those close and those in the back.

QUESTION: Normally it seems that when I'm watching your pictures that the camera is usually objective, letting you see the whole thing; but then occasionally it will switch like in *Mr. Smith Goes to Washington* and become subjective; in other words the camera will actually become one of your characters, and let the audience see what that person sees. Can you elaborate on that?

CAPRA: That's point of view. It really depends. If I'm photographing somebody, and he is looking up here, and I know what he is looking at, then you have to photograph what he is looking at from that point of view just to follow the continuity. You don't disorient the audience. There's nothing that makes an audience more unhappy than to be disoriented. They don't know where you are. If you make a sharp reverse cut for no reason at all, they don't know what happened. So their mood of being with the film and being part of it is broken, you see, that's just bad direction. Whenever you break an audience's mood, you're just asking for trouble. So you use machinery, but it must never be seen. The interest must always be on the actors. That's what the audience is interested in, in the people who are to make these decisions, the actors. But how you get there, that's your business, not theirs. They don't want to know about that.

QUESTION: Leland Poague, in his book [*The Cinema of Frank Capra: An Approach to Film Comedy* (A.S. Barnes, 1975)], says that in your editing style you use a lot of cuts between shots. Is this because of your emphasis on dialogue and the story or do you only use this frequent cutting in scenes where you're trying to build suspense?

CAPRA: Well, you follow the interest. That is the guideline there. Where's the interest? Who does the audience want to see? Whose face do they want to see react to somebody else coming in the door? What effect is that going to have on them? You follow the interest of what is happening, and if you just use that as the guideline, you'll find that you will do the right kind of cutting. Who do you want to see next? Who do you want to see in that moment? Now these are cuts with closeups. A closeup is an emphasis. You want to get up close so you can see that person's face, the person's eyes. What are her thoughts at this moment? Closeups are for dramatic purposes—not just to speed up or not just for glamour. They must have a purpose. Every cut must have a purpose. One of the principal things about it is to get the smooth flow, the filmic flow, the dynamic of film. You can edit a film so that it flows very smoothly from one cut to another. You don't know where you have a cut; you just don't know. Your interest flows back and forth, back here this way and that way, and it's just wonderful the effect you get when you do it right. The audience doesn't know it or have to know anything else. They remain fascinated by what is going on. That's what you should try to accomplish. There are many ways to put scenes together. Many, many ways. But only one or two are worth a darn.

QUESTION: How many cameras did you use?

CAPRA: Mostly three.

QUESTION: Three at once?

CAPRA: Yes, but there are a lot of problems. You can light one camera; and if you light two cameras, the problem is doubled; and if you light three cameras, your problem goes up geometrically. The problems with three cameras are eight times what they are with one. But it's worth the effort because then you've got that scene photographed from three different angles, and you just intercut those angles at will. You can go from one to another without fear of stopping the pace or the effects of the scene or anything else, because it is one scene being photographed from several angles. And if you have to stop in between and photograph all those angles separately, you're liable not to get the same intensity, the same character of the scene, the same kind of mood of the scene, the same feeling of the scene as when it's photographed all at the same time. And then you pick up closeups from one of the other cameras at the same time that the master scene was being photographed.

QUESTION: What sort of techniques did you use in editing to help bridge a time gap in a story?

CAPRA: All kinds of gimmicks have been used: going from a tree with flowers to a tree with snow on it. A lot of these things you think are necessary, but the audience is so far ahead of you that all these things bore them. So if somebody is going into the elevator on the eighth floor, you can bring him right out of the building on the next cut, and the audience will thank you. They know he went down. It just accelerates telling your story. You just don't have to follow him down, and follow him getting out, and all his long walks. That's unnecessary. They do it in television because they've got to fill up time.

QUESTION: Do you use headlines for bridging a time gap or just going forward?

CAPRA: Information. In a play that used to be done by the butler and the cook talking in the kitchen. They gave you everything that happened the night before: who was what, who was with whom, who slept with whom. They give you a lot of this exposition part. Exposition is dreary stuff, and it has to be made kind of interesting. That is why you have to use your ingenuity to make exposition interesting. I used newspaper headlines and that kind of thing that would have a kind of flow to it. Other people do it other kinds of ways. But the whole thing is how do you tell exposition, what happened. You're in this interval between this sequence and that one, it may be a week or a year. What happened during that time? Tell it short, quick, exciting; make it interesting.

QUESTION: I was amazed at some of the technical solutions you came up with, like how to show cold.

CAPRA: Well, I have a passion for credibility, and I tried to make a film believable, and that starts, of course, with getting very good actors for all the small parts; because if you believe the small people, you're more liable to believe the derring-do of the stars. And, of course, such things as snow that looks like snow, and cold that looks like cold, are made more credible when we see breath of people that are working in the scene. If you get in the 20°s, your breath shows. If you're supposed to be in the 20°s, and there's no breath, the audience knows something is phony about that scene. And in a word they just don't believe the scene, and then they won't believe the story. But if you make all those things credible, and they believe that you're out in the cold or that you're in the Arctic, then you believe everything.

QUESTION: How did you solve that problem in *Lost Horizon*?

CAPRA: I took everybody to an ice house. We hired an ice house and made a studio of it, and threw out the swordfish that were piled up in it, and brought in the actors.

QUESTION: Did you go on location when you made your movies?

CAPRA: Location wherever it was possible. It was too costly then. The equipment was not as fine and miniaturized as it is today, and it was rather cumbersome. If you went out to take a closeup of two people away from the studio, you had a retinue of over fifteen trucks following you. It was a very expensive thing. Now that is all over with. You can make a picture anyplace in the world with the equipment that you can put in a station wagon. And many pictures are shot that way. Interior and exterior, all are shot right on location.

QUESTION: In most of your films, you focus on the average man, your John Doe, your little man, the individual who is typical of everyday life. I guess it's the little man versus the big man, and in many of your films you were against politics or political bosses. Would you go into detail and say why?

CAPRA: Well, about the little man. I like people. I think people are just wonderful. I also think that people are all equal in the sense of their dignity, their divinity; there's no such thing as common man or an uncommon man. To me they're all—each one has something unique. Each one is actually unique. Never before has there been anyone like you. Never again will there be anyone like you. One mold, one young lady. So you're a very unique person, so is he, so is he. You are something that never existed before and will never exist again. Isn't that wonderful? Isn't that something pretty exciting? So I look at you as something that plays part of a great whole, an equal part of everything, or else you wouldn't be here.

That being the case, I just always liked to get down to people that are supposed to be the mob, and I find very interesting people there. I like people, and I get right into them. I use people a great deal for background. I shoot many scenes in crowds because I think people are more interested in other people than they are in anything else. They love the faces; they don't know who the devil they are, but they like them because they are people. You could put a camera inside of a window, let's say a grocery store or a restaurant or a jewelry store, and just photograph the people from the inside window-shopping. And you watch the various faces that come in and look; they're just fascinating. You are an audience by looking at them in the projection room; you can't take your eyes off them. They are interesting per se to other people. That's why I direct my attention to the people or to the actors that are representing people, and they become credible, and they know who they are and then the audiences care for them. The biggest thing is that I want them to care about these people.

QUESTION: Your characters seem to represent certain ideals, like all of mankind should stick together and love and . . .

CAPRA: Well, the advent of the human race has been because of idealists and not because of masochists, or cynics. That's all pretty dry. It gets you nowhere. It's the idealists who walk alone and live alone and swim up the stream.

QUESTION: They're non-conformers?

CAPRA: They're non-conformers. And it's the idealists that are non-conformers. And they're the ones that finally become the folk heroes. I don't know where we're going, but we came up from some kind of a jungle, and we're better off now than we were in the jungles. Some of us have a little more compassion within us and forgiveness within us, and make a kind of an evolution. I don't know where we're evolving to, but the idealists will have a great deal to do with where we're going.

QUESTION: You "discovered" a lot of new talent, like Barbara Stanwyck. What kind of talents did you look for in a prospective actor or actress?

CAPRA: I don't know what I looked for.

QUESTION: Were you just told to go look at Harry Langdon and make something out of him?

CAPRA: Yes! That's right. And we managed to do something with Harry Langdon. But I don't look for anything in people. I look for interest; if they attract me, they're interesting. That's a point in their favor.

QUESTION: I've heard that with Barbara Stanwyck, you would rehearse all the other actors before she came on the set; and when she came on, she just went through it and did it in one take.

CAPRA: She was very difficult to work with because she was unskilled in that she started as a chorus girl and she worked her way to be a kind of ingénue, and she was very, very stage-minded. She had only one performance to give to the audience and that was the performance she gave when she gave it. She'd give the best performance in a rehearsal. And every time she did it again, well, that was new to her, and it would not be as good as the first time she did it, and each succeeding time she did it she would go downhill. Now this was a great problem because you have to rehearse these scenes with other people; you have to see that everybody else knows what they're doing. And then you get an actor that leaves the best performance in the rehearsal. That really creates a problem because then you will not get her best performance on the film. So with her, I realized that she was new and young and fresh and dewy-eyed, and that she would not be able to master this technique that other film actors had mastered: to keep their emotions down in rehearsals and save them for the time when they needed them during the takes. So I just had to invent ways not to rehearse her. And that's where the three camera thing started with me so I'd have more cameras on at one time so really I didn't have to do as many takes with her. We were trying to get all the different kinds of angles, we tried to get all the angles we possibly needed, the important ones in a scene the first time. This created problems in lighting, it created problems with the other actors. They hadn't heard of her; they didn't know—I didn't give a damn whether they'd heard of her or not, I knew she'd be marvelous. Everybody'd stop just to look at her. She really had power—a lot of young, fresh power. She'd make you believe anything she did. So in that way we had to shoot Barbara Stanwyck on her first film, *Ladies of Leisure*, and on a couple of other films; but not too long after that, of course, she learned to control herself, because other directors might not go to these lengths just to baby her and protect that first scene she would do.

QUESTION: You liked characters or actors who played themselves, didn't you? Is that what you were looking for? Gary Cooper on the screen as well as off screen has struck me as almost the character he played.

CAPRA: Well, he'll play that character better than he will any other character. And in a sense every actor puts himself into that part. No two actors would play the same role alike because they are different people. Each one is a unique individual. They have no likenesses at all. And they'd play the same part, but not the same. That's why when I'm casting a part I try to get the actor that I think will do that part as I see that part.

QUESTION: What messages should filmmakers be communicating to the audience?

CAPRA: The message is that we should forget messages. You have Western Union for that.

QUESTION: What ideals?

CAPRA: Entertainment. Just entertainment. It's show business, it's theatrical, it's theatrics. What message have you got for the world? At your age? You're still learning. You're still absorbing stimuli from the outside. You still don't know. You've got opinions, but your opinions will change. You'll go back and forth as you make your way through life. You'll realize that your opinions were probably in a sense prejudiced. And you will find that they will change. So what gives you the right to give the world a message? See? You wait for that message. Don't worry about that message. You worry about entertainment. You worry about making things interesting and tell a story in an interesting way. Never mind the message. That message will come out. If you have anything, it will come out. But it will come out when you can give that message with entertainment; and if you're going to make tracts instead of dramas, people are not going to come to see them. They won't pay money to come and hear tracts, religious, political, or any kind of tracts that you have in mind. But the audience is the main thing you must think about, not the critics. That's the reason we make films; that's the theater. A theater is not a theater without an audience.

QUESTION: I was reading some critiques on your major films by Leland Poague in his book. Do you think that he overemphasizes the sexuality in your films?

CAPRA: I'm not too familiar with that part of Poague's book. You just can't forget sexuality. It is a part of everyday living. It is part of what we live with, and it is part of the great joy of living. I don't think we could eliminate it. I don't think we can downgrade it, nor do I think that we should defile it. And when you see explicit sex scenes on the screen, they are defiling one of the most wondrous things any human being can experience.

NOTE

1. Each year the AFI (American Film Institute) creates a television special for CBS as part of the *100 Years . . . 100 Movies* series. *It's a Wonderful Life* was named the most inspiring American film to date in the broadcast on CBS television on June 14, 2006. "AFI: TV and Events Homepage," http://www.afi.com/tvevents/100years/movies.aspx (8 August 2007).

René Clair

> I think that a picture must be able to be understood by all classes of
> society, which is true, by the way, for the best pictures, if you look
> to the past.

*O*n May 10, 1979, Gregory Mason spoke to director René Clair in a retrospective on the director's career that displays Clair's characteristic generosity and
passion—as Mason notes in his own introduction, "[t]he interview was punctuated frequently with laughter." So unassuming is the director, in fact, that he begins by admitting that he does not keep any of his own films. Some of the interview consists of anecdotes surrounding the production of various films, such
as Clair's admission that shooting on *Paris qui dort* (*Paris Asleep/The Crazy Ray*,
1925) had to be stopped one day because the cast and crew could not afford the
entrance fee. At other times, Clair reflects more generally on his approaches to
his filmmaking over the years, such as his sense of what it means to be "faithful"
to a play. But Clair hardly presents himself as the expert on his own oeuvre: he
is just as likely to confess that he has forgotten something from one of his films,
as when Mason asks him about a scene from *Un chapeau de paille d'Italie* (*Italian
Straw Hat*, 1928) that Clair does not immediately recall. In all cases, however,
Clair's generosity is evident, and he ends by noting that a "picture must be able
to be understood by all classes of society. . . . We should take care that motion
pictures do not lose this precious quality."

Interview by Gregory Mason
Originally published as "René Clair at 80: An Interview," Literature/Film Quarterly
10, no. 2 (April 1983): 85–99.

The best of René Clair's early work combined an almost balletic, slapstick drollery with an incisive satiric wit, whether in such silent classics as *Entr'acte* (1924) and *Un chapeau de paille d'Italie*, or in the groundbreaking early sound films *Le Million* (*The Million*, 1931) and *À nous la liberté* (*Freedom for Us*, 1931). His later work was more reflective, as in the wistful, superbly photographed *Les Grandes manoeuvres* (*The Grand Maneuver*, 1955). With such major box office successes as *Sous les toits de Paris* (*Under the Roofs of Paris*, 1930), Clair gained both the respect of the critics and the affection of the international cinema-going public. His theoretical writings reflected the same crisp intelligence and familiar sense of irony that informed his films. Herman Weinberg praised Clair's *Cinema Yesterday and Today* (1973) as "the most serene, cool and patrician writing on the cinema extant." In 1960, René Clair became the first filmmaker to be elected to the Academie Française.

Throughout his career, Clair struggled to remain free of the influence of the big studios, whether in Paris, Berlin, London, or Hollywood. In the thirties, Joseph Goebbels tried to persuade Clair to move his base of operations to Berlin and to interest him in a plagiarism suit against Charles Chaplin. Infuriated by Chaplin's mockery of Hitler in *The Great Dictator* (1940), Goebbels sought to discredit Chaplin by attacking his obvious borrowings in *Modern Times* (1936) from Clair's *À nous la liberté*. Clair, needless to say, was not interested.

During the interview, Clair reflected on his work with genuine interest but with a certain detachment. He was usually reluctant to interpret his own efforts, a familiar if occasionally exasperating experience for the critic. And reflecting on the course of such a long career, it was understandable that in some cases he had simply forgotten the reasons for artistic judgments made nearly fifty years ago. Indeed, the word "probably" occurred with some frequency on Clair's lips, as if he too were surmising on his possible motives, somewhat in the manner of an outsider. The interview was punctuated frequently with laughter. At one point, Clair applauded with great good humor a gag from *Un chapeau de paille d'Italie* that he had entirely forgotten. But this was the kind of irony he enjoyed.

It was equally ironic to discover how little control Clair, the complete *auteur* of his films in their conception and making, had managed to maintain over the fate of his works after their release. Their cavalier re-editing by different distributors and the insertion of redundant titles by foreign editors was still clearly a source of chagrin. René Clair owned none of his films. This surprisingly diffident attitude toward his own work was entirely consistent with his general view of the cinema. Clair knew that the same process that preserves every gesture and outward sign on a film also freezes it into a quickly overtaken moment in time. He valued preserved film artifacts less than the ongoing film enterprise, at its best a symbiotic process where new films are continually shown to contemporary audiences. For Clair, it was neither the filmmaker nor the critic but the viewing public that was the true arbiter of quality. He saw the broad popular appeal of the cinema as its most important characteristic, making it unique among contemporary arts.

On March 15, 1981, René Clair died in his sleep in his Paris home at the age of eighty-two. As a filmmaker, he brought to the cinema a fine sense both of humor and of irony. As a man, he exemplified the wit and humanitarianism so apparent in his substantial body of work. The cinema has lost another of its pioneers from whom it still has a lot to learn.

MASON: Monsieur Clair, you have enjoyed a long career in filmmaking. Looking back over the body of your work, I wonder how you now feel about it—which, for instance, emerge as your favorite films in retrospect?

CLAIR: It's more a question of which of my films I can still stand to look at, which ones I don't hate.

MASON: Doesn't it worry you even so, that some of your films may be lost forever? I read a couple of years ago that, when the late Henri Langlois of the Cinémathèque Française died, the vaults were found to be almost empty. Have you personally retained prints of at least some of your films?

CLAIR: I have not one piece of my films. I'm not interested in keeping old films. I would perhaps be interested if it were done under the proper conditions, in vaults with the proper ventilation, but that's too difficult.

MASON: What then is the archival situation in France? Do you know?

CLAIR: There are big battles around personal ambitions. The only serious thing in France are the archives of film history, *Les Archives de Film*, because they are just technicians who want to protect and preserve the films. But Langlois and his school were more or less like antiquaries; he kept old films, and the older they were the better it was. He had no idea of protecting or preserving them.

MASON: You wrote in your *Cinema Yesterday and Today* that "what remains of a film creator's efforts is not so much a body of work as the inspiration this work can give to those who follow him." Do you now feel then, that as far as your own films go, they might provide inspiration but that they haven't stood the test of time as artifacts?

CLAIR: That's more or less true, yes. There are some films I made that are still nice to look at, like *Les Grandes manoeuvres*, but on the whole . . .

MASON: Looking back to the start of your directing career in 1923, to *Paris qui dort*: do you recall if you got the idea for this film from the very early French films, like *Onésime Horloger* (1912)? It has a plot that is quite similar.

CLAIR: I never felt that, you know, but probably I was impressed by some old films I had seen when I was a kid.

MASON: You had seen some of these old films by Zecca and others?

CLAIR: Probably. But now it seems I know these films because I have read about them. It's a later impression, you see.

MASON: Is it true that when you were filming *Paris qui dort* you had to stop filming because you couldn't afford the entrance fee to get into the Eiffel Tower?

CLAIR: Quite true. On one day.

MASON: How was the budget? Were you literally just going from day to day?

CLAIR: There was no budget. There was no organization behind me. I was making the film for another director who had become a producer, you see, and he was very happy when I came back with some reels of film because he didn't have too much money at the time.

MASON: So you were using your own money, obviously, to get into the Eiffel Tower, but how about the purchase of the film stock?

CLAIR: No, that was made by the so-called producer. I couldn't have used my own money because I didn't have any of my own.

MASON: Did each of the actors have to pay his or her own admission or something like that?

CLAIR: No, no. We did that for them. (*Laughter*)

MASON: How did you get your cast together for *Paris qui dort*?

CLAIR: I took the people who were given to me by the so-called producer. I met Albert Prejean, for example, while making *Paris qui dort*, and after that I used him as often as I could.

MASON: Apparently *Paris qui dort* has been mutilated many times and there are many different kinds of prints available. There is a company in the United States which offers six or seven of your films for sale, including *Paris qui dort*, and they claim that theirs is the authentic version.

CLAIR: No, there are no authentic versions extant, but the closest to authenticity is the one which now belongs to the Pathé Company in Paris. That's the only one, because the so-called producer Henri Diamant-Berger, before he died, wanted to reissue it, and he had no right to do it without my consent. Then we made a sort of deal, and I took *Paris qui dort* and recut it, as far as I could remember the way it had been originally.

MASON: Did you have any thematic intentions with this film or was it just more of an experiment in stop motion? Some critics have suggested that there's a theme like "Money doesn't buy you happiness" there. When you were making the film, was there anything like this in your mind?

CLAIR: Well, I was interested in showing an example of what the motion picture should be. It's the difference between still and motion, you see.

MASON: And any more complex thematic designs are just something that the critics have put onto it?

CLAIR: They are dreaming the others, yes.

MASON: Turning to *Entr'acte*: again I'm interested in your intentions in this film. Let me suggest some possible intentions, and you can say whether they were there or not. Some playful ones: was there any idea of an homage to Lumière with the spraying of the hose?

CLAIR: No.

MASON: How about Méliès and the balloons going up and down and so forth?

CLAIR: I didn't think of Méliès or Lumière when I made that film, although I admired them very much of course.

MASON: Were there any other kind of "in" jokes, private gags, like the Tyrolean hat, the matches, the camels—were there any special references here, or a comment on anything specific?

CLAIR: No, just improvisation in the Dadaist spirit.

MASON: Would it be fair then to say that there is no narrative intention in your film *Entr'acte*, or is there some narrative intention in it?

CLAIR: With the question of *Entr'acte* it is very complicated, because this film came at the time of the evolution of the Dadaist spirit, just before Surrealism came in. There is a little Surrealism in it, but it is mostly Dadaist. At the end of Dada. I say this in order to show you the spirit of *Entr'acte*. It was not deliberate. I mean I didn't do that just to show dancing, you know, but it happens later that we discover it was between Dadaism and Surrealism. I didn't think of it when we made it.

MASON: When I read certain critics who suggest that there is some complicated narrative scheme in the film, it strikes me that they are plain wrong.

CLAIR: Very often, it is wrong, because the author of a motion picture as well as a play or a novel does something or writes something, but later an explanation comes from a critic which is completely different from what he intended to do.

MASON: I'd like to ask you a question about *Le Fantôme du Moulin Rouge* [*The Phantom of the Moulin-Rouge*, 1925].

CLAIR: It has disappeared, thankfully. It was a very bad film, I think.

MASON: I have seen it.

CLAIR: You have seen it?

MASON: I saw a print in London.

CLAIR: I don't know what kind of a print they would have, because I don't know of any prints that are still around.

MASON: Well, I saw one a couple of months ago at the British Film Institute.

CLAIR: It was very bad. Alright, I forbid to show this film.

MASON: You do?

CLAIR: Yes, because I don't know what kind of copy it would be, it has been mutilated so often.

MASON: Well, let me tell you some of the things that are in this print. Maybe this has been added on. There are several titles in English, long titles that somewhat surprised me. I know that you don't like long titles . . .

CLAIR: Oh no.

MASON: Such things as: "Jacqueline offers some useless advice," and when we see the Moulin Rouge it says "Moulin Rouge where laughter is the password."

CLAIR: All these titles were invented and added by the English editors.

MASON: The main thing that interested me in the film was the reporter, played by Albert Préjean. Although he wasn't the hero, he was kind of the moral center of the film, as well as being the comedian. In the end the main character who had become a spirit gets back together with his fiancée and the courageous reporter is ignored. Everyone in the film is fairly selfish except the reporter, and he ends up being chased away!

CLAIR: I don't remember what I did with him. I haven't seen the film in fifty years.

MASON: How about *Le Voyage imaginaire* (*The Imaginary Voyage*, 1925)?

CLAIR: It has disappeared too. I made that for a company which has since disappeared.

MASON: I saw a print of that in London too, but I have no idea what kind of print.

CLAIR: As far as I know, it was mutilated.

MASON: I'm very interested in different methods of composing. You have written for films, of course, but you have also written short stories, novels, and adaptations for the stage. When you are thinking up a scenario for a film, or when you are working on a short story, would you be working in a different mode? Novelists nearly always work alone it seems. At what point for you in preparing and executing a film was there collaboration with other technicians, only during the shooting, or beforehand too?

CLAIR: Before too. I was always working with an assistant, what I call an assistant, who didn't really help me to write, but I always liked to have someone to whom I could talk, someone to try my ideas out on. This situation does not exist in novels, but it exists on the stage. Many stagewriters work this way.

MASON: If a filmmaker does an adaptation, do you feel that the filmmaker has any responsibility to the source, or do you feel that he can make any kind of use of the source that he wants to? For instance when you worked on *An Italian Straw Hat*, was the question of faithfulness to the source in your mind at all?

CLAIR: No. I admire the play very much, but I didn't try to be faithful to it. The play was written for the stage, and I was writing for motion pictures—a completely different approach.

MASON: So you think that the idea of staying faithful to the source may not be possible; that, if you are going to be faithful to the film medium for which you are after all writing, then you have to ignore the other one?

CLAIR: I think that's the best. After I accepted the idea of a play or a novel, the first thing I did was to close the book and not to look at it anymore. Write as the author would have written it if he had been working for the film medium and not for the stage.

MASON: The actor Paul Olivier is in *Italian Straw Hat*, and to me he somehow seems to epitomize the spirit of the film, just a personal reaction. In all of your films in which he worked, it seemed like you had a special kind of sympathy with him. Was this some kind of immediate rapport or did it just develop gradually?

CLAIR: He became a friend of mine, and when I worked with him I would be thinking of using him in the next picture, you see, and I wrote his parts according to what I knew of him. He was not a real actor, but with me he worked well. He was an entertainer, almost a dancer really.

MASON: One of the very original touches I find in your films is the attention you pay to the minor characters. Often in the major American comedies, everything is focused on what happens to the hero, but in so many of your films there are always these other characters who keep turning up and are always a little bit embarrassed because they can't quite do something. Do you think consciously about these minor characters, and of using them for dramatic purposes?

CLAIR: Sometimes it was a question of improvising while shooting, and sometimes things were prepared and written in before. There was no rule.

MASON: That makes me think of the famous scene in *Le Million*—the rugby scene where a whistle blows and they start throwing the jacket around to the sound of a crowd cheering as in a stadium—did you think that up beforehand, or did you improvise it while filming?

CLAIR: No, no. In that case it was written in beforehand.

MASON: Returning to *Italian Straw Hat*, there are so many objects in the film that seem to take on a life of their own—for instance, when Fadinard is in the wood whipping the horse, the whip catches round the tree and pulls away out of his hand as if by itself; and often it would seem that by the way you framed a shot, as when we see chairs flying through the air with no one throwing them—was it part of your plan to somehow show objects taking on a life of their own?

CLAIR: No. It was just coincidental, or accidental I think.

MASON: My favorite scene in the film is the scene with the umbrella when they come out of the police station and Fadinard is trying to prevent the husband from seeing the hat which is hanging caught on the lamp post. That reminded me very strongly of a Chaplin-style routine. In a scene like that, how detailed would your shooting script have been and how much would have been developed during the shooting by improvisation?

CLAIR: It was probably improvised.

MASON: The whole scene is just hilarious.

CLAIR: I don't remember it.

MASON: Oh, it's just beautiful, because he comes up and pretends it's raining, so as to hide the hat and he puts the umbrella up.

CLAIR: That's a good idea! (*Laughter*)

MASON: Oh, I really liked it. I had a question about the reception of *Italian Straw Hat*. Some writers have suggested that the French public was offended by this picture because you were making fun of them? Do you think that's true?

CLAIR: No. That's just an invention of foreign critics. I heard that too.

MASON: It has also been suggested that, despite the fact that it was a critical success, the relatively poor box office of *Italian Straw Hat* prevented you from filming again sooner. You didn't make another film for about a year, between *Italian Straw Hat* and *Les Deux timides* (*Two Timid Souls*, 1928).

CLAIR: But that wasn't because of *Italian Straw Hat*. The picture was a big critical success. It was because I was looking for a different kind of script. I tried to work on it and it didn't succeed, then I came back to *Les Deux timides*, which I prepared.

MASON: Turning to *À nous la liberté*, I think you're on record as saying that it's the only one of your films that you would have liked to remake. Why is that?

CLAIR: Because I think now that the theme of the film is so rich that I could have developed it in another way.

MASON: How would that have been?

CLAIR: I don't know, because I haven't done it yet.

MASON: When you recut the film, you cut out the park episode.

CLAIR: I didn't exactly do it on purpose, but when the film was shown in France this part didn't succeed very well. The audience was quite cold, and then when I came to Germany to show the film in Berlin, it happened that this part, the park sequence, was just one reel, and some German journalist advised me that it would be better to take this reel out and not to show it, which I did. And then I thought the reel was probably lost, so I don't know whether it was cut voluntarily or not.

MASON: When I saw the Museum of Modern Art print in the United States, it had this sequence in it, but then the print at the British Film Institute does not retain it. Do you prefer to think of the film with the sequence in or out?

CLAIR: Well, it is better to have it in, because it was my first idea, my intention, but I must say that if I would like that film to be seen by the public there were a lot of long scenes in it that were not interesting for the audience.

MASON: One thing that struck me was that the slogan "*le travail, c'est la liberté*" ("Work is freedom") that comes up in the film is exactly the same as the inscription above the entrance to the Auschwitz concentration camp. Was this a common slogan at the time, or was it just a coincidence that it turned up in both places?

CLAIR: Pure coincidence. "*Le travail, c'est la liberté*" is an old joke. It was a famous thing, you know, that the government was trying to teach the people that they "should work, should work"; but I was against the idea that work is sacred, so I made the film to show this.

MASON: How did you intend the audience to take the ending of the film where the workers are just fishing; was it supposed to be straight, a kind of utopia, or was it intended ironically?

CLAIR: It was joking really, it was showing the ideal of the fishermen where nobody would be obliged to work. I knew it from other workers who were fishing instead of working.

MASON: The film unleashed a terrific amount of debate among socialists and communists at the time, didn't it?

CLAIR: I know, I know, especially the communists didn't like it at all, because they felt a little of the Dadaist spirit.

MASON: I like the film because of that.

CLAIR: I do too, but they couldn't stand that about it, and they attacked the film rather violently, and made fun of it; years later, after the war, there is always this thing, the annual festival of the Communist Party, and they asked me to show *À nous la liberté*, if possible! "Of course," I said, "of course!" (*Laughter*)

MASON: You have a very nice quote in your book *Cinema Yesterday and Today*, attacking the notion that all art should be a direct and serious lesson in politics. It was part of an address at the inauguration of the Gerard Philippe Theatre.

CLAIR: Oh yes. This speech was made by Roland Leroy, Secretary of the French Communist Party at the time. He said that we should not forget that workers have the right to be entertained, which of course I heartily applaud.

MASON: May we talk about *The Ghost Goes West* [1935]?

CLAIR: The first picture I made in English.

MASON: Before the filming started, hadn't Alexander Korda the producer suggested that you make *Cyrano de Bergerac* with Charles Laughton?

CLAIR: Yes, but I was horrified!

MASON: Why?

CLAIR: Because *Cyrano de Bergerac* is a play, a real play.

MASON: And he wanted you to film the play?

CLAIR: Yes, and I do like *Cyrano de Bergerac* very much. I think it's a masterpiece of the French Romantic theater. I could not cut all those marvelous lines to make a real film.

MASON: When you started work on *The Ghost Goes West*, were you happy with the project, or were you more concerned to prevent the project from stalling and being stuck with *Cyrano*?

CLAIR: It was more or less like that, yes. I was very happy with the project of *The Ghost Goes West*, but suddenly I found myself in the unique situation of having a ghost as the major character. Some other writers had tried to do it, and couldn't solve the problem. Then Korda came up with the idea of *Cyrano* to please Laughton. He came here (to Saint Tropez) right away and he asked me to do *Cyrano* with him. I was so horrified that I called Alex the next week in London and I told him I had a new idea for the *Ghost*, and that I had solved the problem which was not true. Then I was called back, and during the journey back to London, I said, "Now I must find something," and I worked it out.

MASON: There are a couple of anti-radio gags in *The Ghost Goes West*. In one, there was a suit of armor with a radio inside, and in another the hero is given a barrel of whiskey, but it is really a radio. I was wondering if you had some idea of equating radio, and sound in general with the millionaire Martin as being somehow vulgar?

CLAIR: No, I had no special ideas in mind, but at the time, you know, radio was starting and people always tried to disguise their looks. They were ashamed of them probably. (*Laughter*)

MASON: The next picture you made in England with Maurice Chevalier and Jack Buchanan, *Break the News* (1938) I didn't particularly care for. Do you recall it?

CLAIR: A horrible picture.

MASON: Just after that, you were working on a project called *Une Enquête est ouverte* (*An Enquiry Is Opened*), almost a documentary. Then you started work on *L'Air pur* (*Fresh Air*) filmed with nonprofessional actors and mostly out of doors. It seems that at this time you were changing direction in the way you were conceiving things. You seemed to be taking a definite neo-realist turn at this point. Why did this come about?

CLAIR: I was probably tired of the fantastic and started to explore another style, but I was never successful.

MASON: *L'Air pur*'s filming was stopped by the outbreak of war. How was the work going at the time? Were you satisfied with what was happening? Did you feel comfortable in that medium?

CLAIR: Not particularly. But it is very difficult to say, because the most successful pictures I made, while I was making them, I was not satisfied with. I remember the first time I saw *Le Million* completely cut, before it was shown to the public, I was so disgusted by it that I didn't want to go and see it with the public. Then, when a picture becomes a success, then you like it.

MASON: Do you have any films that you never got to make that you wish you had made, any unrealized projects that you still regret?

CLAIR: Well there are different vague ideas, you know, but I am not much interested in them, because if they were viable, and if I had not done other things, I would have done them, you know.

MASON: So you have a kind of fatalistic attitude: if they got made, then they were good ideas, and if they didn't then they weren't good enough?

CLAIR: No, it's just that there was always a reason to explain why I didn't do them.

MASON: I read that you admire the writer G. K. Chesterton very much. Is his spirit too English for you ever to have considered making a film of one of his books?

CLAIR: No, I never thought of it. When I admire a literary work, I don't think of motion pictures.

MASON: I would like to ask you a question about *The Flame of New Orleans* (1941). When I saw this film it had an opening sequence that I was very suspicious of. It didn't seem like your work. There was kind of a newsreel opening with a voiceover, and the commentator was saying: "This countess is not really a countess." Was this part of your conception to have a big frame for the story, instead of simply starting with the opera?

CLAIR: No, that was written by my friend Norman Krasna. That was Krasna's idea.

MASON: I thought the production values in that film were very high quality, the camerawork especially.

CLAIR: That was Rudi Maté's work. I met Rudi in Paris when he was filming Dreyer's [*La passion de*] *Jeanne d'Arc* in 1928, a wonderful movie. Then I worked with Rudi on *Le Dernier milliardaire* (*The Last Billionaire*, 1934). I was never successful with Rudi; he was one of my best friends, but our collaboration in cinema was not successful.

MASON: But I liked *The Flame of New Orleans*. I love the scene where she is singing the song and they're gossiping about her. Beautifully done. What did you think of the film?

CLAIR: I don't know now if it's as good or as bad as it's supposed to be. I think technically it's very good, but the spirit, you know, was half European and half American, so I don't know. It was my first film in America and I was very much impressed. I didn't know really if the people would like the film. You know, you never do a film alone, but you are always impressed by the atmosphere, the air you breathe. I didn't do any American films which depicted the modern way of life. I was always trying to escape.

MASON: That would account then for the opening title of *I Married a Witch*: "Long ago when people still believed in witches." I understand that you attended a sneak preview of this film, and when you noticed that the audience was coughing in places you subsequently cut out those parts.

CLAIR: Yes, I did.

MASON: That would lead me to think that you're saying: when the public coughs, as it were, they are right and you are wrong.

CLAIR: In a way the public is always right, as long as their attention is considered. That does not mean that they can suggest to you what to do, but they very naturally express their boredom in different ways, and coughing is one of those ways.

MASON: I like what you have written about the importance of the filmmaker appreciating and not despising the public, but I'm wondering if today we still have such a unified public for films. When people try to market films today, aren't they aiming at particular audiences? Isn't "the public" much more divided into different groups than it used to be?

CLAIR: I wonder, I wonder.

MASON: What do you think of television as a medium?

CLAIR: I have never seen a real television show. What you see is more or less imitation or bad theater or bad movies. For instance, I'm against the style of perpetual close-ups in talking pictures, you see. And that will last because it's much less expensive. I can shoot one reel in one afternoon. You take two spots with closeup, closeup, then you just shoot it till you're done. What I have seen on the television screen is something that could be theater or could be motion pictures. I always expect, I hope I will see something one day that belongs to television.

MASON: What about your film *And Then There Were None* (1945)?

CLAIR: A horrible film.

MASON: You didn't care for that one. How about *Le Silence est d'or* (*Silence Is Golden*, 1947)? I loved the part where everyone was given a medal. Was that based on a real event or did you just think up the idea?

CLAIR: I just thought it up.

MASON: It was great. Apparently you had to change the ending of the film because Raimu your leading actor fell sick and had to withdraw?

CLAIR: Yes. He died by the way. We rewrote his part for Chevalier and made it a little lighter.

MASON: Let me ask you a couple of questions about *Les Grandes manoeuvres*. I particularly liked your use of color in this film; for instance, when they first kissed, the shot was composed so that they were surrounded by green plants. It was the only scene in the film, if I remember correctly, where you used the color green. I'm sure you were using the colors very consciously.

CLAIR: Very consciously. I was disgusted that except in two or three articles, nobody mentioned that a special effort had been made with the colors.

MASON: I noticed also that you used the swish pan a lot in this film. Was that something that had just come into the movies at the time that you made use of it, or did you have a particular intention with the frequent use of that shot?

CLAIR: It was just for technical reasons, because at the time, with the color films made in France, they were not very good at making dissolves. I thought about the best way to go from one scene to another and ended up using that.

MASON: I particularly liked the direction in this film. For instance, at the point where they begin to waltz with each other for the first time, there was a long pause before they started which was very effective; and in the scene when she comes back from the church because she thinks that he has been killed in the duel and they meet in the corridor, again with the hesitation and the suppressed emotion, I thought that was really well done.

CLAIR: That was evidently more sentimental than the films I made in my youth.

MASON: Yes, I guess so. Do you like that film among your films particularly?

CLAIR: Yes.

MASON: Apparently you changed the ending. You had an idea for the film that Michele Morgan was to commit suicide, didn't you? That they would open the windows because she had gassed herself, and that Gerard Philippe would see it as he rode by and mistakenly think that she was signalling her consent to him?

CLAIR: I shot the scene which would explain that, and he would go away without knowing that she was dead. It was very impressive, but *too* impressive. For me it is a question of style. As I wrote to Cocteau—Cocteau wrote me a letter, you know, telling me that an ending with the death of a woman would be better—that in this film, dear friend, I tried to be as *discreet* as possible. A scene like that which I had shot was very impressive, but too impressive; it would detract from the general style of the film.

MASON: I interpreted the ending to mean that they were definitely parting. Did you intend any ambiguity in the ending?

CLAIR: No. I wanted to avoid the big scene of separation.

MASON: I know that when you were making silent films you were very impressed by the work of Chaplin, Griffith, and Mack Sennett. During the course of your career, were there any other directors or any other figures in film that influenced you particularly?

CLAIR: Apart from Chaplin, you know, I cannot name anybody because we were all influencing each other. I can't say any one man did it, except for Chaplin who influenced everybody.

MASON: What do you think of the work of Vittorio de Sica?

CLAIR: He was a very great friend of mine, dear Vittorio. He made one very great masterpiece, *The Bicycle Thieves* (1948).

MASON: Most of his films are realistic in style, but his *Miracle in Milan* (1951) reminded me very much of your pictures.

CLAIR: Yes, he told me that when he was directing this film, he always had the feeling that it was René Clair who was directing it.

MASON: How about other Italian directors?

CLAIR: I admire Fellini's work very much, particularly his earlier neo-realist films. *La Strada* (1954) was wonderful, and *Nights of Cabiria* (1957) too.

MASON: How about Antonioni's work?

CLAIR: I think that a picture must be able to be understood by all classes of society, which is true, by the way, for the best pictures, if you look to the past. I am very violently against intellectual motion pictures. I believe that for the first time since the Greeks we have an art or a medium of expression which can touch the lowest public as well as the intellectuals. That is not at all true in the other arts, you know. Music is far too specialized, and poetry is too. We should take care that motion pictures do not lose that precious quality.

MASON: Monsieur Clair, thank you very much.

Eric Rohmer

France is characterized by the very fact that there are nothing but individual cases. Everyone works in his own way. That's what makes
French cinema interesting. There is no common line; there are very
distinct individualities.

In popular and academic film criticism, Eric Rohmer has become shorthand for
a certain kind of cinema—namely, one that seems to privilege dialogue above any
other concern. Whether or not this association is entirely accurate, it is certainly
true that Rohmer's cinema often accentuates the script itself; *Ma nuit chez Maud*
(*My Night with Maud*, 1969), one of the most famous of Rohmer's earlier work,
is probably responsible for this reputation as much as any of his films. Taking, as a
given, this idea of Rohmer's cinema, and citing Rohmer's past discussions of his
ideas on film in his introduction to the *Contes moraux* (*Moral Tales*), Robert Hammond and Jean-Pierre Pagliano here discuss the "relative importance of the script
as opposed to the rest of the film" with Rohmer. Much of the early part of the
interview concerns a comparison between the *Contes moraux* (which Rohmer had
already completed) and *Comédies et proverbs* (*Comedies and Proverbs*) (which, at the
time of the interview, Rohmer had yet to begin). Rohmer is given to frequent
asides and reflections, as when he speculates, "what is cinema in the first person
and cinema that isn't in the first person?" Much of the interview is dedicated to
discussing not only how Rohmer uses scripts but the role of the scriptwriter in
France, a role Rohmer admits he is not completely at ease with: "I believe in the
script," he says, "but I'm wary of script-writers." Finally, he ends by discussing the
difference between plays and scripts as texts, noting wryly, "There are 40,000 directors who want to re-do *The Misanthrope* or *Hamlet*; no one wants to re-make
Citizen Kane [1941], obviously."

   In terms of the historical context of the interview, it was originally published in 1983 but probably conducted at least two years prior to that year, since

Rohmer makes reference to his not having begun the *Comedies and Proverbs* cycle (which began in 1981 with *La Femme de l'aviateur* [*The Aviator's Wife*]). Whether or not the timing of the interview is significant, given Rohmer's being between larger projects and, perhaps, more interested in discussing them reflectively, it is fascinating to see the director, as with many of the interviews in this volume, contemplating making films that we are already very familiar with, some twenty-five years later. Of course, at the time of this volume's being compiled, Rohmer is not only still alive but, like so many of his New Wave peers—Jean-Luc Godard, Agnès Varda, Jacques Rivette, and Claude Chabrol—continuing to make films. In 2007, at the age of 87, he is wrapping production on *Les Amours d'Astrée et de Céladon* (*The Romance of Astrée and Céladon*), an adaptation of Honoré d'Urfé's novel *Astrée*.

Interview by Robert Hammond and Jean-Pierre Pagliano
Originally published as "Eric Rohmer on Film Scripts and Film Plans," Literature/Film Quarterly *10, no. 4 (October 1982): 219–25.*

(Since Eric Rohmer has already spoken of his ideas on film in the introduction to his *Moral Tales*, this interview concerns the relative importance of the script as opposed to the rest of the film.)

HAMMOND/PAGLIANO: What are your current film projects?

ROHMER: Let me give you a bit of information: now that I've written a cycle of films based on original scenarios—what they call in France "author films"—*Moral Tales*—and now that I've stopped for a few years to film *The Marquise of O* [*Die Marquise von O . . .*, 1976] and *Perceval* [*le Gallois*, 1978], I'm going back to a new cycle, called *Comedies and Proverbs*. So you see, my answer can differ depending on the periods. If you had seen me two years ago, perhaps I would have answered differently.

HAMMOND/PAGLIANO: *Comedies and Proverbs* . . . is there a connection with Musset?

ROHMER: Yes, there is. That is, just as you have *Moral Tales* as a title that already existed (especially since Marmontel—whom I haven't read—wrote some *Moral Tales*) you have Proverbs that are a traditional genre. You have them in Shakespeare's *Much Ado about Nothing*; Carmontelle, whom I haven't read, was famous for his proverbs; and not only Musset, but also the Countess of Ségur, who wrote the little book that I always loved when I was small, called it *Comedies and Proverbs*.

But in the last analysis, just as the *Moral Tales* have nothing to do with Marmontel, neither will my *Comedies and Proverbs* have anything to do with the people who managed to write *Proverbs* and *Comedies*. *Moral Tales* is simply a means of stressing the tale side, the narrative side, the story, which I didn't initiate in cinema—since other people had already done that—but that I used in a slightly more systematic fashion. As far as my *Comedies and Proverbs* is concerned, that has another spirit, the spirit of social games, something too of the actors' work. That's what interests me—this new project.

HAMMOND/PAGLIANO: Will there be, as with the *Moral Tales*, variations on a theme?

ROHMER: No, in this case there will not be variations on a theme. Maybe someone will discover a common theme, maybe I myself will discover a common theme, but a priori there is none. I couldn't identify the least theme except that the stories have a rather unhappy ending, but anyway it's an apparent black that is really white, an evil which is a good. The *Moral Tales* ended happily, but that was only a transitory white which was perhaps a black insofar as this happy ending closed, stopped the story, and dropped the character back into his banality, whereas in the *Comedies and Proverbs* the ending is more open. The outcome of the story being played out is more of a failure—as a matter of fact, in general, proverbs are rather negative: like "you shouldn't do that," "there is no reason to . . . ," etc.—but, in the last analysis, it leaves the door open for something more positive. The character has set out on a road which, it appears, is not really his. In the *Moral Tales*, the character felt rather sure of himself—in an often rather pretentious way and which he has been criticized for—but which is attributable to the character and not to the author. (It is pretentious of the character to think of having found his own way and of securing his own happiness. This pretense is part of his character, however, and is not to be claimed by the author.) In my new project, inversely, the character has something more to be pitied for, doesn't know very well where he is going and he goes wrong. But in a comic way, whence the title *Comedies and Proverbs*. Comic, within the limits which I have always drawn, that is, a comedy. . . . You say "*à la* Musset," if you wish, but anyway it isn't exactly the same tone: a serious comedy, a comedy which doesn't have the effect which triggers a laugh in any violent way.

HAMMOND/PAGLIANO: Knowing your current interest in the stage . . .

ROHMER: The fact that I call these films "comedies" and not "tales" shows that the connection with the theater is more specific. In the *Moral Tales*, there was a connection with the novel, the art of storytelling, and here there would be a sort of connection with comedy. Having said this the first, the one I'm about to shoot, everybody is going to tell me: "After all, it's like a moral tale, there's no great difference." The only difference is that there won't be any commentary at all in the first person. There is no character who can say, "I." You can't do that. If you put in a commentary with "I," it would change the tone completely. And there we leave the main character sometimes, whereas in the *Moral Tales* you might say we never leave the main character (except in *Claire's Knee* [*Le Genou de Claire*, 1970], for just a few seconds). I think we'll follow the main character from one end to the other, but we won't necessarily identify with him—or at least we won't imagine at all that the story could be in the first person.

As a matter of fact, there's a point that has always interested me: what is cinema in the first person and cinema that isn't in the first person? It doesn't depend necessarily on whether or not there is commentary. You could very easily make a film in the first person without having any text. There are films in which you'd have liked to introduce a commentary to make things easier, but it's frequently disastrous: it produces a complicity with the character and completely destroys the kind of objectivity necessary for the film. So I think it would be better to make it impersonal, and that is often difficult because at that very moment you have to imagine an observer, and that's not always so easy. There is a Howard Hawks film, *The Big Sky* [1952], where the commentary says, "We." It's a bunch of men. I like that "we." It's not the main character speaking; it's one of the members of the crew so that you get back to a sort of objectivity. It's a simple storytelling device and there you can use short-cuts.

Anyway, in the present project, there isn't going to be any voiceover. So it will be more like a comedy, divided into acts, but that's all the theater there will be. The acting will be cinematographic, but maybe a little more extreme than in the others. In the *Moral Tales*, I had arranged for the acting to be more "in-turned." There weren't any very sentimental scenes. People had the attitude that there was running conversation. There were lots of conversations. In the new series, there are conversations as well, but I think there will be scenes that will be more actors' numbers. That interests me: *The Marquise of O, Perceval*, and my recent experience with the theater have given me a taste for acting. I think that the kind of barrier that has been put up between theater and cinema (and that some people, like Bresson, persist in maintaining) hasn't any meaning anymore.

HAMMOND/PAGLIANO: In that case, the actor has to have a good text.

ROHMER: Yes, of course. I'm writing my texts as I go along. I don't even have all the subjects ready yet. I have a few. I'd like to do more than for *Moral Tales*. I have done the first subject. The text here is very important for me, too. It's a text written from beginning to end, not at all improvised. For the most part, it will be written. But it is quite possible that I may reserve, as in the *Moral Tales*, a few little nooks and crannies for improvisation. Anyway, for the moment, I'm not going down that road; for the moment, I'm writing it all down.

HAMMOND/PAGLIANO: But, the *Moral Tales*, wasn't the greatest part written out?

ROHMER: Yes, it was written out. Sometimes it was written after conversation with the actors. I try to put familiar words in the mouths of the actors, words familiar to them personally. The text is very often made as a function of the actor. So there I'll be doing the same thing. It will be a subject for which I have done some research. I talk with a lot of people . . . you might say I have guinea pigs. In *Moral Tales*, contrary to what you might think, there had been a lot of research.

I've always said that they were not personal stories. In the current stories, the research side will be perhaps still more emphasized; that is, I'm having conversations with the actors themselves and other people who are not the actors, and from these conversations . . . I'm not constructing my story, perhaps because the story is already constructed, but I'm trying to find the tone for the dialogue in order to vary my own tone; for the danger when you are your own scriptwriter and your own dialoguist, is a certain uniformity of tone that is perhaps acceptable in literature or in the theater, but that in film I find tiresome. I like to vary the tone of the dialogues. In *Moral Tales*, I succeeded in varying it enough: for instance, there is no common measure between *The Collector* [*La Collectionneuse*, 1967], which is a language which belongs to the characters themselves and *My Night with Maud*, which I wrote myself as a function of the people I know in a university society, let's say. In *Claire's Knee*, as well, there are ways of speaking that came to me via the characters, either characters who were not French—like the novelist—or young people who have their own language, one that is peculiar to the generation. And so here, too, I'll be using elements like those; in that sense I won't be changing.

HAMMOND/PAGLIANO: So your manner of developing a scenario is a dialectical process: you begin with a storyline, then you shift to conversation-research?

ROHMER: That's rather hard to say. For instance, for the first subject, I started from something very old. It was a sketch. I can tell you quite frankly that I have very great difficulty inventing stories. I had a very fertile period when I was very young, let's say between twenty and twenty-five, prolonged to around thirty. After thirty, I found myself rather dried up. At the time I suffered a lot from this, telling myself I'd never succeed in finding subjects independently. And at the same time I really wanted to make films on my own subjects. Probably that's one of the reasons I've made films (I've explained this in the preface of *Moral Tales*). Why be a filmmaker if you can be a novelist? If you really want to write stories, you write them and then you're happy, and you don't have any desire to make films afterward. The novelists who make films do it perhaps because writing causes them some problems. They want to branch out into something else. The case of Marguerite Duras is quite clear. I think that there is someone who, in the last analysis, has an inspiration which is at once very rich and very limited. She had very few subjects and, at the same time, she redoes those subjects, recombines them, etc.

As for me, my case is a little different. I had written stories, and, besides, in the beginning I didn't even want to make films. I would rather have written a novel. Anyway, I didn't complete it. It's remained in rough draft. I haven't published it. In the '60's I suddenly thought that I might take up some of the stories I'd written a little after twenty-five and that I could make *Moral Tales* out of them. *My Night with Maud*, for instance, was a little, extremely short, short story (I thought I had more of a gift for very short, short stories than for novels.) It wasn't situated anywhere near Clermont-Ferrand. There wasn't the business about Pascal, Christianity, Marxism, absolutely nothing. It was simply a situation: someone was forced to spend the night at someone else's house. *Claire's Knee*—people think that it's the reflection of a forty-year-old on youth, but in reality when I wrote it I was twenty-four years old. I was more the age of the guys in the film than the narrator. As a result, it isn't a biographical story in any way. At that moment, I confess I had wanted to imagine a character that I might have known, a person about forty years old.

After *Moral Tales*, I kept hoping to find subjects, and then I noticed that I had a big problem. At the same time, I had this idea of *Comedies and Proverbs*, and I felt that they needed a common theme. I looked and even found some vague themes, but it didn't really get organized. And then I began to reread what I'd written, not at twenty-five, but before, and that I'd completely dropped. I noticed that there were things there I could use. From the time that you find two or three stories you can make out the others by relationships (opposition, similarity, symmetry, etc.)

So I took a very short story, thinking that I might make a short film out of it, and then I noticed that after all was said and done this story was not short at all and that I could easily make a one and one-half hour film out of it.

HAMMOND/PAGLIANO: Don't you think that novels are too unwieldy to be made into a film? There's too much . . .

ROHMER: I feel that film is nearer to the short story than to the novel. What makes many adaptations of novels bad is that they have had to be cut terrifically. *The Marquise of O*, which is an extremely short, short story and which is followed exactly from beginning to end . . . well, that made a film one hour and thirty-five minutes long. As a result, the scale of length for a film is that of the short, short story.

HAMMOND/PAGLIANO: But you have to expand . . . you must elaborate on the original somewhat.

ROHMER: Well, I am not ashamed of developing ideas. I say to myself that there is a time for the invention of situations and there is a time for. . . . What amuses me, besides, is that all the people who have read this story that I'm going to shoot have said to me, "Now that's a story that depicts the youth of today very well!"

HAMMOND/PAGLIANO: In the last analysis, you have always done adaptations, whether it be Kleist, Chrétien de Troyes, or yourself. . . .

ROHMER: . . . or myself, yes. I don't believe in "direct writing" in cinema. There are not so many examples of that, and in general the films that have been made like that are not among the most successful. There is no such thing as what Alexandre Astruc has called the "camera-pen," that is, anyone who makes a film the way he writes a book. The work in films is always a job of staging, and staging begins by an adaptation of a work which exists by itself in a literary way.

There is no film which cannot exist literarily in one way or another. And the criterion which would state, "This film would be worth nothing literarily; it exists only by the film" is a criterion which is only rarely valid. When all is said and done, I don't see any film for which it would be valid. Even things which are very cinematographic, which renew cinematographic language, *Citizen Kane* [1941], for example, or *Stromboli* [1950]. . . .

HAMMOND/PAGLIANO: Or *Breathless* [*À bout de souffle*, 1960]?

ROHMER: Or *Breathless*. They have literary equivalents. Now, these literary equivalents may be less interesting. What is original in the film would not be so in literature, not in the same way. There is, all the same, a literary existence of those works, their subject can exist literarily and it does exist literarily. *Breathless* is after all a story which wasn't born with. . . . Even if Godard improvised a little, it's a thing which he thought and wrote, after all. There was a script. In other words, I believe in the script.

HAMMOND/PAGLIANO: It does my heart good to hear someone say those words at last.

ROHMER: I believe in the script, but I'm wary of scriptwriters. I find the position of the scriptwriter, especially in France, a very uncomfortable position. Because the scriptwriter, when you come right down to it, is a mender; he's someone who is in the service of someone else, etc. It is better, in France at least, for the director to be his own scriptwriter. We don't have the example, in France, especially today, of a scriptwriter who is really. . . . Scriptwriters are people who come to patch up things, to help the director when he doesn't have any ideas. I think that in England and in the United States it's different. I think that in Italy, too, it's different, that there is an effort to collaborate with the scriptwriter that is more productive than in France.

HAMMOND/PAGLIANO: There are cases, all the same, in France. Gruault, for instance, is certainly more than a mender.

ROHMER: Gruault is after all. . . . Yes, I know Gruault very well, but anyway. . . . It's certain that the Resnais film, *My Uncle from America* [*Mon oncle d'Amérique*, 1980], has a slight Truffaut aspect, that educational side that up to now hasn't been in Resnais. There is a slightly instructional side, that manner of explaining to people, to put within their reach that fastidious side, slightly teacherish like the Truffaut of *Day for Night* [*La nuit américaine*, 1973] or *The Wild Child* [*L'Enfant sauvage*, 1970]. I wondered if that came from Gruault. You can't be sure. It could come from Resnais. Certainly his authority is very, very comprehensive. Resnais's relationship with his scenarists is very individual. I don't believe that there is an example, in French cinema, of anyone who has such a definite personality and who at the same time really needs a scriptwriter.

HAMMOND/PAGLIANO: Yes, they are Resnais films, and at one and the same time Duras films, Robbe-Grillet films, etc.

ROHMER: Right. He is a rather rare case in France.

HAMMOND/PAGLIANO: But you are a rather rare case yourself. A director who is his own scriptwriter doing without any interlocutor.

ROHMER: France is characterized by the very fact that there are nothing but individual cases. Everyone works in his own way. That's what makes French cinema interesting. There is no common line; there are very distinct individualities.

HAMMOND/PAGLIANO: American scriptwriters are very much the servants of the directors. Perhaps more than in France. Professionally it's very difficult to get into the system because the producers have their stable of scriptwriters.

ROHMER: In France, a young author can succeed more easily in doing a film based on his own subject than on someone else's. If you come saying, "I want to adapt such and such a thing," or, "I'm working with a scriptwriter," you won't be taken so seriously. Whereas, in the United States, according to what I'm told anyway, if a new director wants to make a film based on his own subject, he can't. Néstor Almendros, my cameraman, told me about the case of Benton, who did *Kramer versus Kramer* (1979). He told me that Benton had succeeded in making the film only because his own subjects had been filmed before by others. Or, inversely, you won't get to make a film if you don't have a known scriptwriter; whereas, in France you can very well get along without a scriptwriter. In France, at present, I believe that there is not a scriptwriter who carries really great weight, in whom producers can have confidence. And then, in France, the production system is a little different. What counts more and more are the Commissions (of advance on receipts, television, etc.) and the Distributors. Those are the great powers. Beneath, there are the directors and the producers on more or less the same footing.

HAMMOND/PAGLIANO: In your work, on the level of the script, you don't feel the need of an interlocutor, even just to test your ideas?

ROHMER: There are people, like Resnais, who like to talk with someone. For me, my interlocutors are my guinea pigs. It has even happened that my actors have served as my guinea pigs, not for the film in which they played, but for the next film. . . . No, I don't need collaboration. Not at all. I work all alone. I speak to no one. Only when I have finished do I have someone read it.

HAMMOND/PAGLIANO: This manner of working with the actors is also Tacchella's, isn't it?

ROHMER: Tacchella was a scriptwriter before. The position of the scriptwriter is always uncomfortable. The scriptwriter is either a novelist who isn't very much at ease, or someone who wants to become a director. There were once people who were more at home writing with the script. Charles Spaak was really the scriptwriter. Prévert, while not being a real cinema person, had an extraordinary reputation anyway. A Prévert script was a thing which had a value in itself, independently of the director with whom he worked. Nowadays, there are certainly no people of this kind.

HAMMOND/PAGLIANO: I have been astonished to hear scriptwriters in France say, "I am not a writer," or to make a distinction between *écrivain* and *écrivant*. . . .

ROHMER: That whole story is really rather complicated. One thing is certain; that is, that a play is a literary work. It can be produced by anyone; it can be simply read, never played. It is nonetheless a work which exists in and of itself. But there is no script which has the same literary value as a play. Why not? That is a question I keep asking myself without being really able to answer it. The play relies entirely on the dialogue, which has a certain continuity; it makes a whole. If you take a script that has a certain quality, a Prévert script, there must be blanks, moments where the story is handled simply by the acting, by the image, whereas in the theater—at least traditional theater—the moments where the expression doesn't come from the text are really rather rare. But then, in contemporary theater, there are indeed things which seem more like cinema, that's certain. So there I won't theorize; I'll just observe: I don't see many examples of scripts that are the literary equivalent of a play. A play exists independently from a production. It is written. You feel like having the text; people can learn it; others can feel like producing it. But the film script, in general, is made for one production. There are 40,000 directors who want to redo *The Misanthrope* or *Hamlet*; no one wants to remake *Citizen Kane*, obviously.

Federico Fellini

I worked in the streets a lot—like the prostitutes and the neo-realists.
I owe so much to them—*both* the prostitutes and the neo-realists.

$\mathcal{T}$he following interview is more like an essay about the experience of meeting Federico Fellini than a traditional question/answer discussion. (Despite the unusual format of the piece, we feel that the comparative rarity of recorded conversations with Fellini in English merits its inclusion.) Rocco Fumento establishes a visceral sense of the presence of one of Italy's most revered *auteurs*—the Fellini of this piece is magnanimous, full of largesse, yet occasionally and ironically confrontational; impatient with academic posturing and the reception of his films yet socially generous. Fumento's essay is also a touching account of the long-standing professional relationship between Fellini and his assistant, Gianfranco Angelucci, who directed several productions of film and television with Fellini as his mentor. (Angelucci's adoration of Fellini is unqualified in the extreme and the assistant reminds himself "I mustn't confuse the artist with the priest.") The essay seemingly cannot help but feed off, as well as add to, the cult of personality attached to Fellini's name, partly because it documents the difficulty of arranging a meeting with him. References to well-known actors and filmmakers (such as Marcello Mastroianni, Giulietta Masina [Fellini's wife], and Roberto Rossellini) are mentioned as casually as Fellini's characteristically ironic statement that he owes as much to the Roman prostitutes as the neo-realists. Fumento's account is less about Fellini's films, about which so much has been written, then about faithfully representing the experience of meeting the "maestro."

Interview by Rocco Fumento
Originally published as "Maestro Fellini, Studente Angelucci," Literature/Film Quarterly *10, no. 4 (October 1982): 226–33.*

"You've helped others besides Gianfranco," I said to Fellini. He raised a questioning eyebrow, forcing me to say, "Like Lina Wertmüller." He laughed, as though I'd told him some marvelous joke. Then he threw out his arms and raised his eyes in mock despair as he looked first at my wife, seated on a couch across from us, then at Gianfranco, at whom he winked. Gianfranco smiled wryly, apparently knowing what Fellini was thinking. Then Fellini turned back to me and laughed again. "Lina Wertmüller! She tells *everyone* she was my assistant. She worked for me ten minutes—and with no pay!"

Lina Wertmüller may have worked for Fellini for ten minutes, which I doubted, or for ten weeks, which is more likely. The point is he obviously did not care much for Wertmüller and wanted no one to believe either that she'd ever been his assistant or that her work was influenced by his. Critics have accused Fellini of not saying enough in his films. Fellini implies that Wertmüller says too much—that she's too involved in political and social issues, that she's a cartoonist who smothers her viewers in polemics.

Gianfranco tells of his first meeting with Fellini. We, with our wives, were sipping espresso at an outside cafe in the Borghese gardens. "I was a student of literature at the University of Bologna," he said. "One of my teachers thought I might do, as my thesis, a comparative study between film and literature. I went to Rome and this teacher, who knew Fellini and was very fond of him, arranged that I should meet him. This was in the later sixties when students all over the world were in revolt. Two minutes after we met, Fellini and I began to argue and we argued throughout that first meeting."

My own first meeting with Gianfranco Angelucci was somewhat more relaxed. In the early spring of 1980 he'd come to the University of Illinois to give a talk on Fellini and to show a film he'd made on the making of *Amarcord* [1973]. It was an ambitious film, not merely a sixty-minute trailer for *Amarcord*. We saw Fellini picking out his cast, his face very expressive, amused by this performer, bored by that one, enchanted by another. We saw him in conference with composer Nino Rota, with cinematographer Giuseppe Rotunno, with writing collaborator Tonino Guerra; we saw him directing his players in scenes from the film and often what was in the script was changed radically for the cameras. There was so much loving attention paid to Fellini himself (a pensive Fellini, a distracted Fellini, a melancholy Fellini and, now and then, a Fellini whose face broke into a radiant smile when a scene went well) that I suddenly remembered he'd also been an actor, most notably playing the Joseph character opposite Anna Magnani in "The Miracle" [the first segment of Rossellini's *L'amore*, 1948]. And I was also made aware of the fact that the maker of this film was deeply committed to both Fellini the artist and to Fellini the man.

After the film showing I attended a reception for Gianfranco at the home of a colleague. I watched, from across a table burdened with a huge punch bowl, as he talked with others. He smiled a great deal but seemed ill-at-ease. An art professor's wife, slightly tipsy, was asking him about Marcello Mastroianni (she pronounced it Mastrianni, dropping the "o"), who was starring in Fellini's latest film. She was more interested in Mastroianni the offscreen lover than in Mastroianni the actor. A graduate student, who wrote very serious, very cerebral film critiques for the campus newspaper, was obviously irritated by her frivolous questions. Like Mike Wallace on *60 Minutes* he shot bullet-paced questions at Gianfranco about Fellini and "why hasn't he done anything really decent since *8½* [1963]?" Gianfranco smiled and seemed distraught as he turned from one to the other. "Mastroianni nearly ruined *8½* for me," said the young critic. "He's much too handsome." The art professor's wife smiled sweetly at him. "Oh really? Does that prevent him from being a good actor?" Gianfranco backed away from them and that's when I went up to him and introduced myself.

Perhaps it was my name, so unmistakably Italian, that caused him to relax. "So were you born in Italy? Ah, your parents. And what province did they come from? But you've been to Italy. Several times? Not Sicily? Of course you must go to Sicily some day. It is very beautiful. Just last summer I went to Taormina for the Film Festival. Yes, I am tired of answering questions about Fellini and Mastroianni."

"Does anyone ever ask you about Giulietta Masina?" I said. "Not very often, and that's a pity," he said. *"Nights of Cabiria [Le notti di Cabiria*, 1957] is my favorite Fellini film and, I think, it's mainly because of Masina." I said, "I can't imagine anyone else playing Cabiria. She *is* Cabiria. She reaches out from the screen and touches you, very deeply." "Yes, exactly. Now I will write down her address and you must write and tell her what you told me. It will please her so much," he said. "No, I couldn't do that," I said. "She'll think I'm a star-struck adolescent." "No, it will please her very much. You must write to her. I will give you my address, too. You must write to me and when you come to Italy again perhaps I can arrange a meeting with you and Fellini and Giulietta, too."

I wrote to Giulietta Masina and, as Gianfranco said, she was pleased and wrote me a charming letter in return, grateful to be remembered though she hadn't appeared in a film in years. Gianfranco and I corresponded—not regularly, but often enough. Then I read in *Variety* that a Giancarlo Angelucci was about to direct a film, *Desideria,* of which he was also coauthor. I'd received a letter from Gianfranco dated May 27, 1980, in which he'd said, "I'm beginning in these days the preproduction of my film and I really hope to start shooting in the summer."

I wrote and asked him if Giancarlo Angelucci was a relative of his or whether *Variety* had made a mistake in the first name. "Yes, it's me!" he wrote. "They made a mistake, and the title is also wrong." Late in the summer of 1980 he began to direct that film, his first feature film, *Miele di donna* [1981], which translates as *Honey from a Woman* but will be known in English-speaking countries simply as *Honey.*

When I saw him in Rome late in May of the following year, he explained the title to me. It was the images that honey conveyed to him—a thick liquid, sweet and golden and translucent and clinging and moist and sticky—it was in these images that he saw his film, "impressionistically," he said. He told me about the film. A lovely woman carrying a manuscript of a novel enters an editor's office and pulls a gun on him. He must read her manuscript, she says, or she will kill him. Then we are transported to a hotel, the Hotel Desiderio, and slip into a world of erotic fantasy and dreams. When he made the film, he had no great theme in mind, no deep meanings, he insisted, "But you will be able to see for yourself this weekend! It opens all over Italy."

On the day before we were to leave Rome for Florence, Gianfranco brought us to Fellini's office on the Via del Corso near the Borghese gardens where the Via Veneto ends. I had told Gianfranco that I hoped to do a teacher-student story revolving around Fellini and him. Gianfranco was pleased because, he said, Fellini was indeed his teacher. I knew, of course, that he admired Fellini tremendously. No, admired is too tame a word. Loved? Revered? Respected? All of these, I think. Yet I was wary of Fellini. As Malcolm Cowley once said, "Authors are sometimes like tomcats; they distrust other toms, but they are kind to kittens." But Gianfranco was no longer a kitten. He had been Fellini's assistant for eleven years, since *Roma* [1972]. Now his first feature film was about to be released. (He had made documentaries for television as well as two films depicting the making of Fellini's *Casanova* [1976] (and the aforementioned *Amarcord*). It had the makings of a hit, with an international cast headed by Catherine Spaak, Fernando Rey, Donatella Damiani, and a beautiful and talented newcomer, Clio Goldsmith. His collaborator on the original screenplay was Liliana Betti, who'd also been a Fellini protégée.

More than all this, Gianfranco had, only the day before, been invited to show *Miele di donna* at the Venice Film Festival in early September. For a film to be entered in competition at Venice, it could not be shown publicly beforehand. He had spent much of the previous day phoning theater owners throughout the country asking that they postpone showing his film until after the Venice Festival. (The scheduled opening date was a mere four days away.) All had agreed except for several theater owners in Catania and, ironically, in the province of Emilia where Fellini was born in Rimini and where Gianfranco was born in a small town barely thirty miles away. On the morning of the day following our visit with Fellini, Gianfranco was to fly to Catania and then to Emilia to try to change the minds of these theater owners.

Fellini, of course, knew all this. Gianfranco was most certainly no longer a kitten; he was well on his way to becoming a tomcat. But I had been with Gianfranco for much of four days. If there was a father-son, teacher-student rivalry between them, I detected none of it in Gianfranco. I interviewed him on tape as we sipped our espressos in the café of the Borghese gardens. Every time I asked him questions about his own film, he was suddenly talking about Fellini and Fellini's film: How Fellini was depressed when he turned sixty because he felt that truly his youth was behind him now; how critics disliked *Casanova* because Fellini didn't depict the "great lover" as the conventional romantic they'd expected; how Nino Rota's death was a devastating blow to Fellini because not only did he lose the great musical composer of his films but also a very dear friend—"they were of the same mind, the same heart"; how Fellini had just returned from launching *La città delle donne* [*City of Women*, 1980] in New York, a task he disliked but he needed to raise funds for his next film; how Fellini was asked to make this next film in the United States and his refusal to do so. It was obvious that Gianfranco felt Fellini, man and filmmaker, could do no wrong.

I asked Gianfranco about Fellini's reaction when he discovered that Gianfranco wanted to make his own film. "At first," he said, "he was surprised. He did not imagine . . . he could not understand why I would want to make my own films. But after the bewilderment . . . well, maybe he thought I was abandoning him, you know, and I would never do that. He is preparing this new film I spoke of and I shall be working with him again. He came to understand, I think, because the same thing happened to him, more or less, many years ago—you know, when he was with Rossellini. After the surprise, he encouraged me and became my most loyal supporter and seemed proud that I should make a film of my own."

Did Fellini help him in making the film? Offer any advice? "He told me to listen to myself and nobody else. Was that entirely possible? No, of course not. Everything I know about film I learned from Fellini, from watching him, from what he said—from that first day I met him and we argued. It was my idea that the artist, the filmmaker, should be more involved in what was happening in the world, that films should make a statement, a political statement, about injustices and such things. But Fellini would have none of that. I mustn't confuse the artist with the priest. I think he managed to convince me, that very first day, that the honesty of the artist is to follow his own instincts, not something that is, to him, an unknown or maybe a lie. If you ask Fellini today about his work he will say if he wasn't a director he would have been a painter because he works more with light, with faces, with composition than with a story, a plot, or the 'literary tradition' as it is called. He uses cinema to express *himself*; it is very personal. The other directors, not Bergman and, perhaps, not Buñuel, are more tied to the literary tradition. I don't mean to say there are no other fine directors. But their ways are not Fellini's ways. That is why he is misunderstood. His *Casanova*—I think that in ten years it will be considered his most important film. Today critics say it's a failure.

Because it is a dark film, cynical, not what they expected. Fellini did not like Casanova . . . the man Casanova. He read his memoirs and found him boring, incredibly boring. And Casanova wasn't a pleasant man. The romantic lover nonsense. So much of that is myth and legend. At the same time Fellini was turning sixty and, as I said before, he felt sad because he was saying goodbye to his youth. And the film shows that inner . . . depression. The film . . . it was not what they expected at all . . . and they did not expect Donald Sutherland. The backers, they wanted an English-speaking actor. They mentioned, you know, Paul Newman, Al Pacino . . . " He laughed. "Then he met Donald Sutherland in Parma on the set of Bertolucci's *1900* [1976] and he said he liked him, that the face was the face he was looking for."

When one first meets Fellini, one immediately recognizes the outward differences between him and Gianfranco and one thinks of the stereotypical southern Italian male versus the stereotypical northern Italian male. Except for their builds (Fellini is a tall, broad-shouldered bear of a man and Gianfranco is slight), and despite the fact that they are both from the province of Emilia, not quite in the north but still far from the south, they outwardly fit these stereotypes. After the initial surprise of our meeting (he seemed a bit shy, a bit nervous), Fellini was suddenly the extroverted, animated, dark-eyed, swarthy southerner, teasing and flirting with my wife, talking with his hands, his eyes, his eyebrows, and laughing a great deal. Gianfranco's hair is auburn, his eyes are a very pale blue; he is reserved, quiet, very intense, rarely uses his hands and, though he smiles a great deal, he rarely laughs aloud. They embraced with a warmth and affection that seemed both genuine and genuinely touching. The greeting, at least, was not a tomcat greeting.

Fellini apologized to my wife and me because his wife had planned to be there but her jaw was swollen with a toothache. "She has an appointment with the dentist," he looked at his watch, "in less than two hours. Can you stay until Monday? She'll be well in a day or two." We couldn't stay until Monday and he saw our disappointment. "But you'll come back to Rome. Perhaps next year? I promise you will meet her—well, you *must* meet her after that letter you wrote," he said, pretending to be jealous. "And you," he said to my wife. "You don't care that there is this thing between my wife and your husband?" "We've been married for twenty-five years," my wife said. "And we've been married for forty years!" he said. "Is your wife jealous?" my wife [asked]. He said: "I wish she had reason to be . . . *more* reason to be," he added with a broad smile. "But I'm not Mastroianni. I am a one-woman man. Marcello has it all: the women, who always chase him, and a wife who looks away. For more than thirty years she looks away!" he said, not maliciously, but as a man who relishes a bit of gossip.

We were now seated around a large coffee table and Gianfranco had brought out his tape recorder and was setting it on the table, between Fellini and me. "No use bringing your tape recorder all the way from America," he had written to me.

Fellini asked if anyone would like a drink: coffee, tea, beer, a brandy. The others wanted nothing. I asked for a brandy, at eleven o'clock in the morning, because I suddenly realized that I was there, really there, in the presence of Federico Fellini and I needed a brandy.

"So," Fellini said. "You will ask me the same questions they all ask—the film teachers, the scholars. They are so serious with their deep, so thoughtful questions and I show them that I can be equally serious and on the inside I laugh a bit. You're a film teacher and so why do I tell you this! It's because of Gianfranco, I suppose—because *he* brought you here and therefore I don't have to wear the mask." "If you'd rather," I said, "you can just talk. Answer questions that nobody's asked. Now and then I'll interrupt you to ask a not-so-serious question because the brandy has already gone to my head and chased away all my deep thoughts."

He laughed. "In that case I will give you another drop or two. Is that thing running?" he asked Gianfranco, gesturing at the tape recorder. Gianfranco leaned forward and pressed the record button. "So," Fellini said, sitting back in his chair and bringing his hands together as though in prayer. "What bothers me about the scholars, the critics, is that up to *8½* I could do no wrong. They praised everything. They *over praised* everything. I wasn't as good as they said. I was still learning—but you never stop learning, eh? With *8½* they truly gave me a swollen head. Not really, of course, because I knew the film wasn't as good as they said. Then, like one man, they turn against me. *Giulietta degli spiriti* [*Juliet of the Spirits*, 1965], *Satyricon* [1969]—why I'd gone mad! Mad with the use of color, with pretentiousness, with obscurity, and God knows what else, and I was either saying too much or too little."

"These later films," I said. "You believe they are better than your earlier ones? Gianfranco thinks that *Casanova* is probably your best." "Ah, Gianfranco," he said. "That's because you suffered with me so much during the making of that film." "You don't agree that it's your best film?" "The film I am working on now is my best film, my favorite—and therefore, like a father who loves all his children equally, I have no real favorites. But I defend, sometimes very noisily, the films that are attacked the most. That's normal, eh? Isn't that what a father would do?"

"Have you seen Gianfranco's film?" I said. "Only in bits and pieces and so don't ask me what I think. Do I envy Gianfranco? Of course. Not always, but sometimes when I think, with all I've learned, how good it would be to be at the beginning of my career instead of near the end. I've just come back from America—to promote *La città delle donne*. That's what I must do, of course, and it's the worst part because it has nothing to do with filmmaking. Also, to beg for money for my new film. Because of these things I do not envy Gianfranco. Look, tomorrow morning he must fly to Catania and in the afternoon to Emilia, and what for? To talk business, like an executive for Fiat, so that his film will be shown at Venice. So I go to America to get money for my new film. Since *La dolce vita* [*The Sweet Life*, 1960] half, maybe more, of the money comes from

America. They want to know what this new film is about . . . they always want to know, and who can blame them? I tell them I hope to start production in three, four months. "But what is it about?" they say. Like you, here and now, all I can give is the title. Don't ask for more than the title. I wish I could work like Hitchcock. There was an artist, such an artist! Every thing down on paper before the camera turns. Me, my mind is in a constant . . . change. Today I put something in, tomorrow I take it out. Even the title—how do I translate it? *And the Boat Goes On* [*E la nave va*, eventually known as *And the Ship Sails On*, 1983]. Is that right, Gianfranco? Maybe that's all that will remain; maybe even that will vanish. I go to America and it's a problem. Those people with the money, they want me to make a movie in America, eh, Gianfranco? But I'm too old for new beginnings. I feel comfortable here in Italy and especially in Rome and on Roman sets. In the beginning I worked in the streets a lot—like the prostitutes and the neo-realists. I owe so much to them—*both* the prostitutes and the neo-realists. It was mainly Rossellini, as you must know, because I began with him. *Roma, città aperta* [*Rome, Open City*, 1945] was a sensation all over the world and I was happy to be a part of it, no matter how small. I was with Rossellini four, five years, more or less a protégé, like Gianfranco and me, only not such a big age difference. We worked in the streets because we were forced to work in the streets. Now almost every film I make is done on the sets. I can control everything on the sets, especially the actors. When we worked in the streets we were always chasing them out of the bars!"

"In your early films you dealt with low life," I said. "Then, with *La dolce vita,* you switched to high life. Why? Was it a conscious effort to break away entirely from the influence of neo-realism?"

"High life, low life," he said irritably. "I was growing, changing, that's all. It was no conscious effort to break away from neo-realism. I was trying to find me, my own style. In those early days I thought all films had to say something in a social-political way. Gianfranco was the same. It's an affliction of the young. The films I make now are what I feel, not what I think. The critics say that my films don't say enough or say nothing. What should they say? Am I a priest delivering a sermon?"

"Yet *Orchestra Rehearsal* [*Prova d'orchestra*, 1978] is very political."

"Maybe it's political and maybe it's merely about an orchestra rehearsal."

"You know it's not merely about an orchestra rehearsal."

"Of course. All the critics say it's an allegory about the rise of fascism. The film is about an orchestra rehearsal and I wanted it to be both savage and funny—and maybe, *maybe,* it's also an indictment against fascism. What a tremendous joke! All those critics who write that I don't say anything in my films, suddenly they write that I say a great deal in this film. Certainly I can't divorce myself from what's happening in Italy today—well, in the entire world—both politically and socially. But I'm no Costa-Gavras. I don't say this as a slap in the face because every artist must do what he must do . . . and can do, whether his name is Costa-Gavras or Fellini. The critics: they bring me to my knees with *Casanova,* a film that almost killed me, and they raise me up again with *Orchestra Rehearsal,* a little film which, according to them, says big things."

"Maybe *Casanova* was too personal a film."

"All my films are personal. But this *Casanova* . . . They, the people with the money, they asked me to do the film in English and to use an English-speaking star. As you can see, my English is not so good. I was not happy when I made *Casanova* and not only because of my bad English. Gianfranco was my strength. He and Liliana Betti and, of course, Giulietta. They did research for me, Liliana and Gianfranco. It helped me to understand this Casanova fellow, but not to like him better—what an ass, what a bore, what a miserable, unhappy man! But finally I felt I knew him, this aging lover who disguised his stench with perfumes. Then the film received a bad press, mainly in America. Donald Sutherland wasn't right for the role, they said. To me he was perfect! He was what I wanted, exactly. But the Casanova I gave them was not the Casanova they expected, neither the film nor the character. It was such a black film, they said, so morose, so despairing. This new film, *And the Boat Goes On,* they also want me to do in English, but I didn't give them a 'yes' or a 'no.' I say, 'why don't we dub?' and they say the critics don't like it when a film is dubbed."

"You don't object to dubbing?"

"Dubbing is fine, the only answer, if it is done well. We Italians do it well because we dub *everything,* as you must know. We film like in the silent days. Good dubbing isn't a matter of matching lips with the words spoken. People don't look at lips; they look at the eyes! But of course you need good actors and voices that match the faces and the eyes, not the lips. If you're a Sophia Loren, who knows English so well, you can do your own dubbing and everything's beautiful. Even Mastroianni does his own dubbing now that he's learned English. If Americans learn to dub well, maybe European films will be as popular in America as American films are in Europe. Americans are so careful about everything, down to the smallest detail, but not when it comes to dubbing. They do a hack job every time."

"We have a print of *La strada* [1954] at the university," I said. "It was very cheap and do you know why? Because the first reel is in Italian and reels two and three are dubbed into English."

"No, do you hear that, Gianfranco? But that's funny—so very funny!"

"Yes, and of course the students laugh. But they also learn the perils of dubbing. These students, who hate to read subtitles, are forced to admit that the dubbing in *La strada* is terrible, that the voice given to Gelsomina doesn't belong to her face, her eyes, even to her body. It destroys the illusion—the reality of Gelsomina."

"For that Giulietta is partly to blame. She is so unique—and here I try to speak like her director and not her husband—that it's impossible to substitute someone else's voice for hers. In the silent days she would have been great, a very great international star."

"Without a doubt," I said. "Which brings us to *Nights of Cabiria*." "Do you see, Gianfranco? Sooner or later I knew we would come to *Cabiria*. Is it because of Giulietta that it's your favorite Fellini film?"

"No, but I can't imagine the film without her."

"It couldn't have been made without her!" he said.

"For me, in *Cabiria*, everything comes together beautifully—like the tapestries in the Palazzo Davanzati." "No loose stitches?" he said. "No loose stitches." "Listen to him, Gianfranco. He is like your heroine, the way he pours honey into my ear." "All right, there are loose stitches and I know you're laughing at me and more than a bit." "Yes, but you must forgive me. Praise, like wine, goes rapidly to my head. Have I offended you?" "It's the critics, at least some of them, who offend me when they write about *Cabiria*," I said. "It's a circular film, they say. It goes nowhere, there is no progression, unlike *La strada* which is a perfect model of progression. At first glance they seem to be right—the story ends as it has begun, with the trusting Cabiria robbed first by Giorgio and then by Oscar."

"And at second glance you know they are wrong," he said, pouring more brandy into my glass. I plunged ahead, no longer giving a damn whether he was laughing at me or not.

"Yes, they are wrong," I said. "The story doesn't end as it's begun. There's a difference and the difference is reflected in Cabiria's reactions to both incidents. In the first she is furious with Giorgio. He has snatched her purse and pushed her into the river. These are facts she doesn't want to face, but when she faces them she tears up his pictures and burns his clothes. Yet the experience hasn't changed her; she remains essentially the same. The old Cabiria is alive, if not too well, and is still very vulnerable. Later, when she makes the discovery that Oscar also intends to rob her, she *gives* him the money and then rolls on the ground in agony, begging him to kill her, saying that she no longer wants to live. In a sense Cabiria *does* die in that scene, doesn't she? I mean she walks through the forest like a zombie, with no more tears, no emotion at all on her face. A dead person, yes. Then she meets the young singers and they are very much alive. They serenade her and smile at her and say "good evening" to her. Their humanity, their ready acceptance of her, brings a smile to her lips and tears to her eyes as she raises her chin and re-enters life. The ordeal with Oscar hasn't destroyed her after all, hasn't killed her soul. But her descent into hell, her glimpse into the abyss, has made her wiser. She will still love, as she loves Wanda and her other friends; she will still remain a tender, warm human being. As she accepts life, so she accepts *herself* and what she is. And with this acceptance she'll never be eager again to chase after the dream world, the fake world that Giorgio and Oscar represent." I stopped abruptly and finished my brandy with one quick gulp.

"You've been very serious, very intense, and now you think I'm laughing at you," Fellini said. "Aren't you?" I asked. "No, because it's as you say. At the end Cabiria is not what she was at the beginning. And in that last scene Nino Rota's music reflects . . . well, he knew what was in my heart. Oh, we have many wonderful musicians and perhaps Rota wasn't the best. But he was the best for me."

After that he didn't seem much like talking and Gianfranco suggested we leave. They embraced each other again and Fellini wished Gianfranco luck in getting his film to the Venice Festival. But his film didn't make the festival. There were several exhibitors who insisted on showing his film on the scheduled opening date. But when the film was released, Gianfranco was pleased at the reviews, especially that of Alberto Moravio in *L'Espresso,* even though he said the ending was a *felliniana* ending similar to that of *La città delle donne.* He also said the film was highly erotic and in reply Gianfranco said, "It's more exact to say that the topic of my film is concerned with eroticism in that strange country of dream and imagination in which my story lives. I can say that my film is much more psychological than erotic in the strict meaning of the word." Was he disappointed because his film didn't make the Venice Festival? "I really don't mind," he said. "There is a destiny for films as for human beings and perhaps, as Fellini says, it's better, when you finish a film, to think of the next one, without wasting time on things that concern the money people and not the filmmaker." And what of Moravia comparing the ending of his film to that of *La città delle donne?* "For me, that's an honor," he said. "After all Fellini was—I should say is—my maestro."

Richard Leacock

> The process of filming is a process of discovery. It is not a process of
> telling things. It is the process of revealing, discovering.

$\mathcal{I}$n the contemporary context of academic or popular writing about film, one
might be initially suspect of some of the central tenets at the heart of the documentary movement known as direct cinema. The very name, direct cinema,
seems to imply a group of filmmakers who believed that they might, through
careful choice of subject, technology, and technique, achieve a kind of perfect
recording of reality, whereby the filmmaker simply stepped aside and allowed
events to transpire, unheeded. To the casual reader, what could sound more naïve
than this? And yet, as with many moments in film history, once one looks past
the received wisdom on the period and begins examining the particulars, one
finds subtlety and nuance in the ways in which direct cinema practitioners approached their craft (however unmediated each individual filmmaker thought it
possible to capture their subject). Such is clearly the case with Richard Leacock,
as the following interview, conducted by Hamid Naficy in 1977, attests.

Almost from the outset, Leacock introduces his sense of filmmaking as discovery and the important influence of Robert Flaherty in this regard. Leacock frequently muses on his general approach to filmmaking, often employing metaphors
such as sketching or fishing. Yet he is also just as likely to discuss the technology
he has used—what it has allowed him to do and what its possible limitations have
been. One of the recurring motifs is his interest in more personal films—both in
his interest in making them himself and in his sense that the future of documentary lies in personal films. Given the intervening years since this interview, Leacock's predictions in this regard are extraordinarily prescient, since the filmmaker's
personal presence within the film itself has become more and more common (as
Michael Renov's *The Subject of Documentary* [University of Minnesota Press, 2004],

for example, would attest). The interview ends, in a sense, where it began, with an anecdote about Flaherty's *Moana* (1926) and Leacock's sense that "[i]t is full of the delightful reality of life." Such sentiment applies equally to the filmmaker's own thoughts presented here.

Interview by Hamid Naficy
Originally published as "Richard Leacock . . . A Personal Perspective," Literature/Film Quarterly *10, no. 4 (October 1982): 234–53.*

NAFICY: What effect did Flaherty have on you?

LEACOCK: Tremendous!

NAFICY: What were the important things you learned from him?

LEACOCK: I learned to look, and that the process of filming is a process of discovery. It is not a process of telling things. It is the process of revealing, discovering. And in order to discover anything, you have to look, you have to listen. Our films are very, very different, but they are tremendously closely related together.

He saw my first film when I was at school with his daughter, Monica, and somebody showed him the film I made on the Canary Islands when I was fourteen years old. It was called *Canary Island Bananas* (1935). He loved it. And he said, at that time, "One day we will make a film together." And so, ten years later, (I think it was 1945 when I came out of the American Army), I went to see him. He was just getting ready to shoot *Louisiana Story* (1948). He didn't ask to see anything I had done in between. He said "Come on, let's go to Louisiana," and we photographed *Louisiana Story*.

You know, I was not used to directors as the cameramen. They knew the script exactly: "Take this shot, and take that shot." My first day with Flaherty at the shoot, I was amazed. He had no idea. You could easily think, maybe he was stupid. Because he had only a vague idea, he had an impression, he knew what feeling he wanted to get, what impression. So we would start shooting, and it really was a process of looking through the camera. We had two cameras. (He had one, I had one.) And then we would look at the rushes, and we would shoot some more, look at some more, and shoot some more. And we kept changing the way we were dealing. Every sequence was a new problem. It was amazing. He never ever had a set approach on how to do things! It was always new. Every sequence was sort of on the verge of a discovery. It was all completely new, and obviously we had problems. I think he would have loved the new techniques of shooting. He would have loved shooting with this kind of light equipment. He was a filmmaker, he wasn't a director. He hated directing. He didn't want to tell people what to do. He wanted to observe.

NAFICY: John Grierson often criticized him for wasting film, for liking to take pictures only. He once said, "Flaherty's filmmaking ends with taking pictures."

LEACOCK: He was wrong. Grierson never understood Flaherty. Flaherty, I am quite sure, understood Grierson. Grierson was a propagandist and a producer. And we need producers. Grierson played a role, he put some new directors on the map. We need people like that.

NAFICY: As you say Grierson was a propagandist. He said that the filmmaker should be a preacher. And I guess a major difference would be that Flaherty was a discoverer and an explorer, while Grierson was a preacher. Would that be a good comparison?

LEACOCK: Grierson was in fact a preacher. He was trying tremendously hard. That's OK, but it led to some awful bad filmmaking. But Flaherty was in an unfortunate period. Flaherty, I think, desperately wanted sync sound. I think he would have loved it. He was very interested in sound. But the only way we could shoot a film was with disc recorders, big cameras. . . .

NAFICY: How did you do the sound in *Louisiana Story*?

LEACOCK: Disc, synchronous. There were just a few sound sequences in that film, with people talking. And to me sync sound is not people talking. In *A Visit to Monica* (1974) it doesn't mean a goddamn thing.

NAFICY: Just sound?

LEACOCK: Mostly, and I like it.

NAFICY: In *Louisiana Story* all those sequences with the boy and the raccoon, was that conceived in advance?

LEACOCK: It was conceived in advance, but changed enormously during filming. He worked tremendously hard on the script. But it was a conceptual script. It was not close-up, medium shot, long shot, none of that stuff.

NAFICY: What was the conception?

LEACOCK: The relationship with the raccoon, that was written. The drilling of the well, and even the explosion in the well were written. But we had to wait for the explosion for a while, so we tried to fake it. It was terrible. One day the goddamn well exploded. But it was another well.

NAFICY: So the basic things were there, I mean, had been written there. Flaherty had done that after making careful observations, right?

LEACOCK: He went on a study. But in some of his films they were made in the filming. For instance, *Moana*. He had no idea what he was going to film. He just went there with seventeen tons of equipment, his wife, and two children and stayed there for two years.

NAFICY: How do you see the progress in his later films?

LEACOCK: Well, for me the *Louisiana Story* is the last one. Like all documentary filmmakers, he had an identity problem in that period. They couldn't deal with sync sound. It tied them down. Made them rigid. It was a beautiful thing to shoot the *Louisiana Story*. Except for the drilling sequence, which was shot with sound, it was essentially a silent film. And it wasn't till 1960, when we were filming *Primary*, that we were able to jump into the new world.

In 1958 (while I was shooting *Bernstein in Israel* for Omnibus) it became very, very clear to me what the problem was. We had to have a mobile quartz camera, and we had to have a mobile quartz tape recorder, and we couldn't have cables connecting them. It was about that time that I saw an accutron watch because Willard Van Dyke was doing a commercial on an accutron. I remember transistor technology was very primitive at that time. To divide down from a crystal would have taken hundreds of transistors, literally hundreds. The accutron puts out a 360-cycle electric pulse. So we built exactly this particular watch into the back of the camera, and we took 360 cycles and we divided it down to 60 cycles. Then we used that as a chopper and we formed a 60-cycle square wave. Then we amplified that to 120 volts in a transformer. After that we ran a sync motor with the 60 cycles . . . so that it was running exactly 24 frames a cycle, plus or minus one part in 20,000 or so.

NAFICY: This is in the camera?

LEACOCK: Yeah. Then on the tape recorder we did the same thing, we put a watch. That gave us a 60-cycle reference pulse which was recorded on the tape, so when you played back you were exactly in sync with the film . . . essentially what we do today. Nowadays we use DC, crystal with a servo-correcting mechanism. I can never understand why it was so difficult to do this, to get any money. I went to RCA.

NAFICY: Were you alone on this?

LEACOCK: No, there were other people involved, strange . . . for example, Marcel. He wanted to use it for making feature films. He had a feature film that he wanted to do in 35mm—same idea—so he and I went to the chief engineer of RCA, and I explained how it should be done, and with what. And he said "Well, if you boys come up with something, let us know."

NAFICY: So you had the idea and made a prototype?

LEACOCK: We only had the idea. Then the whole Drew team became very interested. Bob Drew was an editor of *Life* magazine. And he and I started experimenting, and he got some money from Time-Life to build the first one, and we went through several different stages.

NAFICY: When did you get the first one?

LEACOCK: The first real one was about 1961 (in *Eddie*) after *Primary*. For *Primary* we still had a cable connected.

NAFICY: Then?

LEACOCK: Then, nothing has really changed since, I mean, it is a little bit better, like CP16. Basically the same thing, done differently now. It is much more efficient, but there is no real difference.

So then the next jump for me was when I came here to MIT, seven years ago, and we rigged up the Super 8 system which I originally used as a teaching tool. We have six or seven of those.

NAFICY: Please describe your Super 8 video transfer system.

LEACOCK: Using the Super 8 camera in sync with a little tape recorder, we record film and tape. We transfer the sound on to 16mm mag film; then using our special Super 8 editing table, we edit the sound and picture together, and finally we transfer the finished picture and sound to 3V4 inch U-matic color video cassette.

NAFICY: What do you teach your students?

LEACOCK: We teach mostly by going out and making films. Some students take to shooting sync sound right away, beautifully, no problem. Others have terrible problems. There are too many things to worry about. So I am beginning to modify my approach. I am beginning to think that video is very useful and getting them to look at it. I am even tempted to go back to teaching drawing. Getting people to see life, very difficult.

What we do mostly is we show quite a lot of films, talk about them, and they decide what they want to do and do it.

NAFICY: Do you emphasize certain things, do you want them to learn something more than just the technique? You know, shooting and . . .

LEACOCK: We want them to do the most difficult thing of all. We want them to see images, films and . . . I am not interested in teaching them how to be an assistant cameraman and all that stuff. You shouldn't do that either.

NAFICY: You want them to see, and to discover things. . . .

LEACOCK: Very difficult. We don't have much success. In the introductory courses maybe we get two or three people, and sometimes we lose them. I had a Japanese graduate student of electrical engineering. He was superb! But he went off to Japan to make more bloody little transistor radios or something.

NAFICY: Is the discovery method, which is based basically on the observation of events, enough for documentary films?

LEACOCK: No, it is the same problem as being a journalist or a writer, and teaching grammar to somebody or teaching somebody to be a writer. And the real problem is that people have a point of view, and they analyze things. I know that I have a particular view about how the world works, and this has influenced my works.

NAFICY: How does that relate to discovering things?

LEACOCK: Well, it gives me a particular view of the world. *Happy Mother's Day* (1963) is a very good example. This film was made for the wrong reasons. I got a telephone call from a friend of mine who was editor for the *Saturday Evening Post*. And he said, "How much would it cost you to make a film about a lady who just had quintuplets?" So I told him $30,000. Joyce Chopra and I, we went down there. When we got there, we got more and more interested in what was happening. And, of course, there was a conflict between privacy and exploitation, family and community and the big wheels in the community, and to us it became fascinating. We made this film in good faith. The editor of the *Saturday Evening Post* loved it, but its publisher hated it. So we gave them back their money.

NAFICY: You have to give them back the money? So the film became yours?

LEACOCK: We also had to give them a copy of everything that we had shot. They, ABC, edited a version of the film that they approved. It is a toned-down film. It said that everything was wonderful. Now, I said some funny things in it because they insisted that they should have narration (sort of high school narration). I think it is a very political film. But most people who believe in political films think it is not a political film.

NAFICY: So then one point you made is that you make discoveries, but you make discoveries based on the point of view you have.

LEACOCK: Yeah, and it is not just a point of view, it is the way you see things. We can't teach people that. We have the same problems teaching attitudes, sensitivity, etc. Flaherty used to say, "How do you teach somebody to smell a rose?" I think you can teach a lot, and you can help people, influence people.
    . . . I think most of my filmmaking is sketching.

NAFICY: Right now, not always?

LEACOCK: No, not always. They were all biographical, true films. Even *Stravinsky's Portrait* (1964) isn't biography, it is much more a sketch.

NAFICY: It is a very good term to use, sketching, because I think it describes what I was trying to drive at. That is the fact that you observe. You have a point of view, or you have a certain attitude or a *Weltanschauung*, as it were. And based on your *Weltanschauung* you shoot something.

LEACOCK: Thanks. Now I want to get more and more personal. But I resist it.

NAFICY: You should not, because you have the wherewithal now, you have the experience, you have the insight. It is a good time to start. . . .

LEACOCK: But it is pretty scary.

NAFICY: It would be. Well, what is your definition of documentary films?

LEACOCK: My definition of what we are doing is to show aspects of the filmmaker's perception of what has actually happened. For instance, Bob Drew, when he first saw my film *Toby and the Tall Corn* (1954) on TV, said it wasn't what the film said; it was as if you have been there. He thought that he was there. And that is mostly what we try to achieve.

NAFICY: Sort of giving an impression of being there. What do you do to achieve that?

LEACOCK: Very hard to say. You select, and it has got to be of interest. . . .

NAFICY: OK, let us put it this way. You want to make a film (you have the urge or you have been given an assignment to do it). What are the processes you go through from the beginning until the film is finished?

LEACOCK: I go on a fishing expedition. Sometimes you catch a fish, sometimes you don't catch a fish. For instance, there was going to be a tremendous flood in Mississippi. They were sure. The biggest flood of the century. We went out there, all of us. We filmed and filmed . . . it wouldn't come up, come up, come up, come up, oh! Jesus Christ! No way to make a film that way. Then, we went to make a film on the Dodgers of Los Angeles winning the pennant. They lost seven games in a row. They finally threw us out, because they thought we were making them lose! We never even developed that film.

NAFICY: So you go on location hunting?

LEACOCK: Joyce and I went to this town [Aberdeen, South Dakota]. We knew nothing about it. We had no idea. We thought we would have to interview the nurses, interview the doctors, interview this, interview that. There was only one interview in the film. A very short one with Mr. and Mrs. Fisher when Joyce asked them a couple of questions. We decided we were going to stop bugging them. We were going to get out of the house, out of the family. We were only going to film in public situations, because they were going crazy. So we sat down and asked them a couple of questions. We asked essentially what they were going to do about it. They answered.

NAFICY: So the first thing to do is find the location, people. . . .

LEACOCK: The problem is you never know whether you are going to get a decent film until you are involved in it. People say, "Oh, such and such is a wonderful subject." My experience is that my best films have been about stupid subjects. Stupid in the sense of unimportant. I mean, *Toby and the Tall Corn*, about a tent theater show—what is so interesting about that? *Happy Mother's Day*, about a lady having quintuplets—what is so interesting about that? *Stravinsky's Portrait* is not about anything sensational, it's just about a man.

NAFICY: What makes these films interesting to you? Obviously, you have to be interested in them to make them.

LEACOCK: Right. But we weren't interested in the situation until we got there. We slowly started to realize, both Joyce and I, what was happening. We were there for three weeks. By the time we left we knew exactly how to edit the film, so it took us only three weeks to edit it.

NAFICY: So, when you became familiar with the whole scene, you decided to start shooting the film. You didn't go there for three weeks to hang around learning about what is going on before you started shooting.

LEACOCK: Naturally. Well, after about the first week we began to realize what was happening, and began shooting.

NAFICY: We are talking in general now, but you can bring in specific examples. After you get to know your subject, you begin shooting?

LEACOCK: Usually we begin shooting anyway. I can't hang around without shooting.

NAFICY: You learn your subject with your camera, to a certain extent?

LEACOCK: Definitely. You learn whether it is interesting, boring, beautiful, or ugly.

NAFICY: How do you shoot? What is your basis for selection, I mean criteria for selecting scenes and people?

LEACOCK: One, what is happening has got to be interesting and two, you have to enjoy it.

NAFICY: Do you think of the audience, the person who might be watching it, whether he is going to be interested in it or not?

LEACOCK: Sometimes. Usually I am scared about it. I usually assume that people won't like it.

NAFICY: How do you see yourself?

LEACOCK: I have always basically been interested in different things you can do with films. Different ways of making films, different things you can do with film. I am not interested in making an endless number of films. You see, I could show you very, very different things. For instance, films that we made for use within the production of an opera. What I am interested in is getting smaller and smaller, cheap personal films, which I am doing on Super 8 and going completely in the other direction.

NAFICY: When you say personal films, do you mean explorative or observatory?

LEACOCK: They can be anything. But I don't have to go to a television station and ask them for money to make a film and explain to them why I am making it. So it has to be very cheap. For instance, *Queen of Apollo* (1970) cost me (out of my pocket) $2,000—because I did it the conventional way. *A Visit to Monica* cost me only $70. I can afford $70; I can't afford $2,000. For $2,000 I have got to go ask somebody for money. Then I have to explain why I want to make the film. Then it has to be on a certain subject they are particularly interested in. Forget it; I want to make films on the subject I am interested in. Painters don't have to, although they used to; they didn't get paid unless they painted the Virgin Mary or Jesus or somebody like that! But painters nowadays paint what they damn well please. I did a lot of work in opera. I am interested in music, in opera. Not singing, but using films within the production of an opera.

NAFICY: You said something about the film *Tread* (1972), which you made of a Merce Cunningham dance raising a lot of controversy. What was the nature of the controversy?

LEACOCK: There were always arguments about how you should film a dance. In most of the dances they want to see the whole stage all the time. And for me that is crazy.

NAFICY: When I was watching *Tread*, I thought that you showed everything. I didn't feel as if you were zooming in too much or that you had too many close shots of people. I thought you moved with the action.

LEACOCK: Probably I missed a lot of stuff. But you know how it is: you can't see all; you see what your eye chooses to look at. Just because you can see everything in your vision doesn't mean that you do. It is a different experience. *Tread* is my version of that dance.

NAFICY: Do other people really believe that you have to show everything? And how do you do that? By putting one camera there, with a 50mm lens or something like that?

LEACOCK: If you do it in 70mm and show it on a huge screen so that you are sitting very close, then it is like you are in a theater. That can work. Then you can select what you want to look at, while you are not really looking at something else. Then it is like being in a theater. That is possible. But with TV it is ridiculous.

NAFICY: I was talking with Joyce Chopra this morning. One of the complaints she had about her kind of filming was the fact that she had to go through the trouble of setting up light and stuff like that. She could have pushed her film in the lab, couldn't she?

LEACOCK: She didn't because she decided not to. During the Drew period we used almost no lights. I like to use no lights.

NAFICY: . . . and using 400 ASA films or . . .

LEACOCK: Four hundred thousand . . . you know that if you can see it you can shoot it, it is getting to be that. The problem is the tyranny of the goddamn television people. The television people are forcing everybody to be respectable. And it is a disaster. The Maysles are using lights because of the tyranny of the goddamn television engineers. They always come up with their scoops and lighting gear. They never take a picture without lights. In broad daylight they use lights! Besides, you know, "Don't wriggle the camera, don't zoom, don't do this, don't do that." They are worse than the movie people.

NAFICY: Yes, the engineers have become the gods of television.

LEACOCK: And the other people are nobodies. It is outrageous, enraging. A great filmmaker makes a movie. They want to run it on television. So who looks at it? It is always some twerp, somebody's assistant, somebody who answers telephones. It is enraging, BAH!! What the hell! Did you see *Monterey Pop* (1967)?

NAFICY: Yes, I did.

LEACOCK: When we finished *Monterey Pop*, ABC sent a little man over. I showed it to him. At the end of the screening, I remember he said, "The film does not meet industry standards." I said, "I didn't know you had any!" Of course, that helped a lot! So we had to spend two years renegotiating our contracts.

NAFICY: Did ABC refuse to screen the film?

LEACOCK: Yes, and the president of ABC was fired. I don't know if that had anything to do with this or not.

LEACOCK: The film I remember really taking seriously was a Russian documentary called *Turksib* (1929). I've never forgotten that film. My first film *Canary Island Bananas* (1935) is a little copy of that. The editing is very derivative: the split titles, the kind of montage. It is imitative . . . no, it is influenced by *Turksib*. We showed these two films together in school. Mine is four minutes long, and the other one is about twenty minutes long. For me, it was a way of telling the children I went to school with in England, where I came from, as I grew up in the Canary Islands. I grew up on a banana plantation. My father still runs it.

NAFICY: Is he still alive?

LEACOCK: Yeah, he is 87.

NAFICY: Fantastic! And he still lives there. You never made any films about him, did you?

LEACOCK: No, I never made any personal films of my life. And this is bothering me. I never made any films about my children, not even home movies.

NAFICY: Why is that, do you think?

LEACOCK: I don't know. I almost thought that it was immoral, that it was somehow frivolous.

NAFICY: Are you a private person?

LEACOCK: I used to be, I don't think I am anymore.

NAFICY: I mean you are vociforous and expressive, but you are probably a very private person. . . .

LEACOCK: I don't think I am anymore. After I got divorced, I changed.

NAFICY: One thing you also said earlier about filming and the privacy of people you film, does this kind of filmmaking make you feel like a voyeur in any way?

LEACOCK: Sometimes. There has been a tremendous shift in personal and sexual privacy. People are not nearly so uptight about bodies. Actually there is a young woman making a film about me. Doesn't bother me in the least bit. I think it bothers her more than me. I get up in the morning, wander around the apartment naked, my girlfriend is wandering around naked, making tea, making the bed, scratching, maybe making love. Political privacy is a very different thing. Depends on the situation. I am not really interested in any kind of privacy anymore.

NAFICY: But the moment you begin to make personal films (as you said you might want to make), you begin to intrude, so to speak, into other people's life. Or they might think you are intruding, or if not they, you might think you are intruding. I was wondering what kind of effect this might have on the process of filmmaking.

LEACOCK: Then it is up to the relationship you have with the person you are filming. I have said, and I still believe it, there has to be some sort of mutual respect. I don't have to like the people I am filming. I sort of like the chiefs in *Chiefs* [1968], but not seriously. I did a film for CBS on the Ku Klux Klan (*Ku Klux Klan—The Invisible Empire*, 1965). I lived with the leadership of the Ku Klux Klan for three months and never had an argument. Obviously, I don't agree with the leadership of the Ku Klux Klan. Now, in that case I was dishonest. But, take a psychiatrist, when he is dealing with a patient. He doesn't get into arguments with his patient about the moral virtue of what he is doing. He wants to find out how the person thinks. And I have much the same attitude. I am not interested in changing the leaders of the Ku Klux Klan or influencing them. I am interested in learning about why they are the way they are. And to me it is more or less a kind of research. That sounds a bit pompous. But it is closer to research than anything I have known. If I can find out an amusingly interesting link between the things they do and why they do them, then I think that is useful.

NAFICY: Do you make any attempt to try and make your subject matter amusing and interesting?

LEACOCK: There's nothing I can do to make them interesting, but boring, God help me!

NAFICY: If they do something interesting and you fail to catch that on film, do you ask them to do it again?

LEACOCK: I tried it. It doesn't work. Joyce and I tried it. In *Happy Mother's Day* we went to the head of a newspaper. He was talking to us and just as I ran out of film, his secretary came running into the office and told him, "The Senator in Washington is on the telephone, talk to him." Obviously it was a big deal so I said to her, "Would you do that again?" And she did. We used to laugh when we projected that piece of the film, it was so grotesque.

NAFICY: Because she was self-conscious?

LEACOCK: Yeah. Hopeless, absolutely hopeless.

NAFICY: So you will not do it because it does not work?

LEACOCK: Also because it changes your whole relationship. Once you start asking people to do things, naturally their inclination is to do it either because they like you or because they want to get rid of you.

NAFICY: So they end up acting.

LEACOCK: So they end up doing what they think you want them to do. So the best thing to do is stop shooting. Don't shoot.

NAFICY: But with you there, with the cameras there and with them having seen a lot of films on TV and so forth, they might think that they should be acting somehow.

LEACOCK: They are bound to, but usually if you wait long enough they end up doing things naturally.

NAFICY: They get used to you, I guess.

LEACOCK: Oh, they can get used to you in five minutes. You go in somebody's office; he is busy. At first he says, "What do you want?" So you put the camera down. You go and get coffee, you light a cigarette. Read the newspaper. He says, "Fuck him, the guy obviously doesn't know what he wants. To hell with him. I am going to do what I am going to do anyway." He changes.

NAFICY: Did you ever establish deep-rooted relationships or ties with your subjects?

LEACOCK: Almost never. The only one was Stravinsky. We were close personal friends. I love that man. Couldn't pick a nicer friend.

NAFICY: Why is that? This kind of filmmaking usually gets you very close to people, in a sense.

LEACOCK: Let us see a few people I filmed . . . Jack Kennedy, Martin Luther King, Boyar (*Kenya*), Bobby Kennedy, Nehru, Eddy Sachs, Mama Cass, Janis Joplin . . . they are all dead. Pete Thomas became a good friend; Stravinsky was extraordinary because it was mutual admiration. We got along, we loved each other, we talked about all sorts of things.

NAFICY: There is a poster of *La Chinoise* (1967) behind you. Obviously, you are interested in Godard's material.

LEACOCK: I am interested in him, but we disagree about a lot of things.

NAFICY: I see, can you explain?

LEACOCK: Yeah, when we first made *Primary* [1960] and our other early films, he wrote some comment about our work. He thinks that I am politically very naive. He said, in fact, that you can learn more about the elections by reading Teddy White's book [*The Making of a President*], than by seeing *Primary*. You learn more about the death penalty by going to *The Anatomy of a Murder* [1959] than by seeing our film *The Chair* [1963]. I suppose, maybe you learn more. But I think he missed the point. He thinks I am very naive. What he says, "He doesn't know which side of the Pyrenees he is on." This was a quote around 1961 that he wrote in an article in *Cahiers du Cinéma*. I think he is best at what I call pure theater, by which I mean, for example, Brecht and not naturalism. I am not interested in naturalistic theater either. I am more interested in Chekhov or Ibsen. That is me, you know, I am perfectly happy to go see *The Doll's House* or *The Cherry Orchard*. But basically I am not interested in naturalistic theater. The whole nineteenth-century tradition was picked up by movies. It has taken a long time for filmmaking to get away from that point (from fake reality). Actually I am not sure, still not sure, what Jean-Luc [Godard] thinks is political. I think he has had a tremendous tendency to be an obscurantist.

NAFICY: Who do you admire in films?

LEACOCK: Well, the people I've worked with. I have tremendous admiration for the work of Resnais, for the wonderful old Spanish filmmaker Buñuel, and Michelangelo Antonioni. At times I very much admired the work of Renoir, of Satyajit Ray, of a great many of the Japanese because they have such strong theatrical elements in their films (they didn't have the inheritance of nineteenth-century naturalism).

Godard, he makes you think very much. He is very difficult. Sometimes obscurantist and sometimes very funny. I like a lot of Penny's [D. A. Pennebaker's] work. I am very interested in what Ed Pincus is doing. I love the work of Jonas Mekas.

NAFICY: What about Stan Brakhage?

LEACOCK: Brakhage, I have more problems with. I like him tremendously, but I have never really made up my mind about Brakhage's films. Some of them I like very much.

NAFICY: He said something very interesting once, and it might relate to your kind of filmmaking too. He said he wanted to have the camera become an extension of his body; and to reach that stage, he would go around and try and practice shooting without looking through the view-finder so that he employed his hand, holding the camera, as though it was his eyes. How do you feel about it?

LEACOCK: Well, of course, if you can get good enough at it . . . Mekas does that too. He is very good at it.

NAFICY: Did you do any of that stuff yourself?

LEACOCK: Not much.

NAFICY: What is your relationship with your camera?

LEACOCK: I wish I didn't have to have one. They are too heavy and too . . . no, I like them. It is very rude to stare at people, but with the camera you are allowed to. You can look at pretty girls, you can look at funny-looking people, beautiful people and get very close to them. And they don't mind.

NAFICY: There! There, your shyness is shining through! Does your love end there or does it continue into editing?

LEACOCK: Oh, I love editing. It is tremendously exciting. You look at all that footage; you sort of remember every single shot. If you sync it up yourself, you learn a lot. And you have to go through from the beginning to the end and it is like going through a maze. You take a wrong turn and oops, you are in trouble! I tend to start at the beginning, the first shot, then I look at the second shot, the third shot . . . all the way through. . . . Pennebaker, too, we don't think about it an awful lot. We think a lot with the subconscious. You don't sit down with a paper-pad (sometimes you do, mostly you don't). All of a sudden you are ready, and you just do it. Then usually I go away, think it over once, twice, and then all of a sudden you are ready. It is very hard to speed that process up. Sometimes it may take a long time. Sometimes, I have known people who have waited for years before they were ready. Stravinsky says that in composing sometimes you have to wait. He says, "Sometimes I am like an insect, I can wait." And it is true in filmmaking too, and in anything creative. You can always make irrational films, blah, blah, blah. But something that really works, flows. . . .

NAFICY: In films of this nature, where there is no specific plot as such (*Happy Mother's Day*), you can't just let the film run on and on and on. You impose structure on it somehow. How true is that in your case? When do you arrive at this structure and how do you fit it in?

LEACOCK: For me, the way I edit is I go immediately to a structure. I don't edit until I have the structure in mind. Some people don't work that way; they put everything together. They make all sequences two hours long and they show it that way. I don't. I make one cut, and then I tighten it. But essentially it is the same film.

NAFICY: The structure is derived by looking at it several times, or by thinking about it or by . . .

LEACOCK: Mostly by just waiting. I don't sit around thinking about it. Obviously, one does think about it. But I don't sit around and worry about it. That is a very difficult thing to teach.

NAFICY: Yeah, everyone has a different style.

LEACOCK: I have a very strong sense of storytelling. I talk that way. If you listen to Stravinsky, it is like his music. It is amazing. He talks in subordinate clauses. It is unbelievable! He talks very slowly, and it is like writing, unlike anybody I have ever heard before.

NAFICY: People's works reflect their personality.

LEACOCK: It is crazy! If you want to listen to music, I don't care where you live, you can get the record of music you want. Or if you want a book, no matter where you live, you can get it.

NAFICY: So you are banking your hopes on a technological answer to your distribution problem?

LEACOCK: There may not be an answer?

NAFICY: Would be, I guess, with the cassettes.

LEACOCK: Cassette system, cable systems maybe. I don't think so. Nobody knows how to make money on cable. Open channel broadcast television is the worst problem because for television they want audiences of millions of people for them to take it seriously. For instance, Omnibus Cultural Program, which was paid for by the Ford Company many years ago, was considered a failure because it reached only nine million people. Now, that's a failure because it was peanuts. You know, in television they are talking about twenty million people.

NAFICY: Some documentary makers have begun to choose subjects that are more popular. Is that because of the distribution problems, or is that because they want to solve one of the basic problems of the documentary films, and that is that if you choose an interesting subject you might come up with an interesting film, and if not, then the film might turn out to be dull?

LEACOCK: This isn't just documentary. Pressure is on story film or narrative films as well. At this point few European or third world films get distributed in this country. Every year a few of them. Only the big, big-budget films get distributed. For me there are two solutions to the distribution problem. One is to make it very cheap to make films. But this is not easy.

NAFICY: And the second solution?

LEACOCK: To make the distribution cheaper and more far-reaching.

NAFICY: You have described briefly what you've done in developing an inexpensive means for producing documentary films. What have you done in solving the distribution problems?

LEACOCK: Not much. That is too big for us. Video disc perhaps, I don't know. Nobody knows.

NAFICY: The cinéma vérité technique seems to force people to move toward more sensational subject matter as opposed to more mundane or routine, day-to-day events. Do you agree?

LEACOCK: No, it is not so much sensational as fitting in with the demands of the big TV networks. They just did a series of documentaries about six American families. And these films weren't all sensational. But they were very superficial, we thought. They were oversimplifications, and they were always worried about information, about it not being difficult to understand what was going on. Look, there are some people who have succeeded. Wiseman has had a lot of success. Let us put it this way, Frederick Wiseman's subjects are not sensational, but quite controversial, and they are designed so that high school teachers will buy them to use in their classes. Very hard to say exactly why.

NAFICY: Joyce Chopra said the same thing to me this morning. She said that her film *Joyce at 34* [1974] was bought by hospitals, medical schools and police departments (and some other institutions you would not think would buy them) to show women in pain and distress. Wiseman's films are about institutions. If you are making individual films, about individual people or situations, the distribution problem will become more acute. . . .

LEACOCK: For instance, the film I made on Stravinsky and another film on Stravinsky made by CBS. The latter sells very well at schools, and you would think that that is so because it tells you how old he is, tells you he was born in Russia, and tells you what happened that night in Paris when they first produced the *Sacre du Printemps*.

NAFICY: You think that films should not give information?

LEACOCK: No, I am not saying that really. My films are made for people who already know the subject matter. My films are almost elitist films. Stravinsky speaks four different languages in the film. He speaks French, German, Russian and English, very little Russian, though. And the French is very simple. But a lot of people say, "My God! He is talking a foreign language!" Now I think this has a very big audience. Maybe thousands of people are interested in that, but not millions.

NAFICY: You don't provide the audience with simple information. Then what do you give them?

LEACOCK: Well, actually there is a lot of information in it. But you have to be at a certain level to understand it.

NAFICY: You have to be beyond biographical. . . .

LEACOCK: It is not an introductory film. This is a film for people who are serious musicians, who are seriously interested in Stravinsky. It is not that obscure. But it is not an easy film. It is a lovely film if you know anything about Stravinsky.

NAFICY: What do you envisage as the future trends in documentary films?

LEACOCK: Well, it seems to be going in the direction of very personal films (the films, at any rate, I am interested in.) We had a big discussion in Buffalo about what is meant by a political film. You see, I think *Happy Mother's Day* was a very political film. If you analyze it, if you discuss that film, whole aspects of our society will be revealed by it.

NAFICY: I think the difference between your films and what is prevalent nowadays in documentary films, is that you show a case, a situation, and your feelings and thoughts about it. But you don't express those outright in front of the camera and are not analytical and dogmatic about it. You present it as a situation. The best approach seems to be to sit down, watch the film and after the film begins to analyze the situation. Today, filmmakers include that analysis, that process, inside the film itself.

LEACOCK: Now, take a film like *Harlan County, U.S.A.* (1977). It is a very interesting film. Everybody agrees that it is a political film. I am not too sure that it is. I think films like that and perhaps *Salt of the Earth* (1953), which is always shown as a political film, tend to be the rituals of the left-wing political people. I don't think that they affect very many people, except to satisfy, in a ritualistic manner, their preconceptions. Now, occasionally you get something—I can't think of any films, but I can think of some books or articles that reveal something that people really don't know about in our society. For instance, the way that poor people live or. . . .

NAFICY: *Harvest of Shame* (1962), would that not be a good example?

LEACOCK: Perhaps, something like that. There are a few films like that, that really do manage to show you something you don't know about, or a book like *The Jungle* by Upton Sinclair, where in the preface to the second edition he said he aimed at the nations and hit them hard in their stomachs because that book caused all sorts of legislation to be written and made into law. I think films are almost always part of an establishment. Occasionally, you get one which is supposedly anti-establishment, such as Barbara Kopple's work *Harlan County U.S.A.*, and *Salt of the Earth*, by all means, but it is not clear to me how those films affect people.

NAFICY: Do your films affect people?

LEACOCK: I don't know.

NAFICY: Have documentaries affected people?

LEACOCK: I hope so. I hope they cause people to think.

NAFICY: But if nobody sees them, or very few people see them because of the problem that is involved in their distribution, and those people who see them have been changed to some extent previously anyway. . . .

LEACOCK: That is the problem! For instance, *Happy Mother's Day* was not shown in this country, except in schools. In Europe it was shown tremendously on TV. In England, for example, it went on BBC. I think a lot of people like it.

NAFICY: Do you think that it is your best film?

LEACOCK: Oh, in a sense, I like bits and pieces of my films. I like a piece of film I have of Artur Rubinstein. I love the Stravinsky film. I love *A Visit to Monica* and may make several in this direction. I have several more I'm working on.

NAFICY: Are they also political, and is it the direction your films are going to take in the future?

LEACOCK: They are political in the sense that maybe people will begin to come to grips with themselves, with their attitudes.

NAFICY: People you will show the films to or the ones you filmed?

LEACOCK: Both. And myself. "Political" is such a bad word, like "propaganda."

NAFICY: Do you mean to make films an active agent for raising your level of consciousness?

LEACOCK: I think so; making and looking can be. I think if people really start looking at films seriously, they will begin to see things they may have never seen before. This is what Brakhage is doing, getting people to begin to look, see.

NAFICY: How can you do that by just making film, if you don't follow it up with discussions or some form of investigation?

LEACOCK: I think that they affect people. They make people see things differently.

NAFICY: They do, but I think the effect will be so much slower than if you, yourself or other people sit down, watch the film, discuss it, etc.

LEACOCK: But I think that, for instance, Flaherty's films—they affected people tremendously! Take *Nanook of the North* (1922). *Nanook* is beautiful, alive, fantastic! Still is. That film works just as well now as it did sixty years ago.

NAFICY: When you saw this film first, how did it strike you?

LEACOCK: Breathtaking! Its directness, simplicity. This man shows you everything you want to see, just as you need to see it. It is disarmingly simple. You get an extraordinary feeling of Nanook's family, of his love for his kids. It is incredible!

NAFICY: Are there any other films that present you with such warmth, openness, a family, a man or people?

LEACOCK: I find that I am very influenced by Flaherty and by Satyajit Ray's *Pather Panchali* (1955). I love all of them.

NAFICY: Does *An American Family* (1973), the thirteen-hour film that was produced by PBS, strike you as a warm and open film about an American family?

LEACOCK: Unfortunately, no. It was done in a TV tradition of a producer running the show. That's no real filmmaking. A producer hires some people to go shoot stuff. Somebody edits it, somebody does this, somebody does that, so it is a big glob! I think there are some interesting things in it, though. I think the filming in *An American Family* was very heavy in the sense that it has lights, LIGHTS! People following with lights, lights! My God! If you want to change the situation, just start turning on lights.

NAFICY: When you are making films about a different culture or a different group of people like the Eskimos, Indians, Iranians, French, or whatever, do you think that, in order to get close to their point of view of their life (because you are a foreigner and don't know their lives, you might misread certain things), that it would be a good idea to show whatever you have shot to your subjects? Something that Flaherty did and something that Jean Rouch did in a different way [he recorded their reactions also and included it in the film].

LEACOCK: I don't think so. The real reason that Flaherty used to do it was that he needed their cooperation in a way that is more than just money. He needed to involve them because it took him years to make a film. To have that kind of involvement he had to sort of cue them into the project.

NAFICY: He didn't want to "fix" the reality he had recorded on film?

LEACOCK: No. Monica and I are now in the middle of adding sound to *Moana*, because that film nobody looks at it. It is crying for sound. It was as if he shot it thinking there was sound. You hear the language, you hear the laughter, you hear the sounds of the scenario. Both of us felt strongly that this film, more than any of his other films, needed sound. So recently we went down to Samoa, with a tape recorder. We went to the same village (Monica was five years old when she was there). It is almost the same, still no water. We saw everything you see happen in that film happen. We decided to show the Samoans the film, so we borrowed a projector and a generator, put it in the back of a truck, and at the village put a sheet on the side of a house and the whole village came that night. Beautiful moon. And we ran the film. They roared over it. Not derisively, I think, not bad laughter. The film is full of little things, mistakes that people make. Like, for instance, in the film they put the turtle on a canoe, and it falls back off again. They howled over it. This must have happened when Bob [Flaherty] showed it to them. The film is not a comedy exactly, but it is a full, jolly, lovely, lively film and the reaction from everybody here [making a long face] bullshit! And Bob must have been horrified when he showed it here, and they all sat so deadly serious. It is full of the delightful reality of life. It is not a serious, long-faced film.

Edward Dmytryk

> If there's anything dangerous in this world, it's a man who thinks he
> knows what the truth is. He'll kill anybody not in support of his truth.

$\mathcal{I}$t can be easy to consign historical figures to the roles to which we have become accustomed for them to occupy, and for many readers, Edward Dmytryk is
likely someone whose part in the Hollywood Ten—and eventual betrayal of his
friends—has labeled him, as Lester Friedman's introduction puts it, "a turncoat, a
traitor, and a liar." Whatever those previous assumptions may be, Dmytryk himself is a fascinating subject, and his candor with Friedman about his involvement
and eventual disenchantment with the Communist Party are useful for helping
readers understand exactly what would lead him to testify beyond the usual mo-
tive assigned to this action: the desire to be employed again. As the interview pro-
gresses, Dmytryk oscillates between narrating the historical events from his own
perspective and reflecting more broadly on such larger subjects as the contingent
nature of truth and the dangers of following those who are all too convinced they
have the final word on it. While this interview may not alter readers' essential
opinions of Dmytryk, it will undoubtedly complicate any easy associations previously held about this historical period and those involved in it.

Interview by Lester D. Friedman
Originally published as "A Very Narrow Path: The Politics of Edward Dmytryk," Liter-
ature/Film Quarterly *12, no. 4 (October 1984): 214–24.*

On September 21, 1947, the chairman of the House Committee on Un-American
Activities (HUAC), J. Parnell Thomas (R–New Jersey), subpoenaed forty-three

members of the Hollywood film community to answer charges about communist infiltration in the movie industry. Among the forty-three were powerful producers like Louis B. Mayer, Jack Warner, and Samuel Goldwyn; successful writers like Clifford Odets, Howard Koch, and Morrie Ryskind; popular actors like Gary Cooper, Ronald Reagan, and Charles Chaplin; and prominent directors like Leo McCarey, Sam Wood, and Lewis Milestone. HUAC began its formal hearings on October 20, 1947, and Thomas opened the proceedings by reading a prepared statement. His Committee's hearings would be "fair and impartial," he declared, adding that HUAC members were interested in finding out "the facts" about communism in Hollywood. Though these hearings lasted only ten days, they ripped apart the thin fabric of civility that shrouded America's dream merchants and divided the industry into vitriolic political factions that remain to this day. The dream factory was suddenly in the midst of a political nightmare.

Nineteen of the forty-three called to testify were well-known leftists. Eventually, eleven of the nineteen so-called "unfriendly witnesses" appeared before HUAC. One, German poet and playwright Bertolt Brecht, responded to the Committee's questions, denied he had ever been a communist, and then returned to his homeland. Citing constitutional guarantees of personal freedoms under the First Amendment, the other ten witnesses refused to answer the Committee's questions about their political affiliations and were cited for contempt by Congress on November 24, 1947. All ten unsuccessfully appealed these charges and served from six months to one year in prison. These men became known as the "Hollywood Ten": Alvah Bessie (writer), Herbert Biberman (director), Lester Cole (writer), Edward Dmytryk (director), Ring Lardner, Jr. (writer), John Howard Lawson (writer), Albert Maltz (writer), Samuel Ornitz (writer), Adrian Scott (producer), and Dalton Trumbo (writer).

Historical circumstances have conspired to link these ten men together, even though their political ideals, professional status, and individual temperaments often placed them at odds with each other. At the time of the HUAC hearings, Lardner, Trumbo, Scott, and Dmytryk stood at the highpoints of their respective studio careers. Lardner, the son of popular author Ring Lardner, had won an Oscar in 1942 for his co-authorship of *Woman of the Year*. By 1945, he commanded a salary of $2,000 per week. Trumbo's even more lucrative contract at MGM guaranteed him $75,000 per script, a figure which made him the highest paid screenwriter in Hollywood. Dmytryk, a prolific director, made twenty-five pictures at this point, including box-office winners such as *Confessions of Boston Blackie* (1941), *Back to Bataan* (1944), and *Till the End of Time* (1946). At the time they were called to testify, Scott and Dmytryk had just released what was to be their most successful film collaboration, *Crossfire* (1947), one of the first Hollywood films to deal with American anti-Semitism.

Two other members of the Hollywood Ten, Albert Maltz and Lester Cole, had what might be described as successful careers on the eve of the HUAC hearings. As a freelance writer, Maltz had won an Academy Award in 1942 for *Moscow Strikes Back* and a special Oscar in 1944 for *The House I Live In*, a documentary about intolerance. Lester Cole's thirty-six screenplays included such hits as *None Shall Escape* (1944) and *Objective, Burma!* (1945). In 1947, his salary at MGM was $1,350 per week.

Three other members of the Hollywood Ten had been far less successful than these six. A popular screenwriter in the early thirties, Herbert Biberman had degenerated into a mediocre author, director, and producer of low-budget films like *One Way Ticket* (1936) and *The Master Race* (1944). Alvah Bessie's work in the forties, which included *The Very Thought of You* (1944) and *Hotel Berlin* (1945), failed to generate much studio enthusiasm or popular interest. Samuel Ornitz's credits were equally undistinguished, writing screenplays for such forgettable films as *Army Girl* (1938) and *Three Faces West* (1940). Though still able to earn a living in the movie industry, Biberman's, Bessie's, and Ornitz's careers were spiraling downward before the HUAC hearings.

John Howard Lawson, however, was something of a different case. Though he had authored a number of popular scripts, including *Success at Any Price* (1934), *Blockade* (1938), and *Action in the Atlantic* (1943), Lawson was almost unemployable in the days prior to the hearings. In the eyes of the conservative Hollywood moguls, Lawson had become the industry's leading left-wing radical. His organization of the Screenwriter's Guild (he served as its first president in 1933), his politically inspired works such as *The Heart of Spain* (1937), his involvement in the Conference of Studio Unions (CSU) strike of 1945, and his other left-wing activities stamped Lawson as a dangerous threat to Hollywood's status quo. By the time of the HUAC hearings, Lawson was a bitter, caustic critic of the studio system and of the capitalistic ethos that spawned it.

In the years following the incarcerations of the Hollywood Ten, much has been written about them, some by the men themselves: Dalton Trumbo in *The Time of the Toad* (1949) and *Additional Dialogue* (1970); Alvah Bessie in *Inquisition in Eden* (1965); Ring Lardner, Jr. in "My Life on the Blacklist" (1961); Lester Cole in *Hollywood Red* (1981). Gordon Kahn, a friend of the Ten who was himself blacklisted, rushed to their defense in 1948 with *Hollywood on Trial*. Another uncooperative witness, Lillian Hellman, remembers the events in *Scoundrel Time* (1976). Academic studies of the witnesses and their time include Robert Vaughn's *Only Victims* (1972), Stefan Kanfer's *A Journal of the Plague Years* (1973), Larry Ceplair/Steven Erglund's *The Inquisition in Hollywood* (1980), and Victor Navasky's *Naming Names* (1980).

The fact that two future presidents of the United States, Richard Nixon (R-California) as HUAC member and Ronald Reagan as a leading spokesman for the Screen Actor's Guild and later President of the conservative Motion Picture Industry Council, played important roles in the proceedings has added interest to the case. Many accounts of the ten days that shook Hollywood clash. Interviews with the men who went to prison convey the same outline of historical dates but give vastly different interpretations of the ideals, motivations, and feelings of the Hollywood Ten.

In this war of words from forces on the right and left of the political spectrum, one man has emerged as the most controversial of all the Hollywood Ten: director Edward Dmytryk. Of all the unfriendly witnesses forced to testify, Dmytryk remains the only one who changed his original position, ultimately becoming a friendly witness for HUAC and retestifying as such on April 15, 1951. For this action, Dmytryk has been vilified. All of the historical studies attack him in some way, calling him a turncoat, a traitor, and a liar. His fellow jailmates have been even less kind. Albert Maltz has assailed Dmytryk in print as a "fawning informer," a "renegade," and a "stool pigeon." Writing to his friend Herbert Biberman on April 12, 1951, Maltz speaks of Dmytryk's actions after his release as "sick and sorrowful and contemptible." Later, in another letter to Biberman on May 3, 1951, Maltz accuses Dmytryk of selling out his political principles in order to obtain work in Hollywood once again. Finally, on May 31, 1951, Maltz tells Biberman that Dmytryk's act of "betrayal" was "nauseatingly ugly" and "the cheapest sellout of the day." Lester Cole's recent book shows that the years have not mellowed opinions toward Dmytryk. Dmytryk's "depraved" performance before HUAC, says Cole, was "so morally degenerate it is impossible to comprehend." Cole passionately concludes his discussion about Dmytryk by saying: "It was he, the Judas, who had violated all moral, ethical, and human laws."

The following segment, part of a longer interview that covers Dmytryk's entire film career, was taped at Syracuse University. Dmytryk reflects back on the events which, three decades ago, forever altered the course of his personal life and professional career. For more on Dmytryk's thoughts, one can check his autobiography, *It's a Hell of a Life But Not a Bad Living* (1974).

FRIEDMAN: Can you tell me how you became involved in the Communist Party?

DMYTRYK: Most of the political activities in Hollywood started during the Depression. It started, to some extent, with the Federal Theatre, with people who came out of New York. I got into it because I was always socialistically inclined. As a matter of fact, the reason I later left the Party was because it wasn't socialistic enough. I got into it during the war because they were the only ones doing anything. They were absolutely the only ones. For instance, they started a People's Educational Center and asked me to come there. I didn't know it was Communist back then. I lectured on a few things and thought it was a hell of a good idea. They were trying to educate people. Then they started doing other things. For instance, they set up an organization to keep soldiers' wives active while their husbands were abroad. I didn't find the Republicans doing that. I didn't find the Democrats doing that. I found the Communists doing that. We had seminars on the meaning of the war at one studio or another at least once a week, organized primarily by the Writer's Guild. I liked that, too. I found out that all the activities I thought were very, very good were actually being organized by hard-core Communists who didn't allow anybody to realize what they were doing. The Communists have always worked on the secretary principle: The secretary does all the work, and if you want to control an organization, you become the secretary, not the president. We actually had very few Communists in Hollywood. I think there were seven. But we were the organizers.

FRIEDMAN: What was the extent of your personal involvement in the Party?

DMYTRYK: I was in the party for perhaps a year, maybe less. I attended about six or eight section meetings; that's all. I was never a very good Communist because one of the very first things I found out was that when you became a Communist you had to follow their discipline. They talked a lot about the rights of the common man, but you had no freedom. You had to take orders from the cell leader. When they tried to get Adrian Scott and me to change *Crossfire* and make it a different kind of story, at a time when it was physically impossible to do so, I said to John Howard Lawson: "I don't think I can take this." He said, "I guess you're right." That was the end of my association with the Party. We had our own meetings almost weekly once the HUAC thing started to break. I missed a few of them when I was making a couple of pictures in England, but I attended them before I left and after I came back. They had Robert Rossen up on the carpet one time when I was gone. Robert Rossen was a Communist. He made *Body and Soul* [1947] and *All the King's Men* [1949], which won him the Academy Award. It was about an American dictator. It painted the picture of a corrupt man in American politics, and you would think that this is the kind of thing that the Communists would have loved. My kind of Communist would have loved it. But I found that they called Rossen up on the carpet for two meetings and gave him holy hell. Finally, in the second one of them, he said, "You bastards are full of shit! You can take your whole goddamn thing and stuff it!" He walked out. Here he made a fine picture, and they were saying he should never have made the picture. But the stupidity of it was, and this is one of the greatest stupidities of the Communist Party, that it was after the fact. There was nothing that could be done about it. The picture couldn't be withdrawn or anything; they just wanted to chastise him. They wanted to show that they were the boss and he'd better knuckle down. This was the way they always worked.

FRIEDMAN: How did you specifically prepare for the HUAC hearings?

DMYTRYK: In one of the earlier meetings, we were talking about the prosecutors asking us if we believed in freedom of speech for the Communists. Of course we'd say "yes" because our case was based on freedom of speech. So, "Do you believe in freedom of speech for the Communists?" The answer is obviously "yes." "Do you believe in freedom of speech for the Fascists?" Well, we debated that one for two sessions. Toward the end of the second session, John Howard

Lawson held up his hand and said, "Okay, discussion is over." He didn't say, "What's the consensus?" Actually, the consensus was about six to four in favor of saying, "Yes, we believe in freedom of speech for everybody." He said, "This is the answer you give. You do not believe in freedom of speech for the Fascists." Naive me, I said, "Why not? We believe in freedom of speech for the Communists. Why don't you believe in freedom of speech for the Fascists?" He said, "We believe in freedom of speech for the Communists because what the Communists believe is true. We do not believe in freedom of speech for the Fascists because what the Fascists believe is false." Now this hit me as wrong. I think one of the reasons I got out of the Catholic Church at eight was because I've always been very anti-doctrinaire. I don't think anybody knows the truth about anything really. I think we hold a momentary truth. Then something comes along, changes it, and it becomes another kind of truth. I hate anybody who tells me he knows for sure how something is. I'm a very positive, arbitrary, opinionated person. I can change my mind. I don't believe, like a born-again Christian, that there is only one way to be saved. This is the kind of thing I began to find out about the Communist Party.

I was out of the Communist Party two years before we went to testify before HUAC in Washington. I was with them on the basis of freedom of speech. The statements we made were chosen arbitrarily. Each one of us chose a particular thing, again just arbitrarily, or we were assigned one by our lawyers. (We had about three Communist lawyers and a couple of non-Communists, by the way.) Adrian and I went to our lawyers, one of whom was a liberal Republican, and we said. "Look, we're not Communists any more. How about if we just go and testify and say, 'Sure we were Communists.' What about it?" He said, "No, you can't do that. We must have absolute solidarity." That's the first thing at our very first meeting that we decided on. But we were guinea pigs, which is the thing I resented. We were not allowed to use the Fifth Amendment or anything else.

FRIEDMAN: You are the most controversial of the Hollywood Ten, basically because of what you did after you came out of prison. Most commentators conclude your motivations were purely economic: the quickest way to get work again in Hollywood was to turn on your old buddies, to inform on them. How do you feel about these charges?

DMYTRYK: At the hearings themselves my stomach began to burst as I realized what was happening. The first day the unfriendly witnesses hit the stand, I knew I was not with them, not in prison, not after I got out of prison, but at that time. The question from then on and for the next two and a half years or more, 1947–1950, was how do I do it? When do I do it as gracefully as possible? It was not if I was going to do it or not.

The Communists said that when I got out I had been offered a $500,000 contract with Louis Mayer. I never talked to Louis Mayer. Never worked at

MGM until years later when I made *Raintree County* [1957], and that was just a one-picture deal. Louis Mayer wasn't even there. Jesus Christ, I wish I had the chance to turn down a deal like that. I didn't have a buck. I didn't work for a long time. Even after the recantation before Congress, nobody gave me any offers. I finally made a picture for the King Brothers, *Mutiny* [1952], for $5,000. The only reason I did that was to prove that I could make a picture, even a B-picture for the King Brothers, that could go out in the theaters and the American Legions wouldn't boycott it. After that, Stanley Kramer came to me with a four-picture deal.

FRIEDMAN: After you recanted, the Leftists must have reviled you.

DMYTRYK: No question about it. I had some very interesting experiences. I'd run into one of the old boys, and the first look was always a look of recognition. The hand would start to come out and then, and as soon as they recognized it was me, the hand quickly went back, the face sobered up, they would turn and walk off. I made a point of looking at them and saying hello. I didn't care about communicating at this particular point. I didn't name any names that hadn't been named, that they didn't know about. I'm not using that as an excuse because the principle is still the same. But nobody lost a job because of me.

FRIEDMAN: Yes, but their jobs were lost.

DMYTRYK: They had been lost a long time. The Black List was very long. But they weren't lost because of me. In other words, I didn't name anybody they didn't know about and who hadn't been on the Black List before. I have no guilt feelings at all, although I understand why a lot of people look at it very badly.

The Communist Party was supposed to be an open party, a legal party. If I belonged to the Boy Scouts and somebody asked, "Who else is in your troop?" I'd tell him. This was a legal party to which you were allowed to belong. Actually, they never got anybody for being a Communist. They got them for all kinds of other things, but they never put us in jail for being a Communist. They put us in jail for not cooperating with Congress, for not answering questions. Later they changed their tactics, by the way, because the old chairman went to jail; they got a new chairman and made sure he was very polite. I went to a couple of the sessions and saw them on T.V. They never shouted again. They were quite polite. As a matter of fact, the other Communists who appeared before them, whom I knew, shouted at them. They never sent anybody to jail because they all pleaded the Fifth Amendment. Everybody accepted that the Fifth Amendment implied guilt. So if we had pleaded the Fifth Amendment, it would have implied guilt. But we said we could win on the First Amendment. If we had won on the First Amendment, then we'd be heroes today.

FRIEDMAN: How did you feel about those people who forced you to name names?

DMYTRYK: Let me tell you a little story. When I was in Rome, Irene Papas asked me to write a short note to the Greek government. Melina Mercouri had been goddamning the Greek Junta all over Europe that year. They finally confiscated her property, and she got absolutely livid. I said to Irene, "I won't do it. This a battle, and if Melina fights the Junta, then the Junta, as much as I hate it, has a right to fight her. They have a right to take away her property if she's going to be nasty to them." If you are going to get into a battle with somebody, you've got to accept the consequences. You're going to get wounded, you're going to get shot, and you can't be unhappy with them. In a decent war, and there is such a thing, you're not angry at the soldier you kill and he's not angry at you. You kill him for various reasons. I was in a war. Those guys were fighting their battle. I lost. They won in this case. I don't know whether they will win in the long run, historically, or not. I never felt any angry feelings. The only guy I ever felt any anger for was DeMille. I hated the son of a bitch for many reasons. He was the leader of the whole thing backstage, a vicious man. But how can you get mad at anybody? You get in a battle, and they beat you. If you get in a tennis match with somebody and he knocks the hell out of you, beats you three sets straight, do you get mad at him because he did it? You take your chances.

Still, I feel very strongly that they were wrong. I felt sorry for Gary Cooper going up there and saying, "Yep." He's a very decent man, and he was forced by his friends to go up there and "yep" all over the place. Sure, he's a conservative. Some of my best friends in Hollywood have been very good Republicans. Dick Powell is a very good friend. Humphrey Bogart was a good friend. I hated some of the guys like Sam Wood on a personal basis. But most of them were very decent people who simply believed something that was pretty far to the right of us. How the hell do you hate them? It's a war. People take sides. Only history tells you whether they were on the right side or the wrong side. Very often history tells you what you thought was the right side is the wrong side fifty years from now.

FRIEDMAN: If you could, what would you have done differently?

DMYTRYK: I probably wouldn't have done anything differently. I've often thought about it. I thought maybe I should have gone to England. Some of the things that happened in this country bothered the hell out of me, and England, in my opinion, is the most democratic country in the world and a very pleasant place to live, in spite of certain kinds of problems. With hindsight I might have said, "That's the easy way out all the way around."

FRIEDMAN: What role, if any, did the unions play in this situation?

DMYTRYK: The CIO was trying to take over the unions in Hollywood. The CIO, at that time, was a liberal union. Of course, it is no longer. It's probably to the right of A.F. of L. now. But in those days, the CIO was a different formation, a vertical union, a very liberal union. In fact, some of its constituents were run by Communists. We had the painter's union in Hollywood, run by a Communist. The studios thought if the CIO took over Hollywood, they would be in trouble. Hollywood was very comfortable with the A.F. of L. unions and with all our guilds: the Directors Guild, the Writers Guild, the Screen Actors Guild. At that time, I had helped form the Editors Guild which later became a union simply because it couldn't get what it wanted as a guild. But there's no question that they got scared as hell of the CIO.

I think the real reason, the real basis, for breaking up the Communist or the left wing element at Hollywood was the union situation. Hollywood depends on the public approval, and they're scared to death of it. The dreadful point is that it's their version of the public approval that counts. In other words, they assumed that the public disapproved of Ingrid Bergman when she went to Italy. They found out a few years later that the public didn't at all. But they assumed it, and as a result, would not use Ingrid. They assumed a lot of things. In other words, they're frightened. What was the phrase: "Nothing is as frightened as a million dollars?" Hollywood is frightened and always will be of what they consider to be public opinion, even though there is no such thing.

FRIEDMAN: How much did the gossip columnists help fuel the fires?

DMYTRYK: Let me illustrate my answer with a personal story. I was in jail and the warden called me into his office. He said, "I wanted to show you this before you hear about it from somebody else." I guess he was afraid that I might try to escape. Walter Winchell had an article that Jean Dmytryk is divorcing Commie Eddie Dmytryk who is serving a jail sentence for contempt of Congress. Well, of course, it was absolutely untrue. Jeannie called Winchell and told him it wasn't true and to please retract it. He laughed at her. I'm mentioning Winchell because he appeared in all the best newspapers. He wasn't exactly Connolly from *The Hollywood Reporter*.

These kind[s] of things happened constantly. For instance, I had a meeting with Louis Armstrong, whom I idolized, at Phil Bird's in Hollywood one time. He was playing a concert there with his group, and I went there with another guy from RKO who used to play. We spent a lot of time talking together. The next day in the press there was something about Louis Armstrong and myself having a big thing, that I was racist, and that I had called him names. There was absolutely nothing to it, but Connolly hated me. Connolly was a good, Catholic columnist who hated me as an ex-Communist. This was the awful thing that happened. I couldn't win. To the Communists I was a renegade. To the right wingers I was an ex-Communist, and once a Communist, always a Communist. There was a very narrow path down the middle for the few people who didn't give a goddamn or who took me on my own.

FRIEDMAN: Who were some of the people who stuck by you when you got out?

DMYTRYK: Dick Powell, essentially. While I was in jail, he gave Jeannie a second lead in *Cry Danger* [1951] and was castigated. He was certainly a solid guy when I got out. My agent was too. That's about all. And both those guys are Republicans. But they were the old-fashioned Republican; the kind of Republican who believes in personal freedom. You know there are some very good Republicans. I hate to say this, but there are. The old-fashioned Republicans. The Lincoln Republican is not necessarily a bad man. I think he may not be a man for the times because the times won't permit that kind of Republicanism anymore.

FRIEDMAN: Did those who named names, so to speak, or went before the committee and cooperated, associate together?

DMYTRYK: No, we didn't form a little group, not by any means. Many of them I'd known all my life. Bud Bridges I've known all my life, but I didn't see him after that. In fact, I didn't even know that he had appeared again before Congress until some time later. I worked with Lee Cobb after he had done that, and we talked about it for a while because we had a mutual friend who was a Communist and there were certain problems. We worked together, but after that I never saw Lee Cobb again. Larry Parks was a friend of mine. He'd been a friend of mine long before. I didn't even know he was a Communist until we got together, hadn't had the slightest idea, and we were friends for a very long time. We remained friends afterward. But we rarely talked about this particular situation.

FRIEDMAN: Were their reasons for cooperating the same as yours: their total dislike for the party?

DMYTRYK: No, I don't think we felt that way. I don't think any of us felt such a dislike for the party that we wanted to organize. I think we'd had enough of organizations and enough of pooling together to do something like that. As a matter of fact, I didn't want to join any other organization again; I didn't want to be told what to do, or have somebody direct me into certain organized directions. I work for ecological and environmental concerns, but never through official organizations.

FRIEDMAN: Do you think they recanted for the same reasons you did?

DMYTRYK: Yes, I definitely do. I think very few, if any, recanted because they felt they could get work. Larry Parks knew he wouldn't work again. And he didn't have to. His business manager convinced him to take his money and put it into apartments. He was a very wealthy man. He had apartments all over the place, and he didn't have to act. He didn't do it for that reason. I don't think Lee Cobb did either. You see, it was a "Catch 22" situation really. You get associated with something like that and unless you can come out publicly against it, you will always be associated with it. And you don't want to be associated with something you hate.

FRIEDMAN: But by naming names you've now simply become part of something else you hate equally as much.

DMYTRYK: I've become a renegade, but I won't become a right-winger. This is a mistake that some of the right-wing organizations made. They asked me to talk to them. Not long ago a fundamentalist preacher in Glendale, California, called me and said, "We want you to come when you're out here in California and speak to our congregation." I said, "Now wait a minute. Understand me. I'm an extreme left-winger. The reason I got out of the Communist Party was because they were too far to the right for me." The American Legion has asked me to speak. I find myself to the left of all my students. I'm constantly preaching revolution of one kind or another to them.

It had nothing to do with politics. It had to do with finding that the Communist Party is a rigid, dictatorial party that will do anything to stay in power and is in no way, no matter how often they call their countries a "democratic republic," a democracy, and never will be. Now, of course, they say you can have a dictatorship for so long and it will gradually change over and become pure socialism. They thought they could do it in about fifty years, if I remember. It's been over sixty years, and they haven't been able to do it. They've become more rather than less rigid. They will never do it. This system is just not going to bring about socialism, any kind of socialism. Let me give you an example.

Just a couple of blocks from the main motion picture studio in Budapest, there's a statue of a man of the proletariat, the working man with the leather jacket. This is the aristocrat of the Communists, you know, the working man. I went into the studio there and up to the offices. I came down with one of the bureaucrats who runs the studio. I just took a walk around the studio to see the stages and things. Everywhere I went, the workers as they passed us would tip their hats, like the old English peasants. If they didn't have a hat, they literally pulled a forelock. I said to him, "I thought these people were supposed to be the masters. I thought they were the rulers." He just laughed. I worked with the people there. I was there for six months. My disillusionment with the system was great. The girl I had as my assistant cutter was supposed to be a cutter. She said: "There's just no sense in working here; there's just no place I can go. My son can't get [in]to college because I'm not a member of the Communist Party. He's very bright, high IQ, but he can't get in." She herself was making $90 a month, which is a standard wage, $3 a day. Everywhere I went, I found this kind of hypocrisy.

FRIEDMAN: Do you still have any reverberations from that all?

DMYTRYK: I get reverberations all the time.

FRIEDMAN: I mean professionally.

DMYTRYK: Yes. Sure. The liberals have come back into power in Hollywood. People like John Houseman were sympathizers but never really did anything solid at all, never had enough courage to become Communists. But they became very highly critical of anybody who was right wing or against Communism.

FRIEDMAN: Have you ever had any offers to go back?

DMYTRYK: To Hollywood? Oh, Christ, I turned down a million dollars in salary last year. I was sent two scripts. My rate now is a half million a picture, and neither script was any good. For one of them, the money was already in escrow. I run into these kinds of things. But I've made my peace with it. I know that I will until the day I die. I don't know whether anybody will ever approve of my actions historically; I know that a lot of people will disapprove of them.

FRIEDMAN: Do you think the pendulum has gone back now with Reagan in office and the Moral Majority going after TV?

DMYTRYK: I think it's very apt to. I'm scared to death of the Moral Majority. I was telling my students a couple of weeks ago that this is your McCarthy era. I'm afraid it's going to be. This is another terribly doctrinaire group of people who think they know the truth, and if there's anything dangerous in this world, it's a man who thinks he knows what the truth is. He'll kill anybody not in support of his truth. I think we're coming into a very dangerous period, this time from a religious element.

FRIEDMAN: Reagan seems unwilling to forsake them.

DMYTRYK: He'd take the Ku Klux Klan if they supported him. He'd take the Communists if they'd support him, except he knows that they're not big enough. Now I know Ronnie very well. My wife made a film with him, and I've known him for years. The one thing we've always said about Reagan, even in the old days, is that he doesn't have enough profundity to be a governor or a president. He's very glib, sharp, and fast, but every answer is simplistic. Look what he did with the fundamentalists about evolution: he said at that religious meeting that he had his doubts about the evolution theory. I damn near dropped dead because I'm sure even Ronnie is too smart for that. He's not suddenly going to go back to the biblical theory of creation. There's no question he's an opportunist. But again, that's the state of the politics in this country today. No first-class mind runs for the presidency. The presidency is for mediocre people who will be pushed by other people. The bright people don't run for the presidency; they run for the positions behind the presidency. That's a fact. I've had some friends who've run for office, and I've learned a few things from them. And I've known office-holders, God knows. The compromises you have to make, the pressures, are immense. You just have to do it; otherwise you're not there.

FRIEDMAN: Do you see the Hollywood Ten as an isolated incident in our history?

DMYTRYK: No, it's the kind of thing that happens in this country once in a while. It's the kind of thing that happens in almost every country every once in a while. These kinds of battles have to be fought constantly, not only in the field of politics, but in the field of ecology, of environment, of living standards, of racial tolerance, of education. This was just one of those battles. The pendulum keeps swinging back and forth, back and forth. It has happened before in this country. More people have gone to jail than in between 1947 and 1951, far more people. There have been times in the past, and there will be again. Believe me. I hope not under Ronnie, but it's possible.

Wes Craven

One of the things that the horror genre does at its best is [to] express that rage that Kurtz expresses at the end of the river, a sort of primal scream, and it's done by people who are in one way or another outside the usual mainstream of art who figure they have nothing to lose.

$\mathcal{T}$his interview is contemporary with Wes Craven's work on the first of several *A Nightmare on Elm Street* films. Having been socially ostracized for directing horrors, Craven ironically rejects the title of "horror film director," emphasizing ways in which his films interrogate American "myths" (of the "normal" family, of social cohesion, of undefeated heroism), arguing that the violence of his films is "incidental" in relation to the moral and thematic concerns of his work. Craven speaks of the rage he gives voice to in his films: rage as primal as Kurtz's last scream in *Heart of Darkness*; rage as response to the daily violence he sees in American society; rage as critique of the unrealistic "Hollywood view of violence" and as an interrogation of the sort of cinematic heroism (typified by John Wayne) that cannot answer the contemporary, political, personal, ideological, and sociocultural violence perceived by Craven. The interview predates a new wave of horror films, arguably inaugurated by his own highly self-conscious and sometimes shockingly playful *Scream* movies which paved the way for other postmodern horror-satires (such as the *I Know What You Did Last Summer* series) and numerous Hollywood remakes of horrors, ironically including Marcus Nispel's 2003 unfavorably reviewed remake of a film for which Craven expresses great admiration: Tobe Hooper's *The Texas Chainsaw Massacre* (1974). Scott Foundas criticizes Nispel's film for its "*Scream*-like self-referential abyss,"[1] the *Scream* series having become synonymous in his review for satirical, crude, and superficial intertextuality literalized through violence. This interview is a timely reminder of the thematic intentions behind Craven's work in the 1970s and 1980s at least, intentions much more confrontational than the ostensibly self-satisfied, self-conscious satire of the *Scream* movies might prompt us to perceive.

Interview by Christopher Sharrett
Originally published as "Fairy Tales for the Apocalypse: Wes Craven on the Horror Film,"
Literature/Film Quarterly *13, no. 3 (July 1985): 139–47.*

Wes Craven—along with Tobe Hooper, George A. Romero, David Cronenberg, John Carpenter, and Brian De Palma—is part of the "new wave" of the horror film that emerged in the 1970s. A graduate of the distinguished Writing Seminars of the Johns Hopkins University, Craven left a teaching career to pursue filmmaking. With the assistance of producer Sean Cunningham, Craven directed his first feature in 1972; known as *Last House on the Left* [1972], the film (adapted from Bergman's *The Virgin Spring*, 1960) became a transitional work of the horror genre. Craven describes the film as "the next logical step after *Psycho* [1960]," inaugurating an attitude toward horror that would be developed in Hooper's *The Texas Chainsaw Massacre* [1974], Carpenter's *Halloween* [1978], Romero's *Dawn of the Dead* [1978], and Cronenberg's *They Came from Within* [also known as *Shivers*, 1975], *The Brood* [1979], and *Scanners* [1981].

A subsequent project, *The Hills Have Eyes* (1976), achieved wider recognition for Craven, focusing new attention on the horror film's traditional theme of psychopathology. The equation of horror with pervasive social crisis—the chief characteristic of Craven's films—has had the effect of transforming the genre, causing it to drift away from monsters and the supernatural. *Last House on the Left* and *The Hills Have Eyes* share in common the notion of a collective barbarism overtaking the middle-class values of American society frequently lauded by genre art. *Last House*'s story of a couple's revenge for the brutal murder of their daughter and their subsequent descent into savagery (even outstripping the cruelty of their attackers) turned on their ear conceptions of the family idealized by the conventions of Hollywood cinema. *The Hills Have Eyes*, which Craven describes as his version of *The Grapes of Wrath*, depicts society entering into a New Dark Age in the tale of two families (one "civilized," one "barbaric") clashing on the fringes of the American frontier, now portrayed as a wasteland. By combining classical myth with renovated conventions borrowed from the Western and melodrama, Craven addresses the undercurrent of repression and consequent backlash in American society that the mainstream cinema tends to rationalize or gloss over. With *Last House on the Left* and *The Hills Have Eyes* the horror film abandons the Gothicism of the works produced by the Universal and Hammer studios, preferring to show its atrocities in broad daylight rather than Expressionist shadow. More important, the horror film after Craven operates as social commentary, detailing the malaise and sense of a disrupted social contract in the post-Vietnam, post-Watergate period (this role has been discussed in Robin Wood's articles for the monograph *The American Nightmare*).[2] While more recent projects (*Deadly Blessing* [1981], *Swamp Thing* [1982]) have enjoyed less popularity, Craven's contribution to the horror film already seems landmark. His current work includes an ABC television film entitled *Invitation to Hell* [1984], and *A Nightmare on Elm Street* [1984], a project based on Craven's original script.

The following conversation took place as Craven was completing work on *The Hills Have Eyes 2*, a sequel to his 1976 film scheduled for release in the summer of 1985. He discusses his career and the horror film's role in the conservative 1980s.

SHARRETT: Do you perceive a bias on the part of mainstream media reviewers against the horror film?

CRAVEN: I think there is. I don't know how to account for it, except that it may be a kind of visceral reaction on the part of the general public, perhaps because of the increase in everyday horrors, on the news. Also, I think some of the excesses of the horror genre have come to represent the genre itself to these people who simply don't see many films. They see them all as blood-and-guts films, slasher films. Certainly a few people in the genre contributed to that impression.

SHARRETT: So you feel that critics can't or won't distinguish between slasher films and films that use violence to communicate ideas?

CRAVEN: Yes, except that there aren't very many that *do* communicate very much right now. When *The Texas Chainsaw Massacre* came out it received some good reviews, including in *The Village Voice*. The same applies to *The Hills Have Eyes*; even *Last House on the Left* has had its share of champions. But I would say that ninety-five percent wanted to lynch me and the rest of us.

SHARRETT: Regarding *Hills Have Eyes* and *Last House on the Left*, can you talk about some of the ideas influencing those films?

CRAVEN: By and large it was the European cinema that contributed to my thinking about film. A variety of directors from Truffaut to Buñuel, that rather massive oeuvre, had the strongest influence on me. I didn't go to a great deal of movies as a kid. Aside from this my greatest influences were memories of the family and what it was like to grow up. As you know, both *Last House* and *Hills* are strongly involved with issues regarding the family, and I suspect this will interest me for some time to come. I have an upcoming project about a girl and her family, actually a group of three families, which picks up the basic theme. For me this is a very interesting idea. *Deadly Blessing* was not my original script, of course. While I found it technically interesting I was not particularly interested in the substance of it, except for the general theme of religious repression. But the film wasn't intrinsic to me, sort of part and parcel of me the way *Last House* and *Hills* were. In both of those films so much of what happens, even down to the names of characters, was derived from personal experience. Not that I had known those specific kinds of monsters, but that my feelings regarding family dynamics came through very strongly in those films. The idea of hiding something so as to avoid showing weakness only to create a more serious weakness—this was something I recall very vividly from ordinary experience.

SHARRETT: You're probably aware that a few critics, including Robin Wood, see the contemporary horror film as a form of reaction against bourgeois society, in the sense that the current films show the consequences of various forms of repression. Do you feel that your own films have a consciously ideological thrust or are they more on the order of personal statements?

CRAVEN: I wouldn't separate the two. I think the films are ideological although I don't go into a film with the attitude of attempting to make a statement. Inevitably certain things come out that I suppose express a specific position. One thing I think my films do express—and this is shared by some of the more recent horror films—is a sense of rage. This is something not very easily expressed, not normally found in the American cinema. Rage against the culture, against the bourgeoisie or whatever you want to say. It may be rage against the horror of life itself. Certainly one of the things that the horror genre does at its best is express that rage that Kurtz expresses at the end of the river, a sort of primal scream, and it's done by people who are in one way or another outside the usual mainstream of art who figure they have nothing to lose. When I did *Last House* I was in this situation. Nobody knew me, I had quit teaching, was living in New York, letting my hair grow and just letting all the stops out. I wasn't thinking about making a political statement as much as letting myself go in the freest way possible to see what comes out. At the same time I was very aware politically.

SHARRETT: So you think your cumulative experiences of society coincided with a more unconscious ideological development?

CRAVEN: Yeah. At first I never thought I was in an arena for making any sort of political statement. I came out of a period where I wrote poems and short stories which were involved with the period surrounding the war; nothing much happened with any of that stuff and I'm sure all of it would now seem very pompous and pretentious. Finally Sean Cunningham told me to write a horror film and pull out all the stops, just go nuts. I found that when I finally did that I wasn't concerned with chopping people's heads off. What came out of it seemed like a strange mixture of Grand Guignol and an entirely new statement. I don't mean to flatter myself but as I look at it now it seems the next logical step after *Psycho*, and of course in this period *Texas Chainsaw Massacre* comes along and a new attitude toward horror develops.

SHARRETT: Your films have been read in part as a criticism of the way society displaces violence as well as a more general critique of American myth, including the frontier experience and the image of the family. Do you think these approaches are valid?

CRAVEN: In general, yes. The nuclear family has been under siege for at least the last twenty years, with profound effects. The sexual revolution and the subsequent backlash are factors, along with the Vietnam period and the destruction of the nice idea of "the people next door," the idea of fair play and all of it. I think the reality of the world is simply encroaching on American myth and that it must be redefined by that ragtag group of people who are not part of the Hollywood mainstream. They must at least play a part in reexamining this myth. I certainly felt this around the time of *The Hills Have Eyes*; one phrase that kept coming up was that we were doing "fairy tales for the apocalypse," and this was before I was conscious of *Apocalypse Now* [1979]. When I was speaking of Kurtz earlier, I was referring to *Heart of Darkness*, which did have some effect, I think, on my attitude toward the horror film. But more importantly, I think the horror film has become a specific way of digesting the horror that really is all around us; it's just never ending. You can't look at the annual issue of *Life* magazine without seeing piles of dead bodies, people being machine-gunned as a matter of course. It seems to be a time when people are being ground up in huge tectonic movements, these continental, psychic, cultural collisions. I don't think anybody buys the John Wayne image of how we confront violence, both collectively and in the individual. We can't kid ourselves that Lt. Calley was some sort of a monster; he was the most ordinary of guys.

SHARRETT: He was just, part of an ideological process.

CRAVEN: He was just thrust into a reality that the myth did not serve. Before Vietnam the image of war was of the front line, which is the good guys vs. bad guys myth that fell apart. There is no longer any such myth when you see civilians being killed all around you and this is being transmitted regularly by the media. The only way to survive this is by an enormous cynicism unless you are ready to confront the myth. I also wanted to confront the idea that the average citizen is incapable of violence, that he or she is supposed to turn the other cheek. In both of my early films much of the violence is carried out by the "whitebread" types, the middle-American families. I always resented the way Hollywood glossed over this, although it's a more predominant theme today perhaps. Still, Hollywood's view of violence remains pretty unrealistic.

SHARRETT: Hollywood's view of violence is still more or less antiseptic while the culture itself is increasingly violent.

CRAVEN: Well, it produced Reagan! Here is the most antiseptic sort of person who in his own way is nudging us toward the abyss. These are the people who really worry me. I mean, they give millions of dollars to their minions in El Salvador without any sort of human rights qualifications. This kind of thing is what scares the hell out of me.

SHARRETT: It's another way of covering up one reality with an idealism that is essentially hypocritical. They make references to "democracy" instead of coming straight out with their real interests, which are economic.

CRAVEN: Sure. They want to preserve the white man's playground and the cheap labor.

SHARRETT: To get back to some themes in your films, I'm interested in the names given to the cannibal family in *Hills*, the Roman-astrological names of Pluto, Mars, Jupiter. Is this part of a general sense of barbaric regression?

CRAVEN: Well, they were planetary names and absolutely primal. The family, Jupiter's family, was absolutely outside the normal skein of earth societies. They represented bodies of great force, tremendous power. On the other hand, of course, is the idea that the cannibal family is a mirror image of the "whitebread" family, the Carters, and that each member of the Carter family has a correlate in Jupiter's clan. I also wanted people to confront this basic xenophobia by showing that a group of seemingly reprehensible people can be like anyone else in one's experience of so-called normal, everyday, middle-class life. Papa Jupiter has his own wife and sons. Their behavior is not at all different from the behavior of Carter and his sons, although Jupiter is first seen as the aggressor.

SHARRETT: Do the Roman names, with their association with the origins of civilization, give Jupiter's family stronger moral connotations than the Carter family?

CRAVEN: I thought they had a certain morality in the sense that there was nothing devious about them. They made no pretense. I think in particular of the speech by Jupiter to the dead body of Mr. Carter.

SHARRETT: When he says over the campfire, "Your dog made sport of my blood, you pig—I'll kill your kids for that."

CRAVEN: Exactly. It is a basic scene wherein one culture supplants another. It always seems that it's the barbarians at the gates and the end of civilization, and all of a sudden they are the ones who end up being civilization. I was approaching this in terms of totally amoral forces, as part of what seems to be the human freight train. One can think of the Mayans vs. the Spaniards, the American Indian vs. the pioneers. I was not looking at this aspect of the film from a political standpoint. People just seem to grind up other people, in the same way that animals eat other animals to grow stronger.

SHARRETT: That speech to the severed head of Mr. Carter seems like something from Seneca.

CRAVEN: Yeah, very much. He's saying "I'm going to get you right down at your seed." I was thinking of the Greeks and of *The Oresteia* in particular, where a cycle of reciprocal violence goes on and on until someone steps in and says it has to end, that the cycle of revenge must stop. On the one hand, I wanted to deal with that great, purging feeling surrounding violence, but, on the other hand, I wanted to show that the idea of reciprocal violence must be halted, this whole idea that "I'm gonna get those sons-of-bitches who blew up my neighborhood." This mentality seems to be at the heart of much of the violence internationally right now.

SHARRETT: In *Hills* this resolution comes when Bobby goes off with Ruby, the daughter from the wild family.

CRAVEN: Yes, and in fact I carry this further in *Hills 2*, with Bobby marrying Ruby, suggesting a new cycle in time.

SHARRETT: The violence in your films centers on the theme of cannibalism, which has become a major theme in the horror film of the '70s and '80s. How do you regard this as an element of the horror film?

CRAVEN: There's a peculiar thing about cannibalism. Obviously it's one of the last taboos, but there's also something intellectually very appealing about it, in that it's absolutely direct, an absolutely honest way of going about the idea of someone killing someone else. It goes directly against the tradition of portraying violence in an antiseptic way. Even on the news there is the basic tendency to show people being put into plastic body bags and sort of carefully tucked away on a shelf somewhere, as if the bloodshed never happened. Grenada was a recent example. Cannibalism is much more direct. The cannibal takes the other person's strength, the person's vital fluids. It's symbolic but it also strikes a chord about the nature of violence. The person's essence is being taken. It's a good opposite not just to the way violence is portrayed in movies, but to the whole notion of how we "knock somebody off," even in a business sense. Cannibalism tends to expose the casual aspect of all of it.

SHARRETT: Some critics regard cannibalism as a theme, as a portrayal of the logical consequences of capitalism, people feeding off of each other.

CRAVEN: Well, it's a changing of violence from something that is socially acceptable and manipulable. Even in the military, violence is very mechanized, very dehumanized. People are not asked to view its consequences or its connections to any larger system. When it does begin to confront them square in the face it's terrifying, as in the Vietnam experience, which people are still trying to "deal with."

SHARRETT: I'd like to move to another area regarding violence in the horror film. While many mainstream reviewers have attacked the genre almost out of principle, it has also come under attack from feminists and other progressive factions who hold that the horror film's violence is directed primarily at women. How do you respond to this?

CRAVEN: I think I've always been sensitive to this in my own films, always conscious of it as an issue. Certainly the horror film has traditionally shown a great deal of mayhem directed toward women, but on the other hand, I never felt that this was an inaccurate depiction of the violence that is directed against women in our society. Again, the horror film has been more honest about this than most genres. In my own films women have certainly had extremely important roles and have really been the most insightful and strongest characters. Phyllis in *Last House* is one of my strongest people. Ruby in *Hills* is a central figure in many respects. The issue of violence directed at women could be aimed at any genre. There's always a line where something becomes mere exploitation.

SHARRETT: But where do we draw the line? Some people have argued *Maniac* [1980], *Friday the 13th* [1980], and other films of the slasher sub-genre have some purgative function and reveal something about the nature of violence, but few of these films contribute anything new to the horror film itself.

CRAVEN: I don't want to sound glib but I don't bother myself with this debate. A similar debate goes on about pornography, the same debate from the '50s and '60s. I think these things sort themselves out. Films that serve no purpose to society just disappear, except perhaps to a very small segment. I don't happen to believe that movies cause people to go out and commit violent acts. Of course people who live very hermetic existences and consume these films as a steady diet might be influenced, but I suspect they are being influenced by boxing or cock-fights or whatever, which I suppose is not a new argument. I'm not really an expert on the subject of violence. In general, I don't go to violent films, *never* go to slasher films. I'm much more interested in psychic violence, in the denial of terror, in family dynamics. The violence itself is almost incidental to me. I go to see horror films on a very spotty basis. I'll see anything done by Tobe Hooper. His *Texas Chainsaw Massacre* simply amazed me. I'll see anything Cronenberg does. But these guys have very special visions; the question of violence is again almost incidental. Cronenberg doesn't even regard himself as a "horror director," and I share the same feeling.

SHARRETT: Another criticism leveled at the horror film is its deep pessimism. Many of the films, including your works, *Texas Chainsaw Massacre*, and Cronenberg's films, seem to deal with a world verging on chaos, without any suggestion of a solution to the crisis.

CRAVEN: I don't think that's necessarily true with my films. Both *Last House* and *Hills* contain characters who offer the possibility of change. Change is one thing I have a basic faith in. I *don't* think 1984 has to be *1984*, that apocalypse is now, that we have to face off with the Russians. I suppose I might differ with other genre directors in this. Hooper's *Texas Chainsaw* is an epochal work; it somehow caught extraordinarily well that insanity that's always at the fringe of American society. It is finally a very dark film. He deserves to be remembered for this film if for nothing else. But, no, I don't think there's a consistent pessimism to my own work, certainly not in later films like *Swamp Thing*. *Swamp Thing* was my script and I do regard it as part of my work and reflective of changes I've gone through in my own life. There is rage still present in my work, but I look forward to other projects that don't necessarily express the same rage as *Last House* or *Hills*. How much can you say about rage? My thinking about art and life still depends, I suppose, on someone like Camus. I believe in shaping something out of existence, in taking responsibility.

SHARRETT: But the importance of *Last House on the Left* and *The Hills Have Eyes*—and other horror films of the '70s—resides at least in part in the way they reflect a specific outrage and pessimism about the traditional view of the family, the frontier, the whole civilizing experience as previously portrayed in film.

CRAVEN: Oh yes, certainly the traditional vision has changed. Too many walls have collapsed to support that particular roof. I *do* believe in the family. I mean, I just got married and want to have children. At the risk of sounding simplistic, I do feel that a few human institutions are important. I wouldn't have dealt with them at all if I felt otherwise. If we discover a certain amount of rage in examining these institutions, it's obviously because they have some emotional significance to us, otherwise we could brush them off very easily. I think that some of the myths about what constitutes a man and a woman, what religion is or isn't, what patriotism is, are issues which have changed profoundly. American myth as previously conceived— John Wayne at Iwo Jima, the flag, good guys vs. bad guys—all this has to die, because as it is applied to the real world it clearly doesn't make it; it's failing every time. It didn't make it in Vietnam. It's not making it in Lebanon. The basic working model for a lot of us making horror films comes almost out of Mao Tse-Tung. I mean, no one is that rigid in their thinking, but it does become a question of a few people who aren't in the mainstream being able to get out there and swim with the fish. You do things on a very, very small budget, hitting and moving on.

SHARRETT: Which brings me to the question of the declining popularity of the horror film. Both the audience and the industry seem to be together on this, since few horror films are being released right now and very few are commercially successful.

CRAVEN: Well, you know, I have a list of topics suggested for film projects. The list was published by a major studio. Off-the-wall love stories are in, off-the-wall comedies are in, small films about families are very big, any film with an uplifting theme is very big. Vietnam is definitely *out*, and the horror film is way, way down the list. No interest, absolutely none.

SHARRETT: That's incredible, compared to what was going on five years ago.

CRAVEN: If I were to be introduced in the general studio crowd as a director of horror films, it would be equivalent to being introduced as a bomb-thrower or worse. People move away from you. I'm serious. It is not a well-liked genre out here. Even if you do get money to make a horror film, people in the industry really don't want to have very much of an association with you.

SHARRETT: It does seem that with the Reagan Administration there is a general reversion to the '50s, with the tremendous success of films like *Flashdance* [1983] and all this light-hearted, escapist fare.

CRAVEN: I'm not sure how it works. It may be valid to say that the images being put out there are what basically construct the mind-set of society. Right now it might be a question of putting "positive" images out there rather than something controversial. To be fair to all sides, there is also a point where people simply can no longer tolerate something like the horror film because it is *so* rageful, so down, so bereft of human warmth. Things are so bad today that people may not want to plunk down five dollars to see two hours of rage and horror when they can see it on the cable news every hour and don't even want to see that. On the whole I think Hollywood simply tries to anticipate trends in society to capitalize on them. I guess *Flashdance* is one example, because the industry could see the whole new dance craze and the exercise craze, combined with that particular form of optimism. The peculiar thing is that every so often a horror film makes it. Occasionally a slasher film of the *Friday the 13th* variety will make it while a film like *Videodrome* [1983] can't get off the ground. No one wants to know about it. I don't know how that works. *The Dead Zone* [1983] was rather successful because of the name of Stephen King, I would suppose, although it also represents some of Cronenberg's best work, and I admire all of his stuff tremendously. I think we have to recognize also that very *few* horror films are successful in the way that *E.T.* [1982] or *Star Wars* [1977] is successful. I don't know of any horror film that could get that kind of an audience and show that kind of profit today.

SHARRETT: Could audience rejection of the horror film be tied to the general attitude of "Let's put Vietnam and Watergate behind us?" Do audiences reject films with very volatile, contentious ideas?

CRAVEN: Could be, and the joke is that these things were never really confronted in the first place! I've not yet seen a film that deals with Vietnam realistically, in terms of its true horrors, and I've seen them all. Even in the novel, I haven't seen anything that deals with the real implications of the war. On the other hand, I think it's necessary to say that few horror films are really contentious, and not very many embody real ideas. The ones that do contain ideas are usually not treated very seriously except by film teachers and students, or by people disposed toward serious thinking. While I feel that *The Hills Have Eyes* contains some important ideas, I could count on one hand the people who have congratulated me for the intellectual content or the innovations. I still get the usual knee-jerk sort of reactions like "Gee, it was really neat the way that guy fell off the cliff." People who look at the horror film politically forget that there's still an enormous gap between watching a film like *Hills* or *Videodrome* or something and getting involved in social action. After all, films are just visions, just dreams. There is some worth in looking at them in a larger context and analyzing them, but I don't know how many people are interested or prepared to do that.

SHARRETT: One last question about themes in your films. *The Hills Have Eyes* looks very much like an anti-Western. Was it so intended?

CRAVEN: When I wrote the original script I was thinking of a new version of *The Grapes of Wrath*. In that draft, people were leaving New York because of the really horrendous pollution. It takes place just before the 1984 primaries, in other words right about now. People are trying to escape the pollution and going from state to state; each state has a check point and you have to hold a passport. No one is allowed in California because it's one of the sunbelt states but everyone wants to go there because fuel prices are so high. So you have this middle-class family trying to sneak into California in their trailer via the desert and they're set upon by this tribe. I was talked out of that opening, and of course much of it was window dressing, but you do have *The Grapes of Wrath* and this modern Western.

SHARRETT: It's great how Jupiter's clan lives off the scrapheap of another civilization, the society left over from a John Ford film.

CRAVEN: Yeah, I wanted to have even more of this sense of the tribe using Army surplus and Air Force surplus, with the jets flying overhead. Originally I wanted the wild family to have a cave built out of shell casings, but the budget stopped this from happening. Money is always the question!

NOTES

1. Scott Foundas, "Review of *The Texas Chainsaw Massacre*," *Daily Variety*, 17 October 2003, 12.

2. The full citation for this monograph is: Robin Wood and Richard Lippe, eds., *The American Nightmare: Essays on the Horror Film* (Toronto: Festival of Festivals, 1979).

Marcela Fernández Violante

> I can't go to a commercial producer because they would not be interested in my projects. They want to make films about singing prostitutes having fun.

The following interview with Marcela Fernández Violante was conducted in 1987, in confluence with the beginnings of a new wave of work by Mexican women directors. Several films directed by Mexican women directors—Marisa Sistach, Busi Cortés, Guita Schyfter, María Novaro, and Dana Rotberg—have been given domestic *and* international release since this interview: a heartening pattern of development in relation to Violante's representative difficulties in terms of getting her own work shown. A recent book entitled *Women Filmmakers in Mexico: The Country of Which We Dream* by Elissa J. Rashkin (University of Texas Press, 2001) focuses on the logistics as well as the cultural significance of filmmaking by the directors above who, like Violante, are concerned with questions of national identity and cultural tolerance, as well as challenges to hegemonic and patriarchal order through cinema. Although Violante has directed more than ten acclaimed feature films to date (including several since the time of this interview), it nevertheless remains difficult to access her work in the United States, partly because they have never been given release beyond film festival circuits (excepting the DVD release of *Cananea* [1977] in 2004).

In this interview, Violante discusses processes specific to filmmaking in Mexico, the "problem" of the homogenizing influence of Mexican television schedules as well as theatrical distribution, both of which are dominated by American productions, and the more specific cultural concerns of her film *En el País de los pies ligeros* (*In the Country of the Fast Runners*, 1981).

227

Interview by Andrew Horton
Originally published as "'We Are Losing Our Identity': An Interview with Mexican Director
Marcela Fernández Violante," Literature/Film Quarterly *15, no. 1 (January 1987): 2–7.*

Marcela Fernández Violante is the only woman currently directing films in Mexico. A professor of film at the National Autonomous University of Mexico since 1970, Violante has completed four feature films and has won numerous "Ariels" (the Mexican equivalent of the Oscars) as well as receiving recognition abroad at festivals including the Museum of Modern Art New Directors Series in New York, and festivals in Cuba, Russia, and Czechoslovakia.

De todos modos Juan te llamas (Whatever You Do, You Lose, also known as *The General's Daughter,* 1976), her first feature, is based on the 1926 Cristero War (a religious civil war in Mexico). It is a sensitive portrayal of the role of the military in Mexico drawn in part from her own past: her father was a general, and she grew up surrounded by military personalities.

In 1976 she completed *Cananea,* a film that concerns the true events surrounding an American capitalist, William C. Greene, who opened a copper mine, Cananea, and exploited the workers and the land in 1906.

Misterio (Mystery, 1980) is a contemporary tale scripted by novelist Vicente Leñero from his novel, *Studio Q.* It is a self-reflexive story of a TV soap opera star who confuses the scenes in his own life with those on the television screen. Violante sees this work as an allegory of the alienation of contemporary man as heightened by mass media. *Misterio* won eight of the twelve Ariel awards for 1981 and the Jury's Special Award at the Mystery International Film Festival held at Cattolica, Italy, in 1982.

Her most recent film, *En el País de los pies ligeros (In the Country of the Fast Runners,* 1981), is a children's story about a suburban middle class Mexican boy who becomes best friends with a Tarahumara Indian boy during a vacation in the mountains of northern Mexico. The film documents not only the friendship, but how much the Mexican boy has to learn from the native culture.

The interview took place in January 1983, in New Orleans as she was appearing at a Festival of Mexican Cinema held at Loyola University. Full of nervous energy (she uses her hands most expressively), Violante, a dark-haired attractive woman in her early forties, fielded a wide range of topics. The following is an edited transcript of her remarks.

HORTON: How did you get started in film?

VIOLANTE: I studied at the film school of the national university. Since the film school was founded some nineteen years ago, the Mexican industry has tended to use directors trained by film schools. It happened that the student films I made won awards, maybe not because they were so good, but because the rest of the films were so bad! So they thought my films were almost out of this world. (Author's note: One of these short films is a documentary called *Frida Kahlo*, a study of an artist who had been married to Diego Rivera. It received an Ariel as best documentary of 1971 and the Silver Goddess award from the Mexican film critics.)

HORTON: Can you briefly suggest what you have to go through to make a film in Mexico today?

VIOLANTE: We have a problem with the financing of films. The Mexican film industry is the oldest in Latin America because the Lumière Brothers sent filmmakers to Mexico when Diaz was the dictator in power. And they remained such a long time filming folklore that they trained Mexicans to use cameras. So the Mexican film industry is divided into two trends. One is very, very commercial, making soap operas, for instance, for the illiterate people who live in the rural areas and in the big cities. And then there are the films that have started to be made in the last ten years as a result of the government's interest in having films that are of cultural interest. The State interest in film has slowly been diminishing because of the change of policies that every new president and his cabinet impose every six years. So there is very little continuity, and an increasing cultural gap between the social classes.

When I finish a script, I must go to a film industry official in the government. I can't go to a commercial producer because they would not be interested in my projects. They want to make films about singing prostitutes having fun. Besides, their own children have been trained as film directors, to have everything kept "within the family." This official tells me to leave the script for him to read. But often he (or any other official) does not read it. They give it to someone else. And after this, you may or may not get help. Thus if you want to make a film right away, you have to think of a very cheap project. That is what I am trying to do now.

Finally, if the first official does approve your script, he must give it to the Board of the Direction of Cinematography in order to secure authorization in censorship. This is a very "abstract" Board since you never find out who is on the Board.

HORTON: Have you personally had trouble with the censors?

VIOLANTE: No. Maybe they have not read my scripts page by page. I have been lucky. And if I have a chance to improvise and add something later, and they do not catch it, it is their problem since they have the power also to cut a film! But everyone is not as lucky. Many Mexican directors tend to censor themselves. I feel they should take the risk. Perhaps we have this problem because we are too humble or insecure since we are part Indian, part Spanish.

HORTON: Do you have more trouble than other filmmakers because you are a woman?

VIOLANTE: Maybe. But I will have trouble making *any* film. You see, in order to have power and to be respected in Mexico, you must be well known internationally. In my case I have been on the jury at Moscow two years ago and just recently in Havana. So I am an important person for the industry. They feel it is best to work with a well-known "prestigious" woman director, and then they are able to say how pro-feminist they are because they support me.

HORTON: Does the government control your film once you have finished it since they have put up the money for it?

VIOLANTE: I wish they did. That is, I wish they chose where to send it and so forth, but they don't. What they do is put it on the shelf! I ask them, "Why don't we send it to Cannes or Moscow or elsewhere?" And they say, "We don't have enough money to put on English subtitles." And when I ask why the film is not shown in Mexico, since it was completed a year ago, they answer that, "We have a lot of Mexican films waiting for distribution. You have to wait in line." But *E.T.* [1982], for instance, is playing in thirty movie theaters at the same time in Mexico. These are not privately run theaters. They are run by the Mexican government. The government controls this and prefers to have *E.T.* play because they will make more money than they would from a Mexican film.

HORTON: How are you viewed by male filmmakers in Mexico?

VIOLANTE: You have to belong to a directors' union if you wish to make films, and, if you write films, to an authors' union. Finally, after six years in the union of being treated like the worst boy in class, they accepted me. You know why? Because I take shorthand and type! But this is very useful to me. In fact I am the secretary of both unions. Not I get to know a lot because I ask questions. Now they have learned to respect me and with this respect comes the beginning of love, love in the very open sense.

HORTON: How did you become involved in your most recent film, *In the Country of the Fast Runners* (also known as *El niño rarámuri—The Raramuri Boy*) about the friendship of a middle class Mexican boy and a Tarahumara Indian boy?

VIOLANTE: I was shown a script, a first script, by a young writer which was about the Tarahumara Indians of northern Mexico. It was a rough script, but I talked to the writer and we became good friends as we rewrote it. When I insisted, we went and lived with the Indians for a week because I didn't feel the writer knew enough about the Indians.

We learned a lot. You see, there are seven million Indians in Mexico and they speak fifty-seven different dialects. Most of them do not know Spanish, so they do not communicate between tribes very much or with Mexicans. Many Indians have moved to the cities to find work, and Mexicans often laugh at them when they watch them struggle with their first contact with city culture. So I wanted to see what would happen if we reversed the situation in which it would be the Mexican boy who would look foolish and who would have a lot to learn from the Indian.

In the film, the Indian boy (played by a real Tarahumara) shows the city boy how to fish, how to protect himself from snakes, and so on, and in the end, the boy from the city wants to live with the Indians rather than return to Chihuahua.

It's a film for children. I want the audience to stop being so prejudiced about the Indians and to start learning from them. After all, we are an Indian country.

HORTON: What do you see is the greatest problem in your country which film-makers should address?

VIOLANTE: We are losing our identity. Mexico is a colonialist country and con-sumes foreign products more than home products in all aspects. We have four pri-vate television channels and two cable stations and all we see are American series, often dubbed into Spanish. Both cable stations are in English and ninety percent of what is shown in the cinemas is American films. We used to get films from the whole world—Japan, Europe, but not anymore. We even seldom get films from South America. Just the United States.

The problem with television is that it reduces the cultural level and conforms to a dangerous uniformity for all tastes. It also promotes the "American Way of Life," thus reducing the sense of national pride. Thus the values and ideals por-trayed in the Mexican culture tend to disappear.

HORTON: What will your next film be about?

VIOLANTE: I want to do a film about a divorced woman in Mexico today. First I must research that personally. I am divorced, but my situation is very particular so I can only use my experience partially. I am interested in a common middle class woman. I had sampled about ten different women and interviewed them. I have transcribed everything onto file cards so that I can write the script. I want to do this because we have a trend in Mexico to misunderstand women. They are de-spised if they are divorced. They are also despised if they are unwed mothers. Mexico is still a male-oriented society and not even professional women are well accepted yet.

HORTON: You are the only practicing woman director. Are there other women in other aspects of filmmaking in Mexico?

VIOLANTE: There is one editor, but no camerawomen. There are a number of women producers; I don't know why. And there are about three screenwriters. In the past there were two other women directors.

HORTON: Would you work outside Mexico if given the chance?

VIOLANTE: Yes, I would. You have to give yourself opportunities. I like the chal-lenge. I mean this in all aspects of life, not just film. Many are afraid to say "yes" so they say "no." I would like to say "yes."

HORTON: Finally, do you consider yourself a feminist filmmaker?

VIOLANTE: I am feminine, that is, I am a woman. I love women, but I believe what Rilke says, that women and men resemble each other more than we are willing to admit. That's why I love men too. I am interested in the problems of all people, not just one group. Anyhow, *Frida Kahlo* and *The General's Daughter* (*De todos modos Juan te llamas*) are feminist films.

Alain Robbe-Grillet

In the cinema, I've always been lucky, in that there have always been producers who asked me to make a film. It's strange!

*I*n 1989, Royal S. Brown conducted an interview with the famous French filmmaker, scriptwriter, and novelist Alain Robbe-Grillet. Although he was a major part of the French film culture of the 1960s, Robbe-Grillet is not always immediately associated with the French New Wave; as Brown points out in his introduction, the writer and director "has remained something of an outsider." And yet, despite that outsider status—or perhaps because of it—Robbe-Grillet is candid and generous with his interviewer, though not always with other figures. Beginning with a provocation from Brown, for example, Robbe-Grillet launches into a response to one of his critics, saying her words are "remarkably stupid!" before admitting, only a few moments later, that "[t]here's no point getting upset over" comments such as those. After this initial opening, Robbe-Grillet discusses Jean-Luc Godard before moving into his own films, citing what frustrated him while making *L'Immortelle* (1963). All the while, Robbe-Grillet transitions easily among seemingly distinct elements of the filmmaking process and his own history with it; for instance, a discussion of why he never finances his own films ("I've never put a penny into a film") moves into the set design for *Le Jeu avec le feu* (*Playing with Fire,* 1975), and eventually becomes a discussion of doubling. (On this last point, readers who know Robbe-Grillet's work will not be surprised to see here a reference to the Latin American author Jorge Luis Borges.) Robbe-Grillet also spends a great deal of time discussing his use of music in his films and how it sometimes has "a kind of initiating role" for his conception of the narrative. Finally, after a brief discussion of editing, Robbe-Grillet speaks openly about the directors he admires, a reminder that, despite our conceptions of the artist working in isolation, filmmakers have always exchanged

233

ideas by simply going to the theater to see what their peers have been dreaming about.

~

Interview by Royal S. Brown
Originally published as "Alain Robbe-Grillet," Literature/Film Quarterly *17, no. 2 (April 1989): 74–83.*

Few creative artists have led their careers on the fronts of two substantially different arts. One who has is Alain Robbe-Grillet. While more prolific as a writer—he is the author of around a dozen novels, a collection of short stories, and numerous theoretical articles, and he is currently at work on the third volume of his autobiography—Robbe-Grillet has also written and directed eight films in addition to the famous—and infamous— *L'Année dernière à Marienbad* (*Last Year at Marienbad* [1961]), for which he wrote only the screenplay. Early in his career, Robbe-Grillet became recognized as one of the principal theoreticians and spokespersons for the so-called *Nouveau Roman* (New Novel) movement in France. Much of his earlier literary theory can be found in the collection of essays, published in 1963, entitled *Pour un nouveau roman* (*For a New Novel*), the next-to-last chapter of which also briefly examines the cinema. As a filmmaker, however, Robbe-Grillet has remained something of an outsider, even though it is certainly possible to see him as a part of the "New Wave" that shook up French—and world—cinema as of the 1960s. Yet the writer/director has proven to be every bit as eloquent a spokesperson for a "new cinema" as he has for the "new novel." On March 6, 1989, I had the occasion to talk with Robbe-Grillet in New York City, where he teaches two courses—one on literature, one on film—every three years at New York University. The first question I asked him addressed a criticism that is often leveled at his films and, in reverse, at his novels.

BROWN: Marie-Claire Ropars-Wuilleumier has written, in *De la Littérature au cinema* [Armand Colin, 1970], that "Robbe-Grillet's films are in fact put together just like his novels: but they don't produce the same effects, for they are seen and not read: for one to give sensorial perceptions the same possibilities that one gives to literary signs, one would have to organize them dynamically. But Robbe-Grillet does not concern himself with this at all, absorbed as he is by his desire to find in the cinema the culmination of his literary theory." What is your response to this perception?

ROBBE-GRILLET: It's remarkably stupid! This critic isn't someone who is particularly sensitive to modern cinema. And I don't think she's really interested in my novels either. And so, she can be counted with those who, appreciating neither my novels nor my films, condemn my novels in the name of my films, and condemn my films in the name of my novels. This is a common habit within this type of feeble criticism. There's no point in getting upset over it. If I understand what she's trying to say, what she calls a "dynamic organization" is probably what Bazin called "life," which is quite ridiculous, since the ideology of "life," according to Bazin, is in fact a very linear narrative. He finds it dynamic because it's linear. These critics find anything that breaks with this linearity as preventing dynamism. Furthermore, I've never been preoccupied with trying to put my literature into film, because for me, the raw materials of the cinema are something completely different from the raw material of the novel, of literature. Even the dialogues cannot be the same in literature and film, from my point of view at least. What I find funny is that this kind of critic is quick to appreciate in the cinema "authors" who are nothing more than failed novelists, such as Truffaut and a number of others like him. And so there's no way I can discuss this kind of problem with these critics, because neither the cinema nor literature has for them and for me the same meaning. The dynamic effects that I create in my films are quite obviously not considered by her to be dynamic effects, because for me, dynamic effects, as Eisenstein has explained it, are "shock" effects and not in the slightest "continuity" effects. But there's nothing serious in all this. You have to let people write according to their ideologies, it doesn't bother me. And Marie-Claire Ropars-Wuilleumier certainly hasn't said loathsome things about my films. She's quite calm, particularly in comparison to certain other critics. But one has the impression that she simply doesn't grasp this kind of narrative structure. But that's not her fault!

BROWN: I was surprised to read what she had to say about your films, since she has written quite profoundly on Godard, it seems to me.

ROBBE-GRILLET: What I've read by her on Godard is perhaps interesting. But I have the impression that she's not speaking of the same Godard as I am. She's much more comfortable writing of the narrative technique of *À bout de souffle* [*Breathless*, 1960] than of *Prénom Carmen* [*First Name: Carmen*, 1983], for instance.

BROWN: You prefer *Prénom Carmen*?

ROBBE-GRILLET: Of course. There's nothing wrong with *À bout de souffle*. But there's a screenplay by Truffaut that Godard completely respects, and so the strong cinematic effects show up in spite of the narrative project. I very much like Godard's films from the *Deux ou trois choses que je sais d'elle* [*Two or Three Things I Know about Her*, 1967] and the *Made in U.S.A.* [1966] period, because here he breaks definitively with the traditional storyline, which he respects in *À bout de souffle*, which simply rejuvenates the tradition. *À bout de souffle* remains a historically important film, but it has a certain "in" quality to it as well. In other words, the film owes some of its popularity to a certain understanding of young people who, while not necessarily delinquent, had gotten off the beaten path and who couldn't find an identity, which Belmondo does quite well. But this isn't what's interesting cinematically in Godard. When the *Nouveau Roman* came into being, in the fifties, the "in" thing was not the *Nouveau Roman*; what was "in" was Françoise Sagan, a kind of sensitive capturing of a new *mal du siécle*.

BROWN: In discussing *La Belle captive* [*The Beautiful Prisoner*, 1983], you speak of its inspiration as coming from images and sounds that you had in mind. How is a Robbe-Grillet film born? If it's strictly out of images and sounds that your films take shape, are the possible narratives in your cinema spontaneously generated from these images and sounds, or are there at least traces of narrative ideas as of the moment the egg is fertilized, so to speak? For instance, did the doubled Orphic myth of *L'Immortelle* take its form only from the audio-visual paradigms that you had in mind, or had you conceived of it from the outset? Might Hitchcock's *Vertigo* [1958], which has an Orphic structure almost identical to that of *L'Immortelle*, have influenced you? (I know that you especially like Hitchcock's *Rope* [1948].)

ROBBE-GRILLET: No, I like *Vertigo* a great deal. It's one of the Hitchcocks that I like, because the screenplay is quite well done, and since the film doesn't "talk" all that much, whereas Hitchcock's major shortcoming are those interminable dialogues, which, in fact, one finds in most Hollywood cinema from that era. I have no idea whether *Vertigo* influenced me or not. I don't even know when I saw *Vertigo*. Anyway, you ask how the film is born. First of all, I'd like to separate *Marienbad* and *L'Immortelle* from the other films. In *Marienbad* and *L'Immortelle*, the first of which I wrote only the screenplay for, the second of which I scripted and directed—in both of these films, I completely wrote out the sequence of shots, without numbering them in *Marienbad*—Resnais did that—and numbering them in *L'Immortelle*. In other words, I had written out a technical decoupage that was respected when the films were edited, as the law requires. With *Marienbad*, this isn't a major problem, since I didn't direct it. But with *L'Immortelle*, while I was shooting it, I felt a kind of frustration. In other words, I was bothered by the fact that I had to reproduce something that was pre-written . . . bothered because I realized that, at best, the film was going to be what I had written. I would never be able to surpass what had been written, and in fact it could turn out being worse. I should add that I had already begun work on *L'Immortelle* before *Marienbad*. The producers had offered me the chance to make a film, provided I did it in Istanbul. That was fine with me, since I knew the city well. I had even met my wife, Catherine, there. Then the revolution came and I did *Marienbad*, after which, while Resnais was shooting the film, I went back to Turkey to complete *L'Immortelle*. At any rate, I suffered the consequences of pre-writing *L'Immortelle*. Since that time, I've "written" my films less and less. By "less and less," I mean that the film is born in the same way as the images that take shape, immediately accompanied by montage structures. In other words, not just sequences, but structures within which the shots are arranged with absolutely no consideration of "sequence." And it's the same thing with the sound, which is immediately important to me. Within the project that begins to take shape in my head, there is almost always some real setting that inspires me. This real setting is the train in *Trans-Europ-Express* [1966] and, in *L'Homme qui ment* [*The Man Who Lies*, 1968], it's that huge forest that is so impressive, with its perfectly straight tree-trunks reaching toward the sky for miles and miles, that separates the Ukraine from Slovakia and Poland, in other words High Tatra. That's where the project was born. The Slovaks wanted me to make a film in Slovakia, and so I went there. And it was there, suddenly, in those lost forests, where the only buildings are the ruins of castles, that I realized that this was the place where I would shoot my film. The film was born in that forest and of that forest, so to speak. And the main character is born of that forest in exactly the same manner. In other words, the conception of a novel, in spite of what Madame Clair whatever-her-name-is believes, is not in any way comparable to the conception of a film, because the conception of a novel takes place within the structuring of sentences, independently of any idea of where the action takes place, how it takes place, etc.

BROWN: Wasn't *La Maison de Rendez-vous* [novel, 1965] inspired by a trip to Hong Kong?

ROBBE-GRILLET: Fed by my trip to Hong Kong, inspired too. But it's the narrative structure that pre-exists. In the cinema, on the other hand, there is almost always a generating setting [*un décor générateur*], a natural setting.

BROWN: That doesn't seem to be the case in your recent films such as *Glissements progressifs du plaisir* [*Successive Slidings of Pleasure*, 1974] or *Le Jeu avec le feu* or *La Belle captive*.

ROBBE-GRILLET: Ah, *Le Jeu avec le feu* was for the Paris Opera! For a long time I had had the idea of transforming the Paris Opera into a high-class brothel, and I was able to realize this project thanks to a producer who needed an expensive film from me! Producers who want expensive films are producers who don't have any money. And so they want the film to cost as much as possible, since they get paid along the way. A producer who has money makes the film with his money. A producer who doesn't have any money makes the film with money from banks, various institutions, etc. The more the film costs, the more their percentage is worth. Even if the film is a costly failure, they get their share faster.

BROWN: You helped finance *Le Jeu avec le feu*, didn't you?

ROBBE-GRILLET: Not at all!

BROWN: I say that because William F. Van Wert, in *The Film Career of Alain Robbe-Grillet* [Redgrave, 1977] notes that "This film is perhaps the most 'personal' of all his films in a very pragmatic sense, in that, for the first time, Robbe-Grillet largely financed the film himself."

ROBBE-GRILLET: Never! I've never put a penny into a film, *a fortiori* into that one, which was extremely expensive. Anyway, a *décor générateur*: something has to take place there, and in general, it's a real place that I find easily transformable into

a dreamscape. In that sense there's something in common between those transparent, glass-filled railroad cars of the Trans-Europ-Express at the time the film
was made, the phantom forests of the High Tatras, and the Paris Opera, with its
bizarre transformations, since you think you're entering a bedroom and all of a
sudden you're in this immense opera house where they're rehearsing *Il Trovatore*.
So, the place plays an important role. Then, with the place as a point of departure, things begin to take on a structure, a structure that directly results from
whatever the setting in question can produce. For the forest of *L'Homme qui ment*,
the forest that I had chosen for my film, I had been told numerous stories about
the last war. In the villages, one finds monuments to those who died, with lists of
names of the heroes in the resistance against Germany. But these are phony lists,
and everybody in the villages knows it. One finds on the lists people who were
traitors, and there are heroes who weren't put on the lists, because these are the
official lists of the Soviet socialist power, and there are people that simply cannot
be placed on the list. And there are people on those lists who everybody knows
were in fact traitors. This ambiguity between the traitor and the hero immediately interested me, perhaps because of the Borges short story entitled "The Traitor and the Hero," in which the traitor and the hero are the same character. And
so you can see how the forest and the traitor-heroes who were activated there, so
to speak, during the last war were suddenly able to produce the theme of doubling of the traitor and the hero, the same character who can be both the one and
the other. And, in the same manner, the entire film becomes based around structures of doubling. In the same way as there are serial structures in *L'Éden et après*
[*Eden and After*, 1970], here we have structures of doubling, so that each scene is
produced twice in two different ways. There's a kind of "doubling" narrative
structure, if you will.

BROWN: Except for the death of the father, which happens only once, since it's
an initiatory narrative as well, isn't it?

ROBBE-GRILLET: Are you sure that the death of the father happens only once?

BROWN: Completely.

ROBBE-GRILLET: I might be able to find a way around that!

BROWN: I had meant to ask you whether you had envisaged it from the beginning as an initiatory story since, one way or the other, the father must die in order to be replaced by the son.

ROBBE-GRILLET: Of course. It goes without saying that these Freudian structures
stand out immediately, with a greater or lesser dose of irony. At any rate, there are
numerous references to doubled characters. I've often mentioned the character of
Boris Godunov, who is both the Tsar but at the same time the Tsar's assassin. And
he's pursued by a false Tsar who claims to be the real Tsar, etc. etc! And so the
story is fed in that manner, if you will. And with Trintignant in particular, there

was the participation of the protagonist as the events took form, since the film was hardly written out at all. So . . . *L'Immortelle* was written out entirely, *Trans-Europ-Express* was written out a good deal less, *L'Homme qui ment* was hardly written out at all, and *L'Éden*, as you know, wasn't written out at all, there was only the chart of the series. You said that, in my more recent films, the setting seems to have been chosen afterwards. And I answered that, for the Paris Opera, that wasn't the case. *Glissements* is a bit different, since the setting is abstract. It had a prison cell constructed in a studio, and there's a kind of abstraction in the setting. For *La Belle captive* I remember one thing that was quite important, and that is that I wanted to shoot this film, but I couldn't make up my mind to do it, since I couldn't find a setting. My assistants proposed this and that, and I would say, "No, that isn't it." And then, suddenly, just before the shooting began, perhaps a week before, I visited, totally by chance, a place called the Villa Gounod at Saint-Cloud, which had the advantage of being one of those places that is in ruins and that can therefore be torn down, built up, and changed around, and it was right around the corner from the L.T.C. film lab! I liked this villa right away. And it's as of the moment that I had that villa in my hands that the film took its shape. I visited the villa with my cinematographer, Henri Alekan, and we immediately imagined things for this villa. And I decided to shoot the entire film in the villa. In other words, the film takes place either entirely in someone's mind or else in diverse settings—a nightclub, a clinic, etc. Since it takes place entirely in someone's mind, everything takes place in the same setting. We modified the bedrooms from one day to the next. You'll remember that there's a completely black nightclub and a completely white clinic: well, it's the same room! The house was used to such a degree, in fact, that even the motorcycle and the car, which seem to be moving outside in the night, were brought inside the house so that we could light them the way we wanted, and so forth. We built a partition and we brought that huge car into the house so that we could set up those disconcerting lighting effects, which are obviously not possible with a real car in a real setting, in other words a car on the road, illuminated only by the floodlights from a tracking car, which has no creative potential from the lighting point of view. Indeed, sculpting light was one of the organizing plans for this film. There's only one scene in the film that I don't like, and I'm sure it's because it wasn't shot in the villa.

From my point of view the scene is a failure. It has a kind of cutesy realistic quality to it. It's the scene in the café when Walter sees in the daily newspaper the photo of Marie-Ange. There's a kind of strange waitress who looks like a vampire. I don't like this scene; I find it a failure precisely because of the way in which it presents things. And it isn't by chance that the scene isn't in the house; it's in the café that was nearby, a real café next to the Seine. On the other hand, Henri de Corinthe's house, a house that is supposed to be in another place—and the exterior is, in fact, a different house, also in Saint Cloud—as soon as one enters it, it's the Villa Gounod. And the house of Van de Reeves, the old professor, is once again the interior of the Villa Gounod, and quite often the same rooms! The underground passage through which you get into the clinic is in the basement of the Villa Gounod, the clinic where one arrives is the Villa Gounod, everything! And I like that, because of this kind of dream-like unity within the entire setting, except for the café, which almost seems for me to be in another film. There's almost always a scene that seems to belong to another film. In *Trans-Europ-Express*, the boy, Mathieu, seems to be acting in another film. He doesn't act at all like the others!

BROWN: In *La Belle captive*, you use the Schubert Fifteenth Quartet, which Walter describes as if it were the Fourteenth, whose title, "Death and the Maiden," would work perfectly well for *La Belle captive*. You also use Wagner's *Das Rheingold*, which you had slowed down, and Duke Ellington's "The Mooch." What was your musical conception for the film?

ROBBE-GRILLET: For the Schubert quartet, I had always had the idea of using the Fourteenth as the film score. You'd hear it throughout most of the film, but always justified by realistic effects. In other words, Walter listens to the music in his car. I rarely use film music, but here there is a film score, and it's inserted into the diegesis. But I had never tried the music with the film until I got to the rough cut. And then I made perforated copies of the Fourteenth Quartet, and it didn't work at all! Not one of the movements, not one of the scenes! It just didn't work. I was rather depressed by this, and it was Catherine [Robbe-Grillet's wife] who said to me, when I got home, "You ought to try the Fifteenth." I didn't even know there was a Schubert Fifteenth Quartet. And she said, "It's much less known, but it has a much more 'popular' side to it than the Fourteenth." I tried it the very next day. She got the recording I needed, the one made by the Alban Berg Quartet, a wonderful recording, and I tried it the next day. And it was extraordinary. It seemed to have been written for the film's images. In other words, when there were certain visual effects, the music actually highlighted them! When he wakes up in the room and finds traces of Marie-Ange, who has disappeared—the jewelry, the blood, the broken glass—each time Schubert creates an effect. We didn't play round with the music at all. It's almost completely uncut! I was fascinated by this, and so I decided to make it look as if the hero thought it was the Fourteenth!

BROWN: The film is filled with parallel universes.

ROBBE-GRILLET: Of course! Fourteenth, fifteenth. . . . Music has quite often played a kind of initiating role for me. I was thinking "Death and Maiden" while I was making *La Belle captive*. Afterwards, I realized that it wouldn't work. The clearest case of this is in *Le Jeu avec le feu* in which, from the outset, there was the Paris Opera as the setting, on the one hand, and, on the other hand, a kind of triptych structure I had imagined. In other words, the structure here wasn't one of doubling; instead, all the elements in the film had to be triple. In many cases, not much remains of this structure. For instance, there were three animals that were supposed to play very important roles: the horse, the dog, and the cat. The dog remains quite strongly, the horse as well, but the cat almost entirely disappeared, because he was a rotten actor! And from the outset, there were three different kinds of music, three musical domains. These domains were chosen ahead of time for their dissonance, if you will. These were: the third act of *Il Trovatore* (I used *La Traviata* in *Trans-Europ-Express*, where it plays a rather strange role. Do you know what *La Traviata* means? It's strange: it's an Italian title that's never translated, and nobody understands what it means! It means "the one who has left the beaten path." The train! The train, which does not follow its normal path, and which therefore does not conform to the laws. I had a lot of fun with that little play on words with *La Traviata*, particularly since, when you hear the musical effects by Verdi, you see the various railroad switches mingling, crossing paths, etc.). *Il Trovatore* is an extremely obscure story, and much more interesting from the psychoanalytical point of view, no doubt. It's quite difficult to tell the story of *Il Trovatore*, but it's a story about child switching. The witch Azucena, wanting to take vengeance on the Duke, who had perhaps had her mother burned at the stake, or something like that, kidnaps the Duke's young son so that she can throw him into the fire. But she makes a mistake and throws her own son into the fire instead. And so the entire story is based on this "game with fire" [*le jeu avec le feu*], in a certain way, and it will shed its light on Verdi's entire score. The "Fire" aria that you hear at great length at the beginning of *Le Jeu avec le feu* is Azucena's story about the fire. There are even images of fire. The scene of the "burning child" is, furthermore, in *Le Jeu avec le feu*, and it's one of the scenes that I find quite successful. The child, in Freud's text, is "*das kind*," and so you have no idea whether the child is a boy or a girl. Ordinarily, the child is treated as a boy, but, obviously, I made it into a girl. And the girl is Christine Boisson. It was one of her first roles. She became a star later on. She plays one of the two women in Antonioni's *Identificazione di una donna* [*Identification of a Woman*, 1982]. The Freud story is as follows: the child dies of fever (the fire), and the father sits wake over his child, who lies dead in its coffin. In the film, it's Jacques Doniol-Valcroze who plays the father, sitting in a chair at the foot of the bed. Dead tired, the father falls asleep, the candles fall on the bed, and the bed begins to burn. And one doesn't realize whether it's true or whether it's the father's dream, for at that moment the child wakes up and violently reproaches his father for having fallen asleep, etc. The last line is, "Don't you see, Father, that I'm burning?" Around the same time, I was already interested in the story of the "Fiancée de Corinthe," which produced *La Belle captive*, which is based on a story by Goethe that also ends in the line, "Don't you feel how I'm burning?" Goethe's entire text is in *La Belle captive* when the ghost of the young woman appears, draws nearer, and says, "Don't you recognize me, your fiancée . . . ," etc. The actress does that quite well. And it ends in the same way by "Don't you feel how I'm burning?" And so that's a theme that passes from one film to the next, while also passing from Freud through Goethe. And so that's it for the first theme, the first musical domain in *Le Jeu avec le feu*.

The second domain is a dance. It's a Brazilian song by Chico Buarque, sung by a black Brazilian woman named Elisete de Cardoso who is not at all well known in France but who was a big star in the very popular milieus of Brazil. Do you know that there are "sonotheques" throughout the world that record the voices of writers? There are traces of my own voice in Göteborg, in New Zealand, in Brazil! And so the sonotheque in Brazil gave me, in exchange, someone else's voice, which took the form of non-commercial recordings that had been made with great care during public performances by Elisete de Cardoso. The song is called "Carolina," and it constitutes something completely different from Verdi's music. It's a piece for bandoneon and mandolin filled with something completely different from Verdi's music. It's a piece for bandoneon and mandolin filled with dance rhythms, very Brazilian, and quite well sung by Elisete Cardoso.

The third domain, which needed to be in strong contrast with the first two—chose a German military march from the Wehrmacht. It isn't a Nazi song, as people have claimed: the song comes well before Hitler. They were singing it during the realm of Wilhelm II! And there's nothing warlike in the words. It's one of those "boy scout" songs that German soldiers have been singing forever and which says, "In the marshes there's a timid little flower that's called heather . . . " but sung in a strongly accented march rhythm. And I was able to get a genuine recording from the Wehrmacht. You were able to find songs from the Wehrmacht like that, not just during the German occupation, but afterwards, for the collectors of fascist memorabilia! And so, that was a completely different third domain which, every time it appears, produces specific things in the diegesis. In particular, the Wehrmacht song immediately produces shots of German boots, from the German occupation, something that perhaps represents the father's guilty conscience. One has the impression that he didn't do the right thing during the occupation. But it also brings about the emergence of the spectre of incest, since the entire story of *Il Trovatore* is a story of incest. I had in fact wanted to call the film *Opera Incestuosa*. That was a beautiful title, but the producer didn't want to use it, and he had the right to not use it, since I had used *Le Jeu avec le feu* as the title from the outset. In France, authors have all the rights, but on the condition that there's not something else in the contract. I had put the title *Le Jeu avec le feu* in the contract myself, and it was written that, if the title was changed, all parties had to be in agreement. Anyway, the theme of incest was suddenly fed by the march because of a little-girl impulse on the part of the actress: when Anicée Alvina saw, in the courtyard at the Chateau de Vincennes, the real German uniforms and the young men who were going to wear them, she suddenly put on a little act and said, "I want to have a uniform too!" You don't see that very often, do you! And so now you see her as a German soldier, with her blond hair beneath the helmet, marching along with the rest of them. And so, all of a sudden, the march feeds, quite strongly, the spectre of incest. You can see how the genesis of the film begins to disappear: there's a setting, a somewhat arbitrary structure—the elements that are tripled each time—the very specific case of the music, which has very rich diegetic tie-ins, and the elements, the events of the shooting: all of this feeds the making of the film. Needless to say, some things were written out for *Le Jeu avec le feu*. But it's the process of making the film that produces the film.

BROWN: Since the film was shot in scope, did you have scope images in mind from the outset?

ROBBE-GRILLET: In the cinema, I've always been lucky, in that there have always been producers who asked me to make a film. It's strange! But on the other hand, my films are known for making back the money they cost. In other words, I spend much money, and I have always been conscientious, which isn't the case with Bresson or even Resnais. Anyway, a producer who had no money at all, and to whom I had proposed something, began to ask me questions such as, "Couldn't you have somewhat more expensive ideas?" And so I said, "O.K., I have expensive ideas too, but I rarely talk about them, because I don't like making expensive films." But I had thought of using Michael Lonsdale, and so I said. "We can use Philippe Noiret, for instance. He costs ten times as much!" "Ah! Noiret! Wonderful!" And we shot the film at the Paris Opera. All this completely changed the film. And since we were shooting at the Paris Opera, we decided to shoot in scope. "Ah, yes! Wonderful!" Do you know why scope is more expensive? Because there are tons of things that need lighting. The 1.33 aspect ratio costs the least, since you just have to light one face, two faces. The wider the aspect ratio, the more costly the film, because you have to light various backgrounds, various things that are not the center point of the image, and they all play a role. That's why I used scope!

BROWN: What is the role of Bob Wade in your films, since editing is such an integral part of your style?

ROBBE-GRILLET: It's a considerable role. And I'd like to point out that, since *Trans-Europ-Express*, my editor has always been my continuity person, my "script boy," except in *L'Éden et après*, when he was in trouble with the producers. And so, he's present during the shooting. That's quite important, since, because he knows how I'm going to want to edit my film, I'm able to say to him, when we're in a particular setting, "Are there shots that we should take, that we might need?" And he adds shots. For instance, we had spent a long time shooting Philippe Noiret's horse [in *Le Jeu avec le feu*], because Noiret hated the film. It wasn't his kind of film at all; he only did it for the money. He particularly hated the scenes where he had to touch naked women, which caused him a lot of anguish. He's not a homosexual, but he's quite a puritan. He had these absolutely horrible crises of despair during the shooting. He'd begin to cry between the takes. Seeing this huge man crying was not a pretty sight! And so I asked him what we could do for him, and he answered, "I want my horse." Like Caligula, he's in love with his horse! And so, at great expense, we brought in his horse, right away! And since the horse was there, we shot Noiret on his horse, to make him happy, and of course we had no idea what to do with those shots. I was with Bob one day, and we were trying to find a way to edit the scene in the bathroom where Noiret is washing his daughter. It's a very good scene, but I wasn't happy with it. Narratively, it had no interest, the scene didn't work. I came back to the lab the next day, and Bob said, "I've got something to show you." And he had edited the horse into the bathroom scene! And right away I said, "Wonderful!" So you see, it was a very Robbe-Grilletian idea, but it came from Bob, not from me.

BROWN: And so it becomes an indispensable collaboration.

ROBBE-GRILLET: Indispensable, I'm not so sure, but certainly quite useful. Since *L'Immortelle*, where I hated my entire crew and could only think of how to get rid of them, and as of *Trans-Europ-Express*, I've given a creative role to certain technicians. The cinematographer Igor Luther in *L'Éden et après*. Henri Alekan in *La Belle captive*: they play very creative roles. Alekan would say, "We have to shoot a scene from this angle," and so I'd do the scene for the angle he wanted. And it's the same thing with Bob Wade, who has participated in all my films, from *L'Immortelle* on. Michel Fano (the composer) has participated in all of my films except for *La Belle captive*. I don't think he was entirely happy about this. But I felt that, in the making of the film, I didn't want to use Fano because, in the first place, I wanted to make major use of the Schubert quartet—I had thought the Fourteenth, but it ended up being the Fifteenth—without transformations such as Fano did with *La Traviata* and *Il Trovatore*, where the music is completely cut up and transformed. For this, I wanted large expanses of music, as if the music were carrying some kind of story. And so I didn't really need Fano, all the more so since I also wanted to use some fragments from Wagner, but transformed. Fano refused to transform Wagner. He accepted to do this for Verdi, since he doesn't respect him. But he has a complete devotion to Wagner. My idea was to transform the opening bars of *Das Rheingold*—the famous chord in E-flat—by slowing it down, to transform it into a kind of rumbling, which blends remarkably with the rumblings of the storm and the rumblings of the motorcycle. Fano refused to touch it. Bob Wade is also quite a musician, and he's quite capable of doing these things, and so he's the one who did it. In the films of mine that he has worked on, Fano would choose areas where he wanted to intervene. And so, I would work on those areas with him. But since he works quite slowly and never had the time to do an entire film, major portions [of the sound scores] have been done by Bob Wade and me.

BROWN: I've often thought that the "explanation " given to the couple in *Marienbad* by M concerning the statue could be just as much of a lie—and just as much the truth—as the whimsical explanations given by the protagonist, but that the public and the critics are all ready to believe M, since his explanation seems to be based on "history." Are you making fun of the audience here?

ROBBE-GRILLET: Completely, since these are historical characters who never existed, historical characters I invented. And the statue doesn't exist either. It's a statue that was constructed for the film!

BROWN: Might one say that the role of the woman in your films is to resist rape, not just within the narrative but *by* the narrative? It seems to me that audiences which, most of the time, enjoy being "raped" by filmmakers, are forced by the very structure of your films to take the side of the woman, who refuses to be imprisoned in a line narrative that hides all the myths of a sexist culture.

ROBBE-GRILLET: I would put it a different way. I would say that rape, in my films, is male passion, whereas in the story, usually put together by the woman, it's the trap that draws the man into something, usually death. This is completely transparent in *La Belle captive*, but even in *Marienbad*, it serves to draw the hero toward death.

BROWN: What do you think of other French directors, such as Claude Lelouch?

ROBBE-GRILLET: Ah, Lelouch is certainly much less of a non-entity than Truffaut. Lelouch is a filmmaker, which means that he has cinematic ideas, which is never the case with Truffaut, whose ideas are screenplay ideas. But Lelouch, who's totally scorned, has at each instant quite interesting cinematic ideas. His films grow out of the shooting and the editing.

BROWN: What other filmmakers do you admire?

ROBBE-GRILLET: I've mentioned Godard quite often. I've mentioned Buñuel quite often, all of Buñuel's films, whether the early surrealist films, the Mexican films, or the more recent French films, it's all quite remarkable in its cinematic invention. Antonioni, of course, a great cinematic inventor. And Fellini often—not always, but often.

BROWN: And Jean-Jacques Beineix?

ROBBE-GRILLET: I've been interested by certain films by Beineix, and in particular a film that I find to be a masterpiece and that was destroyed by the critics, *La Lune dans le caniveau* [*The Moon in the Gutter*, 1983]. I find it to be an extremely beautiful film. I saw it twice in a row. It's a remarkable film in its narrative structure, in its images. And for once Depardieu is good, which is rare. There's one moment in the film where the brother and sister are standing on the dock and there's a boat pulling away into the setting sun. It's a dime-store painting! And all the critics screamed, "Ah, this can't be! It's a dime-store painting," as if Beineix hadn't thought of this! It's quite obvious that, at each moment, he's putting together images that are stereotypes like that, stereotypes from our culture.

Robert Altman

If I stepped down off this stage we're on and went straight downhill
to the end, I'd have to look back and say, "I had a great roll."

$\mathcal{I}$n this interview, the late director Robert Altman had recently released his film
Vincent and Theo (1990), to great critical success, when he came to Kansas City to
receive both a Lifetime Achievement Award from the Greater Kansas City Film
Commission and the key to the city. On the latter, Altman jokes, "They used to
lock me up for getting into trouble in this town. . . . They used to throw away the
key. Now, they're *giving* me one!" This opening sets the tone for the highly ener-
getic interview that follows, one that covers Altman's youth and career up until the
time of this interview before focusing on its main subject, *Vincent and Theo*. Altman illustrates his attempts to tell the more familiar aspects of Van Gogh's life in a
new way, sharing anecdotes such as, "I'd come on the set and I'd say, 'I've seen this
before'—and then I'd move the chair and shoot the room differently." As for the
relationship between his mise-en-scène and any attempts at historical reality, he
notes, "I didn't want exact copies, just the—just the *smell* of things," adding later
still, "I'm sure my film is not factual . . . but I hope it's truthful."

The style of this interview is somewhat unusual but highly effective, as John
C. Tibbetts narrates an afternoon with Altman and intersperses responses to questions among reflections on the director's career and descriptions of what his activities are like on this day (as well as those of his son Stephen, who accompanies
them). This approach allows Tibbetts, for example, to narrate a trip to the coffee
shop with Stephen, where the latter notes in an aside, about his father, "He's mellowing out a little bit." The style also allows us to see what a typical Altman press
conference might have been like—a "rapid-fire" "give-and-take," in the words of
the writer, with Altman hurrying the reporters along with exclamations like,
"Next question!" And in many ways, the style here relates to something Altman

246

says much earlier in the piece, in a description of the movies he remembers seeing in his youth: "Those movies just seemed to happen." Such a statement reflects an aesthetic of seeming spontaneity that Altman spent the rest of his career chasing down—a sense of life's unfolding without provocation or direction, much like the interview itself. It's a fitting tribute to the *auteur* of happenstance.

Interview by John C. Tibbetts
Originally published as "Robert Altman: After 35 Years, Still the 'Action Painter' of American Cinema," Literature/Film Quarterly 20, no. 1 (January 1992): 36–42.

"They used to lock me up for getting into trouble in this town," quipped filmmaker Robert Altman as he accepted the Key to Kansas City from Mayor Richard Berkeley. "They used to throw away the key. Now, they're giving me one!"

Altman lived in his native Kansas City, MO, for his first nineteen years. As a boy he raised quite a ruckus, as he puts it; and he made his first movies there (which is, perhaps, the same thing). Now an acclaimed world-class filmmaker, he has returned to receive a Lifetime Achievement Award from the Greater Kansas City Film Commission in the ballroom of the downtown Crown Center Westin Hotel. There is a sense of euphoria in the air that has been growing during the three days of nonstop screenings of sixteen Altman films, press conferences, workshops with area filmmakers and reunions with family members. Altman and his hometown are both on a roll these days. He is fresh on the heels of his latest triumph, *Vincent and Theo*; and Kansas City itself is basking in the glow of the successful completion of two recent theatrical films that had been shot in the area—the prestigious *Mr. and Mrs. Bridge* (1990) and the forthcoming *Article 99* (1992).

"This town and I will have to get together again," he told a press gathering earlier that day. "I haven't shot a film here since *The Delinquents* [1957] in 1955—which I'd rather not talk about! But the future of filmmaking is here in communities like this. We help each other. Companies have to figure things now down to the split penny. We go where it's cheapest and where the artist can get the most return for his time. When I leave here I'll have a whole box of scripts under my arm." He paused with an air of mock drama. He waited a few beats, then—"We'll have to see."

Altman is relaxed, accessible and talkative. His Buffalo Bill beard is neatly trimmed. A white shirt and tie peek out from his zippered navy-blue jacket. He hardly seems the same hard-charging, hard-drinking maverick that barnstormed his way through movie after movie in the early 1970s. With *M*A*S*H* (1970), *Brewster McCloud* (1970), *McCabe and Mrs. Miller* (1971), *The Long Goodbye* (1973) and *Nashville* (1975), he was a prime architect—with other young filmmakers like

Paul Mazursky, John Cassavetes, Francis Ford Coppola and Martin Scorsese—of what Diane Jacobs has called the "Hollywood Renaissance." He was called a "prairie Buddha" by his associates. He referred to himself as the "action painter" of American films. Controversies, disputes, awards and brickbats trailed in his wake. College students appointed him their Vietnam-era voice. Critics debated his unorthodox, looping and elliptical style. While Stanley Kauffmann called him a pretentious blunderer, Pauline Kael praised his idiosyncrasies: "Altman has to introduce an element of risk on top of the risks that all directors take," she wrote in 1981. There was always something protean, even relentless about him. After the failure of *Popeye* in 1980, the big studios rejected him, but he kept going, staging operas at colleges, shooting modest projects like *Come Back to the 5 & Dime, Jimmy Dean, Jimmy Dean* (1982) in 16mm, and filming plays for cable television. Meanwhile—although Altman wasn't counting—the awards were piling up. There were numerous "Best Film" and "Best Director" awards from the New York Film Critics Circle, the National Society of Film Critics, the National Board of Review and the Venice Film Festival (a Grand Prix for *Streamers* [1983]).

"I haven't been back to K.C. in almost 15 years now, I guess; and I come back and don't see the same city." We are talking together in the Presidential Suite on the 17th floor of the Crown Center Westin Hotel. The rooftops, spires and glass ramparts are spread out below us in the late afternoon sun. We have an hour to spend before he greets a sold-out house for a filmmaking workshop. "But I smell it and I feel it," he continues. "This is where I got my 'chips,' my attitudes. I lived on West 68th Street and went to several schools—Rockhurst, Southwest High School, Wentworth Military Academy, and then did a hitch in the Air Force, where I was a co-pilot of B-24 bombers. Restless, I guess." He takes a drink from a tumbler filled with club soda and a slice of lime. That's all he's drinking today.

"Somewhere along in there I saw my first movies at the old Brookside Theatre. Those movies just seemed to happen—nobody made them, you know? And I guess that's the way I still see movies—I want them to be occurrences, to just seem to be happening."

We reminisce for a moment about the fate of the Calvin Film Company, a Kansas City landmark. Established by Altman's grandfather at 15th and Troost, the company had been "home" for every film student and filmmaker in the area for more than 40 years. The building had been razed in 1990. "Actually, I came back to Calvin several times after the war," Altman muses, rubbing his bearded chin. "I'd go to California and try to write scripts, but then return, broke, to Calvin. Each time they'd drop me another notch in salary. Like some kind of punishment. The third time they said it was like the Davis Cup—they were going to keep me!"

In the early 1950s Altman participated in every aspect of filmmaking. "I don't remember actually learning anything," he says; "it was more by a kind of osmosis." For $250 a week he made promotional films for Gulf Oil and safety films for Caterpillar Tractor and International Harvester. "They were training films for me—stuff like "How to Run a Filling Station." They weren't a goal for me, just a process to learn how to do entertainment and dramatic films. It was a school, that's what it was." During these years he met several other young filmmakers who were to form the core of his filmmaking team—writer Fred Barheit and editor Louis Lombardo.

After returning to Hollywood and clicking in the late 1950s and early 1960s on television series like *Alfred Hitchcock Presents, Gallant Men, Bonanza* and *Combat!* (for which he directed fully one-half of the episodes), he was ready to tackle feature films.

"There's always been a sort of division between the feature film business and the television business," he continues. "It's hard to step from one to the other. And that still is the case. But it was a great training ground. I was lucky; it kept me in California. I developed a nice reputation there and learned to stay in budget. But when I did my first movie, *Countdown* (a science fiction thriller) in 1967 for Warner Bros., everything went wrong. Jack Warner fired me. I got a call Sunday night from the studio warning me not to come in because the guard would stop me. I'd been locked out. Warner had looked at the dailies and he said, 'That fool has everybody talking at the same time!' So I went to the studio gate and got my stuff in a box from the guard. Somebody else edited it. Since that and another picture, *That Cold Day in the Park* (1969), you've never seen a film of mine that I didn't keep total control over. And that's why I don't work a lot." He laughs outright.

The criticism about Altman's unique use of densely textured sound and dialogue has always aroused controversy. "But, you know, last Saturday night the Audio-Engineers Society—they are the Hollywood sound people—awarded me their own Lifetime Achievement Award." Altman smiles. It's a Cheshire cat smile. If he were to vanish, that knowing grin would still hover there in the air. "This was the first time it's ever gone to a filmmaker instead of some inventor or process, like Dolby. And that very day I had read a review of *Vincent and Theo* complaining of the same thing—that the soundtrack was so muddled you couldn't understand anything. Like all the characters were played by 'Mumbles' in Dick Tracy. Look, what I'm trying to do is—" he pauses, groping for the right words. "I don't want you to understand everything—not the sound, not the images. What I'm trying to do—and this is what the engineers understood (which pleased me)—I'm trying to present something to an audience where they have to work a little bit. They have to invest something. You don't hear everything somebody says in real life, do you? Maybe you're not really listening or distracted or something. That's the illusion I want. It's a way to get the audience involved and participating in the thing." He spreads his hands philosophically. "But some people don't like it." Another pause. "Anyway, I really worked this out the first time in *California Split* (1974). I used 8-track sound. I said, "They do this in music recording, put a microphone on every different instrument and try to isolate them as much as possible then mix it afterwards. Why don't we do that with the voices on the soundtrack?" So, we developed 8-track tape machines and individual microphones. Which means recording everything and then mixing it later. I can take a person's sound down or push it up. That way, I don't have to go back for post-synching, looping of lines—you know, bringing the actors back in to match their lip movements. When you do that, the acting is gone."

Clearly, Altman still relishes the role of iconoclast. That memorable spurt of movies in the early 1970s took the cherished genres of war story (*M★A★S★H*), western (*McCabe*), detective thriller (*The Long Goodbye*) and the caper film (*California Split*) and turned them inside out. "When I look at a subject and see how it's done, I think, it doesn't necessarily have to be done that way. Like *McCabe*. What a collection of stereotypes! There was the gambler down on his luck, the whore with the heart of gold, the three heavies (the giant, the half-breed and the kid). Everything there you've seen all your life in westerns. The audience can supply most of the story already! That left me free to work on the backgrounds and the atmosphere and the details. The same thing with *The Long Goodbye*. That was a Raymond Chandler story. To this day I've never finished it. I could never figure out what was happening! And I didn't much care. I thought, Raymond Chandler used his plots the way I do—just as an excuse to hang a series of thumbnail sketches on. I had fun dropping the 1940s character of 'Philip Marlowe' into the attitudes of 1973, into a time of marijuana and brownies and health food. He was out of place and that was a great chance for some thumbnail essays of our own of what the culture and society at the time looked like."

One genre that he tried to avoid—and couldn't—was the biopic, or film biography. "*Vincent and Theo* was offered to me and I didn't even want to read it," admits Altman. "I didn't want to make that kind of picture. I don't like those biographical things. I just don't believe them, for one thing. But they kept pressing me to make it and I said, at last, 'OK, you let me have artistic control on this and do whatever I want to do and I'll make it.'"

The results have been spectacular. As *Variety* reported April 27, 1990, "Seldom has an artist been so convincingly or movingly portrayed on screen." Although it got no Oscar nominations (a grievous sin of omission) it has found the largest, most enthusiastic audience for an Altman film since *Nashville*. For Altman, the movie was a process of avoiding traps. (He frequently describes filmmaking as avoiding hazards and traps.) "For example, at first I didn't want to use any of the Van Gogh paintings at all," he explains. "I wasn't going to show them. And I wasn't going to show him actually painting, either. Finally, I realized I had to show them, but I decided to show them as a kind of 'evidence.' We'll treat them roughly (like he did). We'll have them lying around, people stepping on them. Vincent himself destroys some of them. I wanted the audience to say—'Oh, that's worth $82 million dollars!'—and then somebody steps through the canvas! That's great!"

Our laughter attracts the attention of a young man who has just wandered in from the hallway. He has chiseled features and curly dark hair. He is Altman's son, Stephen, who was the production designer on *Vincent and Theo*. Stephen was born in Kansas City in 1956 and, although he was reared by his mother, Altman's second wife, he began working with his father (he calls him "Bob") on sets and props at age eleven. Stephen claims he can look back upon his father's films and discover his own "fingerprints," evidence of his own presence—like the pay telephone he managed to insinuate into every picture (and which now adorns a wall in his Paris apartment). He describes himself as part scavenger, part prop master and part set dresser. ("Anything an actor touches is a prop," he explains. "If he drives a tank, it's a prop. If he eats cornflakes, it's a prop. If it's something just sitting on the set, then it's set dressing or background.") It was he who arranged for all the reproductions of Van Gogh paintings and sketches seen in the movie.

"They were all done by students at the Beaux-Arts in Paris or in Holland," explains Stephen, whose research into the ateliers and galleries of Van Gogh's time has made him into something of an art historian himself. I ask him where the paintings are now. "Oh," he looks sidelong at his father. "The producer has a lot of them. I know somebody else who keeps some of them in his office." He pauses meaningfully, still grinning at his father. "But I don't have one."

Altman pushes his way into the pause. "Those darned paintings—I'd find the sets would look just like them—the sort of thing you see in the Vincente Minnelli picture, *Lust for Life* [1956]. I didn't want that kind of competition. So, I'd come on the set and I'd say, 'I've seen this before'—and then I'd move the chair and shoot the room differently. I didn't want exact copies, just the—just the smell of things." Stephen nods. "On all the Dutch scenes, we wanted a kind of lighting with an 'old Masters' look—with the light from above, northern light. When we went to Paris, we wanted a gray, impressionistic feel. And when we went to Arles, we had to have a bright shining light."

Altman's eyes twinkle as he leans forward. "Although, if we'd have had to shoot a rainstorm in the sunflower fields, we'd have done that, too. I'd read a lot of stories about David Lean waiting weeks for snow in *Dr. Zhivago* [1965]; but in my experience, you're lucky to get the crew together at all. So if you're out there and it's raining, you just change the script from 'sunshine' to 'rain.'"

Robert Altman's laugh fades after a moment. He continues, more seriously. "I wasn't so much interested in showing Van Gogh's creativity as in showing the pain that this guy went through. You have to remember that nobody ever smiled at Vincent Van Gogh. But there was some compulsion to just keep doing what he did, until he finally couldn't stand it anymore and just shot himself. Only in combination with his brother, Theo, was Vincent a complete person. They were connected in some way. That's the story I was trying to tell. You know, people expect movies like this to blow trumpets when a painting is made. But Vincent did not have a great deal of talent. He was not a great draughtsman. It took him a long time to learn how to draw and paint. He taught himself and he worked hard. He copied other people and didn't start any schools. He couldn't paint from his own imagination, just from what was in front of him. He had a lot going against him. If anybody was going to make book and ask which of these painters at the time would sell paintings for millions, like I show at the London auction at the beginning of the movie, nobody would have voted Vincent." He pauses again. His next words come slowly. "I'm sure my film is not factual," he says, "but I hope it's truthful."

I ask about the final sequences in the movie. Rarely has a person's self-destructive impulses been more harrowingly portrayed on film. "I think that when Vincent mutilated his ear, it was a cry for help, for attention," says Altman. "When he went to the asylum for a year, he met the daughter of the man who ran it. But when he rejected her advances, he realized he didn't belong, that he couldn't make it in life, and by that time he abdicated and wanted out."

"There was a dramatic, unexpected moment on the set during the ear mutilation scene," volunteers Stephen. "You know it's a moment that audiences have been waiting for. But when Tim Roth (the actor portraying Van Gogh) cut the ear, suddenly he did something none of us expected. He held on to the razor and suddenly brought it close to his tongue. We just shot it once and, Tim surprised everybody with that. I guess he didn't know what to do at that moment, but he felt he needed something else. He didn't tell anybody in advance. It was scary."

"Maybe not so unexpected, though," growls Altman. "I get a lot of credit for having the actors improvise all the time. When we go into rehearsal, I encourage as much improvisation as I can get. And we find out what works and what doesn't work. But by the time we actually shoot the scene, it's very well rehearsed. The secret lies in letting the actor give the good performance. That's what Tim did. I can't teach anybody to act. My job is like a cheerleader's, really—trying to set up an atmosphere and a focus of energies so the actor becomes the most important part of the collaboration. Get them to trust you and take some chances. Get them to know that you won't make them look bad. If they can't say a line in the script, we'll change it."

Our conversation is interrupted by a ringing telephone. It's time for Altman and his son to repair downstairs to the hotel lobby for a workshop with area filmmakers and students. For the next two hours Altman's high spirits continue unabated. As he mounts the platform to the applause of the crowd, he jokes, "I think I forgot my lines!" Peering out at the crowd, he mutters, "You know, the actor's nightmare is to find himself in a play and not know his lines. Hell, I don't know this play!" But he fields the questions beautifully. It is obvious that he loves audiences and respects them.

At times the give-and-take is rapid-fire. Examples:

QUESTION: "Are you really a control freak in your movies, like they say?" (The questioner is too young to have seen Altman's first pictures during their first run.)

ALTMAN: "Let's put it this way. Making a movie for me is getting people to work for you who are shooting the same film you are shooting. In *Fool for Love* [1985] we started with a wonderful cinematographer named Robby Müller. After six days of shooting I fired him. I said, 'I can't do this. I'm sure you're shooting a beautiful movie, but it's not the movie I'm making.' So we started over again. Next question!"

QUESTION: "Have you ever tried to make a movie somebody else's way?"

ALTMAN: "I can't do anything but what I do. If I tried to, I'd fail. Next."

QUESTION: "Do you have a particular style?"

ALTMAN: "I don't know what my style is. I'm the last one to say what it is, I think. What I secretly think about myself might be wrong. I didn't know what anybody was talking about when they said my first seven films had 'the Altman signature.' I was just trying to do things totally different from one film to another. Now I look back at them and see my fingerprints all over them. You can't keep your hands clean."

QUESTION: "What do you think of critics?"

ALTMAN: "A lot of people see my films and say, 'I don't get it.' But I've created at least a cult following. That's not quite enough people to make a minority!"

QUESTION: "What is your favorite among your films?"

ALTMAN: "I won't fall into that trap. They are all your children. You can't choose."

Later, while he's surrounded by the crowd for some last questions and pictures, I steal away to the coffee shop with Stephen. I tell him I'm amazed at his father's easy amiability. This is not the same Altman, I tell him, that stormed through critics, press and audiences alike twenty years ago.

"He's mellowing out a little bit," Stephen admits, stirring his coffee. "He used to be a hard drinker. He never drank on the set, but he'd drink a lot and rip into people. Usually they deserved it. But I think it's better now. He's looser. He's not trying so hard. He's had a lot of experience. Hey, he's done more films consecutively now than anybody else working today. I think he's the best director I've ever worked with. He's very tough and very difficult and at the same time can be the easiest and nicest. Anybody can disagree with him on the set, but he'll tell you, 'Anybody can make a suggestion, but only give it once.' He won't easily admit it if he's wrong. He has some funny quirks. People might sit around and talk and it won't seem like he's listening; and then the next day he'll come up and say, 'I had this great idea. We'll do this and that.' And everybody will sit around and say, 'Good idea, Bob!'"

After the ceremonies that night, Altman rejoins me for a wrap-up of our interview. He has to leave early the next morning, he explains, to return to his editing studio in Malibu, CA. He describes the studio as a kind of support environment. "I have lots of people there to help. Primarily, I can get into an environment where I have everything I need. Like being in a submarine. We have a cook who comes in. That way I can keep everybody there. We'll work six days a week, 12-13 hours a day. I like the intensity. I just can't do it leisurely. It's the process that's the real reward."

There are many projects in the works. He will begin immediately editing footage, for Japanese television, he has shot backstage during a performance of the Broadway musical, *Black and Blue*. "Like I first wanted to do with *Vincent and Theo*, I decided to ignore the show itself and get the fatigue on the faces of the dancers as they come back offstage. All those smiles and energy would collapse as soon as they hit the black. I'm dealing here with errors and frailties."

Another project is the long-cherished *L.A. Shortcuts* [which became *Short Cuts* (1993)], a script he and Frank Barhydt adapted from stories by Raymond Carver. There have been problems lately in getting the financing, but Altman hopes at last the project is in the gate. It sounds like a kind of West Coast version of *Nashville*: "There's a big cast, 27 main actors, who all lead different lives. They don't necessarily affect one another, but their lives all criss-cross. You know, Frank Lloyd Wright said that Los Angeles was made when the continent tipped and all the people without roots slipped into the southwest corner!"

Even more tantalizing are hints at other movies. His highly praised television series, *Tanner '88* [1988], made in collaboration with comic strip guru Garry Trudeau, may have a sequel just in time for the next presidential election. "Let's run Tanner again in 1992," cracks Altman. "Somebody's got to run against those guys!" And he confirms something his son Stephen had told me—that he plans to make a movie called *The Player* [released in 1992]. "Oh, yes," he grins, "that's another thing about an artist at work. It's about a studio executive who murders a writer. And gets away with it. We'll get in some shots and make the producers hate us! That's all I'll tell you."

He pauses a moment. The ballroom has almost cleared and some members of the Altman clan still living in Kansas City—a whole contingent of cousins, uncles and nephews—are waiting for him. Doesn't this man ever get tired??? "But with all these projects there are still those that fail, that don't get made," he continues philosophically, apparently in no hurry to leave. "Like *Rossini, Rossini*." I start in amazement. Robert Altman making a movie about the great Italian opera composer . . . ? "Sure," he says, as if reading my thoughts. "This was to be our 'big' film, not *Vincent and Theo*. *Vincent* was going to be just a warm-up for it. Stephen and I worked on it for over six months, traveling through Italy, scouting locations, dressing sets, hashing out the script. Then, things got very strange. We'd be called back to Rome several times; and finally we were told the movie had shut down. Then I got fired. Somebody else finished it."

Clearly, the aborted project meant a great deal to him. It's the sort of disappointment and pain that tempts me to compare Altman's career with his most recent subject, Vincent Van Gogh. But no. Altman rejects—almost peremptorily—the association. "I can't summon up the fortitude of somebody like Vincent. I've had a good deal of personal adulation in my life and a great deal of success. But I think if I ever made a film and people got up and walked out of a theater before it was over, I'd never make another one. I couldn't change my films to anything else. I don't make mainstream, 'shopping mall' kinds of films, like *Pretty Woman* [1990]. I'm not an 'in demand' commodity. If I stepped down off this stage we're on and went straight downhill to the end, I'd have to look back and say, 'I had a great roll.' Some people liked my work—I can at least find a couple. But the minute I don't find anybody, then I'm stepping off."

No compromises. No prisoners. After more than 35 years of making films, he still can thumb his nose at the naysayers. He can still say brashly, "There's them and there's us." There's no question that "them" still means the Hollywood establishment, the grownups, the crowd; and that "us" means those who grew up loving his movies—those who felt young and special just watching them.

Wayne Wang

I'd like to keep myself honest by bouncing between the mainstream film and the personal, independent thing with rough edges.

$\mathcal{W}$ayne Wang is among the most well-known Chinese-American *auteurs*, and this interview focuses on his most celebrated film to date: *The Joy Luck Club* (1993), a film recognized as a potential "breakthrough for films about Asians in America."[1] The narrative complexity of *The Joy Luck Club*, featuring meticulously interconnected storylines, has more in common with Wang's under-discussed *Smoke* (1995) than the linearity of his other recent, more generically predictable films (such as the mother/daughter road movie *Anywhere But Here* [1999] or the especially lucrative, romantic comedy *Maid in Manhattan* [2002]). In this interview, Wang discusses the logistics of directing many stories within one film; the film as homage to his own parents' histories; working in partnership with Amy Tan to adapt her novel upon which the film is based; the personal as well as epic resonance of the film as it reflects Wang's belonging to, and being torn between, two cultures that are embodied by the women of *The Joy Luck Club*.

Interview by John C. Tibbetts
Originally published as "A Delicate Balance: An Interview with Wayne Wang about The Joy Luck Club," *Literature/Film Quarterly 22, no. 1 (January 1994): 2–6.*

Born in Hong Kong in 1949, Wayne Wang grew up in a bilingual household. His father, an engineer, was fluent in English and imparted to him a passion for American movies; and his mother, a painter, encouraged him to pursue painting. After graduating from a Jesuit high school in 1967, Wang went to Oakland, California, where he earned a B.F.A. in painting and a master's degree in film and television from the California College of Arts and Crafts. He plunged into film-making, dividing his time in the next decade between filmmaking in San Francisco and Hong Kong. *Chan Is Missing*, which he co-wrote, produced, directed and edited on a budget of $22,000 in 1982, was his breakthrough picture. An edgy, seriocomic account of life in San Francisco's Chinatown, it played in many mainstream theaters and garnered critical praise.

With *Dim Sum*, which premiered at the Cannes Film Festival in the Director's Fortnight section in 1984, he consolidated his growing reputation as a spokesperson for Chinese-American generational conflicts. It told a sensitive story of the problems between a Chinese mother and her American-born daughter. It was nominated for a British Academy Award in the Best Foreign Film category.

Subsequent films include *Slamdance* in 1987, starring Tom Hulce, Mary Elizabeth Mastrantonio, and Harry Dean Stanton; *Eat a Bowl of Tea* in 1989, a screwball comedy shot in Hong Kong; and *Life Is Cheap . . . but Toilet Paper Is Expensive* in 1990, a film he refers to as an "experimental mix" of the samurai and thriller genres.

The Joy Luck Club has been dubbed by Richard Corliss as a film of "epic radiance." Based on Amy Tan's 1989 novel, the title refers to a mahjong-playing group of four Chinese women—Suyuan (Kieu Chinh), Lindo (Tsai Chin), Ying Ying (France Nuyen), and An Mei (Lisa Lu)—who live in San Francisco with their American-born daughters—respectively, June (Ming-Na Wen), Waverly (Tamlyn Tomita), Lena (Lauren Tom), and Rose (Rosalind Chao). The stories of these eight women unfold in a complex series of interlocking flashbacks, and the action ranges from past to present, generation to generation, from Imperial China to San Francisco. The relations among these women are just as complicated—nourishing, suppressive, selfless, and self-centered. It's a tour-de-force of voices, each seamlessly joined to the other, each contributing its thread to the huge tapestry.

The following remarks from Wayne Wang are excerpted from an interview with this writer on September 6, 1993, in Kansas City, Missouri. Despite a grueling promotional tour, Wang was fresh, enthusiastic, and in a high good humor. His youthful appearance made him seem at least ten years younger than his forty-four years.

He obliged me at the beginning by speaking for a few minutes in Mandarin Chinese for a broadcast I was preparing for Voice of America. He explained that Mandarin is the common language of China. During the Mao regime it had been selected as the language that would be spoken by everyone. He explained that his knowledge of the language and his background in Hong Kong stood him in good stead for making *The Joy Luck Club*.

WANG: Well, any director could shoot in San Francisco's Chinatown, I guess, and even in the Chinese locations, like Beijing, the Shanghai Film Studio, and to remote country villages. Although I speak Mandarin, I had lots of problems communicating with the people there. But at the same time, I understand the Chinese culture. It's part of my consciousness, part of my history. If anybody else had wanted to do this, he would have had to spend a lot of time researching the subject, and even then the subtleties of the culture would have been too confusing.

TIBBETTS: This isn't your first film to deal with several generations of Chinese and Chinese-Americans, is it?

WANG: *Dim Sum*, obviously, comes to mind, because that one's also about a mother-daughter relationship. There's one other film that I completed in 1989 called *Eat a Bowl of Tea*, which is about a father-son relationship, set after the war in 1949. That one is in some ways also very much related to *The Joy Luck Club*, because it's about a generation gap, the Chinese-American culture, the particular period where actually the Chinese were not allowed to bring their wives over. It wasn't until after the war that the GIs could use the GI Bill to bring their wives over. And that was the introduction to the Chinese-American families. In that sense it's related to the roots of *The Joy Luck Club*.

TIBBETTS: Do you see recent Asian-American films, like *Joy Luck* and Ang Lee's *The Wedding Banquet* [*Hsi yen*, 1993], especially, becoming as popular as the martial arts and ghost-story genres?

WANG: It's true the family genre seems to be very popular now. I guess the American audience is becoming interested in seeing movies about Chinese-Americans—although elsewhere in the world the ghost stories, the action films, and the kung fu films seem to be more popular . . . I think we're still pretty much a country of immigrants, some older and some newer than others. Stories about immigrants and the different generations and how the parents may be closer to their roots in their own history, and the kids are not. Those things concern all of us and are very strong, universal themes that way.

TIBBETTS: Tell me how you came to the project in the first place.

WANG: I was given Amy Tan's book, read it, and found it very moving. It was familiar in the sense that the stories reminded me of stories I heard while growing up. And yet at the same time it was very universal. Not just about Chinese, but about all immigrants. I also liked a lot of the details in the book that were true and visually oriented. I called up Amy—we both live in San Francisco. We got together informally, got to know each other, and formed a relationship and eventually a partnership.

TIBBETTS: Was the task of telling so many interlocking stories at all intimidating?

WANG: Yes, actually. And don't forget there are not just eight characters telling a story, but that each story has its own past and present. Sixteen stories! At first I was very worried about that, that it was very complicated; that it would be very tough to pull off. But we also connected up with a very experienced screenwriter, Ron Bass, who won an Academy Award [Best Writing, Original Screenplay] for *Rain Man* [1988], and he came in and had good ideas about how it would work: using the simple structure of a dinner party to see one of the daughters off to China to visit her twin sisters. Using that to introduce all the mothers and daughters. And also to use narration to bridge things and get more information across.

TIBBETTS: It's dazzling. But as easy as it is to watch, it must have been terribly complex to write the script.

WANG: Yes it was. I think we took a long, long time trying to figure out how many stories we were going to tell and what kind of emphasis we wanted in the sixteen stories. And how to get into the stories in an elegant and simple way. That was the major part of the first step in the scripting process. Later on, in the cinematic sense, we had to make sure that each story had a different look; that the flashbacks to the near past and far past had a different look. Those were all things that were very important. They may not be obvious to the viewer, but subconsciously it will make a difference to them.

TIBBETTS: And there's such a delicate balance you maintain between the tragic and the comic elements. Everybody talks about it as an "eight-handkerchief movie," but it really is quite funny in places.

WANG: I especially like the scene where Andrew McCarthy goes to have dinner with the parents of his girlfriend (Rosalind Chao as Rose). He doesn't understand anything about their customs and the affair is a disaster! Ms. Tan told me that scene grew out of experiences she had had. And when I read it I remembered different things in my own background where a Caucasian had to cope with the Chinese "Emily Post" kind of things. It's funny how such small details of table etiquette can create such serious problems!

TIBBETTS: On the other hand, other scenes are heartbreaking, like the drowning of Ying Ying's baby.

WANG: Forgive me if I laugh when I think about it, but we found a baby who actually loved the water very much. The mother was great and we used her hands as doubles. And it worked out nicely, the baby was so natural it was amazing. This baby really loved the water. It was a tough scene to film, though.

One of the saddest scenes, though, was June's reunion in China with her two older sisters. When we were filming the scene, what was amazing was that during the rehearsal the whole row of extras could hear the dialogue. They were completely in tears. An older woman came up to me later and told me she had had to leave her baby during the war and had never found it again. She really broke down. There's a lot there that the Chinese can identify with. Chinese-Americans in their own way can identify with this daughter, June, because her story is going back to your own roots, going to your home, and finally doing something for your mother. In another sense, for any daughters watching the film, I think they would be moved by it: because in the end it's about fulfilling your mother's wish. That's what that scene is all about.

TIBBETTS: The problems of the daughters don't seem particularly serious, after all, when they are compared to what their mothers had to go through.

WANG: I'm forty-four years old and my generation has been very lucky. We haven't been through major wars or major tragedies, so to speak, in terms of having been bombed by another country, having to escape from our own country, having lost family members, giving up babies—all that kind of stuff. And we live in a way a very self-centered life, our generation. And our problems are quite minor compared to what my parents in China have gone through. And I feel like sometimes I forget about that. And through this film I feel there's a lot we can learn from the dramas, tragedies, and sufferings that our parents have gone through. And what they've gone through to get us to this country and bring us up and all that. On the one hand, it's a burden, their expectations on us; on the other hand, we need to learn from their history and past, because that's where our roots are.

TIBBETTS: What a contrast this strikes with some of the pictures by a filmmaker like, say, John Hughes, where the parents are idiots. Where the teenagers deride their elders.

WANG: That goes back to my own generation being so self-centered. I think a lot of films actually serve to please that in a sense—we look at our parents and we laugh at them because they're so old-fashioned. They have certain ideas that seem very strict. We've lost the value of trying to understand where all that has come from. Some of it is old-fashioned, but if you understand the essence and where they come from, there is a lot of value to them. Take for example a scene in the movie where the daughter has to cut her own flesh to make a soup for her mother who's dying. I think I could in a sense say that's a stupid ritual; but in another sense, I look at it and can say that's a really strong thing about how much respect you show for your parents, which doesn't exist anymore.

TIBBETTS: Do you feel sometimes like your characters, poised between generations, between the Old and New World? Is that a potentially tragic dilemma?

WANG: I think my parents definitely fit that description. My dad has always wanted to become an American. And he finally became an American just a couple of years ago. And now he's kinda—he doesn't feel like he belongs here, either. He's a big baseball fan, football fan, all that good American stuff; but he feels there's something that's not his home here. He wants to move back to China, now that it's opened up. It's very strange to be caught between those two poles.

TIBBETTS: Rich material for a filmmaker who wants to deal with people and not guns!

WANG: (laughs) Yeah. Right. In my next movie I want to deal with guns! (laughs again) . . . But it's even more complicated than that. For me it's having to choose how to shoot my movies, too. Just as I'm kind of pulled between Chinese and American traditions, I'm pulled between the smoother, polished kind of film-making and the very rough, underground kind of filmmaking in *Chan Is Missing*. Actually, when I returned to Hong Kong for *Life Is Cheap . . . but Toilet Paper Is Expensive*, that was also very rough in a way—a true kind of "guerrilla filmmak-ing." I'd like to keep myself honest by bouncing between the mainstream film and the personal, independent thing with rough edges.

TIBBETTS: Anything you can say about some of the formative influences on your filmmaking?

WANG: Yes, actually when I was preparing for *The Joy Luck Club* there were three directors that I consciously looked at right at the beginning of pre-production. Because I felt that *The Joy Luck Club* had elements of these three directors. Ozu and Satyajit Ray were two who portrayed human emotions in such a simple, truthful way. David Lean was a third one, because a part of this movie is very epic and very big. Because *The Joy Luck Club* is not only a personal, little movie, but it opens up into a very epic scale. In that sense it has both of those worlds in the same film.

NOTE

1. Todd McCarthy, Review of *The Joy Luck Club*, *Variety*, 13 September 1993, 32.

Franco Zeffirelli

> It irritates me that some people want art to be as "difficult" as pos-
> sible, an elitist kind of thing. I want to give these things back to the
> people. All my training has been a preparation for the one medium
> that can do that, the motion picture.

*J*ohn C. Tibbetts's interview with Franco Zeffirelli makes a useful as well as
ironic companion piece to the interview with Baz Luhrmann. Both directors are
regarded as *auteurs* overseeing all aspects of production, both are famous for directing opera as well as film, both have directed adaptations of Shakespeare
specifically shaped in terms of appealing to mass, contemporary audiences (in
the interviews of this book they both speak in terms of democratizing Shakespeare). Though they have each directed Shakespearean films with liberal cuts to
the original texts, they both speak of the playwright and the tonal complexity
of his work with great reverence—here, Zeffirelli speaks of "sudden" and potentially uncomfortable humor in *Hamlet* in a way that recalls Luhrmann's discussion of the Shakespearean tendency to mix high tragedy with humor. Zeffirelli's *Romeo and Juliet* (1968) arguably spoke to his generation much in the way
that Luhrmann's adaptation of the play speaks to his. Despite this, Zeffirelli has
been openly critical of the "fun and games" and contemporary setting of
Luhrmann's *Romeo and Juliet*.[1]

For Zeffirelli, it is possible to "break the classical barrier" through casting actors (such as Mel Gibson in the role of Hamlet) who might draw in new audiences, who can perhaps mitigate the impact of a potentially alienating mise-en-
scène designed, in accordance with the play's setting, to connote an "authentic"
sense of place in a time now distant. The subtlety of Zeffirelli's approach is fore-
grounded in this interview in which he discusses the subdued palette of his *Hamlet* connoting a "medieval-primitive look," the expressionistic use of light forming

a suitably understated context for the language that is, in Zeffirelli's view, less "Baroque" than that of *Romeo and Juliet*. The restraint of Zeffirelli's *Hamlet* predictably contrasts with his colorful, rambunctious film of the Shakespearean comedy, *The Taming of the Shrew* (1967), but it makes a more fascinating contrast with Kenneth Branagh's adaptation of *Hamlet* (1996), which features an extraordinarily elaborate, nineteenth-century mise-en-scène to offset Branagh's inclusion of the "full" Shakespearean text. Along with establishing Zeffirelli's comparatively understated approach to adapting *Hamlet*, this interview reveals the backstory in casting Gibson and the difficulty of securing financial support for the film.

Interview by John C. Tibbetts
Originally published as "Breaking the Classical Barrier: Franco Zeffirelli," Literature/
Film Quarterly *22, no. 2 (April 1994): 136–40.*

As Franco Zeffirelli recalls in his autobiography, he was born a bastardino, or "little bastard," near Florence in 1923. Unable to take the name of his biological father Corsi, he was a *nescio nomen*, or "no name." Later he took the name "Zeffirelli," which was adapted from a reference in an aria in Mozart's *Cosi fan tutte* to the *Zeffiretti*, or "little breezes." He studied architecture as a student and later fought in the Resistance in the hills around Florence during World War II. He claims that his ambitions to work in stage and cinema were confirmed by a screening of Olivier's *Henry V* [1944] and by a subsequent association in the 1940s and early 1950s with mentor Luchino Visconti. He became a successful opera director, guiding the careers of such luminaries as Maria Callas and Joan Sutherland. But his theatrical films, including the Shakespearean cycle—*The Taming of the Shrew* (1967), *Romeo and Juliet* (1968), *Othello* (1987), and *Hamlet* (1990)— have established his reputation for general audiences.

Zeffirelli has been frequently criticized for a style he describes as "lavish in scale and unashamedly theatrical." Yet, undeniably, his pictures (which also include *Brother Sun, Sister Moon* [1972], *Jesus of Nazareth*, 1975, and *Endless Love*, 1984) have appealed to a mass audience with their blend of flamboyant imagery and spectacle with scrupulous care and craftsmanship. Arguably, more viewers have encountered grand opera and Shakespeare through his films than through the work of any other contemporary artist. He is the complete filmmaker who oversees every aspect of the design, story, and production. It was Laurence Olivier, who, during the filming of *Jesus of Nazareth*, said of Zeffirelli: "No matter what we do, in the end Franco has the scissors!"

I met Franco Zeffirelli in December 1991 on the occasion of a series of press interviews he granted during the premiere of *Hamlet*.

TIBBETTS: Is Shakespeare a "hard sell" these days?

ZEFFIRELLI: Impossible! We tried to interest studios here, but they weren't interested at all. We had to go the independent route. I don't know why they were nervous, we had had great success with *The Taming of the Shrew* and *Romeo and Juliet*. I remember more than ten years ago when the people at Paramount told me that Shakespeare never worked in the movies. Now you are young and you may not know that when I had done *Romeo and Juliet* a few years before, it had resurrected Paramount from the ashes! No matter, they just decided that Shakespeare doesn't work. You go to them with figures and a track record, but they don't listen. The way we did *Hamlet*, finally, was to go with three different companies, including Nelson, Carolco, and Sovereign Pictures. Barry Spikings, with Nelson, is English and I've known him for years. He's been a great fan and friend of mine. When we got Mel Gibson and Glenn Close, he was the one who finally said, "Come on, let's do it!"

TIBBETTS: How important was getting the Gibson name?

ZEFFIRELLI: It was vital. But it was a two-edged thing. On the one hand, for anything with Gibson you can find financing; on the other hand, you get people who doubt, who say, "Gibson, Gibson as Hamlet?" For Gibson it was extremely risky. He was very brave. He put his career on the line. Imagine if we did not succeed, he might be the joke of the industry. He has a new audience now. His fans go, too. But I tell you, it took great nerves from Mel.

TIBBETTS: Was it also a risk when you did *Taming of the Shrew* with Burton and Taylor?

ZEFFIRELLI: They were at the peak of their careers. Richard Burton was the most famous Shakespearean actor of his time. Elizabeth Taylor was the greatest beauty of the day. It was extremely easy. It was supported by him, personally, and by Columbia. The big problem was later with *Romeo*. Despite the success of *Taming of the Shrew*, when I immediately suggested a little, lean *Romeo*, instead of a big fat budget thing—just a crust of bread—everybody said, "No way." I wanted to prove that Shakespeare can work without the big names.

TIBBETTS: How difficult was it to bring *Hamlet* in at just over two hours?

ZEFFIRELLI: The kind of story we wanted to do automatically meant some areas of the original play became unnecessary. They fell away by themselves, like dried branches. I never cut down so little from the first assembly to the final version than I did here. At first it was two hours and forty minutes. We cut down only half an hour. Unheard of. My first cut of *Romeo and Juliet* was five hours twenty. And we came down to a little over two hours. I'd love to go back to my original!

TIBBETTS: Describe your first meeting with Gibson.

ZEFFIRELLI: I come from the city of Machiavelli. I know one thing: In the heart of every actor, no matter how big or famous, there is this thorn, this stinging thing, that they wish to do Shakespeare. I talked with Dustin Hoffman before and I told him I was going to do *Hamlet*. He asked me, "with whom?" I told him, "Mel Gibson." Dustin just almost fainted. He told me, "My dream has always been to play Hamlet!" Everybody wants to do Hamlet. So you can be sure that you hit a note there, you ring an alarm, a bell, in the ears of every actor. He will not say no. With Mel we had a brunch, which turned into a lunch, and then into a tea and dinner. We separated and he was convinced.

TIBBETTS: Did anything about Gibson come as a surprise to you?

ZEFFIRELLI: I was already informed that he had done some Shakespeare when he was young. I also was madly in love with his voice. It was something I liked, perhaps because of my operatic training, whatever. And his voice is a magnificent, bronzed, rich voice. There was something in him that made me very, very excited about the possibility. It was mainly that he could be a sixteenth-century character. He looks like a young Michelangelo now, with his hair and beard. The classical structure. And the humor. He's capable of a very nasty humor! That's one of my main regrets in the adaptation—that we did not trust ourselves enough to put in more humor. Because Shakespeare knew perfectly well what he was doing. He injected a sudden humor. Perhaps people are uneasy about *Hamlet* now, though—they don't know if they should laugh or not.

TIBBETTS: Generally speaking, what are the challenges in bringing Shakespeare to a modern audience?

ZEFFIRELLI: I think it's making the language acceptable [so] that you can understand it, that it's almost colloquial. You look at Shakespeare's earlier plays, like *Romeo and Juliet,* and a much more baroque language, a more flourishing language than, say, *Antony and Cleopatra* or *King Lear.* I think our actors have done this miracle. They have to speak a language that is beautiful, yes, but more "primitive" and spare, in a way. Look at the scenes with Paul Scofield. You're not aware of a "classical barrier" between you and him. He speaks in a way that you understand every single word. And Mel, for all his realism, he makes "To be or not to be" not a poetical aria, but a real suffering and a real problem that you understand. People who are not familiar at all with the speeches tell me that for the first time they understand it. In trying to make it clear to himself, Mel helps others to understand it better. That was for me the main problem. The story is already so magnificent!

TIBBETTS: Is reaching a mass audience your biggest priority?

ZEFFIRELLI: You know, I think culture—especially opera and Shakespeare—must be available to as many people as possible. It irritates me that some people want art to be as "difficult" as possible, an elitist kind of thing. I want to give these things back to the people. All my training has been a preparation for the one medium that can do that, the motion picture.

TIBBETTS: Let's get back to *Hamlet.* Have you ever staged it before?

ZEFFIRELLI: I did it on stage in Italy with a superb cast and brought it to the Festival des Nations in Paris. Later we toured it to Russia and Eastern Europe. That was in 1964. Always I wanted to bring it to the cinema. Either the actor wasn't ready or I was not, or the money was not . . . Every project has its own season.

TIBBETTS: In *Hamlet* you achieve a distinctive kind of "look" with cinematographer David Watkin. Tell me about your work with him.

ZEFFIRELLI: I like always to work with him. We did *Jesus of Nazareth* together. I had lost my cameraman, Armando Nannuzzi, who had become a director himself. David knows how to re-create the look of the "Old Masters." He can make a "still life" out of each set. I enjoy how we worked out a special kind of light for the dueling scene in *Hamlet*. We shot in that huge area with light coming in from openings in the walls. Then we took huge white sheets and placed them from one end of the hall to the other to bounce the light, to reflect it back into the scene. Even the white shirt of Hamlet became a kind of reflector and you can see the light on Laertes's face brighten when he gets closer. An extraordinary effect. All of this is possible too with special lenses and the film stock. And we kept the colors to a more black-and-white look, yes?

TIBBETTS: Quite a difference from the charge that you usually work in highly saturated, vivid colors!

ZEFFIRELLI: Color is devastating here, but in this way: I keyed the whole movie to mostly grays and ash colors, a "medieval-primitive" look, the look of a society that is brutal and made of stone. Whenever a few rich colors do come out, the effect is even more vivid. In that sense, this is one of the most colorful films I've ever done—but only because the few rich colors stand out so much from the grays. That way, you become inebriated by those colors.

TIBBETTS: Hamlet himself continues to fascinate us, doesn't he?

ZEFFIRELLI: Hamlet really was a window opened onto the future. He invented the "modern man." You'd like to meet him personally, if you could, today, because he'd be so exciting and interesting.

TIBBETTS: Some film critics complain that Gibson's character is too old compared to the relative youth of Glenn Close's Gertrude.

ZEFFIRELLI: They don't know what they're talking about! They absolutely don't know what they're talking about! Hamlet here is 33, or 34, which at that time was a mature adult. His mother is still young enough to be exuberant sexually, a wildcat who wants to have sex with her new husband at every minute, behind every pillar. She's so hungry for sex. She must be around 45. And that fits very well. She could have had Hamlet at a very young age, you see, even as early as thirteen—which was common to that time because women were married as soon as they were capable of having children. It works perfectly for us.

TIBBETTS: In your autobiography you say that from childhood the world of theater has always represented something larger than life. Can you recall an example of that?

ZEFFIRELLI: We've been talking about the Middle Ages, yes? Well, I grew up in the Tuscan countryside, which has always had for me a taste of the real Italy of the Middle Ages. I spent summers watching the traveling troupes of performers who would come and perform. They kept lamps on the floor in front of them which would throw diabolical shadows on the walls behind them—something I often do in my movies. They told stories and acted them out with shouts and blows and gestures. I have always felt these players were the true descendants of the world of Boccaccio, and I've always believed more in their fantasies than in anything else.

NOTE

1. Zeffrelli claims that "the Luhrmann film didn't update the play, it just made a big joke of it. But apparently the pseudo-culture of young people today wouldn't have digested the play unless you dressed it up that way, with all those fun and games" (Brook, Peter Hall, Richard Loncraine, Baz Luhrmann, Oliver Parker, Roman Polanski, and Franco Zeffirelli, "Shakespeare in the Cinema: A Film Director's Symposium," *Cineaste* 24, no. 1 (December 1998): 48–55 (54).

Martha Coolidge

I just want to understand people. I think that's the source of drama
and the source of complexity, conflict, and resolution. So I certainly
hope that I'm appealing to universal kinds of truths.

*M*artha Coolidge and her films have received numerous awards: a year after this
interview she received the "Crystal Award" from Women in Film[1] and two years
after this interview she was elected the first woman president of the Director's
Guild of America in its 66-year history. This interview focuses on Coolidge's
Rambling Rose (1991), her most celebrated film to date. Coolidge describes the
process of adapting Calder Willingham's novel (of the same name), making connections between the South of the past (as he represents it) and her New England background while also respecting the details of difference.

Coolidge speaks of "universal kinds of truths" in her work which nevertheless represents specifically nuanced, psychological studies of complexity, conflict,
and resolution. Her films are united through a lightness of touch which sometimes belies their serious subtexts: the comedy *Real Genius* (1985), for instance,
focuses on teenage geniuses who unwittingly involve themselves in the creation
of destructive laser technology (a story resonant with the contemporary context
of worldwide debates over the future of nuclear power) which is offset by the unusually, infectiously clownish presence of a young Val Kilmer and the finale in
which the laser technology is used to cook a massive pot of popcorn.

Here Coolidge also discusses how particular autobiographical experiences influence her films: the humanism of her mother; the death of her father which left
the family of several children socially vulnerable (inspiring the director to "identify
with outsiders"); her own spiritual beliefs. The style of *Rambling Rose*, a film almost
entirely in flashback, is designed to imitate the forms of light that Coolidge associates with her processes of remembering or recalling scenes from her own past.

268

This interview establishes an understanding of Coolidge which transcends individual film productions: her preference for the flexibility of independent filmmaking despite budgetary constraints, the socially driven nature of her work, and the discrimination she has experienced as a female director *despite* her success.

Interview by Lorna Fitzsimmons
Originally published as "Respecting Difference: An Interview with Martha Coolidge," Literature/Film Quarterly 27, no. 2 (April 1999): 149–54.

Relaxing in the Adolphus Hotel in downtown Dallas, Martha Coolidge put her feet up, joked briefly, and quickly cast politics into the conversation. In Dallas to receive the USA Film Festival's Great Director Award, Coolidge was the first woman to be admitted among the ranks of Altman, Cassavetes, Stone, Wiseman, Cukor, Capra, and other Great Directors in the festival's 24-year history. Supported by Texas governor Ann Richards, a staunch proponent of the Texas film industry, Coolidge grew emphatic about her concern for the advancement of women in film.

From her semi-autobiographical docudrama on date rape, *Not a Pretty Picture* (1975), to her popular feature about a single mother, *Angie* (1994), Coolidge's work provides a tragicomic exploration of women's struggles to find themselves. Less extreme than Duras's [screenplay] vision in *Hiroshima, mon amour* (1959), perhaps, her interpretations of women's lives similarly explore the double-edged effects of interdependency. Often tormented by the past, rambling like Rose within destructive dependencies, Coolidge's heroines struggle to survive the morass of others' narcissism. Coolidge has studied the telling details of bonds that bind, bringing to her films a tireless resistance to intolerance and a puckish curiosity about the uncanny.

FITZSIMMONS: Many Southerners seem to appreciate the sense of the South that you convey in *Rambling Rose*. As a New Englander, was it difficult for you to make this film?

COOLIDGE: Southern culture, particularly the South of the past, is so much a part of America and so much a part of at least anybody who reads. It's such a part of my life, even though I'm a New England yank. I felt the setting of Calder Willingham's book was the South that I knew or had heard about. When I travel to the South, I often feel that it's very hard to find that South anymore. But through the Southerners I've known, as well as their literature, I feel as if the South was a part of my youth. And, not only that, I had a long talk with Calder about this. It seems to me that whatever class you would call Mother and Daddy in *Rambling*

Rose—upper middle class WASP?—is widespread. So, New England and the deep South have deep similarities. The language is not the same. The language is the poetry of the South, which is special and something I love and New England doesn't have. But, on the other hand, Calder currently lives in New Hampshire, which is no accident. We talked about this a lot. There is such a similarity between New England and the deep South of Calder's youth that there are really strong parallels within that particular class of people. So, for me, the realities of the family, the structure of the family, the talk around the dinner table, the kind of values, that is, the intellectual values—the value of thought, the value of reading, anything from politics to freethinking—are similar. Calder's story seemed all a part of my grandparents' tradition and my grandparents are exactly the age of Calder's parents in the book. Of course, the mother and father of the book and the film are portraits of his parents. It is totally autobiographical in the sense of the reality of the characters.

FITZSIMMONS: Autobiographical for Calder but also for you?

COOLIDGE: Yes, for me it was re-creating the visits to my grandparents' home and an idea of how my father grew up.

FITZSIMMONS: There are tensions in several of your depictions of family life that seem figurative of larger struggles, so that the domestic battles and declarations of independence appear allegorical of macroscopic conflicts. Do you see your focus on the family as a metaphor for American society?

COOLIDGE: I don't know that I've ever really intentionally done that. However, on the other hand, I do know that, in my approach to my work and to helping actors work, you start with a microcosm, and when that is specific—truthful—then it automatically expands into a macrocosm. And that is absolutely a rule. So detail, detail, detail—if you start with detail you will reach the abstract. Curiously enough, I don't necessarily start with an idea in detail. I do think in very sweeping abstract shapes, but then when you execute something, you execute it in detail. That's why, for me, the more specific I made the South the more real that was, and people will identify with it, and the more interesting the movie becomes. Being abstract or vague is a choice made in a lot of movies. For example, [The] Witches of Eastwick [directed by George Miller, 1987] is a totally New England story, but somebody made a decision not to use New England accents, not to make it feel New England but to make it sort of American. Well, it immediately doesn't feel real to me. So you dismiss it at a real level, even though there are many things about the movie I enjoy. But in terms of choices, in hitting a specific spot, they made a classic movie choice of not being specific, and I find that causes an area of disbelief or dismissal. In *Real Genius*, for example, I wanted all the math and the physics to be real. To this day, mathematicians and physicists love this movie because in most movies, the makers seem to think nobody understands the technical material anyway, so they'll just do gobbledygook. What does that mean? First of all it means the actors know it's not real. The actors know. So they are acting as though it's real, but they know that it's not real. In *Real Genius*, on the other hand, I sent all my actors to a real laser lab with a real mathematician who explained to them in lay terms how to really act around a laser. They actually took lab classes with the laser and learned how to handle the equipment. So, by the time the actors got to the movie, they knew everything was real—a completely different kind of conviction. So even the audience, who doesn't understand the math, I think still has a sense that it's real. Curiously enough, lasers on those same principles have been developed since then. But we were careful. Even though all the math and theory was correct, we were careful to create a laser that couldn't be made, because we didn't want to can somebody someday. (Laughs.)

FITZSIMMONS: It's clear that the appeal of your work is also due to your knack for tapping undercurrents considered from a psychoanalytic perspective.

COOLIDGE: I hope so. I take a very psychoanalytic approach, hopefully complex. And in fact, I have made a lot of psychoanalytic presentations. I've been asked maybe three or four times to do presentations.

FITZSIMMONS: Is there a particular area of psychoanalytic thought that interests you?

COOLIDGE: Not specifically. I am interested in people. I've studied people from every angle that I could. That includes psychology and all the way to behavior and acting. I've studied virtually every kind of acting technique as well as deep psychological approaches. I just want to understand people. I think that's the source of drama and the source of complexity, conflict, and resolution. So I certainly hope that I'm appealing to universal kinds of truths. And again, I believe that you start with a specific and then people will find their truths in your work. For example, in *Real Genius*, I think it was the first time I consciously realized that for me the greatest evil is people who simply don't regard other people as humans. When people start putting themselves above other human beings and think they can afford X losses and if they lose $150 million on a nuclear war they will have won, as if these are acceptable losses, when they start referring to human life that way and start feeling as Professor Hathaway does in that film—that he is kind of above the students and he doesn't have to tell them what he's doing, and that he can supply the CIA with a weapon to knock people off at will—people are functioning on a not-needing-to-let-anyone-know basis within their own little clique within the government. This kind of superiority is very dangerous. The source of most of the evil in our society is groups of people who think they are better than others and do not include themselves with the other people. It's a "we can lose them—we don't need them" mentality.

FITZSIMMONS: Certainly, there is a lot of holier-than-thou in the history of American thought.

COOLIDGE: In the history of the world. We enslave these barbarians because they don't matter.

FITZSIMMONS: Would you say then, that part of the social role of film is to exert a leveling influence?

COOLIDGE: I believe that. It's not what everybody thinks, but that's what I'm trying to do. I really call myself a humanistic filmmaker, not specifically feminist, but humanistic.

FITZSIMMONS: Does that mean promoting equality? Respect for people of all kinds?

COOLIDGE: Yes, respect, good old respect for all people. In my mind, it goes back to my grandmother. She said respect was the most important thing. I sat down and edited that documentary [*Old-Fashioned Woman*, 1974] for a year and I must say that there is an enormous amount of wisdom in the way of looking at the world that she was raised with. If you can function with respect toward everyone and yourself, she said, it would be a different world.

FITZSIMMONS: It's clear from the tremendous characterizations of older women in your films that you had a great attachment to your grandmother. What other childhood influences helped shape your humanistic perspective?

COOLIDGE: My mother is extremely liberal. My father comes from a Republican Coolidge political family. My early childhood memories are of complicated, conflicting political debate at home. My mother was an extreme liberal and an extreme humanist. My grandmother believes in tremendous social work. That's what a woman did in those days. So there is a great sense on both sides of the family of service to the community as well as political and social concerns. My mother was certainly as concerned with society as much as politics. I think that early influences—exposure to certain kinds of concerns—stay with you for the rest of your life. You can wander away from them for a while, but they come back.

In the end, my father died and I was raised to really care about people. My mother constantly talked about the common man and whatever meaning that had for her, the concern took on a new meaning for me. We had very little money; my mother was a single parent.

FITZSIMMONS: What age were you when your father died?

COOLIDGE: I was just nine, with my siblings all younger and my mother pregnant. We had a rough couple of years there, to say the least. It gave me an understanding of being in social standing and then out. I really walked both sides of a social fence. So it was these things that made me identify with outsiders.

FITZSIMMONS: Intertwined with your sympathy for outsiders, several of your works show a transpersonal or paranormal perspective. For example, characters speak about communicating through supersensory means. In *Crazy in Love* [a film made for television in 1992], Georgie feels she has a "magical" means of knowing when her husband is in trouble. In *Rambling Rose*, the mother's belief in the "fourth dimension" is also parapsychological, albeit from the perspective of spiritist myth. Is this transpersonal theme of special interest to you?

COOLIDGE: I try to reflect life as I see it and experience it. And I think that perhaps the fact that these things come up is because women are more concerned with them than men. So they may not appear in men's movies, but they are going to appear in women's movies because, when I think of the women I know, a lot of them are involved with these ideas, whether it's astrology or some sort of spiritual pursuit. In the case of Calder's work, the mother in *Rambling Rose* is a portrait of his own mother. According to my research, there is a great tradition in the South of spiritual pursuits, particularly among women. It is considered a healing. Diane Ladd is from the South and I felt her portrayal of the role to be a very accurate portrait of this. I feel it's important that we spend some of our time thinking about these things.

In the case of *Crazy in Love*, this idea is an example of Georgie's neurosis. Georgie believes that she has this kind of power. She's wrong, her husband isn't screwing around on her, but she's convinced herself, as many people convince themselves, that certain signs mean certain things. On the other hand, I've had some experiences where I've certainly had communication or unexplainable contact with people through a sort of parapsychological means. That I can't explain.

FITZSIMMONS: Would that be with people very close to you?

COOLIDGE: Well, yes. My brother had an accident with his hand and my hand went numb. I was 3,000 miles away and did not know what was happening to me. I can't tell you how many people I've met that have had things happen like this. So, do I believe there are things that connect us that we don't understand? Yes. Do I believe that I know what they are? No. I can't make any rules. I'm not propagating a philosophy or spiritual approach. I know many women are involved in these things. These things are worthy of us looking at. I think that they should be in movies.

FITZSIMMONS: Of course, from a psychoanalytic viewpoint, Jung would speak of this as releasing the "feminine," the "anima," which to more recent psychologists might imply greater right-hemispheric functioning.

COOLIDGE: Yes, what's extraordinary in Calder's work is that, on one level, his writing about females is idealized. In a certain sense, you could call it a male fantasy. But, on the other hand, he has such extraordinary ability to observe. He loves women so much and his anima is so strong that his characters and his themes are so far above what you mostly see. His themes are extraordinary, way on a higher plane than most. But, of course, the truth is that another director could have taken that story, made Rose a bimbo, and still have made a movie.

FITZSIMMONS: You said you felt inspired by the story the moment you read it. What were the main elements of the novel that really attracted you?

COOLIDGE: There were several. Extraordinary language and dialogue. The themes were clear. It was a story that was deeply, deeply about love. Real human love. Love way beyond the average—real caring. And also it showed the magic of humanity, the magic that a woman, like Rose, who has been so abused, who is a classic victim of sexual abuse, could still be an extraordinary person. I believe that if you look in all areas of the world, out of hell-holes emerge saints. It's one of the great human powers. People have extraordinary resiliency and resources. She is one of those and this is an extraordinary family, but they need a little help. She comes in and their humanity is improved. And a huge incredible lesson is learned by Daddy which is priceless.

FITZSIMMONS: Your striking use of light in that film really enhances the characterization of Rose.

COOLIDGE: Yes, the whole concept of the film was light. Rose was light. So everything came from that, such as the way we designed the house. I made the house incredibly dark. It's darker than a house would've been in that period. And it has great big windows without curtains, just lace because I wanted the light to pour into the house as she entered. Essentially, it gets lighter and lighter. These windows just have beams of light coming into the rooms. The image I had when I started the movie, which was curiously enough shared and seen by my cinematographer separately from me, was a screen door of a kitchen with a beam of yellow light coming through, hitting a kitchen table like my grandmother's with a bowl of fruit on it. Just the way you remember from your childhood. Since the whole film is about a memory, I wanted every image to feel like a memory—to burn into your way of thinking. So we heightened the things that you would remember—like light. And we built the set to be able to do that and then selected the times of day. The bridge that Rose crosses was oriented in a particular way. We had to shoot Rose at a certain time of day to get the light behind her. Our whole shooting schedule was designed around where geographically the things were and where the light was.

FITZSIMMONS: The locale certainly contributes a lot to the atmosphere of *Rambling Rose*. Is it your preference to shoot on location or at the studio?

COOLIDGE: For that film, we did both. The home is a set. There's a great, great control that you can exercise on the set. So there are many reasons to shoot on the set. But when you go to locations you get a kind of energy and kind of reality that you can't get on the set, faking it in Los Angeles. Well, you can say, we'll find some house that looks like Tara in Los Angeles. But the trees aren't the same. The moss would have to be fake. In fact, when my art director went out to look for the location in North Carolina, I said if we can't find it there we'll find one in Georgia. He found that house and as soon as he found that house, I knew we had the movie.

FITZSIMMONS: It must have been demanding shooting on location for your island films.

COOLIDGE: Yes, I have made three films set on islands. For *Crazy in Love* the island was a great, lucky find. It was a low budget production, up in Seattle. We couldn't find a waterfront property with several houses on it. So finally we sent some men out in airplanes, and they shot stills from the air. They could have driven around and around there forever; there is so much complicated coast line. The problem is, if you take too many ferry boats for too long, it's going to cost so much. So we decided on Bainbridge Island and finally found this nook. The people there were extraordinary. They were really cooperative, and it was a great place to shoot. But there wasn't a single hotel on the island. So we ended up renting something like 42 beach houses, and this was in season! I can't tell you what a nightmare this was.

FITZSIMMONS: *Crazy in Love* was made for cable television. What have been the relative advantages of working in television, independent film, and Hollywood in your experience?

COOLIDGE: Well, television would fall last on the list. It's very tough for a director. Television is not a very satisfying place if the director enjoys the way a movie is shot. The reason that a lot of directors enjoy working for the larger budget television shows like HBO and TNT is because they have the freedom of dealing with more serious material—sometimes, not always. And that's great. A lot of filmmakers want to deal with important subjects. A lot of film just won't let you do that. So, directors will take a cut in salary and a tougher schedule to do something more meaningful. It just shows you that there really are sincere people working in the business who want to deal with something important. There are certainly subjects I would do for television because they would reach the audience and would have something to say. For example, I was really interested in *Who Killed Lisa?*, the story of a couple in New York where the husband beat his child to death. That would be an extraordinary television event, which shouldn't really be a feature. And I think it's really an important story to tell because, the implication is, where does responsibility lie? As a society, we do see these things happen where we have rules and regulations to protect the privacy of the family. But, on the other hand, social workers, teachers, and neighbors could not seem to interfere and that situation went on for years until it had a tragic ending. So I really wanted to do that project.

Still, I would rather do independent film any day of the week. But, if you just do independent film, then you can be limited—pigeonholed—into a more restricted budgetary and marketing pattern. So the point is to do big budget pictures in Hollywood film because they reach many people and you have a chance to really do a broad spectrum appeal picture. And I want to do those. For my soul, though, I prefer independent filmmaking. The corporate structure of Hollywood filmmaking gives it an inflexibility. This is changing slowly, though, because of the influence of other media, which is forcing more flexibility into the Hollywood system. Competition with other art forms is making the Hollywood style change. I believe new thinking will emerge in Hollywood, but not overnight.

FITZSIMMONS: Your rise to prominence within the film industry must have been challenging. Do you think discriminatory conventions against women are breaking down?

COOLIDGE: Now that I'm older I realize that discrimination against women is absolutely everywhere and absolutely constant. But it can take subtle forms that you may not be aware of. It's involved in every part of the system—in subject matter, audience attendance, and interaction with the crew. But, being a woman can sometimes be a plus when, for example, male producers hire you because they want a "woman's touch." On the other hand, many men have problems dealing with female authority figures. I had to fire a production designer because of this attitude problem.

But, again, things are changing slowly. Every success by a woman helps every other woman to succeed. My advice to new directors would be to become the best there is at storytelling and helping actors. Technical know-how isn't enough; you have to know how to interact with people.

NOTE

1. The purpose of the Los Angeles-based organization Women in Film is "to empower, promote and mentor women in the entertainment and media industries" and "the Crystal Awards were established in 1977 to honor outstanding women who, through their endurance and the excellence of their work, have helped to expand the role of women within the entertainment industry." (Women in Film Homepage, http://www.wif.org/index.php?option=com_content&task=category&sectionid=4&id=14&Itemid=38 [8 Aug. 2007].)

Terence Davies (and Olivia Stewart)

The whole point of drama is to make us empathize—in this case, with what is, essentially, a tragic story. In tragedy certain small things happen. In tragedy, it's always the small things.

$\mathcal{I}$n a recent interview preceding a retrospective showing of his films at the NFT (National Film Theatre) in London, Terence Davies expressed surprise at the celebration of his films which are, in his words, characterized by "modest budgets" and "modest intentions."[1] Davies grew up in a large, working class Liverpool family, a context remote from the worlds of utopian song and color in classical Hollywood movies, movies which entranced him as a child. In this interview with Linda Cahir, Davies refers to the intoxicating extravagance of the films directed by Douglas Sirk, "very sentimental" stories which are "refracted" in Davies's own, unsentimental journey toward representing emotional and social truth. This interview focuses on *The House of Mirth* (2000), a film which appears superficially antithetical to the rest of Davies's work through its comparatively lush, period, painterly mise-en-scène offsetting the star power of Gillian Anderson. However, the economy as well as the restraint with which the film records both violent and tender experiences connects it with his other work. Cahir's interview with Davies and Olivia Stewart (his long-time collaborator and producer) focuses on the process of adapting and making interpretive changes to Wharton's text, the use of music (always crucial in Davies's work), indirect connections with Davies's other films, the power of the film in contradistinction to Martin Scorsese's adaptation of Wharton (*The Age of Innocence*, 1993), the difficulty of financing the film through nine sources, casting and directing Gillian Anderson in the lead role of Lily Bart. Davies reportedly cast Anderson after simply seeing a photograph of her, never having seen *The X-Files*, unaware that his *The Long Day Closes* (1992) was one of her favorite films.[2] It is mystifying that the happy accident of this collaboration, at the heart of an extraordinary and virtually unanimously lauded film, has not been followed by further funding for Davies's work.

Interview by Linda Costanzo Cahir
*Originally published as "*The House of Mirth*: An Interview with Director Terence Davies and Producer Olivia Stewart," Literature/Film Quarterly 29, no. 3 (October 2001): 166–71.*

[Editor's note: The following interviews in person with Davies and Stewart were conducted in New York City on September 19, 2000.]

The British director Terence Davies and the producer Olivia Stewart have been a collaborative team for over fifteen years. Their partnership is responsible for *Distant Voices, Still Lives* (1985), *The Long Day Closes* (1992), and *The Neon Bible* (1995). Davies's earlier films comprise his "Liverpool Trilogy": *Children* (1976), *Madonna and Child* (1980), and *Death and . . . Transfiguration* (1983).[3] His work is characterized by a highly visual, rather than verbal/visual, approach to subject. Intimate and introspective, exacting and elegant, Davies's films are auto-biographical studies of family love and the legacy of family violence, of gender and sexuality, and of integrity and loneliness. Throughout his films, remnants of Davies's memory reel in elliptical constructions, tender sequences of shots that are fragmented and juxtaposed, in a manner that evades all sense of linear narrative.

In contrast, Edith Wharton's *The House of Mirth* is a conventional story, de-cidedly linear in structure and traditional in plot elements. A period piece set in wealthy turn-of-the-nineteenth-century New York society, the story centers on the demise of Lily Bart, a social beauty trained to one end: to inveigle, then hook a wealthy husband. Skilled in that way, but not constituted, ethically, to carry it out, Lily dies, impecunious and alone. The literary world of *The House of Mirth* is far removed from what we know and admire in Terence Davies's work: his gentle rummagings through the personal past of post–World War II working class Liverpool, his splintered, looping, non-linear rendering of innermost memories.

I spoke with Olivia Stewart, the producer of the film, about Davies's deci-sion to take on Wharton's novel, a work so antithetical to his own. We spoke both by phone and in person, where, just prior to the New York Film Festival press screening of the film, I met with her over coffee at Burke and Burke, and where, punctuated by sips of espresso, she considered Terence Davies's choice to make *The House of Mirth*.

STEWART: *It was brave of him, very brave. Most directors would have kept to the proven formula. He departed—radically—from it; and, while that initially made him nervous, Terence needed a change. He needed to expand. I told him that he should try something completely different, a period piece, perhaps. He came to me with* The House of Mirth, *a book which he has loved for fifteen years. He told me that he would love to film it. I thought it was a very good idea and that it was time for him to move in a new direction.*

Olivia Stewart had high artistic involvement with the film, not just financial and organizational involvement. I asked her what made her interested in this particular project. Stewart responded that Wharton's understanding of society was the dominant element.

STEWART: *The world of* The House of Mirth *is a blatantly vicious one, quite insidious—cruel. And mean, very mean.*

As Stewart spoke, I thought about Terence Davies's other films and his scenes of domestic brutality that are so unforgettable. I asked her: "Davies could have been drawn to any number of novels, period pieces, linear in structure. Why, specifically, *The House of Mirth*? Was he drawn to the violence it enacts—the novel's understanding of the brutality that people are capable of committing?"

STEWART: *No, no. I don't think so. Terence loves women; he was drawn to that book because of the women, and he just loved Lily Bart. He was drawn to its opulence, too, I think.*

Filmed in nine weeks, largely in Glasgow, and on a budget of $8 million (roughly, for example, Martin Scorsese's promotion and distribution budget for *The Age of Innocence*), the film, nonetheless, has a handsome look. Intelligent choices, that reduce production cost, were made. For example, a key scene, set on a yacht off the coast of Monte Carlo, is shot with characters lounging in deck chairs in front of a blue screen and a canvas that affect the ship's awnings. A more expensive production may have lingered on the opulent details of the yacht and the vistas of the Mediterranean coast. The *House of Mirth*'s less extravagant, more minimalist approach works well. While maintaining authenticity of locale, it politely insists that the audience focus on what is important: not on the distracting details of wealth, but on the dynamic currents and undercurrents occurring among characters. I asked Stewart about the film's financing.

STEWART: *In spite of Terence's skill as a director and the great cast we had, in spite of the wonderful source material and an extraordinary script—a script whose quality does not often land on people's desks—despite all this—it was not easy to raise money. We ended up with nine financiers, which made it all very complicated to deal with. Eventually, we got to make it, but it was a very hard thing to get off the ground and it shouldn't have been. You mentioned Scorsese's film, which, I have to say, is gorgeous. It is almost perfect. On a smaller scale, though, ours is just as lovely. Terry's way of filming is a particular way: formal and intimate, a chamber piece, not an orchestra. And he is not distracted by large set pieces [implying, as Scorsese seemed to have been in his film].*

I agreed. Scorsese's *The Age of Innocence*, certainly strong—handsome—in its technical achievements, was too reverential of the "large set pieces"—the entitled, monied world that it was filming. The movie softened the social malevolence present in the novel, and, consequently, softened Wharton's criticism of that malevolence. I asked Stewart about this.

STEWART: *Yes, I think he [Scorsese] did soften it. I can see how a director or an actor could become slightly awed by those surroundings—how that kind of wealth could have a restraining effect. It could have had that effect on Terry, too, but he didn't let that happen.*

The film has a lovely look, what many critics are describing as a "painterly quality." Much of that took is due to the casting and to the portrait-like way in which the actors are shot, most notably Gillian Anderson as Lily Bart; Laura Linney as Bertha Dorset; and Eleanor Bron as Mrs. Peniston, all of whom provide strong performances.

STEWART: *Yes. Gillian was wonderful; I am glad that you thought so, as was Laura. Although I had a lot of involvement in the casting, I have to say that, at first, Laura was not quite what I had in mind. In casting the part, I would have gone much more down the line for Bertha—for much more an obvious bitch. But all that false saccharine Laura brings to Bertha—she got it absolutely right, absolutely. She makes us cringe, cringe!*

Eleanor Bron has an interesting connection to the period of the film and to its look. When she was younger Eleanor Bron looked exactly like Lady Agnew [of Lochnaw], who was painted by Sargent. When they had the big Sargent exhibition in Edinburgh, she was invited to open it. We didn't know this, at first. So, it all comes full circle when Bron, Lady Agnew's look-alike, appears in a film that has a Sargent-look, a look Terry consciously wanted.

But Terence did not only direct the film, he wrote the screenplay. And, I think that screenplay is just beautiful. In writing it, he had the utmost fidelity and respect for Wharton's work.

Edith Wharton's novel is not the usual story, in which plot supports image. In *The House of Mirth*, action frequently is not external and self-explanatory. Drama often occurs off-page, in the implied, subterranean world of insinuation. Significant acts and choices are intimated, not denoted or enacted. Conflicts are largely internal. Ambiguity of situation and of motives pervades the novel.

Implied action, internal conflict, and motivational ambiguity are three things that a novel can do well, but which film, in particular, finds more difficult to convey. (Much in the same way as a film can convey an abundance of visual information, very efficiently, while a novel cannot do this with the same inherent ease.) After the New York press screening of *The House of Mirth*, I met with Terence Davies and asked him about the particular difficulties presented in bringing this novel to the screen and about the departure from his film style that this new movie represented.

DAVIES: *I wanted the discipline of a linear narrative. To use a musical analogy, I wanted to see if I could write a good tune. But, I am not interested in linear narrative in the sense of things that happen next. I am interested in what happens emotionally next and how you can relay this in film. And, yes, yes, yes, the book often is ambiguous, very much so. I do love the nature of ambiguity, where you can hold two things in your mind at the same time, one or the other of which can be true; but, it is very, very difficult to get that kind of ambiguity in film. It is one of the areas that film is just not good at. Just as it's not good at interior monologue—there's no visual equivalent, except, maybe, for the voiceover, which falls flat because it is not as subtle, unless it's very, very well done, as it is in* The Age of Innocence, *which, I think, is a masterpiece.*

Lily's death is an example of this ambiguity. Was it intentional or accidental? The book keeps that somewhat ambiguous. It is harder for film to maintain that kind of ambiguity, unless a voiceover actually says: was Lily's death intentional or not?, which would be just silly to do. In shooting the death scene, I can tell you, the only direction I gave her [Anderson] was to quote from Keats: I told her "What Lily is thinking is to cease upon the midnight with no pain" [quoting "Ode to a Nightingale"]; and her eyes filled with tears and I said, "let's do it." There are times when you can not give any direction, at all, or the minimum of direction and you just let it happen. The first take was good, very good, but no chloral came out of the bottle! So, I calmly said, "Let's do it again."

And Gillian was wonderful. I wanted it [the film/the character shots] to have the quality of a John Singer Sargent portrait. I thought she had those same qualities and the same kind of beauty as Greer Garson. And, she's very good at doing small things with her face and eyes.

Throughout *The House of Mirth*, the specific ways that Davies frames shots (respectful closeups and poised two-shots) and the way that the camera alternates between remaining static and delivering slow, lingering pans create the sense of intimacy that is, in part, Davies's signature. Davies's past work is also praised for its use of music. Often operating ironically, music heightens the sentient intensity of a scene or amplifies—complicates—meaning. Davies chooses popular or well-known songs that we cannot help but associate with other experiences. This causes meaning to ramify in curious ways. Most notably in *The House of Mirth* is his use of Mozart's well-known "Cosi fan tutti."

DAVIES: *When I knew that there had to be a transition from America at the end of the season to Monte Carlo it had to be something that had all that yearning for hope that had been dashed. That aria has it: two young women, wanting their lovers to come back. But also a transition from a rain-soaked Hudson River to that wonderful light upon the Mediterranean water, just full with sensuality and implied sex. I wanted all that and I found that "Cosi" had it.*

You are the sum of all you hear and see. I grew up on what then were called—ter-ribly, I can see now—"women's pictures," which my sisters took me to and which I loved, as well: All That Heaven Allows *[1955],* Magnificent Obsession *[1954], and* Love Is a Many-Splendored Thing *[1955]. Shlock! But absolutely wonderful! Of course, I was influenced by them; they went into the psyche and came out refracted. Again, if I could use a musical analogy, it's like the "trill" in eighteenth-century music, particu-larly Mozart. It begins as decoration, but by the time you hear it in Mahler it has be-come very dark, full of angst, but it's still a trill. So are all the things in your own psy-che. I did love all those old movies. They went into my psyche and came out refracted and distorted in some way. Many of them were very well crafted, visually succinct, even though they were very sentimental.*

A very non-sentimental aspect of Wharton's writing is the anti-Semitism which exists throughout the society of *The House of Mirth*. However, the film makes no reference to this social sickness that Wharton's novel exposes. Why?

DAVIES: *I found the anti-Semitism the most dispiriting thing about Wharton's work, in her later novels, as well. I deleted it. I simply could not bring myself to write it or to direct an actor to do it.*

While Davies fully omitted any reference to anti-Semitism, he added the most wonderfully abrupt and unforeseen moments of humor: visual and verbal wit—pure waggery, comic flourishes, and sly camera-flirtations with naughti-ness.

DAVIES: *The humor? My own—even the dialogue! Score: Lions one, Christians zero.*

While the humor is largely Davies's, the movie is allegiant to the plot de-tails of Wharton's novel. Exceptions to this would be: 1) that the characters of Gerty Farish and Carrie Fisher are combined into a composite; 2) that Lawrence Selden lacks the complex shading and governing plot value that he has in the book; 3) and, that a scene is inserted (which is not in Wharton's novel) in which Lily Bart, at the "end of her tether," tries to blackmail Bertha Dorset with the love letters that she had written to Lawrence Selden. This last change will incite the most contentious challenge to the film made by loyalists to the book.

In the novel, Lily will not stoop to extortion, even though to do so would save her. She will not respond in kind to the avaricious, insidious, cruelty of her world. In Wharton's work, the finest quality in Lily's character triumphs; and, while she does die, what is most significant in Lily is not destroyed by her soci-ety's malignancy. In the film, it is. In adding this scene (i.e., Lily going to the Dorsets' home, with the clear intention of extorting them), the film, arguably, al-ters not only Wharton's character, but also the final pronouncement that Whar-ton is using that character to deliver. The change that the movie makes is a curi-ous one, an alteration made more radical because it is inserted in a film that is so otherwise respectful of the novel, as literally written. When Davies was writing the screenplay, did he see the inclusion of that scene as a radical departure from the novel?

DAVIES: *No, I don't think it is. But, reading a novel is not the same as watching images that pass before you at 24-frames-per-second. It is a different experience. [In film] we have a charging story—images rushing forward—and we cannot turn back and reread something that may have been confusing. That added scene clarifies the drama. The whole point of drama is to make us empathize—in this case, with what is, essentially, a tragic story. In tragedy certain small things happen. In tragedy, it's always the small things. For me it felt right that she has the letters and then she goes there, and—a seemingly small thing—they're out. They're not there. There is something extraordinarily moving in that, for, had she gone the day before, they would have been home. The consequence of that is that, having pitched herself up to blackmail—something she wouldn't have done well anyway—she realizes that the moment is gone. The moment—the one in all our lives when we either catch something or we have to let it go. And it's never repeated, which is why she throws the letters on the fire. Which is also not in Wharton, either. I wrote that in. It's a kind of resignation because she thinks, if I had done it, I would have ruined him [Lawrence Selden], socially, and I love him too much. Fate conspires to make the Dorsets away. I thought that was a good cinematic bit of poetic license.*

I also asked Stewart about the added scene.

STEWART: *When you watch that scene and you know that she is going to the Dorsets, you assume that they are going to be there; and when they are not, it is so tragic. In going there, I don't think she loses the moral high ground. I think she becomes human. A lot of people's reaction [to Lily] is that she is not that sympathetic. The whole thing about it is that the process is humanizing. And, it plays with your own moral position. You, yourself are conflicted. You admire her [for her moral high ground], but you also desperately want her to do something about saving herself. And most modern audiences would say, "Why doesn't she just help herself?" But when she tries to, she is inept, incapable of looking after herself. That is one of the things that Terry shows; but, more so, he shows the tragedy. And, first and foremost,* The House of Mirth *is a tragedy.*

Wharton, herself, may even have concurred, as is evident in the tragic deterioration and death of her protagonist, Lily Bart.

In a letter written to her friend, Dr. Morgan Dix (rector of Trinity Church in Manhattan), who had just read *The House of Mirth* and had suggested that her novel was a "terrible but just arraignment" of "social misconduct," Wharton stated: "No novel worth anything can be anything but a novel 'with a purpose,'& if anyone who cared for the moral issue did not see in my work that I care for it, I should have no one to blame but myself."[4]

However, what is the "moral issue" in Wharton's novel? For the filmmakers of *The House of Mirth,* the moral issue is the tragic consequences of that "social misconduct." They show how beneath the lovely veneer of gentility, rectitude, and refinement is a rapacious and grasping, immoral and self-interested junta, which annihilates anyone who threatens its status quo. Throughout the film of *The House of Mirth*, society is a visually lovely, but insidious and treacherous, infirmity of destruction, one that is corrupt and, even more lamentable, corrupting. The strength of the Davies/Stewart film is its resolute boldness in showing the fullness of the destruction that that society causes: it indifferently lays to ruin Lily's innate decency.

In having Lily attempt to extort Bertha with the love letters, something she resists doing in the book (she will not compromise her moral code), the film accomplishes what it sees as the "purpose" of Wharton's novel, its "moral issue." It lays to view the tragic, vile power that a vile society has to waste and ruin that which is good. The filmmakers' interpretation of *The House of Mirth*, even while it is so respectful of the details of Wharton's novel, is not a traditional one, and it may not jibe with most readers' views; but it will guide them, intelligently, to an alternate way of thinking about Wharton's novel, insisting—as perhaps all great film translations of literature should do—that we consider other legitimate ways of reading the book in addition to our own.

The House of Mirth, in keeping with Terence Davies's other films and Olivia Stewart's collaborative importance to them, is a thought-filled work, one alternately joy-filled and sorrow-saturated in its understanding of human nature. The screenplay is a fascinating work on its own. Incorporating approximately two-thirds of Wharton's writing and one third of Davies's own, its dialogue is a seamless integration; and, while written in words, the screenplay is predominantly visual, permeated by choice visual cues.

The design of the movie, itself, is handsomely exacting—wonderfully meticulous—often classical and balanced in its construction, with the kind of beauty—fine, elegant, and subtle compositions—that imprints on memory.

"Your film is intelligent and lovely, and I am sure that people are going to like it very much," I told Davies.

The normally loquacious Davies did not say a word. He just smiled at me, quietly looked up through his glasses, and then he laughed, roundly, a laugh filled with good-natured mirth.

NOTES

1. Jason Solomons, "Film Weekly" podcast: Interview with Terence Davies, *The Guardian*, 12 December 2007.

2. Trevor Johnston, "Even my therapist hates my father now: *The House of Mirth* is new territory for director Terence Davies," *The Independent*, 1 October 2000, 2 (Culture).

3. Stewart worked as a production assistant on *Distant Voices* and then progressed to unit production manager on *Still Lives*. Although released together, the two films were shot more than a year apart. She was the producer of *The Long Day Closes* and *The Neon Bible*.

4. R. W. B. Lewis and Nancy Lewis Wharton, ed., *The Letters of Edith Wharton* (New York: Simon & Schuster, 1988), 98–99.

Patricia Rozema

I liked that it wasn't just another tea party . . . I liked the implied
parallel between the captivity of women and the captivity of slaves.

*H*iba Moussa's interview with Patricia Rozema focuses on the director's adaptation of *Mansfield Park* (1999), a film released in a wave of Austen adaptations, a few years after the especially ostentatious display of period mise-en-scène in the six-hour BBC television series of *Pride and Prejudice* (1995). In its stylistic economy and comparatively understated mise-en-scène, Rozema's film echoes Roger Michell's *Persuasion* (1995) and Ang Lee's *Sense and Sensibility* (1995) as well as anticipating Joe Wright's more recent *Pride and Prejudice* (2005).

Rozema's films (such as *When Night Is Falling* [1995] and *I've Heard the Mermaids Singing* [1987]) tend to focus on the emotionally-charged, explicitly creative experiences of women. Her *Mansfield Park* self-consciously represents the central character of Fanny as a writer, performing the implicit "author function" of Austen within the film as well as being a kind of stand-in for the female *auteur*, one who (like Rozema's camera) is able to stand "outside" her immediate context to observe the sometimes condemnable other characters. The tone of Rozema's film is consistently one of detached compassion (in the way of Lee's *Sense and Sensibility*) rather than of romanticization. She probes the ideologically disturbing backstories of the characters' upper-class lives, foregrounding (in her words) Austen's "implied parallel between the captivity of women and the captivity of slaves" upon which the hegemonic order of imperialism depends.

In this interview Rozema specifically mentions the influence of Edward Said's essay, "Jane Austen and Empire," which highlights issues of the slave trade referred to in the novel. Said's post-colonial reading of the text has, like Rozema's film, been criticized as anachronistic as well as misleading because Austen's novel makes little direct reference to the slave trade, focusing attention much more explicitly on the bildungsroman of Fanny. In an article on *Mansfield Park* for *JASNA* (*Jane Austen Society of North America*), for instance, Melissa Burns concludes that Said's analysis perverts understanding of Austen's text through adopting a "twentieth-century perspective" in weaving *Mansfield Park* "into a debate to which [it] does not solidly belong."[1] Such criticism is implicitly answered through Rozema's argument that "interpretation is impossible to avoid." Furthermore, Rozema's unsentimental and candid approach to adapting Austen might be seen as an important corrective to prettified adaptations of Austen which gloss over the social realities Austen is famous for confronting (albeit with irony): a prime example is the most recent, mainstream adaptation of *Emma* (1996). Like this version of *Emma*, a fanciful new film about Jane Austen's private life (entitled *Becoming Jane* [2007]) feeds the romanticized cult of personality surrounding the author, insulating her experience as well as her words. Conversely, Rozema's film interrogates the discomforting social and cultural truths of Austen's upper-class characters in *Mansfield Park* without forfeiting irony or compassion or love in her telling of the story. The reprinting of Moussa's interview is thus a timely reminder of Rozema's under-discussed film.

Interview by Hiba Moussa
Originally published as "Mansfield Park and Film: An Interview with Patricia Rozema," Literature/Film Quarterly *32, no. 4 (October 2004): 255–60.*

Patricia Rozema is a Canadian film director whose adaptation of Jane Austen's *Mansfield Park* produced a torrent of varying receptions, ambivalent at best, denigrating at worst. The novel itself is not highly popular with Austen readers/critics and it was adapted only once for the BBC and broadcast as a miniseries in 1983 before Rozema released her vision of the novel on film in 1999. This interview is meant to interrogate the choices behind her clearly politicized interpretation of the story. Since she is both the screenwriter and director of the film production, Rozema embodies an interesting case of the reading, envisioning, and rewriting process of literary classics like Austen's and representing them in the twentieth century's most popular medium, the cinema, which has its own methods of communication. In this interview, I investigate Rozema's reading of the text, the ideological stances that informed, affected, or shaped her reading experience, and her position in relation to the issue of fidelity to the original text, which is still at the core of any critical assessment or indeed general reception of film adaptations of classic/canonic works of literature.

Our dialogue took place through written correspondence and I received the answers to my questions in March 2003, when Rozema was busy working on a film and I was still researching Austen and film adaptations in England. I hope this interview sheds some light on the stages of filming *Mansfield Park* and highlights some of the central issues regarding film adaptation in general, and that of Austen's novel in particular.

MOUSSA: What factors do you think make a book adaptable?

ROZEMA: The moral core of the piece needs to be built into the turns of events themselves, not just the prose description of those events. Some novels declare themselves in their interpretation of events and some, the ones that are more easily adapted, declare themselves in the very fabric of the causal relations.

MOUSSA: How much do socio-historical circumstances, whether those shaping the time you read the book or the time the book was produced, affect your reading and understanding of a novel?

ROZEMA: They affect me very much. In fact, that is what I added to *Mansfield Park*, the movie. I felt like we couldn't fully understand Austen's subtle statement about captivity if we didn't know that the issue of slavery was raging in every home in Britain at the time. And I felt morally obligated to explain that the extraordinary amount of leisure time these people enjoyed was purchased with the sweat and blood of slaves in the West Indies.

MOUSSA: Do you think that studying literature at a university prepared you for the role of adapter and do you think that it is a prerequisite for a successfully well-informed screenplay?

ROZEMA: The more you know about different parts of life, the richer your work can be. Acquiring some analytical skills around novels definitely helps.

MOUSSA: What is the main purpose behind adapting literary classics in your opinion?

ROZEMA: To examine stories that bear re-examination. Tales that are rich in humanity need to be re-interpreted. Re-fashioning them into a different media expands the complexity of our understanding. Collective re-awakening.

MOUSSA: How important is fidelity to the original text when you want to adapt it?

ROZEMA: Fidelity is critical. The movie should have a different title if it serves an entirely different purpose than the original text. But you cannot underestimate what a radical thing it is to change from one art form to another. An author slaves to start with just the right word, phrase, sentence, and paragraph. The sounds of the words are crucial. But all the demands of words and prose are lifted when you make a movie. The physical presence makes many unnecessary and some necessary ones impossible. So you serve two masters as an adapting filmmaker: the author's intention and the needs of film. Sometimes "fidelity" can mean only focusing on one day of a story told over twenty years in a book. That said, I do sometimes think that if I had changed the title just slightly to say "Letters of Mansfield Park" or "Mansfield Park Revisited," I could have saved myself some grief and managed to get people just to look at it as a movie first and then evaluate its relationship to the original text second.

MOUSSA: What kind of changes do you make when rewriting the text?

ROZEMA: I make the written word conform to habits of speech. Shorter sentences mostly.

MOUSSA: Do you think that reading a novel and re-presenting it from a post-modern point of view and culture entail the risk of imposing meanings and implications that are foreign to the novelist and the novel itself?

ROZEMA: Yes. But the whole enterprise is a "risk." But some stories need to be retold, over and over and over again, with this spin and then that. Fairytales are changing all the time. The strongest, most important ones will be retold with postmodern and then post-postmodern interpretations. Interpretation is impossible to avoid. It must be openly declared by the filmmakers (writer and director) but "imposing meaning" is impossible to avoid—just selecting the moments we do from a novel is a form of imposed meaning. The effort must be made not to run counter to the novelist's intent, but then the fact of interpretation must be embraced.

MOUSSA: *Mansfield Park* as a literary adaptation makes, in my opinion, the least interesting of all Austen's novels a most interesting film version. What made you choose *Mansfield Park*?

ROZEMA: Thank you. I was attracted to the open acknowledgment of slavery in the novel. I felt like I could bring something new to the canon of Austen movies. I liked that it wasn't just another tea party. I felt for Fanny, the injustice with which she is treated right from the start. I liked the implied parallel between the captivity of women and the captivity of slaves.

MOUSSA: Some critics think that *Mansfield Park* is difficult to adapt to film mainly because of the nature of its tone and its main character. What problems did you encounter with the text when writing the screenplay and what risks were you bearing in mind when adapting it?

ROZEMA: I did think that the character as written would be too slight and retiring and internal and perhaps judgmental to shoulder a film. So instead of just arbitrarily adding contemporary characteristics to her personality, I became obsessed with Austen herself. I wanted to know everything about her intentions and journey as a writer. It was clear that *Mansfield Park* was a hugely autobiographical work so I thought I'd add some of the "teller into the tale." I would include Austen, as I understood her, into the character. I tried not to change her behavior in interaction with others. I just allowed the audience into a privileged place inside her mind by making her a writer. *Mansfield Park* without any alteration would make a lousy film. I knew that. But I thought if I could include just a few things I knew about the period and about the author, it would be fascinating. That was the goal.

MOUSSA: Did you read the book as a literary critic, a screenwriter, or a director?

ROZEMA: As a human being.

MOUSSA: To what extent does your identity (nationality, gender, and class) affect your reading and presentation of this classic text?

ROZEMA: I connected to her as a woman. I connected to her experience of starting out life poor and ending up rich (my personal history). I connected to her rage about not being considered central to the real social story. I connected to her insecurity around more educated and elegant individuals. I felt like she was a barely noticed Canadian at a British function.

MOUSSA: Why do you think Austen is so popular for contemporary audiences and for screenwriters?

ROZEMA: She's one of the best writers in the English language. She understands people. She's extremely funny and her stories are exquisitely structured. Everyone can find themselves in her stories. She tells "romances" but with such an unsentimental voice that we never feel tarnished. We will always be concerned with who sleeps with and marries whom, but without all her economic, psychological, and social layering, it would be mere soap opera.

MOUSSA: How did you assimilate your role as a director and screenwriter when you were writing the screenplay, especially in relation to the specific and different natures of film and novel?

ROZEMA: I have a short memory. I write it, then as a director I execute the writer's plan. Once in a while I change but I trust what I came up with in the quiet contemplative moments more than the hurly-burly of the set. I just try to make it authentic in every way, even the magic.

MOUSSA: The film obviously adopts and presents a political voice, specifically feminist and postcolonial, and you mentioned before that you read some criticisms of the novel before re-writing it. Did you read Edward Said's essay, "Jane Austen and Empire," on the novel before writing the script?

ROZEMA: Yes, I was very influenced by him. I don't think, however, that Austen was as unaware of her imperialism as he suggests. I do agree with him that *Mansfield Park* is more about Antigua than it is about England.

MOUSSA: Did you think of your audience when writing the screenplay *Mansfield Park* and visualizing it from a director's point of view?

ROZEMA: Yes and no. I just try to please myself and hope that I'm normal enough that it will please others. I knew it could function for some merely on the domestic romantic comedy level and for others more like myself on a political level. I try to make it simple and strong and true for those who don't wish to know that there is really sugar on the pill.

MOUSSA: Did you make any changes in the script while the film was being shot? In other words, were there any scenes that looked good on paper but were disappointing in live action and had to be changed?

ROZEMA: Not really. I stuck pretty much to the plan. The only big change was going back two months after principal photography had ended and shooting the scene with Sir Thomas Bertram (Harold Pinter) confessing the error of his ways to his dying son, Tom. We felt we needed that resolution otherwise the issue of slavery was never really addressed or completed. What I had originally thought was just a kind of social theme that was always present (the slavery accents) somehow became a subplot and needed resolution. That is what that scene was.

MOUSSA: The film has received varied reactions among academic critics. How would you react to some who think this is a completely "unfaithful" version or "against the spirit of Austen" or "not in tune with the novel?"

ROZEMA: I would disagree. It is definitely a free and openly interpretive version but I think that if Austen came back as a filmmaker in 1999, she might have adapted her novel into a film in the same way I did. I believe that.

MOUSSA: I see the film as an academic rather than mainstream adaptation of Austen's novel (mainly because I could feel a theoretical spirit in it). Do you think that makes it slightly elitist? And how does that reflect on its popularity or status?

ROZEMA: I don't think of it as academic. I'm not an academic. It is informed by my research and theory but no, I intended it to be a tale told from one heart to another.

MOUSSA: To what extent do you think Harold Pinter's presence in the film added to its critical/academic tone, if it did at all?

ROZEMA: He probably lent it a little credibility with some; his presence might have alerted some to the film's political leanings. But he's not a big draw in suburban mall culture.

MOUSSA: The film is being used in seminars on the novel in universities and colleges teaching Austen, especially in relation to postcolonial theory. To what extent do you think your version is also useful for educational purposes and how do you feel about adaptations playing that role?

ROZEMA: I feel honored. I think it is quite useful educationally partly because one is forced to read the novel. I don't pretend to have redone the novel (as some filmmakers absurdly claim) in film. I think both the film and the novel are rich territory for postcolonial theory.

Moussa: Was Mansfield Park's first appearance to Fanny as "Gothic" meant to contribute to its dark and mysterious side or to the tradition of the novel in Austen's time?

Rozema: Both.

Moussa: Why did you put the responsibility on Tom (rather than the more "moral" Edmund) to illuminate the dark side of Mansfield Park and its owner?

Rozema: It would have been Tom's struggle as the eldest. Would he follow in his father's footsteps?

Moussa: What future do you envision for Susie as Fanny's successor in the main house?

Rozema: Questioner of established suppositions.

Moussa: The film's end, interestingly, is not a closure in the traditional sense. How does that relate to Austen's neat closing of the narrative and what does yours aim to achieve or say about the consequent lives of the characters?

Rozema: Hmmm. I think it's actually quite a traditional ending. The flying about with the camera was meant to embody that suddenly distant tone Austen takes when she sums everything up. Perhaps I don't understand.

Moussa: Do you think Sir Thomas repents at the end despite the fact that he is investing in a newer and surely milder form of enslavement, that of tobacco?

Rozema: It's a partial redemption for jolly old England. Slavery may have been abolished but there were lots of other imperialistic shenanigans after that. That line was me trying to not tie things up quite so sweetly.

Moussa: If you were to adapt another Austen novel, which one would you choose and why?

Rozema: I wouldn't. I think I did the most interesting one. And I think that most of the others really should be read and not watched.

Moussa: Would you consider other literary classics to adapt? If yes, which ones and why?

Rozema: Yes, *The Picture of Dorian Gray*. But I haven't figured out how yet.

Moussa: As a cinematic product, did you ever think of the film as a risk in terms of reception and box office returns?

Rozema: I try to make a film that engages people I respect—then I let the gods and the distributors have their wicked way with the thing.

Moussa: Were you involved in the casting and what aspects in terms of actors/actresses did you think were crucial for the success of the film?

Rozema: I was totally responsible (in consultation with my producers) for the casting.

Moussa: Did the producers want any changes done to the original draft/script?

ROZEMA: It was too long at first and I had to cut a million pounds out of the budget just before shooting so that made me become more and more economical and eliminate any experimental scenes. I was lucky to have extremely smart and literate producers: David Aukin, Allon Reich, Sarah Curtis, and Harvey Weinstein.

MOUSSA: What conditions affected the production most?

ROZEMA: Chance. Weather. Actors' moods and love lives. Jonny Lee Miller was divorcing Angelina Jolie and not very happy about it. Frances O'Connor was separated from her long-term boyfriend and open to romantic negotiation, shall we say. Harold raged about all the waiting. The weather rarely cooperated. The size of the cast made quick changes or rethinks very hard, it was like steering a big ocean liner. I wanted to use starlings in Portsmouth but they are of nervous disposition and probably would have died in the boxes, so we used white homing pigeons but the animal wrangler somehow got stuck with non-homing pigeons and they just stayed there, on our set. Also the language itself had to be checked and double-checked for historical accuracy so there was no ad libbing. I got meningitis during the shoot and everything had to be shut down for a time while I recovered in hospital. Various amusing issues like that.

NOTE

1. Melissa Burns, "Jane Austen's *Mansfield Park*: Determining Authorial Intention," *Persuasions On-line* 26, no. 4, http://www.jasna.org/persuasions/on-line/vol26no1/burns.htm (30 July 2007).

Richard Linklater

> What I think I'm always going through in that process is that magi-
> cal moment in filmmaking where the text and the ideas and the con-
> cepts of the movie meet in the people who are physically manifest-
> ing them.

*W*hen thinking of the sensibility of director Richard Linklater, it's almost impossible not to invoke his first major feature, *Slacker* (1991). The meandering
conversations, the marginal characters, the willingness to push the medium's
potential, especially through long takes and tracking shots, and the tonal shifts
from humor to tragedy (and back again) are all qualities that mark a Linklater
film. And yet, when one examines his body of work, one sees a director constantly pushing that sensibility into new ground, whether it's the high-school
nostalgia of *Dazed and Confused* (1993), the claustrophobic interrogation of
Tape (2001), the youthful romance of *Before Sunrise* (1995) and the more complicated reunion of *Before Sunset* (2004), the trippy, philosophical mindbender
of *Waking Life* (2001), or the mainstream comedies of *The School of Rock* (2003)
and *The Bad News Bears* (2005). In short, while calling something a Linklater
film may not define a subject or genre, it's likely to indicate a film that has a
genuine curiosity for the world and for the cinema, as well as a compassion for
all of its characters, especially those to which the cinema—and the world—
rarely gives enough.

In 2006, Linklater released two adaptations: *A Scanner Darkly*, based on the
Philip K. Dick novel, and *Fast Food Nation*, based on the nonfiction book by Eric
Schlosser. Late in the summer of 2006, David T. Johnson spoke with the direc-
tor about his adaptation of *A Scanner Darkly*.

Interview by David T. Johnson
Originally published as "Directors on Adaptation: A Conversation with Richard Linklater,"
Literature/Film Quarterly *35, no. 1 (January 2007): 338–41.*

JOHNSON: Could you talk about when you first came across the text and why it made such an impression on you?

LINKLATER: I . . . um . . . wow. Let's see . . . I got to Philip K. Dick kind of late. You know, I wish I could say I started reading him as a teenager or something like a lot of people I've met along the way, but I really didn't. I wasn't a big science fiction guy (or I put him in that category). I caught up to Philip K. Dick in my mid-twenties—a girl tried to give me *VALIS*, and I had heard about him for a long time and I'd seen *Blade Runner* [1982], so I really didn't have any excuses. [*Laughs.*] So I read *VALIS*, which is an interesting one to start with, and then I started working backwards and forwards and picking up more, so it's kind of a blur—I read *Scanner* in there somewhere. But I didn't think of it as a movie—I really didn't. And even of all of those, I wasn't thinking any of them were movie ideas, probably because at that point I was not at that phase of making my own movies, really. I mean, I was working on my very early movies—the idea of adapting a Philip K. Dick [book] was so far from me. I remember it was Wiley Wiggins [on the set of *Waking Life*] . . . saying he thought *Scanner* would actually make a really great movie . . . and so I went back and read it . . . , and I just saw it from a whole different perspective, [one] that was much more adult, reflective. Having lived through a lot more of my life, it was more poignant to me as an autobiographical piece about loss—something I couldn't quite relate to in my early or mid-twenties. It resonated with me at this point; it felt more important, now that I figured out who I was as a filmmaker. You know, I felt like, that's a movie I could make—I felt like it was mine to make, in fact. The view of the book is my view of the world too—very comedic and very tragic.

JOHNSON: That brings to mind the end where you reproduce Philip K. Dick's "Author's Note" about the people he's lost in his life.

LINKLATER: I thought that was very important to keep that in there. I had to fight to keep that in the movie.

JOHNSON: Oh really?

LINKLATER: Yeah, you know—a lot of people don't get it. Not people personally but people who are thinking for other people—i.e. executive types in Hollywood. But I don't know, I felt that that really hit home that these were real people in his life and in all of our lives. I said everyone who works on the film had their own list, and we all do. We all do. You can't live too long in this culture and not be acquiring your own list of casualties who you feel in an almost unfair way went way too soon.

JOHNSON: The next thing I want to ask you about is the setting of Anaheim, California. Why do you think that's an important setting both for the novel and for your film?

LINKLATER: Well, I've never lived there, and as far as I can tell, it's a very different city than when he [Dick] lived there in the seventies. But, I think Anaheim and the other cities referred to, Santa Ana and things like that, I think that they have a place in the American psyche. Anaheim, Disneyland, Orange County—it seems like ground zero of something in the US psyche, I'm not sure what—some kind of straight world. . . . [It's] interesting he would live there. He spent time in the Bay area of course, but I always found it fascinating that he lived there. Wasn't it J. G. Ballard that lived in the suburbs of London? I mean, people think I'm strange—I live in Texas. But I always found it interesting that he lived there. And often, I saw pictures of crappy little apartments and places like that, but that was home, you know, for him. I just felt it was important to honor that because that's where the autobiography was, and I felt that it still holds up today.

JOHNSON: In thinking about that biography, I know you worked with [Dick's] daughters a good bit. What were those initial meetings like?

LINKLATER: They were always very supportive. I think they wanted to meet me and talk to me about it because this book in particular—they knew how personal it was to their father, and they treated it differently than just optioning one of his 120 stories that people want to buy and make movies out of. This one, I could tell meant more to them. . . . They had read the script and we were sort of heading down the road, but we didn't have the total signoff or anything—so I flew up to the Bay Area and met with them. And they're really wonderful ladies. And [Isa Hackett] pointed at my script, and she said, "I'm really so glad that you left this in"—she was pointing to the dedication at the end. And she goes, "Just so you know, this was my father," because [Dick] put himself on the list, but then she goes up the list and goes, "Oh, and this was my mother." I was like, *O-kay*. And then I could only deduce that of course she was one of those little girls who lived in that house. . . . She visited the set when we were shooting—you know, [the daughters] were around as much as they wanted to be. But they visited the set, and I said, "Is this your house?" And [Isa] goes, "Yeah, I lived here. We moved out, and those guys moved in!"

JOHNSON: Well let me talk a little bit about the rehearsal process with you. In past interviews I know you've talked about that process being fairly consistent and also involving a fair amount of collaboration with your actors.

LINKLATER: Yeah, absolutely. The script is a really good place to start, and the story is the same—we didn't change any major architectural aspects of the structure of the story. But what we did and what I think I'm always going through in that process is that magical moment in filmmaking where the text and the ideas and the concepts of the movie meet in the people who are physically manifesting them. And when you cast a movie correctly—and in this case, energetically, with these creative collaborators like Robert Downey Jr., Woody Harrelson, Keanu [Reeves], Winona [Ryder]—I mean, they all brought a lot to it. You wouldn't get this cast and then tell them to say their lines and hit their mark the way you wanted them to. I wasn't interested in that. I really wanted them to collaborate. And so, to varying degrees, they all jumped in in-character and contributed quite a bit. . . .You know, we added a lot more about New Path, I thought we had to make that clearer, and Downey really had a lot to say. It was fun to work with him on his character because he had a lot of ideas; he could think big about the whole movie and his character. I'd say, "Well, we've got to really make it clear, even though Freck isn't going to hear you, necessarily—you're on two different wave-lengths here—[but] what you say, I think, is very important. It needs to resonate within the movie that you're onto them—you're onto everybody. You're onto Arctor; you're onto New Path. You're smart. And they're onto you."

JOHNSON: Well, [these actors] seem to have great chemistry. I'm thinking about the bicycle-gear scene especially.

LINKLATER: Yeah, that scene is its own little set piece. And I think that's the kind of scene that would be cut out of a traditional adaptation or a traditional movie. And it almost got cut out of my movie. I mean, I never wanted it to—I felt it was such an essential scene—but it's one of those scenes you have to fight for. Because people could say, "I know it's a funny scene, but we could cut it for the sake of pacing, and you wouldn't miss it. . . . It doesn't move the plot along, it doesn't advance the storytelling." So much of Hollywood screenwriting and storytelling is all about keeping a highly toned or a sharply structured story. You're supposed to chip along, one thing into the next, everything important, you know—all that by-the-book storytelling. But I've always been allergic to that, especially in a piece like this that's so fundamentally a character piece. A scene like that says so much about our characters and the environment they live in and the mutual wavelength they all exist on that binds them together. So that [scene] seems in a way essential—not in a narrative sense but in terms of the overall movie, as a character piece.

JOHNSON: I know you've talked a lot about your influences in the past with some of the '60s arthouse cinema, particularly when you were first discovering film. Do you find yourself going back to certain filmmakers, or do you find you want to discover new ones? Or is it a combination of both?

LINKLATER: You know, my cinematic thinking over the years—it just changes. . . . It's just like literature, or something you read in your early to mid-twenties meant something to you, now in my mid-forties I read something and it's like, wow, it's a whole new book to me, just like it's a whole new movie. . . . And your appreciation can go up even more or down—you know, you see it in a different way. You can't help but see it in a different way. It's kind of an endless lifetime project of trying to see as many great films that are out there. I've got a thirteen-year-old now—we watch movies together, so it's fun to see things through her eyes as she's discovering movies. We watched *Vertigo* [1958], and we watched *3 Women* [1977] this weekend. She's catching up with things I think she's vaguely ready for but she's really interested in it. So it's fun to visit these films anew. But that said, I think anyone who loves movies is open to inspiration from anywhere you get it. You know, I've always enjoyed all kinds of movies—I'll watch documentaries, I'll watch films from all over the world—pretty much whatever you can get your hands on, whatever is out there. I'm not too systematic about it.

JOHNSON: Are there any specific filmmakers right now that you feel are under-appreciated?

LINKLATER: Maybe I don't have the right perspective on that, about under-appreciated, you know, I don't know. But I think that the fact that if you're even getting films made means you must be appreciated on some level by somebody or you wouldn't get to make films. [*Laughs.*] I think the under-appreciated ones are the really talented people who aren't getting to make films at all, for whatever reason. So that would be under-appreciation. You know, people have put me in that category a few times. They'll say, [*imitating someone else*], "Why aren't you bigger?" I'm like, you know, I know a lot of people who would kill to be in my position, so I feel like I'm doing just great. No complaints here.

JOHNSON: [Going back to *A Scanner Darkly*,] did your sense of the novel change as you found yourself working through the film—through the process of making the film?

LINKLATER: Well, certainly, the adaptation was probably trickier than it looks on the surface. It was a tonal issue more than anything. . . . Once I decided, in the spirit of the novel . . . to reflect our present moment—and I feel like the subject matter very much reflects our present moment—but then set it in this near future, this vague "seven years from now"—once I decided to do that, then it was a process of culling out, I would say, getting it set in this century a little more. . . . You know, Philip K. Dick had had some pretty bad rehab experiences at one place, and I think he based a lot of New Path on that. And I think the tone [of rehabilitation] has changed a lot from back then—I forget what that was called—where they reduce you, they're really rude to you, and all that. We're so much more of a touchy-feely world right now—they're no better for you now than they were back then—but they just do it with a different tone, so I changed that a little bit. [Now] New Path would have a smilier face attached to them but [be] equally evil. More evil. I think we have more examples in our culture right now of this kind of quasi-governmental, public/private institution, kind of a Halliburton-esque type company.

. . . [In general], it's truly scary, the kind of rhetoric that comes up, but it's all couched in such terms that if you're not thinking at all, which they're kind of counting on. It sounds good, and you can go about your day okay about stuff. Someone's in charge, someone's taking care of it, we're good. Someone's counting on you really not having any analytical ability, and I think they count on about sixty percent of the population being in that category. Whether it's ability or interest—I won't say ability, because that implies people are stupid, which I don't think they are. I just think it's interest. They don't want to know.

JOHNSON: Let me ask you one last question. Are there any other adaptations that you'd be interested in doing for a future project—things you've had on the back burner for a while or things that have been floating around in your head for a while? I know you've got *Fast Food Nation* [2006] coming out this year.

LINKLATER: There was one thing I was working on—I don't know if it's going to happen or not, I hope it will. It's called *Last Flag Flying*—it's a follow-up to the book [Signet Books, 1971] and the movie, *The Last Detail* [1973], written in the late sixties. So it's the same three guys, thirty-four years later. The author, Dale Thompson, wrote a follow-up novel that addresses the Iraq war and what happened to those three guys and what they're doing now. It's really fascinating . . . they end up on a similar road trip for very different reasons, and you just kind of catch up. It's three old guys hanging out—it's my kind of movie!

Baz Luhrmann

Shakespeare wrote for everyone, from the street sweeper to the
Queen of England: they all had to get it. And it's why I revere him
so much as a story-teller because he was dealing with a supremely
alive, real audience, who had to be absolutely and totally arrested
into the story. They didn't come quietly.

Interview by Elsie M. Walker

Baz Luhrmann has made three films to date: *Strictly Ballroom* (1991), *William
Shakespeare's Romeo and Juliet* (1996) and *Moulin Rouge!* (2001). These films, mar-
keted as the "Red Curtain Trilogy," have already established Luhrmann's status as
one of the foremost Australian *auteurs*. The films are united through their combination of theatricality and cinematic complexity, the audaciously postmodern
exuberance of their mise-en-scènes, their emphasis on musical eclecticism
(though only *Moulin Rouge!* is identified as a musical), and their emphasis on self-
conscious storytelling. The films are also united in self-consciously, paradoxically
combining excessive materialism and self-evident commercial imperatives with
nostalgic, high Romanticism. *Romeo and Juliet* is one of the most financially successful Shakespearean adaptations to date,[1] yet the film itself applauds belief in the
fundamental value of love "beyond the market."[2]

This interview took place on July 9, 2000, when I met Luhrmann at the
headquarters of his production company Bazmark: the House of Iona in Sydney,
Australia. He had finished post-production work on *Moulin Rouge!* for the day:
the interview was at approximately 10 at night. When I arrived at the luminously
lit House of Iona I found myself standing before two enormous iron gates. Given

my short stature, I was intimidated by the intercom system that was positioned above my eye-line. I was about to stand on tip-toe to announce my arrival when the gates silently, mysteriously, and slowly opened before me: I realized that someone unseen had seen my approach. There was a pale round face at the window: the face of, as I learnt later, Luhrmann's assistant affectionately know as "Dubsy." I made it down a cobbled path, like something from *The Wizard of Oz* (1939), lined with extraordinary foliage and a prominent palm tree. Dubsy opened the enormous front door and escorted me through a main entrance hall with a massive staircase reminiscent of the one featured in the Capulet mansion of Luhrmann's *Romeo and Juliet*. He then led me to a room with bright red walls, velvet-covered sofas with splendidly-detailed cushions (like props in *Moulin Rouge!*), and walls featuring shiny awards for *Strictly Ballroom* and *Romeo and Juliet*. I was dwarfed by the splendor of the room which was itself like a kind of set. Luhrmann then entered, wearing an immaculate brown suit and a Yankees baseball cap. The sheer opulence of the House of Iona, the almost performative display of objects within it, along with the apparently studied paradox of Luhrmann's dress (the informal accessory with a suit) led me to expect a performance from Luhrmann that would make it difficult for me to get the candid, unrehearsed responses I wanted. While Luhrmann made versions of several comments I had already read or heard in other interviews, he was exceptionally generous in his excitable and exciting responses to my questions about *Romeo and Juliet*, particularly questions concerned with tonal complexity and music which had not been discussed in previous interviews.

My transcript of the interview reflects Luhrmann's multi-clause, rapid-fire and multi-directional speaking rhythm. His speech seemed almost as quick as the editing of his films. He described various processes involved in the making of *Romeo and Juliet*: selling the idea to financial backers, pitching the film for a contemporary young audience, self-consciously translating Shakespeare's words in visual and contemporary terms, making a stylistically ambitious film reflective of Shakespearean tonal complexity, and structuring the film in terms of music.

WALKER: I think the academic world was quite slow to appreciate your film and quite distrusting of it—perhaps because of its popularity.

LUHRMANN: I think that's probably true. And much more so in the United States than in England. Because the Americans by their very nature are very suspicious of Shakespeare because there's a massive pretension there that they fear, they're insecure about it. And particularly the academics tend to revere backwards to their most loved production that they saw in the 1960s or some time. You're right there, although I know I did a show recently, for the BBC or ITV . . .

WALKER: The Southbank Show?

LUHRMANN: Yes. I know there was a guy from Oxford University and I thought he had a surprisingly clear take on it.

WALKER: I remember that, at the centenary conference about Shakespeare on screen (in 1999), your film was being spoken of as a landmark production whereas people were suspicious of it before then.[3] And I was wondering why you think there might be that kind of shift.

LUHRMANN: I think firstly that any film, when you release it, you know you have to go through this big mechanism called marketing. First of all, I could spend hours talking about the history of the film but just so you have an understanding, it wasn't like I said, after making *Strictly Ballroom* (and I have a five-year quite extraordinary deal with Fox so I can sort of make what I want), "I want to do a funky *Romeo and Juliet.*" I didn't say "funky *Romeo and Juliet,*" but when I wanted to do a Shakespeare and I said in modern dress they didn't go like "What a great idea, that is a great idea, you know we must do that, that's amazing." That photo of Leonardo [DiCaprio, on the wall] was taken here in Sydney a year-and-a-half before I made the film. So D. came down here and we really had to make a video version of it to convince the studio to give the money. So, what I'm saying is, having invested what they saw as an enormous amount for a Shakespeare—because studios have not tended to do Shakespeare, independent studios have— then selling it became a thing of absolutely nailing your audience. So they sold it very precisely as a youth market picture and as a sort of MTV *Romeo and Juliet.* Now, this is how distant that is from our process. Our process, my process was, I wanted to investigate the *myth* and the *fact* of Shakespeare and I wanted to tell the Shakespearean piece, a Shakespearean piece, in the way in which perhaps Shakespeare would today if he were here directing a film. And every choice we made was based on two years of meticulous research about the Elizabethan stage. So, for example, on the Elizabethan stage as you would well know, Shakespeare would use very low comedy and cut it with very high tragedy and popular song.

WALKER: Wild juxtapositions.

LUHRMANN: All the time. See you've got to remember that a thirteen-year-old boy was playing Juliet. So, you've already got this very heightened deal. Now you'd have two stand-up comics come out and say "Do you bite your thumb at me, sir, oh I do bite my thumb at you."

WALKER: That's a scene [the first fight scene from *Romeo and Juliet*] that can really fall flat in stage productions and on film. And you did something quite incredible with that scene, with all the Western allusions and the action movie conventions . . .

LUHRMANN: Again it comes back to Shakespeare because . . . Shakespeare would do *anything*. He wasn't a thematic teller. He didn't think, "well I'm doing a tragedy, so it must all be in a certain color and a certain rhythm." He said . . . the audience, an audience as you would well know of 4,000 in a city of 400,000, next to the bear-baiting and the prostitution, who are mainly drunk, incredibly violent, and unbelievably noisy. He had to shut them up with jokes and *then* hit them with an emotional twist. Our cinema audience is much closer to his audience than an audience in a theater today. They're a rowdy, noisy bunch who aren't going to be easily won over. So, we had to us the same aggression of device to shut them up. So, for example, we relate to many movies that they would know, subconsciously, like we were specifically quoting a Morricone Spaghetti Western in the beginning and then when Romeo's out in the desert we're specifically quoting *Giant* [1956], the James Dean [film]. The way in which Leonardo looks is a combination of Kurt Cobain and James Dean. So, we specifically quoted that in the style. The world of the film—we spent a good year researching social and economic realities of the Elizabethan world, then translated them into a tear-sheet of twentieth-century images. So, we took an image that said religion and politics are mixed up together, so you get the giant Christian cross and religious symbols, a world where the wearing of a weapon gave you status—suddenly it starts to look like a South American city. We went then to Miami, we actually started in Verona oddly enough. We then went to England, did the English research there, then went to Miami—because Miami, for us, was the closest kind of city to an Elizabethan city—hot.

WALKER: And then you ended up in Mexico.

LUHRMANN: Finally shooting in Mexico. But if you think of that environment, even though it's a heightened world—you've got a hot, sexy environment, full of religion, signs and symbols and Miami, where there is a schism, 50 percent of the population speaks Spanish as their first language and there's a gang temperature there. So to answer your first question, I think initially, just by the publicity of it, academics thought "oh, Shakespeare-lite" or "funky Shakespeare." When they finally had a look at the work, if you know anything about Shakespeare, you had to start to register that a great deal of meticulous research . . . that the ideas of execution came directly from the Elizabethan stage.

WALKER: I suppose nowadays people in theaters tend to behave a bit like a congregation rather than, as you say, the rambunctious crowd of . . .

LUHRMANN: Well Shakespeare wrote for everyone, from the street sweeper to the Queen of England: they all had to get it. And it's why I revere him so much as a story-teller because he was dealing with a supremely alive, real audience, who *had* to be absolutely and totally arrested into the story. They didn't come quietly.

WALKER: But many of them were presumably also attuned to a particular way of speaking, a particularly condensed way of speaking. In connection with the language, I wanted to ask you how you made cuts to stick to the "two hour's traffic." And, how did you go about making the text visual?—because it seems to me that you incorporate so many of the images that Shakespeare conjures textually. So can you describe that process?

LUHRMANN: It's a good question. One thing, remember this: first, language. One of the great criticisms we sometimes get is, oh, but you know, you've got people gabbling in American accents and, you know, Latin accents. But remembering that when Shakespeare was acting people probably spoke more like that, with a very round sound. And I think it's Anthony Burgess—he's the most interesting person on this (I think he's a linguistic person)—[who explores] the concept that the Americas were settled by Elizabethans and in fact I think it's irrelevant whether it's an American accent or whatever: the truth is you probably couldn't understand the play if it was performed in its original sound but, leaving that aside, what most critics get obsessed with is really a modern invention, the clipped R.P. [received pronunciation] voice beautiful. So, that goes out the window. Secondly, in the cutting, one thing that Craig [Pearce] and I adhered to was that we cut, we reconfigured scenes but we kept the language. Even Zeffirelli changed the "thee" and the "thou" and he changed some words, there's additional dialogue. But every word in that piece is by William Shakespeare. We have reconfigured, and moved and cut to compress.

The genius and the paradox of Shakespeare is that they'd come on in their basic clothes and they'd pick up a sword or thing and go "I'm a king." And the other great thing is, why he's so cinematic in a sense, is that because there were no . . . most people's idea of great Shakespeare is nineteenth century, you know: big sets, pantaloons, or Leslie Howard climbing up a big piece of scenery[4]—

WALKER: A disastrous Romeo!

LUHRMANN: Disastrous but unbelievably funny, nice pond in the balcony scene and that's about it.

WALKER: And the feet off the floor in the bedroom scene because of the Production Code.

LUHRMANN: Anyway, the point is, having said that, Shakespeare's great success is his rhythmic scene changes—like film. And how he does it is he'll write: "What news of the king?," "Here comes the messenger!" (and you know he's outside). He's got that massive, fast cutting already in the language so it's about visually realizing the world and one of the interesting examples of that is maybe a digression from the questions but . . . Say, if you take the balcony scene—I mean taking the absolute truth of that scene but converting it into a modern situation—basically, he's looking up at the girl's room and he's saying, "oh God, oh I'm so in love with Juliet, oh my God, a light's come on, oh God it is Juliet, oh my God sweet angel, if I could . . . " and then he clambers up there and then she discovers him and then they almost touch, and it's a push-me, pull-you scene and it would have been hilariously funny because a thirteen-year-old boy would've been saying, "Oh Romeo, Romeo" and the nurse and all of that—so it's high comedy as well.

WALKER: But then there are accounts of really convincing, moving performances by boy actors—

LUHRMANN: That's nothing. I've seen a fifty-year-old man play a ten-year-old child and you weep. It's only the actor's power but nonetheless the scene is rich in comedy and yet the beauty of their romance. And the death scene has it too, strangely. The actual moment of death, maybe that doesn't, but in the actual Shakespearean text there's a retelling of the story and there's a joke in there because they had to recount it, maybe because people left to go the bathroom or something—I think it's the Prince who says something like "you go on too long." There's a gag in there to break the tension. So, I'd say that he uses the device anyway of at the most serious moments having comedy.

WALKER: Which, I think, would be true of many parts of your film as well.

LUHRMANN: That's a style that we utilized all the way through it, and purposely, and it's something I'm utilizing in this next film I'm doing [*Moulin Rouge!*, 2001].

WALKER: Can you tell me about how you sold the idea to financial backers. Did you tell them, for example, how eclectic it would be?

LUHRMANN: I already was in a deal with Twentieth Century Fox for five years. I don't have to make films. They didn't want to do a Shakespeare, they said, "You know, we really like the idea—set it in Miami, young people great, but do you think you could do just one thing?: change the language."

WALKER: So how did you persuade them to keep it in?

LUHRMANN: Well, I basically am a fairly persuasive chap and I brought Leonardo down and we shot a whole chunk of it. And then when they actually saw the boys get out of the cars with the guns and say, "Do you bite your thumb at me sir?" they went "Oh I get it, it's like gangs, it's gang language." And that's in fact what we're doing: when you've got an urban gang film you've got someone saying "Hey mother-fucker, you're so bad" when they mean good or whatever so that use of language [is connectable with Shakespeare]: I mean this is a man who invented one-quarter of the English language so the extraordinary elasticity and invention in the mouth we related to street gangs and they got that very strongly. Finally, they gave in and it wasn't that much money for them: fifteen million they gave me and I ended up with twenty.

WALKER: So, a comparatively small production.

LUHRMANN: Tiny. And it made a lot of money.

WALKER: Why do you think that the film spoke so deeply to the predominantly young audience?

LUHRMANN: I think the piece speaks to young people anyway. All I did was find a way, and remember Shakespeare didn't write the story, that myth has been with us forever—youth in conflict with society, the extreme danger of absolutism of idealistic love and youth. The great point of the piece is that if the incumbent generation propagates hate of any kind—racial hate, hate over religion, sexuality, whatever reason—it will come back on them. And the greatest loss is that you lose your children over your hate. It comes around in a circle. That is, for me, the ultimate idea in the piece.

WALKER: I was curious to know your take on a line of the Chorus' first speech: "Doth with their death bury their parents' strife." Did you take that as absolutely true or did you want to cast some doubt on that? Because it seemed that the ending of the film was quite open.

LUHRMANN: You're quite right. I think traditionally there is a scene where there is a conclusion with all the characters. But it was just rhythmically better for this film to finish with the death. And so, it seemed better to say, "And of course, their death resolved the conflict." But there is a real argument, and a genuine and a fair one that we . . . I actually shot the whole scene with the parents arriving and the priest telling the story. Finally, because of film and clarity you get, it just seemed unnecessary.

WALKER: An unnecessary coda.

LUHRMANN: Yeah.

WALKER: Can I also ask you about the music in the film? Because I was interested in how you think your experience in directing opera might have influenced this film?

LUHRMANN: I see music in life actually. I'm sort of with Pythagoras. I almost think the very matter from which we are made is musical and, in terms of storytelling (that's what I do, it's my work, and my life really), I see music as the great great asset, a tool of it but, also, I think it's a force that bonds all humanity. So it was important to find musical language. The language itself is musical so it's important to find a musical language, a musical way of using popular music. Shakespeare used popular music on the stage so I wanted to find a way of using popular music as a way of opening the door into the language. I'm working with the same team now except for Nellee [Hooper]. I worked with Thom Yorke of Radiohead—we all work together. He wrote "Exit Music" especially for the film. To me, all movies are a piece of music in that they have rhythm and structure and rise and fall and then you have other movements, if you like, which are the tracks within them.

WALKER: Can you describe the process of fitting the film to music or fitting music to the film?

LUHRMANN: Traditionally, what you do in a drama is you shoot your film and then you sort of add music a bit like you add wallpaper. But we write our music *into* the film. So, for example, when you see the little boy singing "When Doves Cry" as a hymn that's written in the script: "A young boy who looks like a young Stevie Wonder sings with the choir." I write the music into the script.

WALKER: So did you have Craig Armstrong's "O Verona" in your mind when you made the film?

LUHRMANN: Actually, no, to be real about that, what happened was then you'd have other templature music that you'd cut to so, of course, [in the case of] "O Verona" you don't have to be much of a musicologist to tell that our template would've been "O Fortuna." There's been a big problem with the Orff estate so you couldn't get "O Fortuna" and so, I actually worked with Marius de Vries (it was actually Maz that got that together with Craig), we inverted it and just created our own version of "O Verona." But even then, for example, "Pretty Piece of Flesh" is Shakespearean text but as a kind of rap.

WALKER: So what kind of brief did you give these music people?

LUHRMANN: They're rock 'n' roll so it's very unusual for them to work in this way and take so much time out, but that's just the bottom line for people who want to work with me—they come to Australia and they live here and work with me.

WALKER: So what was the rationale behind using such an eclectic soundtrack?

LUHRMANN: The reason is very specific. What I like about soundtracks is they're like mix tapes and actually each musical idea was specifically . . . a lot of people put soundtracks together by basically saying "well let's just put a whole lot of groovy tracks together and we might sell some tickets to the film." But mine are put together based on every track must serve the story. So "O Verona" is clearly needed there. And you need a track about the boys doing their thing and "Pretty Piece of Flesh" makes sense. You want a really naïve little moment . . . Now the Cardigans track had been around . . . That song "Love me, love me" becomes Juliet's theme. And then we extrapolate the set pieces through the score, throughout the whole piece. So, for example, "Kissing You," the Des'ree piece which she wrote specifically for the film becomes the score in the balcony scene . . .

WALKER: Yes, I've picked up those relationships that he [Craig Armstrong] had woven into the score and the various different motifs . . .

LUHRMANN: We write it exactly like an opera. It's the same thing I'm doing with *Moulin Rouge!*. You set up a primary theme, a song or aria, and then you thematically weave that through depending on what the action is. So, it's exactly like an opera. But remember that he [Armstrong] did it with Marius de Vries and Laura Ziffren. But he actually writes the dots.

WALKER: Tell me how the final film differed from your original intentions. I mean were there big surprises during filming and were there things that changed substantially during filming?

LUHRMANN: Okay, they're great questions and you know time never really helps. Let me say this, on every film we make we go through an incredibly thorough process. In fact, we've been pretty low-key about it but I've only made two films in ten years and I spent about three years just making them, researching. Because I love researching and to live the life of the work. So, if you were to see all the early drafts, all the incarnations of it, you would be shocked and surprised by how many different developments we had. We had one version where we had mock Elizabethan ads in it and devices to try and help clarification. And some of the plotting was quite different. But if you read the very early treatment I did and then look at Craig's and my drafts they are essentially the same idea. But there was a time, for example, when the whole scene in Mantua was set in the coast off Miami, with speedboats going forwards and back and the coastguard arrested them. In shooting, surprises, yes . . . people got very sick . . . but one very simple change I can think of, when we first developed the film: she [Juliet] was put in a tomb, the Capulets' tomb, and people came to visit her there, in a family mausoleum. So we went to Miami and we found these fabulous mausoleums and we copied one of them. So we were down in Mexico and I kept doing the staging in the mausoleum and whichever way I looked at it—you know, people coming in, stone building, round—in a very already artificial film it just seemed *so* artificial. And I just couldn't figure out why I couldn't make the scene work. I kept looking at the set and then I realized that the problem is that mausoleums are theatrical sets. By their very nature they're not naturalistic real rooms, they're theatrical rooms, they're stylized, like theater sets: stylized theatrical sets. So, at the same time, we found that very extraordinary church in Mexico with the Jesus on the top—it really exists. Do you know that the whole end scene was filmed in a church, a real church and the only stipulation was that we didn't blow her head off on the altar? Because we had to shoot on the altar. So there's a tiny little trickle of CGI blood out of her but basically, it was shot, all of that, in a real church in Mexico City and we dressed it. So, then I thought, what if they just leave her in state overnight in the church to be buried overnight. And no one's ever questioned that. I think Romeo gets the priest, there's the chopper, and he breaks his way in . . .

WALKER: But once Romeo enters the church, the noise and other characters (besides Juliet) fade away. I remember that someone asked me, "how is it that they just disappear?" But you forget about the other characters: they become temporarily unimportant. When did you decide to have Juliet wake up just after Romeo has taken the potion?

LUHRMANN: Ah! That's a good question. Actually, in doing my research I found that in the nineteenth century they used to do lots of big re-writes.

WALKER: Echoing the one by David Garrick?[5]

LUHRMANN: Yes, like the Garrick—she has to wake up and do a big speech. Her part wasn't big enough. It's a sort of Sarah Bernhardt.

WALKER: Or like Pyramus and Thisbe?!

LUHRMANN: Yeah, a Pyramus and Thisbe gig and she'd wake up and do a twenty-minute . . .

WALKER: I die, I die, I die!

LUHRMANN: But I always thought, actually, how there was something good in that. I actually wonder if Shakespeare found it a bit hard to do too much with a thirteen-year-old boy kissing and . . . I'm sure they were extraordinary and beautiful but probably it's harder to do. Juliet does seem to be low-key at those moments. . . . There's always a reason why they're never truly together isn't there? Maybe that's a presumption. Either way, I thought it would be great, it's the most emotional scene. He comes there, she's dead, he dies, she wakes up, she dies. So, I just thought by extending the moment there'd be this very dramatic, final realization. It compresses it doesn't it?

WALKER: I think if you have the full Shakespearean text all of that happens very quickly but if you've paired down the text it seems rhythmically right to—

LUHRMANN: Extend that moment.

WALKER: Yes.

LUHRMANN: So, you know it's really a staging thing. Finally, productions are interpretations, everyone just does their own interpretation. I think that in any death moment, seeing the person that you love just before you die is a strong moment.

WALKER: So many people know the story already that it reinstalls the shock.

LUHRMANN: I've been in audiences in LA and they've gone "she's waking up, oh she's gonna be okay" because they don't know the ending—you'd be shocked how many kids in the US don't know the ending of *Romeo and Juliet*!

WALKER: So do you think you'll ever make another Shakespeare film?

LUHRMANN: Maybe . . . For the moment I have other things I have to attend to. Each piece comes from its own particular journey and they relate very specifically to my life and what I want to investigate or express.

NOTES

1. Luhrmann's *Romeo and Juliet* was number one in its first weekend at the United States box office, making over US$11 million on 1,277 screens. The film, which was made for about US$20 million, grossed over US$147 million worldwide. "Box Office Mojo" (Burbank, California), http://www.boxofficemojo.com/movies/?id=romeoandjuliet.htm (July 14, 2007).

2. I quote Catherine Belsey who writes that love is finally "a value that remains beyond the market" (72). As Belsey writes, "The postmodern condition brings with it an incredulity towards true love" but when it seems that everything else can be bought, love "becomes more precious than before because it is beyond price, and in consequence its metaphysical character is intensified." In postmodern culture love is "infinitely uniquely desirable on the one hand, and conspicuously naïve on the other" (1994, 73). After all,

postmodernism "repudiates the modernist nostalgia for the unpresentable, ineffable truth of things" (77). Catherine Belsey, *Desire: Love Stories in Western Culture* (Oxford: Blackwell, 1994).

3. At "Shakespeare on Screen: The Centenary Conference" (Málaga, Spain on September 21–27, 1999), there were nine separate presentations on Luhrmann's film alone.

4. The 1936 film version of *Romeo and Juliet* directed by George Cukor starred Leslie Howard (Romeo) and Norma Shearer (Juliet). The film came out when the Production Code (or Hays Code) was in effect and which had to be obeyed if a picture was to receive the office's "seal of approval": amongst many things, the Code forbade scenes in which a couple was in bed with more than two of their four feet off the floor.

5. Here I refer to David Garrick's now notorious, eighteenth-century adaptation of *Romeo and Juliet* (1748) which, like Luhrmann's film, has Juliet waking early in the tomb scene and makes cuts that focus more attention on the lovers throughout the play. Unlike Luhrmann, however, Garrick also added lines of his own for the lovers in the final scene.

Index

About the Editors

Elsie M. Walker earned her Ph.D. at the University of Sheffield (United Kingdom). Her doctoral thesis is about adaptations of Shakespeare's plays to film, and her work on this subject has been included in several anthologies, including: *Peter Greenaway's "Prospero's Books"* (2000); *The Concise Companion to Shakespeare on Screen* (2006); and *The Literature/Film Reader* (Scarecrow Press, 2007). She has also published articles in *Kinema, Entertext, Literature Compass, English in Aotearoa* (the New Zealand English Teachers' journal), as well as in *Literature/Film Quarterly*—the leading academic international journal in adaptation studies for which she is now coeditor-in-chief. Elsie Walker co-runs the cinema studies program at Salisbury University, Maryland, where she teaches courses on international cinema, film theory, literature and film, film genres, and soundtracks.

David T. Johnson earned his Ph.D. in English with a concentration in film studies in 2003 from the University of Florida. He is coeditor-in-chief of *Literature/Film Quarterly* at Salisbury University, where he co-runs the cinema studies program and teaches courses in film history, literature and film, and other related subjects. His research interests include cinematic accidents, documentary, adaptation studies, and film sound, and his essay on Abbas Kiarostami's *Close-Up* (1990) will appear in the forthcoming volume *Lowering the Boom: New Essays on the Theory and History of Film Sound* (2008).